THE TAX MAN COMETH

LAND AND PROPERTY
IN COLONIAL FAUQUIER COUNTY, VIRGINIA

Tax Lists from the Fauquier County Court
Clerk's Loose Papers

1759-1782

Compiled by
Joan W. Peters,
C.G.R.S.

HERITAGE BOOKS
2008

HERITAGE BOOKS
AN IMPRINT OF HERITAGE BOOKS, INC.

Books, CDs, and more—Worldwide

For our listing of thousands of titles see our website
at
www.HeritageBooks.com

Published 2008 by
HERITAGE BOOKS, INC.
Publishing Division
100 Railroad Ave. #104
Westminster, Maryland 21157

Copyright © 1999 Joan W. Peters

All rights reserved. No part of this book may be reproduced or transmitted in any form or by any means, electronic or mechanical, including photocopying, recording or by any information storage and retrieval system without written permission from the author, except for the inclusion of brief quotations in a review.

International Standard Book Numbers
Paperbound: 978-1-58549-408-8
Clothbound: 978-0-7884-7538-2

To William D. Harris, Clerk of Court, and
Mrs. Gail H. Barb, Chief Deputy Clerk
of the Fauquier County Circuit Court
for their steadfast dedication
to the preservation
of the colonial records
of Fauquier County, Virginia.

TABLE OF CONTENTS

Preface

Foreword

Introduction …………………………………………………………	i-xxxviii
Abbreviations ………………………………………………………	xxxix
1759-001 Thomas Marshall's Tithable List …………………………	1-3
1759-002 George Lamkin's Tithable List ……………………………	4
1759-003 John Marshall's Tithable List ……………………………..	5
1759-004 Added Tithables to Existing Lists …………………………	5
1759-004 Added Land Taxes …………………………………………	5
1765-001 Tithable List ………………………………………………..	6-7
1766-001 Gilson Foote's Tithable List ………………………………	8-11
1767-001 John Kirk's Tithable List …………………………………..	12
1768-001 Armistead Churchhill's Tithable List ………………………	13-15
1768-002 John Kirk's Tithable List …………………………………..	15-16
1775-001 William Grant's Tithable List ………………………………	16-20
1777-001 John Moffet's List of Tithes, Land & Wheeled Carriages in Leeds Parish …………………………………………………….	21-26
1778-001 Thomas Keith's Tithable List ………………………………	26-32
1778-002 William Pickett's Tithable List ……………………………..	32-34

TABLE OF CONTENTS

1782-001 William Blackwell's Property List	35-47
1782-002 Charles Chilton's Property List	48-61
1782-003 John Blackwell's Property List	62-76
1782-004 William Heale's Property List	77-106
1782-005 Personal Property List	107-117
Index "A" Tithables 1759-001 to 1778-002	118-144
Index "B" Slaves & Slaveholders 1759-001 to 1778-002 Tithable Lists	145-167
Index "C" Tithables 1782-001 to 1782-005	168-188
Index "D" Slaves & Slaveholders 1782-001 to 1782-005 Tithable Lists	189-222

PREFACE

This is a book about Fauquier County Virginia's colonial and Revolutionary war tax lists. These tax lists were discovered during a 1994 sixteen month grant project, funded by the Library of Virginia. The purpose of this grant project was to mend, flat file, label, arrange, store and index the earliest paper records of the County. These records, known as the "clerk's loose papers" were stored in the vault in the Courthouse basement. Tri-folded, jacketed and bundled together with red tape, the papers were packed into narrow 4"x 12" metal woodruff drawers, and arranged chronologically, by drawer, from the earliest papers of the 1759 county court through the cessation of the court, in 1904.

One of the record groupings associated with the preservation grant project related to Tax and Fiscal records. The records in this series portrayed the work done by the Justices who took the lists of Tithables from Fauquier's residents and by the Sheriff and other officials who took in the actual taxes and were responsible for their transmission to the colonial capital.

The colonial tax lists (those lists taken before 1782) were loosely termed " Tithable" Lists and often included both property and land; during and after 1782, these lists were divided into two distinct tax lists: personal property tax lists and land tax lists.

Fauquier County is only one of a handful of Virginia counties whose colonial tax lists have survived down to the present day. Natural disasters like fire, flood and war have all contributed to the dearth of colonial tax records, on a county level, available for historical and genealogical study. So, unfortunately, has indifference and neglect. After all, these are just old records – old, torn, moldy, dusty records, at that. Too often, neither the public nor overworked staff of county court houses see the connection between preserving these old, musty, torn records and actually being able to use them for family research.

The tax lists transcribed in this book fit the description given above. Some lists were dirty and flaking. Others were hard to read because the ink had faded. In some instances, the paper had been folded and refolded so many times that it was tearing around the folds. In other instances, the lists were on large, unwieldy heavy sheets of paper which had been folded and refolded to enable the clerk to store them in the woodruff drawer. A few lists were in absolutely pristine condition. Very few. These lists, had, after all, lain, unsuspected and forgotten amongst the rest of the clerk's loose papers in the vault.

Clerk's whose names we have forgotten (or perhaps never knew) had stored the tax records, for safekeeping, with the rest of the court papers. As other clerks came along and moved records about, the early tax records got shuffled around to make room for other records. In time, they became the forgotten residents of the vault, quietly awaiting their re-discovery . Most needed some sort of preservation in order to ensure their use by historians, genealogists and family historians.

The 1994 preservation grant team rescued them. There were nineteen lists in all: four for 1759; one for 1765; one for 1766; two for 1768; one for 1775; two for 1778; and five lists for 1782. These nineteen colonial lists have been transcribed and are presented here for the first time.

Foreword

The Tax Man Cometh was written with two purposes in mind. First, to make Fauquier's hitherto unpublished colonial tithable lists available to the research public; secondly, to provide an explanation for the tax and fiscal laws that brought the tithable lists into being.

This book was designed to meet the needs of a broad spectrum of people. Family historians, professional genealogists, historians, African-American family researchers as well as anyone interested in colonial Virginia history all will benefit from the information found here.

These tax lists and the historical background surrounding their evolution will assist any one interested in tracing their family's colonial Virginia roots. African-Americans who are looking for ways to find eighteenth century forbears, whether slave or free, will find these tax lists enlightening. Historians wishing to delve into the intricacies of Virginia's colonial tax and fiscal legislation will find the Introduction especially helpful. Those of you who are interested in Virginia during the colonial period will find an engrossing and fascinating story relating the correlation between the colony's need to expand westward and her need to pay for that expansion in the form of taxes and a sound fiscal policy.

The book is organized into a three parts. The first part includes a Preface, a Foreword and an Historical Introduction and Abbreviations. The second part is devoted to the transcription of Fauquier's nineteen hitherto unpublished colonial tax lists, taken between 1759-1782. The third part contains the Indices.

There are four distinct indices associated with these tax lists. The first two deal with the listings for the 1759-1778 tax lists. There is an index for tithables and another, separate index, for slaves holders and slaves. The last two indices are both associated with the 1782 tax lists. One is for tithables; the other for slave holders and slaves. The 1782 lists are treated separately because 1782 was a transition year as the state's General Assembly began the process to move the commonwealth's tax and fiscal policy towards peacetime needs.

There are also some Caveats identified with the creation of this book. Caveats deal with certain underlying assumptions as well as warnings and cautions relating to the data found in the tax lists. They are a sort of "Be aware that the author has…"

The names in these lists are spelled exactly as they were written in the originals *except* for the "*f*" whose modern equivalent is the short stem "s" as found in names like "Rose" or the "*ff*" which today is the double "ss" found in names like "Jesse". There are no modern equivalents for those eighteenth century letters on today's computer keyboards. So, for indexing purposes, the modern equivalents "Rose" and "Jesse" and like names were used instead of "Ro*fe*" or "Je*ffe*"

When the name on the tax list was undecipherable it appears as [???]; when the name was illegible, it appears as [illegible].

Bracketed page numbers (e.g. [page 1]) mean that page numbers and/or column numbers were not found on the original lists. The same holds true for the word tithes, when the number following the tithables' name obviously referred to the number of tithes in his household. Generally speaking, any work appearing in square brackets should be looked upon as an inserted word, placed there to make the meaning or context clearer.

Abbreviations in the transcribed tax list are exactly as they appear in the original lists. However, I have taken the liberty of modernizing and spelling out the abbreviated names in the index. Common abbreviations and their meanings are found after the Introduction.

Sometimes eighteenth century handwriting is very DIFFICULT to read! The words "o" and "e" often looked alike as did "e" and "l", especially at the end of a name. The letters "r", "w", "m", and "n", when appearing in the middle of a name, presented special challenges. Then, there was the legibility issue. Some of these hands were beautifully done and easy to read. Others were barely legible.

One last warning, regarding the indices. Remember that the indices in this volume are only as perfect as human error allows. Inaccuracies and mistaken identities *always* seem to find their way into lists of names. It is quite likely that, given the vagaries of eighteenth century handwriting, and the condition of some of the original documentation, some of those pesky little mistakes have crept into this transcription and index. Please know that I have done what I can to eliminate these kinds of annoying interpretative errors.

Finally, some acknowledgement is due to the following people: This book could not have been written without the substantial help, encouragement, and support of my husband, Bill Peters. I would be remiss, too, if I did not thank my good friend and colleague, Karen White for her words of encouragement and her unflagging support for this project. Thanks too, go to William H. Harris, Clerk of the Fauquier County Circuit Court, Gail H. Barb, chief deputy clerk of the Circuit Court and to Phyllis Scott, a deputy clerk employed by the Circuit court in county's record room.

Joan W. Peters, C.G.R.S.
Broad Run, Virginia
October, 1999

INTRODUCTION

A. Historical Overview

When Fauquier County was formed from Prince William in 1759, Virginia found itself in the midst of a global conflict known on the European continent as the Seven Years War. England and France faced off as they continued their traditional enmity in the European phase; while in the American colonies, it was the British and the colonists with their indian allies against the French and their indian allies.

This war was just one of a long series of Continental wars into which the British dragged their colonies. In 1739, the colonists found themselves fighting against the Spanish at the siege of Cartagena in Spanish America along the Spanish Main. Of the 1,500 strong expeditionary force made up of Georgians, South Carolinians and Virginians who set out under the direction of the British, 600 returned home, victimized by Spanish cutlasses, incompetent British commanders and tropical disease.

Then, in the 1740s, Britain and France fought over portions of Canada in the war the colonists called King George's War. During that war, an expeditionary force from Massachusetts invaded Canada and successfully besieged the French fortress of Louisbourg, known as the "Gibraltar of the North". Unfortunately, the British gave back the fortress to the French at the conclusion of this war, as part of the European settlement of the conflict. [1]

When the French and Indian War erupted along the Virginia frontier, the colony found that it needed to secure its frontier in order to keep open the gateway to lands west of the Appalachians into the fertile Ohio valley. Tobacco planters were especially interested in this land, now dominated by the Algonkian indians. The planters hoped that speculation in the Ohio lands would replenish income lost to a glut in the tobacco market and would provide an alternative for the exhausted soil of their Virginia plantations.[2] As settlers pushed the bounds of Virginia's frontier further and further west, they ran into stiffened Indian resistance to the loss of traditional hunting grounds and sacred ancestral lands.

During the French and Indian War, Virginia's legislature had two goals with regards to a tax and fiscal policy: 1) to protect, defend and secure their frontiers against marauding indians and their French allies and 2) to provide funding for the colonial infrastructure on a local level in the form of the public levy.

Each county had public expenses; paying for the maintenance of the poor is just one example; paying for the upkeep of the gaol and county court house is another. The clerk of the county court kept an account of these kinds of expenses in the form of the "county levy", which he recorded scrupulously in the county's minute books. Tithable persons paid the county levy in tobacco at a rate established by the colonial legislature.

Fauquier County has five tithable lists that have survived from the French and Indian War period, all taken in 1759, during the year in which the county was formed. Thomas Marshall's 1759 list of tithables appears to be complete. The remaining four lists are not. Unfortunately, no other lists have survived in the Clerk's loose papers between 1759 and 1763.

Nevertheless, there *are* six colonial tax lists for Fauquier County that date from 1765-1775. During this period, the colonies were officially at peace with their neighbors. The 1765 tax legislation dealt primarily with the collection of the public levy on the county level. In 1768, the legislature repealed some earlier taxes because the duties on tobacco, carriage wheels, writs and ordinary licenses, collected in that year, were thought to be sufficient to cover the needs of the civil government.

Be that as it may, Virginia's borders were still the target of indian tribes who had become increasingly alarmed at the expansion of the white man into tribal hunting and burial grounds. The tax and fiscal legislation for this period dealt with the indian threat and ways to pay for a burgeoning civil county and colonial bureaucracy. Taxes were raised to help pay for determining the boundary between the colony and the Cherokees in 1769.

As Virginia moved closer to joining the other twelve colonies in declaring their independence from Britain, their tax and fiscal policy reflected their concerns with defending the frontier and paying their soldiers. In 1775, tax legislation was ratified to pay for the colony's militia expeditions against the indians. Treasury notes were issued again with the express purpose of paying for the defense of Virginia.

In 1776 Virginia became an independent state, As such, the legislature struggled to fund and support a war for independence and, at the same time, endeavor to ensure a stable fiscal policy. This tax legislation, in many ways, went to the heart of a newly independent state at war.

The legislature had to wrestle with other means to raise new taxes to fund and supply the militia, support the Continental army, find foodstuffs for families whose husbands and/or sons were now in the army, set up a new state Navy, and build new fortifications and new ships for defense of the state. Inflation was rampant. Paper money, Congressional and state treasury notes and a lack of a unified coinage dogged any attempts to come up with a consistent fiscal policy.

At the same time, the war was not going well for the colonies. It was not until October 1777, when the Americans defeated the British at Saratoga, that the American cause began to move forward. The old British enemy, France, formally recognized the united colonies as the United States, an independent nation in December 1777. In February 1778, France and the United States became wartime allies, providing close commercial ties with the newly independent states.

While these negotiations were going on, American troops were languishing at Valley Forge. The two opposing armies were at a stalemate. Battles were fought when conditions were auspicious for one side or the other. Throughout 1778 the British would win a victory only to have the Americans counter with another. The war was to drag on for another three years before the American's decisive victory, with French help, took place at York town.

Virginia's tax legislation during the Revolutionary war cannot be examined without utilizing the war as its backdrop. Although this wartime legislation does not make for easy reading, it *is* necessary to understand how the war efforts motivated Virginia's tax and fiscal policy.

Inflation and increased demand for funds to prosecute the war all but shattered the tax collection process. The printing of paper money by individual states, the disappearance of hard coinage due to hoarding and payments for imports and the resultant widespread counterfeiting led to such inflation that the commonwealth considered recalling *all* paper money. If this measure was taken, the legislature thought, it would at least *limit* future liability.

A barter economy arose, using grains like wheat, corn and barley, as acceptable taxable items. Forgery was addressed by death without benefit of clergy. The official acceptance of Spanish dollars as legal tender in October 1782 helped form the basis for a permanent unit of currency which was inherited by the new republic in the form of the dollar bill.

Fauquier has three wartime tax lists that were found in the Clerk's loose papers: A 1775 tithable list and two 1778 tax lists. Fighting ended in October 1781 at Yorktown; the British Parliament voted to end the war in February 1782. The war did not officially end until September 1783 when the Treaty of Paris officially recognized the independence of the former British colonies.

Between the end of the fighting in 1782 and the signing of the peace treaty in 1783, the colonial legislature began the process of converting to a peacetime tax and fiscal package. Fauquier has five of these tax lists, taken in 1782, that have survived. These are included here as well.

B. Virginia Colonial Tax Legislation 1759-1776

1. 1759 Tax Legislation
- **Overview**

In February 1759, Virginia's colonial legislature contended with one over-riding issue in terms of a tax and fiscal policy: how was Virginia to raise money to secure, defend and protect their frontier?. Virginia and the rest of British North America were still fighting the French and their indian allies for control of its colonial borders.

The 1759 tax legislation, then, was directly associated with military manners. The legislature allowed for an increase of up to 1000 men for the militia regiment, garrisoned at Pittsburgh. Public money, not to exceed L28,000, was to be used to defray the costs of recruiting, clothing, feeding and subsisting these forces until the following December.

This legislation gave authority to either the Governor or the commander-in-chief of the Virginia forces stationed at Pittsburgh to order the regiment to march, join, and fight under any of the King's forces in any offensive the British might wish to take.

Realizing that once the militia went on the offensive with British forces, the Virginia frontier would be left defenseless, the Legislature provided an additional 500 men to be raised, divided into five companies, under the command of a lieutenant-colonel, four captains, ten lieutenants and five ensigns. These companies were to be employed for the protection of the frontiers; they were not to be incorporated with the king's forces. Indeed, these new companies were not to be sent out of Virginia at all.

In order to raise the requisite number of men in a timely fashion, the legislature authorized the payment of a military bounty of L10 to each man enlisting in the regiment that was at Pittsburgh and L5 to each man enlisting in the companies of men who were to protect Virginia's frontier. Public money, not to exceed L16,000 was to be utilized for the payment to protect the frontier.

Since there was not sufficient money to pay the claims and arrears of the militia and damages done by the Indians, the Treasurer was authorized to pay these claims out of tax revenues.

a. Tax on Tithables
Every tithable person was to pay a tax or duty of two shillings to the sheriff of the County on or before April 10, 1765. A further tax or duty of 2 shillings was to be paid, for every tithable person, on or before April 10, 1766. Another tax or duty of 4 shillings was to be paid for every tithable person on or before April 10, 1767.

These taxes were to be paid in 1761 and for the next three years (i.e. 1762, 1763, and 1764) according to legislation passed the previous year in 1758. The articles of the 1758 legislation were included in the 1759 tax legislation as it related to the payment, collection and accounting for these taxes or duties.[3] In this way the local tax collectors would understand clearly what was to be collected and thus could carry out this new legislation.

b. Tax on Tobacco and the issue of Treasury Notes
In addition to the tithable tax of 2 shillings, a duty of 2 shillings for each hogshead of tobacco delivered from the colony's warehouses between October 20 1764 and October 10, 1767, was to be paid by their owner or proprietor. Since all the taxes imposed by this act could not be collected in time to pay the militia, the legislature decreed that the Treasurer could issue treasury notes – two thousand of these notes were to be in L5 notes, signed by Peyton Randolph and Robert Nicholas; another two thousand were to be in L2 notes, also signed by Randolph and Nicholas; and fifteen thousand notes were to be in 20 shilling denominations, signed by Benjamin Waller and Philip Johnson.[4]

c. The Public Levy

In the same session, in February 1759, the legislature passed another act for raising the public levy. Six pounds of tobacco was to be paid by every tithable person in the colony, "for the defraying and payment of the public charge of the country"; this levy was to be collected from April 14, 1757 to February 22, 1759.[5]

Both the public levy and the tithable taxes were passed in February 1759. Fauquier County was formed in May 1759. Thus it was incumbent upon the County Court of Fauquier to appoint persons to take a list of tithables so that the County could begin collecting the 1759 taxes.

3. 1760 Tax Legislation
- **Overview**

This tax legislation was also directly associated with the protection of the Virginia frontier. In March 1760, the colonial legislature provided L20,000 to extend the terms of the men serving in the Virginia militia from May, when their enlistment ended, to the first day of November. In this legislation, 300 of these men were to be retained and stationed for the defense and protection of inhabitants on the south western frontiers of Virginia; the remainder of the regiment could be assigned to the British forces and under British command.

The legislature also found that it might be expedient to have a small body of the forces thus allocated on foot *after* November 1st in order to protect and defend the frontiers from "any insults... offered .. them by ... neighbouring Indians and to keep such Indians in awe."[6] So the Governor or Commander in Chief of the militia were given the authority to extend the service of these men from November 1759 to April 1, 1760 and to employ them in either offensive or defensive operations. Public funds were to be used to pay the men as long as the sum did not exceed L20,000.

a. Land Tax

The taxes for these military manners were allocated as follows: first the legislature allotted for each land holder a tax of 1s 3d for every 100 acres of land, using the base rate for land holders with greater or lesser acreage. Land holders were to pay this tax on or before April 10, 1767 to the Sheriff of the County in which the land was found.. Another tax or duty of 1s 3d for each 100 acres was due on April 10, 1768, also to be collected by the Sheriff in the County where the land was located.

b. Tax on tithables

A further tax or duty of 2s was to be paid for every tithable person in Virginia to the sheriff of the County where the taxpayer had his residence on or before April 10, 1769. Thus, the legislature initiated a land tax and a poll tax to be used to pay for the defense of the frontier.

c. 1760 Treasury Notes

Since the taxes imposed by this act could not be collected in time to pay the troops, the Treasurer was given the authority to issue Treasury notes. 1,800 of these notes were to be in the form of L5 notes, signed by Peyton Randolph and Robert Carter Nicholas. 1,800 more were to be issued in L2 notes, also signed by Randolph and Nicholas. 5,333 of these notes were to be issued in 5 shilling notes, signed by John Randolph and 5,334 of the notes were to be issued in notes worth 2s 6d, also signed by John Randolph.

All these notes were redeemable on October 10, 1768 and would then be paid by the treasurer. The notes had the force of legal tender and could be utilized to pay any debt whatsoever, except for the King's quit rents.[7]

4. 1761 Public Levy

In March 1761, the legislature dealt with the public levy. L6 of tobacco was to be paid by every tithable person within the colony in order to defray and pay the public charge of the colony; this was the public levy from February 22, 1759 to March 6, 1761.[8]

So the Burgesses changed the tax picture somewhat in the March term of 1760. There added a land tax to the traditional poll tax while they left the public levy unchanged.

5. 1762 Taxes Legislation
- **Overview**

This time, the March 1762 tax package passed by the colonial legislature dealt with raising as many as 1,000 men for the security and protection of the colony. Each person who enlisted was to receive a military bounty of L10.

These 1,000 men were to be formed into ten companies, under the command of a colonel, lieutenant-colonel, major, seven captains, twenty lieutenants and ten ensigns. A chaplain, paymaster, surgeon, two surgeon's mates, an adjutant and a quartermaster were also to be part of this new call for men.

The militia companies, at the direction of the Governor or Commander in Chief, could be untied to any forces sent to the colony's assistance by the British or by any of the neighboring colonies. The militia companies could be marched to "annoy or attack the enemy" as the British thought fit and proper.

Since the King had ordered that British forces should be filled with these new recruits and has directed the Governors of the colonies to procure levies for that purpose, the Virginia legislature decided to go along with these general orders and contribute men to the British effort. However, the legislature placed a string on this recruitment, saying that only 268 men would be used to fill in the British forces. Each man enlisting in the British service was to receive a bounty of L10.[9]

The legislature decided to raise L30,000, to pay for the raising, clothing, subsistence and other expenses, of the 1,000 men raised for the security and protection of the colony and to use these funds also to pay for the recruitment of the 268 men into the King's service. The term of service for both units was to end December 1, 1762.

a. Tax on Tithables

The taxes to pay for these military recruits were to be paid by each tithable person in the colony. Each tax payer was to be paid an additional tax or duty of 1s to the sheriff of the County where the tithable was listed; the tax was due on or before April 10, 1764; furthermore, each tithable person was to pay an additional tax or duty of 1s to the Sheriff on or before April 10th of the next five years (i.e. 1765-1769).

b. Tax on lands, tithables & wheeled carriages

In November 1762, the legislature acted to consolidate the tax legislation into one package. This was due to the perpetration of fraud by sheriffs of various counties when they collected taxes imposed on lands, tithables, and wheeled carriages for the support of the present war.

In order to prevent this occurrence, the legislature decreed that "every owner or proprietor of lands within this colony... shall at the time appointed to take the list of tithables... deliver to one of the justices appointed to take such list... by the court of the County wherein such land shall lie, an exact list of his or her lands, according to the quantity mentioned in the patent or deed... " If part of the land has been sold or transferred, then the land holder is to deliver the reduced quantity of his acreage to the court.[10]

If the land holder failed to list his acreage, then every one so doing "shall be adjudged a concealer, and shall forfeit 20 s for each hundred acres of land ... so concealed."[11] Moreover, the sheriff or tax collector had to collect, levy and account for the taxes due for the concealed land. The land holder could elect to list lands that lay in two counties in the county where he held the most land.

Every owner of a coach, chariot or other four-wheeled carriage, except for a wagon, and every owner of a two-wheeled chair or chaise, was to deliver to one of the justices appointed to take the tithable list, a list of every wheeled carriage in his ownership. Anyone who failed to do this was to pay L3 for every four wheel carriage he neglected to list and 30s for every two-wheeled chair or chaise he did not register.

The Justices taking the tithable lists in 1762 were to deliver these lists to the clerk of the County court; if the Justice failed to return the list, he was to pay L100 for not returning the list of tithables. Once the Clerk of the Court had received the Tithable lists, he was to turn the lists over to the Grand Jury for the November Court. The grand jury was to examine the list and present in court every concealer of land, tithables and wheel-carriages. Summons were to be issued and were answerable at the December Court without benefit of a jury.

Before the last day of November, the County Clerks were to make out and deliver, or cause to be delivered to the treasurer

"a fair and exact **list of the tithables, lands and wheel-carriages, taken in his County; distinguishing upon such lists, in an alphabetical order, and in proper columns for that purpose, the owners or proprietors names, the number of tithables, quantity of lands, and the number and sorts of wheel carriages, belonging to every such owner or proprietor**, respectively; and such clerk shall also deliver, before the time aforesaid, another such list to the sheriff of his county..."[12]

If the County Clerk failed to deliver these lists to the Treasurer, he faced a penalty of L25 for each failure. The legislature mitigated the impact of this omission by allowing Clerks of the county courts 400 pounds of neat tobacco annually from their County levy as payment for prompt return of the lists. If the Treasurer discovered that there were arrears in taxes owed the Crown, he had to direct the Clerk of the Treasury to transcribe the lists in arrears and transmit them to the Sheriff for payment. It was then up to the Sheriff or his deputy to collect the arrears in taxes. If the deputy neglected to do so on or before June 10 of each year, then the general court or the county court, upon a motion from the sheriff, could issue a judgment against the deputy and his security for all the money and/or tobacco the deputy is charged with collecting.

c. The 1762 Public Levy

Once the land tax, tithable lists and wheeled carriage taxes had been taken care of (in great detail!), the colonial General Assembly turned its attention to the public levy for 1762. They laid a tax of 7 pounds of tobacco on each tithable person within Virginia for defraying and paying the public charge of the colony. The public levy was to be enacted from March 6, 1761 to November 2, 1762.

- **Summary of 1762 Taxes**

There were three different tax packages passed in 1762, if one counts the November public levy as a tax. The first package involved the raising of L30,000 to recruit and equip a force to protect the colony and another smaller force to fill out the British army forces. Tithable persons were to pay a 1s tax on or before April 10, 1764, 1765, 1766, 1767, 1768 and 1769.

The second tax package, passed in November 1762, was initiated to prevent further fraud by sheriffs or tax collectors in various counties in collecting taxes on tithables, land and wheeled carriages. This legislation laid down stiff penalties for failure to return tithable lists, taxes due on the amount of land held by land-owners or proprietors and taxes owed on wheeled carriages and chaises. It lay out in precise fashion the form of the tithable lists to be returned to the Treasurer. The lists were to be in alphabetical order with information laid out in columns regarding tithables, quantity of land, and the number and sorts of wheeled carriages owned by each tithable person.

The third tax package, also passed in November 1762, dealt with the public levy. Now every tithable person was expected to pay 7 pounds of tobacco, instead of the previously apportioned 6 pounds of tobacco, for defraying and paying the public charge of the colony.

The French and Indian war officially ended in 1763 at the Peace of Paris. Britain received, as spoils of war, Florida from Spain and Canada from France. France had to cede the Louisiana Territory to Spain.[13]

Meanwhile, the British and colonial legislatures had to deal with a more dangerous peacetime threat: defending the colonial frontier against the incursions of indian tribes formerly allied with the French. The indians of Canada and the trans-Appalachian west were numerous, powerful and hostile. Moreover, the tribes of the Ohio valley never had been decisively defeated in any of their battle with either the colonial militia or with the British army. While the indian allies of the French may have been proclaimed nominal subjects of King George in 1763, it was the indians who remained in possession of the forests west of the Appalachians.

In the summer of 1763, the Indians overran frontier forts and advanced deep into Pennsylvania and Virginia in what has come to be known as Pontiac's conspiracy. The tribes killed more than 2,000 people – more than were killed in the French and Indian war! The British army, with help from colonial forces, regrouped and defeated Pontiac at Bushy Run near Pittsburgh.

By this time, tax payers in England were growing increasingly tired of providing funds for colonial frontier defense and westward expansion. So, the British government drew an imaginary line along the Appalachian mountains, between the sources of the rivers emptying into the Atlantic and those that flowed into the Ohio-Mississippi River system. The British colonies were not to proceed west of this imaginary line. Speculation in lands west of this line was forbidden and a freeze was placed on land sales west of the Alleghenies and Appalachian mountains.

In Virginia, this Proclamation was greeted with disdain.
No one considered the Proclamation Line as anything more than what one young land speculator, George Washington, called 'a temporary expedient to quiet the minds of the Indians.' Too many Virginia planters and influential British politicos dreamed of riches from Ohio Valley real estate to consider the freeze permanent. Indeed, two newly appointed superintendents of Indian affairs immediately began to purchase territory from the western tribes. The southern part of the line was redrawn within a few months, and regularly over the next decade, trans-Appalachian lands were opened to speculation and settlement.[14]

6. 1764 Tax Legislation
- **Overview**

Before the French and Indian war, Britain had been content to "make do" with their colonial administration so long as mercantile interests remained profitable. By 1764, however, the annual costs of colonial government had jumped to more than three times its prewar level. Britain's national debt approached L130 million due to the debilitating effect of carrying on a two front war: one in Europe and another in the colonies. British landowners were already paying 20 per cent of their income to the government so a British tax package calling for higher taxes to pay off the war debts was out of the question. So were modest increases on taxes on liquor; when the British tried to increase the small tax on cider, the day-to-day drink in southwestern England, village riots ensued.

So the British turned their attention to the American colonies for revenue. Britain's prime minister, George Grenville calculated that the average English tax payer paid an annual tax of 26 shillings; a British subject living in Virginia paid only five pence. Since the colonies had gained the most from the French and Indian wars, Grenville reasoned, they should also do their part in paying off the British national debt and find ways to meet their own expenses.

Virginia's colonial legislation after 1763 did indeed attempt to find ways to pay for the burgeoning colonial infrastructure. The legislature focused on developing a tax package to fund three new counties added to the organization of the colony since the end of the French and Indian War: Charlotte and Mecklenburg, in 1764 from Lunenburg; and Pittsylvania, in 1766 from Halifax county. Legislators were also concerned with the infrastructure of four other counties added during the war: Loudoun, in 1757 from Fairfax; Buckingham, in 1758 from Albemarle; Fauquier, in 1759 from Prince William; and Amherst, in 1761 from Albemarle.[15]

- **1764 Public Levy**

In October 1764, the colonial legislature determined each tithable person was to pay a tax or duty of 46 pounds of tobacco to defray and pay the public charge for the colony *and* to secure the pay and expenses of the militia drawn out into actual service for the defense and protection of the frontiers against the incursion of Indians. This public levy was to go into effect from November 2, 1762 to October 30, 1764.

The sheriff of the Virginia counties was to be responsible for the collection of the public levy; he was required to give bond at the February 1765 Court for the collection of the levy. Once the tobacco levy was collected, the Sheriff was to sell it – sheriffs for the counties of Fauquier and Loudoun were to sell the tobacco at Dumfries on the court day of Prince William County in July 1765. The money collected from this sale was to be turned over to the colony's Treasurer.

If the sheriff failed or neglected to sell the tobacco levy, or didn't account for or pay the money to the Treasurer by September 10, 1765, then the County Court, on motion by the colony's treasurer, could take out a judgment against the sheriff and his securities for the tobacco or money. If the sheriff failed or neglected to give a bond and security for collecting the public levy, then the court was directed to appoint someone else who would collect and sell the tobacco for the public and to pay the money to the Treasurer of Virginia. The appointee had to give bond with security and was held liable for the same penalties as the sheriff if he failed to collect and sell the tobacco and turn the money over to the Treasurer.[16]

7. 1764 legislation altering the Court day for Fauquier and other counties

The legislature changed the court day for Fauquier due to the inconvenience occasioned by the justices, merchants, attorneys and others who had to attend the County court. Previously the Fauquier County Court had met on the fourth Thursday of every month, beginning in May 1759. After March 1765, the court for Fauquier County was to meet on the fourth *Monday* of every month.[17]

8. 1765 Tax Legislation
- **The 1765 Public Levy: An amendment to the 1764 Levy**

In October 1765, the colonial legislature amended the 1764 act that assessed tax payers with a 46 pound tobacco levy to defray and pay the public charge and to pay the expenses of the colonial militia. The amendment was necessary because many of the tax payers did not have 46 pounds of tobacco that the sheriff could sell for the public good.

Instead the legislature said that each person would be at liberty to discharge so much per poll of their public levy, as was intended to be sold for the use of the militia, at the rate of 12s 6d per hundred. The inhabitants of Fauquier were at liberty to discharge this levy at the rate of 36 pounds of tobacco per poll.

Since many of the Sheriffs had exacted great prices for tobacco from many of the tax payers who had already discharged their public levies, these people were then entitled to some relief from the levy. The legislature fixed this amount of relief. The sheriff was to render an account of what tobacco or what money he has received and proceed to sell the tobacco or pay the money according to his account and the directions of this act without shifting or exchanging the one for the other. If the sheriff failed to follow the stipulations of this legislation he was liable for a penalty of double the value of the money or tobacco thus shifted or exchanged.

The legislature made allowances for the public levy to be paid by crop tobacco and stipulated the way the tobacco was to be sold and set penalties for violating these stipulations.[18]

9. 1766 Tax Legislation
- **The 1766 Act to direct the collection of the public levy in Fauquier for 1765**

The sheriff of Fauquier County had been unable to give security for the collection of the 1765 tobacco levy. So this public levy had so far gone uncollected there.

The November 1766 legislative session took care of this oversight when it decreed that the Sheriff was to use the Tithable list of 1764 for the tobacco levy and the two 1765 public levy acts described above as his authority for collection.[19]

- **The 1766 Act for raising a public levy**

In November 1766, the colonial legislature changed the amount of the public levy. Now, each tithable person was to pay 8 pounds of tobacco (rather than the 46 pounds or 12s 6d per hundred allotted as payment in 1765) to defray and pay the public charge of the colony, being the public levy from October 30, 1764 to November 6, 1766.

The sheriff of each County, was to give bond and security for the due collection and payment of the public levy at the court of his County in the May or June Court, 1767.

10. 1768 Tax Legislation
- **The repeal of the 1760 land and the 1762 poll-tax due in years 1768 and 1769**

The legislature repealed the 1760 land tax and the 1762 poll tax along with an additional land tax of 9d per hundred acres of land for the relief of the garrison of Fort Loudoun in Cherokee country in 1768 because it appeared that earlier taxes collected nearly equaled the issuance of treasury notes from 1754-1762. It also appeared that " the duty on tobacco, the taxes on wheel carriages, writs and ordinary licenses, which by law are to be continued for two years, will be abundantly sufficient to make good, so that the land and poll-tax imposed by the above...acts of assembly... may and ought to cease..."[20]

11. 1769 Tax Legislation
- **Overview**

In 1769, the colonial legislature turned once again to effecting a tax policy that would hopefully contain the indian threat to her borders. The legislators voted to raise L2,500 sterling to help defray the costs of running a boundary line between Virginia and the Cherokee country. As soon as the boundary line was established between Virginia and the Cherokees, the Treasurer could pay the expenses of negotiating and running the boundary line.

At the same time, the legislature attempted to stabilize the colony's currency by seeking the right to import copper money, up to L2,500 sterling worth, as coinage for Virginians to use for change and small payments. If the King allowed copper coinage to be used in Virginia, then the Treasurer was given authority to purchase it.

There were also large sums of money due from the public for individual claims in the colony. In addition, large quantities of tobacco had been either damaged or destroyed in the public warehouses. Thus, money could not be raised by the duties already imposed;

The legislature had found from previous experience that taxes on process, ordinary licenses, wheeled-carriages slaves, (due to expire in February 1770) and tobacco were not as burdensome as the poll tax previously assessed on Virginia's tax payers. So, they decided to lay these taxes for 1769.

a. 1769 Taxes assessed on slaves, carriages, ordinary licenses, process and tobacco

The legislature assessed taxes on these six commodities: 1) slaves: a duty of 5 % on the purchase price of all slaves imported or brought into Virginia for sale, over and above the duty already laid on slaves, was added to the tax laws. 2.)20s duty for each coach, chariot and other four-wheeled carriages (except for wagons), 3.) a 10 s duty for every chair and two-wheeled chaise, payable on or before April 10th each year by the owner or proprietor when he delivers a list of his tithables to the justices appointed to take such lists. 4.)a 20s duty for every ordinary license-- this was to be paid to the Clerk of the Court by the person obtaining the license; 5.) and 2s 6d for every original writ or writs in any action or suit at common law, and subpoenas in chancery suits and certain other court process -- to be paid by the plaintiff to the Clerk of the Court.

Finally, there was a further duty on tobacco—this one for 1s 6d per hogshead for each hogshead of tobacco passed and delivered out of the several warehouses in Virginia that was to be shipped in January 1770[21].

b. 1769 Act exempting free negroes, mulattos and Indian women from payment of levies

The legislature also went on to repeal an act, instituted in 1748 which declared that all free negro, mulatto and Indian women of the age of 16, except Indians tributary to the colonial government and all wives of free negroes, mulattos and Indians as tithables.

This act *exempted* all free negro, mulatto and Indian women and all wives, other than slaves, of free negroes, mulattos and Indians from the payment of any public, county, or parish levies. This exemption was to go into effect as of June 9, 1770. There was a proviso attached to this repeal: that the execution of the act was to be suspended until the King's approval was obtained for this legislation. Since women were not taxed ordinarily, this act recognized the necessity for not taxing wives of free negroes, mulattos and Indians.[22]

12. 1775 Tax Legislation
- **Overview**

Virginia once more attempted to stabilize their frontier and to pay their militia. This year had seen colonial successes at Lexington, Concord, Bunker Hill and the Massachusetts and Vermont militias' successful siege of Fort Ticonderoga. Virginian George Washington was sent by the second Continental Congress, then meeting in Philadelphia, to take command of the colonial troops in Boston and bring order to the city. Thomas Paine had just published his pamphlet *Common Sense*. It appeared likely that open rebellion was a reality; that a war with Britain was on the horizon. Throughout the fall of 1775, more and more voices called for independence.

Making arrangements to pay for the defense of Virginia was uppermost in the minds of the colonial legislators, in the event that war should break out between the colonies and Great Britain.

- **Taxes raised to defray expenses against the Indians and taxes raised to pay the militia**

The 1775 legislature appointed commissioners to settle the militia accounts occasioned by Virginia's expedition against the Indians; they also approved a report from their committee on public claims. However, since the funds in the public treasury were inadequate to pay those claims, the legislature appointed commissioners to settle all the accounts relating to the militia and issue warrants to the treasurer for payment.

While the commissioners were settling the militia accounts, they were also charged with determining the pay for militia officers according to rates already established by the council and legislature. This July legislation also took care of payment to wounded officers and soldiers and for that part of the militia called minute men. The treasurer was to pay, from public funds, on warrants from committees of safety the sums needed for wounded officers and soldiers and the costs of training the minute men contingents of the local militia. No warrants were needed to pay public creditors.[23]

a. Taxes on wheeled vehicles

The legislature raised this money via these taxes: First, an annual tax or duty of 40s on each coach, chariot or 4 wheeled carriage (excepting only wagons); second, a 20s annual tax on every chair or two-wheel chaise. Proprietors of these carriages were to pay the tax before June 10, 1776. This tax was to continue for seven years. (i.e. through 1783) 2.)a tax or duty of 3s 9d for every tithable person, to be paid on June 10, yearly, by a tithable person, if a free man; The tax was to be paid by a parent or guardian, if the tithable was a minor; The master or owner of servants or slaves was to pay the tax on tithable servants.[24]

b. Taxes on Land

Finally, a tax or duty of 4s for every hundred acres of land, and after that rate, for a greater or lesser quantity, also due annually on June 10th by the proprietor or by the parents or guardian, if the owner was a minor. This land tax was to be paid in the County in which the land was located. The land tax was to begin in 1777 and continue for six years. (i.e. until 1783)

Each person chargeable with these new taxes was to give to the Justices of the County court or person appointed to take the list of tithes his list of tithables a long with a list of his or her wheeled carriages and the amount of acreage held within the County.

The sheriff or tax collector was to account and pay these taxes, after allowing for insolvents, to the Treasurer of Virginia on or before November 20th each year.[25]

c. Taxes on ordinary licenses, marriages, writs

In addition, the legislature found additional monies by these taxes: 1) a tax or duty of 40s for every ordinary license; 2) a tax or duty of 40s for every marriage license; 3) a 2s 6d tax on court process (writs, Chancery subpoenas, petitions and the like) These taxes were due in April and October every year.

Sheriffs or Tax collectors were required to give bond with sufficient securities, in reasonable penalties, payable to Robert Carter Nicholas or to the Treasurer. If Sheriffs or Tax collectors fail to carry out their duties and collect and settle the accounts, then the County court could give judgment for the penalty of his bond.[25]

d. Treasury Notes

Since there was not enough public money in the Treasury to pay for the defense of Virginia, the Treasurer was authorized to issue Treasury notes.[26] Treasury notes were a time-honored way of handling the lack of money in the Treasury – it had already been used as a source of revenue during the French and Indian war.

C. Virginia's Wartime Tax Legislation during the first years of the Commonwealth 1776-1782
1. Overview

This section deals with the taxation policy of the newly independent commonwealth from 1776-1782. By this time, the colonies had declared their independence from Britain and their intention to be part of a Confederation of united states. They were at war with Great Britain and wartime conditions prevailed. Virginia was expected to support the war effort with troops, ships and military fortifications.

As the war wore on, the commonwealth found that the monies in the treasury were insufficient to sustain the war effort. In addition, there was a flood of almost worthless paper scrip and paper treasury notes issued by the Congress and by the individual states. The commonwealth realized that they had to come up with a better and more permanent way to borrow money to pay for both the war effort and for the expenses associated with running their newly created, independent state. The treasury notes were not working. What was needed, the legislature realized, was a new fiscal policy.

The legislature also realized that they needed a new and innovative tax policy so that the Virginia could pay for its responsibilities towards a successful military conclusion to their war with Great Britain. They also realized that once the economic situation became stable, the new taxes could be used to help run the infrastructure of the commonwealth.

2. 1776 Tax Legislation
• 1776 Taxes to support and maintain Virginia's military forces, army and navy

The legislature realized that further provisions were necessary for the maintenance of Virginia's regular forces, minute men and militia employed in defending the frontiers. Added to the militia forces was the necessity to pay for the expenses of Virginia's infant navy – building warships, furnishing them with seamen and marines, providing armament and the like. The legislature also had to deal with public claims from distressed residents. Needless to say, the treasury's funds were proving inadequate to deal with the pressures of the impending war with Great Britain.

a. Taxes on Tithes

New taxes were needed. The Convention initiated these additional taxes: 1) an additional tax or duty of 1s 3d to be paid by every tithable person in the colony to the sheriff or tax collector of the County where he is resident on or before June 10, 1777; 2) a further tax of 1s 3d for each tithable person for the next six years, (i.e. through 1783) beginning June 10, 1777. 3) an additional tax of 1s for every 100 acres of land, to be paid on or before June 10, 1777. A further tax of 1s for every hundred acres of land was to be collected by the sheriff or tax collector in the County in which the land was located for the next six years. (i.e. through 1783).

The Convention provided, once again for the method of payment and for the issuance of Treasury notes to cover any insufficiencies in the Public Treasury.[27]

b. 1776 Tithable Lists

The newly established, independent General Assembly, in October 1776 dealt with the matter of tithable lists because in some counties, no lists had been taken of those liable for taxes. Now, the legislature gave the courts the authority to divide the County into precincts and appoint one of the justices for each precinct to take the list of all tithables in their jurisdiction. The Justice had to give public notice of his appointment as the person to take the list of tithables in his precinct and had to indicate where and when he intended to take the list. This notice could be in form of an advertisement attached to the doors of meeting places and churches in his precinct.

Each person, when he gave his list of tithables to the Justice, was to include a list of wheeled carriages subject to taxes according to the earlier tax legislation.

Once the lists of tithables had been taken, the Justice was to deliver the list of names and numbers of tithables to the Clerk of the court. The Clerk of the court was to then set up fair copies of these lists in the Courthouse to make sure that the lists were accurate.

In addition the legislature dealt with consequences and penalties for justices who failed to take the lists and with tithable persons who handed in inaccurate lists of their tithes and/or their wheeled carriages.[28]

• 1776 Taxes to raise money for building fortifications, building, equipping and maintaining a Navy and for defraying expenses of the civil government

In October 1776, the legislature found that it had to raise money for a number of matters associated with the defense of the Commonwealth in this first year of the war for independence. Military forts were needed and an army had to be raised and equipped. The state needed to build, equip and find sailors and marines for new naval ships. Finally, the legislature needed to find ways to discharge the previous year's public debt as well as to find new ways to defray expenses of the civil governmental establishment for the coming year.

a. 1776 Tax on wheeled vehicles, tithes and land

The only way to accomplish this was to raise more taxes. First, there was to be an annual tax of 4s on every coach, chariot or four-wheeled carriage and 20s for every chair or two-wheeled carriages, wagons and carts only accepted. Second, the legislature continued the poll tax, this time at 5s for each tithable person; they continued, too, the tax on land at 5s per hundred acres. These taxes would be due on June 10th each year, beginning in 1784 and to continue until 1790.

The tax on carriages was to be paid by the proprietors thereof; the tax on tithables by the tithable himself, if a free man, or by his parent or guardian, if a minor; or by masters or owners of all slaves and servants. The tax on land was to be paid by the proprietor or parents or guardians in the County where the land lay.

The person charged with the taxes was to also give, along with his tithable list, a list of wheeled carriages and acreage to either the justices of the County court or to the person appointed to take the lists. The legislature also provided for penalties for failure to take the lists and for the consequences to the tax payer for concealing either carriages or acreage.

b. 1776 Tax on Ordinary Licenses, marriages and writs

Further more, those wishing to run an ordinary were to be taxed 40s for an ordinary license ; those wishing to marry were to be taxed 20s for a marriage license. The legislature also continued to tax court process (writs and chancery subpoenas) at a 2s 6d rate.[29]

- **Summary of the 1776 Tax situation in Virginia**

The two 1776 tax packages dealt primarily with raising money to sustain the military effort of Virginia against the British. Taxes were raised to support and maintain the army and infant navy and to deal with claims for damage to property. In the fall, additional taxes were assessed to raise money for the erection of military fortifications and to recruit and maintain the militia. Since the money raised in 1775 was inadequate to discharge Virginia's previous year's public debt and insufficient to defray the civil infrastructure's upcoming expenses, more taxes were needed.

The first tax package continued the poll tax on each tithable and the land tax on the proprietors or owners of land in the Commonwealth. The legislators extended the land and poll taxes through 1783 and made provision for a tax on wheeled carriages to be handed in when the list of Tithables was taken. Then, in the second tax package, passed in October 1776, the legislature provided again for the re-institution of the carriage tax and raised the poll tax and land taxes to 5s respectively. These taxes were to go into effect in 1783 and continued until 1790.

At the same time, they levied a tax on ordinary licenses, marriage licenses and continued the taxes on any court process either in law or chancery. Thus, the legislators hoped, the Commonwealth would be able to meet its obligations to it citizenry and to its military efforts in support of the united effort to rid these shores of British rule.

2. 1777 Tax Legislation
- **1777 Taxes for "publick exigencies"**

In 1777, the situation had change perceptively in Virginia vis-a-vis her relationship to the other newly established "states" and to Great Britain. Now, for the first time, Hening's *Statutes At Large* speak openly of the prosecution of the "present just and necessary war for the defence [sic] of our lives, liberties and property…" The Commonwealth had to come to terms with some very real issues: first, the United States and the Commonwealth's issue of bills of credit for large sums of money, which were already in circulation. Because of the volume, and because the bills of credit had flooded the arena of commerce, they had already begun to depreciate in value. This depreciation, legislators were afraid, would injure financially the people who traded in them and would hurt the United States conduct of the war and Virginia's daily operations.

In the words of Henings: ... the great danger of this [depreciation of the bills of credit] [to Virginia and to] the other United States which nothing will so effectually prevent as reducing the quantity, be establishing ample funds for redeeming proportions of it annually, until the whole shall be thereby called in and sunk.[30]

The Commonwealth realized, too, that it was necessary to establish some kind of permanent funding to provide for the repayment of money already borrowed or about to be borrowed by the United States, along with the Commonwealth, for carrying on the war.

For the first time, the Commonwealth instituted taxes for financial reasons, albeit associated with the War for Independence. Hening gives three over-riding financial reasons for the 1777 tax legislation: 1) to make a "just provision" for the fair proportion the Commonwealth ought to bear for sinking the bills of credit of the United States, and of the money borrowed by the U.S., along with the interest charged on this money; 2) the necessity to redeem the Commonwealth's own bills of credit, and payment of the money borrowed with interest; and 3) to come up with a way that all of this can be accomplished with the least amount of distress to its citizens.

a. Taxes on Land

New taxes had to be raised to achieve this. The General Assembly laid a new tax of 10s per L100 value on every owner or proprietor of manors, messuages, lands, tenements, slaves, mulatto servants to age 30, horses, mules, and plate. The tax was to be collected by August 1, 1778. These new taxes were to be collected on August 1st for the next six years (i.e. through 1784)

b. Taxes on income, debt, annuities and quitrents

Likewise, a rate of 10s for every L100 in the possession of one person, was to be paid by that person on August 1st of each year through 1785. The legislature also taxed, at a rate of 2s for every L paid for the amount of annual interest received on all debts bearing interest as well as for the amount of all annuities, including the quit rents owed the proprietor of the Northern Neck.

c. Taxes on Carriages, Cattle and Polls

A tax of 10s per wheel was laid upon all riding carriages; 4d per head on all neat cattle; 5 s per poll upon all tithables above the age of 21, except for soldiers, sailors, and the parish poor. These taxes were also due August 1st and were to be paid each year on that date for the next seven years. (i.e. through 1785.)

d. Taxes on Ordinaries and Marriages

An ordinary licenses now cost L3 in terms of taxes, while a marriage license carried a 20s tax, payable to the Clerk of the County court at the time of granting the license and extending until December 1784.

e. Taxes on salaries and profit

A new tax of 10s for every L100 was placed on all salaries and of the neat income of all offices of profit (excepting, however the military, either in the army or navy), due August 1, 1778 and for the next 6 years. (i.e. until 1784.)

f. Taxes on tobacco exported from Virginia

A tax of 10s was to be paid for every hogshead of tobacco exported out of Virginia by land or water from October 1777 until December 1, 1784.

g. Taxes on Liquor

A tax of 6d per gallon was to be paid on all spirituous liquor hereafter to be distilled in Virginia, payable before December 1, 1784 by the distiller. The tax also applied to any spirits imported into Virginia by land or water.

h. A double tax on citizens not taking Oath of Allegiance to the State

Any one who had not taken the oath of allegiance to Virginia by May 1, 1778 or who should have failed to produce a certificate of the oath, was to pay double the several rates and taxes listed above for property and tithables.

i. Repeal of previous taxes
Section XIV of this act stated that

"land and poll tax, and all other taxes and duties imposed by any former act of assembly or ordinance of convention, and which were payable at any time before [January 1, 1784] shall cease; and that the... acts and ordinances, so far as they relate to the imposition, collection, and payment of ... taxes... are hereby repealed, except so far as may enforce the collectors of any of the ... taxes heretofore due to account for and to pay the same.[31]

- **How the 1777 Taxes were to be spent**

The treasurer was to apply the money coming into his hands as a result of this legislation, first, to the annual payment on the quota the commonwealth owed towards the principal and interest for money borrowed on the U.S. treasury notes. The treasurer was also directed to deduct what came due to Virginia from these notes. The remaining money from the 1777 taxes was to be put towards debt reduction on interest payments for money borrowed by Virginia for commonwealth use and towards the redemption of any treasury notes payable on January 1, 1784.

- **Method of Election of Tax Commissioners for 1777**

Property holders of each County were to meet at the courthouse of their County on the second Tuesday in March each year, for six years, and freely elect three "able and discreet men" of their County. The legislature spelled out the qualifications for these tax commissioners: First they were to be land holders who had the right to vote; second, they had to hold land valued to L800; third, candidates could *not* be a member of any public boards or an officer in the army or navy. They could not be a manager of any public works, or an owner or manager of an iron works or arms factory. They could not be a master in a school or professor in a college. They could not be a clergyman, sheriff, inspector, ordinary keeper or a tax commissioner for the present year.

The legislature set up the way the election was to be held and gave the form for the oath of office, to be taken by the three duly elected tax commissioners.[32]

- **1777 Public Levy**

At the same legislative session, the legislators also looked at how to raise money for the public levy. Each tithable person was to pay 14 pounds of tobacco, either in tobacco or money, at the rate of 3d per pound to defray and pay for the public charge of the country. This levy was to be in effect from February 6, 1772 until December 20, 1777.[33]

- **Summary of the 1777 Taxes**

The tax and fiscal situation for Virginia in 1777 was grim. The war against Britain was not going well. The commonwealth treasury did not have sufficient funds to meet its daily obligations. Added to this was the financial confusion surrounding the bills of credit issued by the new United American States and by the State of Virginia.

It is indeed ironic Virginians, who were as vocal as everyone else in the years preceding 1776 regarding British taxation, should be taxed so heavily and so creatively by the wartime commonwealth legislature. Virginians were paying taxes, among other things, on income (!), salaries (!), debts, cattle, carriages, exported tobacco, slaves and liquor. The poll tax increased almost four fold. Avowed tories who refused to take the oath of allegiance to the commonwealth were taxed at twice the ordinary rate on their property and tithables. In addition, in a separate measure, the legislature laid down a public levy of 14 pounds of tobacco, at the rate of 3d per pound on each tithable person.

3. The 1778 Tax Legislation
In October 1778, the legislature decided to amend the previous year's "act for publick exigencies" for a number of reasons. The taxes raised in 1777 proved inadequate for the needs of the commonwealth. There were inequalities and injustices associated with the valuation of taxable property by assessors. Once more, additional taxes were needed to remedy the situation.

a. **Taxes on Manors, messuages, lands, tenements, slaves, mulatto servants, horses, mules and plate**

The legislature levied an additional tax of 20s for every L100 of value on all manors, messuages, lands, tenements, slaves, mulatto servants to age 31, horses, mules and plate from August 1, 1779 to August 1, 1784.

b. **Taxes on money in hand, and annuities**

A tax of 30s, including the former tax on money, for every L100, was to be paid for all money exceeding L5 in the possession of one person; this tax was due May 1st in each of then next five years. (i.e. May 1, 1779- May 1, 1784).

In addition, a tax of 4s for every pound of the amount of all annuities, including quit rents owed to the proprietor of the Northern Neck, was to be paid August 1st in each of the next six years. This tax did *not* include dower rights or provisions to wounded soldiers or their families.

c. **Taxes on carriages, neat cattle and tithables**

A tax of 20s per wheel was levied on all riding carriages. Taxes of 1s per head were laid on all cattle and 10s per poll was levied on all tithables above 21 years of age. The poll tax excluded soldiers, sailors, the parish poor, wounded soldiers or injuries to public officials in pursuance of their duties. Likewise, slaves and mulatto servants to age 31 were also excepted since they were considered property and had already been taxed at the rate of 20s per every L100 of value.

These taxes were to go into effect August 1, 1779 and to continue for the next six years.

d. **Tax on Ordinary Licenses**

A tax of L6 was levied for every ordinary license taken out and was to be paid to the clerk of the county court at the time the license was granted. This tax was to continue until December 1, 1784.

e. **A tax on neat income of all offices of profit**

A tax of 20s for every L100 of neat income of all offices of profit was to be paid August 1, 1779 and in each of the next five years.

f. **A tax on liquor**

An additional tax of 1s per gallon was to be paid for all spirituous liquors hereafter distilled in Virginia. The tax was to be paid by the distiller. If the liquor was imported into Virginia at any time before December 1, 1784, by either land or water, the tax was to be paid by the importer.

g. **A tax on persons who did not take oath of allegiance to the state of Virginia**

Any person who did not take an oath of allegiance to the State of Virginia, as required by law, was to pay three times (!) the amount owed on the taxes enumerated above.

The legislature left to the counties the method the commissioners and their assessors, limited to no more than sixteen per county, were to pursue in rating these articles of taxation. The legislature went on to specify compensation for the tax officers, damages owed by sheriffs for failure to collect taxes, and other administrative details associated with the collection of these taxes.

This act also specifically exempted any tobacco exported from Virginia or other states for the use of the French West Indies from any duty or tax. Moreover, any tobacco cleared out of Virginia and exported to any of the West Indies belonging to France, was exempted from any duty or tax. Previously, the legislature had taxed hogsheads of tobacco to be exported to the French West Indies. This legislation was necessary to bring the commonwealth into compliance with the French-American trade agreement.

The last item this taxation measure dealt with was the tax on those not taking the oath of allegiance to Virginia.

> ...whereas many good people of this commonwealth, who are well affected to the cause of their country, were prevented taking the oath of allegiance by the negligence of the magistrates, whereby they have been subjected to the penalty of a double tax [now tripled in the 1778 legislation!], as prescribed by an act requiring all the free male inhabitants of this state to give assurance of fidelity and allegiance to the same...[34]

If anyone was able to show the tax commissioners that he had since taken the oath of allegiance, then the county was to refund all but the original tax.[35]

- **Summary of 1778 Taxes**

The taxes for 1777 had not proved sufficient to meet the needs of the commonwealth and the legislature amended the previous year's tax package for public exigencies by raising taxes in all categories for 1778.

Taxes on land and personal property went from 10s to 20s; taxes on money went from 10s to 30s for every L100 in hand; the tax on annuities went from 2s to 4s; the tax on carriages continued to be on a per wheel basis, this time going from 10s to 20s per wheel; The tax on each head of neat cattle went from 4d to 1s per head; the poll tax went from 5s per tithable to 10s per tithable; Ordinary licenses now cost L6, doubling the 1777 tax; taxes on income at 10s for every L100 in 1777 doubled in 1778; the liquor tax went from 6d per gallon to 1s per gallon and the tax trebled for those who did not take the oath of allegiance to the commonwealth in 1778.

In each instance where the tax was raised, the legislature also kept the existing exemptions applied to wounded soldiers, families of soldiers in the army or navy, and officers or soldiers, sailors, and the parish poor or others established as exempt by the county courts.

Interestingly, the 1778 package did not include the previous year's tax on marriage licenses and specifically exempted tobacco exported from Virginia or other states for the use of the French West Indies.

So, we still have a grim tax and fiscal situation as it related to Virginia and its attempts to meet its daily responsibilities in a wartime atmosphere and economy.

4. The 1779 Tax situation
- **Disagreements over valuation of the tax on land and slaves brought about new tax legislation**

In May 1779, the General Assembly met to consider its 1777 and 1778 tax legislation. Apparently, doubts had arisen among the commissioners and assessors of the taxes, especially regarding the tax on land. There was a disagreement, among other things, as to whether the land should be valued at what it would sell for in gold and silver or what it would bring if sold for the U.S. and commonwealth paper bills of credit.

There was a similar disagreement over the assessment of slaves. It was supposed that the assessment on slaves was to be rendered much more equal via the poll tax and was settled so "as to bear the proportion of one and a half per cent to their average value.

- **May 1779 Taxes**

a. Poll tax on slaves
The legislature decided to deal with the tax on slaves through a poll tax. A L5 tax per poll was to be paid for all negro and mulatto servants and slaves. A discount was allowed to the owner for any of his or her slaves who were too old or had a bodily infirmity or were incapable of working. The owner had to show satisfactory proof of these conditions to the tax commissioner. There was a stiff penalty of L50 for concealing information regarding the conditions of slaves.

b. Tax on Money
Doubts also arose regarding the construction on the tax on money: was it intended that the 30s tax per L100 in a person's possession on May 1 be paid for 1777 or begin May 1, 1778? The legislature decreed that this tax was to be paid for money any person had in their possession at sunrise, July 20, 1779 and at sunrise on March 1 of the next five years (i.e. until 1784). No tax was to be paid on Continental bills of credit of May 20, 1777 and April 11, 1778 since that currency had already been stopped by Congressional resolution.

c. Tax on Exported Tobacco

Tobacco exported for the use of any of the West India islands belonging to the King of France was exempted from the tax on tobacco. This brought the commonwealth tax on exported tobacco into conformity with the Trade Agreement between America's French allies and the infant United American States.

Instead, a tax of 30s per hogshead of all exported tobacco was to be paid down to the inspector *before* shipment and paid by him to the treasurer on or before October 25 annually during the continuance of this act.

- **Method of Collection of 1779 Taxes**

The legislature directed the sheriffs or other collectors to receive in payment for any or all of the taxes imposed here receipts for the paper currency of May 20, 1777 and April 11, 1778 that Congress took out of circulation.[36]

a. May 1779 tax on Enumerated commodities

These taxes were raised for two primary reasons: 1) to support public credit and provide for armaments; and 2) to provide for the "more immediate" defense of the commonwealth in relation to Virginia's quota of troops in the Continental Army.

b. Commodity tax on all tithables above 16 years of age

Every man over the age of 16 and every woman slave over the age of 16 (except those adjudged by the county court to be too old, infirm or unable to work) was to deliver to the commissary the following commodities:

1) one bushel of wheat **or**
2) two bushels of Indian corn, rye or barley **or**
3) ten pecks of oats **or**
4) 15 lbs. of sound, clean and merchantable hemp **or**
5) 28 lbs. of inspected tobacco in transfer notes

This tax, payable in any of the above commodities, was due in March 1780. The county court was to appoint two commissioners who were to select a place within the county to receive these goods. The commissioners were empowered to find store houses and employ a commissary there so that they could receive, keep accounts for and store the commodities.

Each person bringing in one of these taxable assets was to be given a receipt for the same. The commissioners could contract with millers to manufacture wheat and rye into flour or meal and to contract for barrels for their preservation.

The commissioners of commodities, as they were styled in the county court minutes, were required to account, upon oath, all the commodities they received, stating, for each person, the quantity and kind of every article received. They were also required to show the quantities of wheat and rye delivered to millers for manufacturing into flour or meal. Then, the commissioners were to take these lists and, with the last list of tithables, put together "distinct accounts of all deficiencies occasioned by non-payment" by the tax payers in the county. They were to charge money for each person so described, estimating the deficiency as if the whole had been in wheat, at the highest market price.

The commissioners were to deliver these certified accounts to the sheriff and tax commissioner on or before May 1st for collection.

This legislation then went on to set out the duties, allowances and liabilities of the commissioners of commodities.[37]

- **October 1779 Tax for raising money supply for service of the United States**

In October 1779 the Legislature met to consider more tax measures in order to cover expenses for supplies owed by Virginia to the Continental congress. Interestingly enough, this tax measure states that the objective of the war with Great Britain was civil liberty. The Continental congress's demand for supplies from the states was rendered to avoid the "ruinous expedient of future emissions of paper money". The thinking in the legislature was that further tax measures could forestall such financial embarrassment.

The legislature felt that there were only two choices: "either to support the common cause by taxation, or having lavished so much blood and treasure, to submit to an humiliating, inglorious, and disadvantageous peace."[38]

These taxes, the legislature said, were necessary to comply with the requisitions and were warranted "by necessity." These new taxes were *in addition* to the current tax package:

  a. **1779 Poll Tax**

  A poll tax of L3 per head was to be paid by all free males above 21 years of age as well as by all white servants (except for those apprentices under legal age). Officers of the line, naval officers, soldiers and sailors in the State or Continental forces were exempt from this tax. So, too, were those who had been exempted by the local county court for the payment of the county levy.

  b. **Tax on slaves**

  A tax of L4 per poll was placed on all slaves, except those exempted due to old age or infirmities by tax commissioners. Both the poll tax on free males over 21 years of age and the poll tax on slaves was due on or before February 1780.

  c. **Tax on wheeled vehicles**

  Instead of taxing riding vehicles by the wheel, as in previous legislation, the legislature now decreed a tax on coaches and chariots for L40 apiece, payable by their owner; Owners of all four wheel carriages and stage waggons used for riding were taxed at L30 for each vehicle they possessed while owners of all two-wheeled riding chairs were taxed at L10 for each riding chair.

  d. **Tax on rum, brandy and spirits distilled from grain**

  The legislature laid an 8s tax per gallon on rum and brandy and a 6s tax per gallon on all spirits distilled from grain as a further means of raising the necessary supplies for the service of the United American States. This tax was to be paid after February 1780.

  e. **Sales Tax on all goods, wares and merchandise**

  The legislature also levied a 2 ½ % sales tax on the amount of sales on all goods wares and merchandise, **except for** salt, blankets, iron, steel, arms, and ammunition imported or brought into this state. This tax was passed onto the consumer.

  The seller had to render an account, under oath, of every sale of goods where the amount of the sale exceeded L1000 within a month of the sale. If the vender failed to do so, he paid a penalty of three times the value of the tax on these goods.

  The reason the legislature gave for passing this entirely new tax legislation was so that the burden of taxes "may be equally borne, as well by the merchants and dealers, as the planters and farmers..."[39]

  f. **Tax on imported goods into Virginia**

  Another 2 ½ % tax was imposed on goods, wares and merchandise *brought into* or imported into Virginia by non-residents of the commonwealth, where the amount exceeded L1000 in value. As in the sales tax legislation, salt, blankets, iron, steel, arms, and ammunition were exempt from this tax.[40]

g. Further measures in this October 1779 tax bill, taken to meet Virginia's obligations to the war effort

The legislature reserved and appropriated fifteen hundred thousand pounds for the payment of the requisitions of Congress. This outlay was to come from the net proceeds of the sales of British sequestered estates. A like sum of another fifteen hundred thousand pounds, was to be taken out of the taxes, which are to be collected this year.

A further L600,000 would be realized in the sales of the specific taxes passed in the 1778 legislative session. That act had laid a tax on enumerated commodities that could have been paid by the furnishing the goods themselves and getting credit according to their value **or** by disposing of the goods and paying the money to the order of congress. Using these measures, the legislature felt confident that the commonwealth would be able to satisfy Virginia's requirements owed to the Continental Congress.[41]

The rest of this October 1779 tax legislation was taken up with the way this tax package was to be administered and covered all aspects of the collection of these taxes.[42]

- **October 1779 Rider to Tax Bill for raising supply of money for the service of the United States**

The purpose of this rider was to speed up the payment of the poll taxes and taxes on riding vehicles. The act enabled the sheriffs, empowered by the previous legislation to collect these taxes, to pay the money directly into the commonwealth's Treasury on or before April 1780.[43] The legislature also made provisions for the advance payment of taxes assessed by this legislation.[44]

- **October 1779 Act to provide further supplies for government exigencies**

Once again, the taxes imposed on the commonwealth's citizenry were not proving to be sufficient for day to day operations of the civil government. Additional taxes were needed.

a. Taxes on property, taxes and cattle

An additional tax of ½ % had already been laid on all kinds of property, assessed *ad valorem* in the previous session. Now, that ½ % tax was extended to include all monies any person had in their possession on sunrise March 1, 1780.

b. Taxes on neat cattle

Owners were to pay an additional tax of 6s 8d per head of neat cattle within the commonwealth.

c. Taxes on ordinary licenses

The additional L40 tax on ordinary licenses was to be paid by the licensee to the clerk of the county court when the license was granted.[45]

- **Summary of 1779 Tax Packages**

There were several striking differences between the 1779 tax packages and the previous ones. The tax on slaves was now to be handled through the poll tax with a straight L5 tax on all negro and mulatto servants and slaves rather than through a property tax based on the value of the slave. The tax on money in hand was clarified – the tax was to be paid for money in hand at sunrise July 29, 1779 and then at sunrise on March 1st for the next five years. Tobacco exported to the French West Indies was exempt from taxation; however, there was a 30s tax per hogshead on all exported tobacco *before* shipment.

The other innovative and new tax package the legislature introduced in the May 1779 tax package concerned the delivery of enumerated commodities. Now each tithable person and woman slave over the age of 16 was responsible for delivering to the commissioner of the commodities tax a prescribed quantity of either wheat, corn, rye, barley, oats, hemp or tobacco

These taxes were instituted to not only support the public credit and provide for armaments; they also helped the commonwealth provide for the defense of the commonwealth in relation to the states' quota of troops to be supplied to the Continental establishment.

In October 1779, a flurry of tax packages were passed, all designed to try to keep up with the state's burgeoning responsibilities to the war effort and to the efficient running of the civil bureaucracy. The poll tax increased dramatically – from 10s to L3 for all free males over 21. The poll tax on each slave was continued, although now the tax was reckoned at L4 per slave. In each instance the former exemptions continued in effect with regards to these taxes on tithables and slaves. Carriages were now taxed by the vehicle instead of by the wheel and there was a hefty increase in the taxes on wheeled vehicles. Liquor was not categorized – rum and brandy were tax a 8s per gallon; spirits distilled from grain were to be taxed at 6s per gallon.

The legislature introduced another innovative package so that the merchants, dealers, planters and farmers might have an equal share in the tax burden. This entirely new tax was a 2 ½ % sales tax on all goods, wares and merchandise. The legislature specifically exempted any goods that could be associated with the war effort: salt, blankets, iron, steel, arms, and ammunition. The tax was *not* paid by the vender. It was paid by the consumer.

The legislature also inaugurated a 2 ½ % tax on all imported goods into Virginia by non residents where the amount exceeded L1000 in value.

Realizing that it was still increasingly difficult to keep up with the commonwealth's obligation to the war effort, the General Assembly reserved and appropriated 1,500,000 pounds from the net proceeds of the sales of British sequestered estates. They also reserved another 1,500,000, to be taken out of the taxes to be collected for 1779.

Moreover, the legislature believed that the State would have a further L600,000 from sales of the specific taxes passed the year before and so were confident that these fiscal measures would allow them to meet their obligations to the successful prosecution of the war.

Unfortunately, this illusion lasted only until the fall session of the General Assembly. Once again, the legislature had to admit that the earlier taxes mandated at the spring 1779 legislative session were not sufficient to run the civil governmental infrastructure. Still more taxes were needed. Tithables were charged a ½ % tax on money in hand; the legislators decided to continue the already imposed ½ % tax on property. Taxes also went up for each head of neat cattle and for ordinary licenses. It was not a good year for Virginia's citizens.

5. May 1780 Taxes
- **An Act to call in and redeem money now in circulation and to issue and fund new bills of credit**

In May 1780, the General Assembly decided to call in and destroy "the excessive mass of money now in circulation. If the state did not call in and redeem this money at its depreciated value, the legislature feared it would increase the national debt thirty nine times greater than it actually was. This would have the net result of subjecting Virginia's citizens to many more years of "grievous and unnecessary taxation." By calling in this money, the commonwealth would then be in compliance with the congressional resolutions of March, 1779 to do this very thing. To do this, the legislature mandated that the taxes raised in October 1779 for public exigencies be used to call in and destroy the depreciated money now in circulation.

a. 1780 Tax on property

To support these measures, the legislature introduced a new tax in place of the old 1779 property tax.

The new tax, to be levied and collected by a general assessment of all and every article of property, used the values and assessment of the tax plan of 1777. Land value was to be based on what it would have sold for, for ready money, in the year 1774, before the revolutionary war, when the economic system was much more stable.

In 1780, this new tax was to be assessed at the rate of L30 of money now in circulation per every L100 of valuation of property as it would have been sold in the year 1774; It was to be paid in three separate payments. The first payment was due on or before January 1781; the second payment was due on or before April 15, 1781 and the third payment was due on or before September 15, 1781.

b. Tax on money, tithables, servants, carriages, spirits, marriages and ordinary licenses

Taxes due between January and September 1781 were to be paid in the paper money of Virginia at the following rates: A tax of 15s was levied on money in hand at sunrise either on October 1, 1780 or on March or August 1, 1781.

A poll tax of L3 6s 8d was to be paid by each white tithable male of legal age, excluding only apprentices who were minors and members of the military or those already exempted by the county court.

Cattle were taxed at 6s a head; coaches and carriages were taxed at L26 6s 8d; phaetons, 4 wheeled chaises and stage waggons used to ride in were taxed at L20; 2 wheeled chaises and chairs were taxed at L6 6s 8d.

Brandy distilled in Virginia carried a tax of 10s per gallon; spirits distilled from grain not taxed before, carried a tax of 8s per gallon.

The tax on marriage licenses was re-instituted – it carried a hefty L10 tax and ordinary licenses jumped dramatically to L200. The marriage license and ordinary license taxes were to be paid to the clerk of the court before the license was issued.

c. Taxes on appropriated land belonging to the commonwealth

A new tax was laid on appropriated lands as well. From now on, L160 per hundred acres was to be paid for all treasury land warrants, except preemptions. This tax was passed in order to fix the price of any unappropriated lands belonging to the state at a rate that would make up the depreciation of money.

d. Provision for payment of taxes

All of these taxes, including money for unappropriated lands, were to be paid in U.S. bills of credit, Virginia bills of credit now in circulation, or in Spanish milled dollars at a rate of 6s each or in lawful gold and silver at a proportionate value. The bills of credit were to be issued on the security of the commonwealth and be received at a rate of $1.00 for every $40.00 of the bills of credit.

In order to sink the money now in circulation, the legislature set the rates for goods offered in payment in lieu of money (like tobacco, marketable hemp, flax and fine inspected flour) The legislature also dealt with the methods for providing sufficient funds for the state if present measures proved inadequate. Provisions were made regarding the duties of both assessors and commissioners of taxes in the respective counties and the duties of the sheriffs in collecting these taxes. Accounts were to be returned to State auditors by the commissioners. Finally the legislation also dealt with salaries to the tax officials responsible for its collection and dispersal to the state.[46]

Other legislation in the same act developed a policy for the redemption of the bills of credit. One hundred and seventy thousand pounds was needed to redeem the bills of credit. This sum was to be raised by the following taxes:

e. Tax on property

A tax or pound rate of 1%, according to value, or 20s per L100 was to be levied and paid on all article of property for the redemption of money now in circulation. The legislature also passed a ½ % tax on every L100 of specie, or 10s for every L100 of property to be levied and paid twice a year in May and September.

f. Tax on Tithables
Every free male above 21 years of age, and all white servants of legal age, except for apprentices who were minors, was to pay 2s.

g. Tax on neat cattle
Neat cattle were taxed at 3d per head.

h. Tax on riding vehicles
Owners of phaetons, 4 wheeled chaises and stage wagons used for riding were to pay 20s for each vehicle in their possession; owners of 2 wheeled chaises and riding chairs were to pay 5s for each vehicle.

i. Taxes on merchants or factors
This was a new tax, for 10s per hundred pounds on each merchant's or factor's stock in trade.

j. Taxes on annual profits of public offices not fixed by salaries and on annuities.
The legislature place a tax of 1s per pound on the annual profits of all public offices not fixed by salaries. The tax was to be rated by the county assessors with the right of appeal to the commissioner of taxes.

A like tax of 2s per pound was to be paid on all annuities, including the quit rents owed to the proprietor of the Northern Neck.

k. Taxes on liquor
Brandy was taxed at 3d per gallon; spirits distilled from grain in Virginia were taxed at 2 ½ pence.

l. Taxes on marriages and Ordinaries
The legislature placed a 5s tax on all marriages and a 50s tax on all ordinary licenses.[47]

The legislature again specified that the above taxes were to be used to call in all the money then in circulation.

- **May 1780 repeal of all other taxes except specific taxes and other legislation**
All other taxes, except the specific taxes, were to cease as of December 31, 1781.

The legislature also dealt with the term of tax commissioners and their allowance and various penalties for commissioners, assessors and sheriff if they failed to perform to perform their allotted duties. The legislature also provided for bonding of sheriffs and dealt in some detail with the punishment that accrued to counterfeiters.

Finally, the legislature provided that the execution of this tax legislation was to be suspended until the Governor received authentic advice that a majority of the states actually approved the Congressional resolution that set up these procedures. Georgia and South Carolina were not included in the majority of states since they were still occupied by the British.

Once the Governor had received notification that a majority of the rest of the states had approved or acceded to the congressional resolutions, the act was to be carried out and a proclamation was to be issued to Virginia's residents for that purpose.[48]

6. May 1780 Tax package to issue and fund money for present "urgent necessities of this commonwealth

The legislature empowered the treasurer of the commonwealth to issue treasury notes in dollars in any amount necessary to run the civil government. The treasurer was responsible for the printing and engraving of these notes on paper that would discourage counterfeiting.

The bills were to be exchanged and redeemed in Spanish milled dollars or the value in gold or silver at the rate of $1.00 for every $40.00 at the Treasury on or before December 31, 1784.

In order to establish a fund which would proved sufficient to redeem these new bills of credit, the legislature came up with still another tax package:[49]

a. A window tax

This was an entirely new tax. Every proprietor of an inhabited house within the commonwealth was to pay a tax of 1s for each glass window in his house. The tax was due in September 1781 and to be paid for the next three years. (i.e. until September 1784)

Assessors in each county were given the responsibility for an exact count of all the glass windows within their jurisdiction and to return that account to the commissioner of tax for their respective county.[50]

b. Tax on land conveyances

This was another new tax. Now, there was to be a 20s tax on each deed of conveyance and mortgage for lands, recorded in any of the courts within Virginia. This tax was to be paid by the grantee. It was due in October 1780 and was to remain in effect until October 1784. This 20s tax applied when the land being conveyed amounted to 400 acres or more.

A tax of 10s, to be paid by the grantee, applied when the land being conveyed or mortgaged was under 400 acres. It, too, was due in October 1780 and was to remain in effect until October 1784. Town lots, the legislature said, were to be taxed at the 20s rate.

The taxes were to be paid to the court with the admonition that clerks would not entered the conveyance into the record without the tax payment.[51]

c. Tax on exported tobacco

An 8s tax per hogshead was placed on exported tobacco, to be paid by the exporter, on tobacco leaving Virginia by either land or water. If the tobacco agent intended to export tobacco by land, than they were to make an application for this to the clerk of the county court where the tobacco was to be exported. The tax was due at the time of application. A penalty of L500 per hogshead was assessed for exporting tobacco contrary to this act.

If the tobacco was to be exported by water, the tobacco agents were to pay the 8s tax per hogshead to the inspector of the warehouse where the inspection of the tobacco took place. If the tax was not paid, the tobacco was not to be delivered.

Upon enactment of this legislation, tobacco inspectors were to take an oath to collect and account for money received for the exported tobacco in front of the county court. In addition, tobacco inspectors were to take out a bond with security. The tax money for exported tobacco was due, annually, in May and October and was to be transmitted immediately to the auditors for public accounts. Finally, the legislature repealed any duty heretofore imposed upon the exportation of tobacco, thus leaving only this new tax as the tax on tobacco.[52]

d. Tax on imported liquor

A tax or duty of one penny per gallon, was to be paid by the importer of each gallon of rum or other spirits imported into Virginia. The tax was due on October 1, 1780 and to continue in effect until October 1783.

If the liquor was imported by land, then the importer, at the time of his arrival into Virginia, was to apply to the clerk of the that county to give him an accurate account of the quantity of liquor being imported. The importer, at the time of handing over this account to the clerk of court, then was to pay him the tax for each and every gallon so imported into the commonwealth. In the event that importers circumvented this act, they were to be liable for confiscation of all liquor in their hands. Whoever informed on the importer's effort to avoid the tax was to be paid 5s per gallon for his information.

Captain or masters of ships bringing spirits or liquor into Virginia by water were to pay the one penny tax to the naval officer in whose District the ship was to enter, *before* the liquor was opened. The captain had the option of taking out a bond, with security, to pay the tax within 30 days thereafter.[53] The legislature laid down the detailed penalties for non-payment of this duty[54].

- **Method of payment for May 1780 taxes to fund money to supply the present "urgent necessities of this commonwealth"**

These taxes, imposed to help pay for governmental expenses during 1780, could be paid in one of four ways: 1) in Spanish milled dollars at the rate of 6s each; 2) in other gold or silver coin at a proportional value; 3) in bills of credit, issued at the rate of forty paper dollars for one Spanish milled dollar; 4) in like proportion for other gold or silver coins.

The legislature noted that the notes or bills of credit circulated by this act, could be used only to pay for the taxes raised under this May 1780 "urgent necessities" tax bill. When the bills were received into the Treasury, they were to be burnt. The gold and silver received into the treasury, as payment of these taxes, were to be used *only* to redeem the paper bills of credit which remained outstanding.

The final section of this act dealt with the penalties and punishment associated with forging and/or counterfeiting any bill of credit or treasury note issued as the result of this tax legislation.[55]

During the same legislative session, the legislators realized that some of the counties were delinquent in the payment of the specific tax on commodities and passed legislation to allow for this.[56]

7. October 1780 Tax legislation
- **An act to explain and amend the act calling in money...according to March 1780 Congressional resolutions**

Since there was some doubt as to the construction of the May 1780 tax legislation dealing with redeeming paper money according to the March Congressional resolutions, the legislature decided to clarify the situation.

The Treasurer could exchange the money emitted by this act for money currently in circulation. However the paper money to be issued for governmental necessities was to be exchanged at the rate of $1.00 of new money for $40.00 of the old money.

Taxes on assessed property were to be paid in three equal payments: L30 on January 1781, L30 on April 15, 1781 and L30 on September 15, 1781.

All taxes imposed prior to this legislation, except specific taxes, were to cease and be discontinued as of December 31, 1780.

Since a majority of states had not approved the March 1780 Congressional resolution calling in the states' paper money, the legislature went on to detail the value of their paper money. Money issued by both May 1780 acts were to be considered legal tender with a rate of exchange at $1.00 to $40.00 of the money now in circulation.

The legislature then dealt with how the money was to be appropriated and other fiscal measures.[57]

- **October 1780 Tax legislation for procuring a supply of money to continue the war**

The legislature realized that they needed a further distribution of paper money until the other 1780 acts went into effect. So the Treasurer was given permission to issue treasury notes in dollars for any money necessary for public necessities The sum of new money was not to exceed 6 million pounds, unless a public emergency would render issuing further sums.

If new funds become needed, then the Governor could authorize, with the advice of the council, a sum totaling no more than 4 million pound. The Governor would lay the need before the General Assembly who would provide its redemption. The Governor, with the advice of his council also had the power to stop the distribution of money should the necessities of the commonwealth permit.

These bills were to be exchanged and redeemed in spanish milled dollars, or their value in gold or silver at rate of one for forty at the Treasury on or before December, 1790.

In order to establish a fund sufficient to redeem these bills of credit, the October 1780 legislative session lay these taxes on Virginia's residents:

a. Taxes on lands, slaves and other property

A tax was to be imposed on lands, slaves and other property within the commonwealth, via general assessment, adequate to that end and collected so as to redeem all the bills of credit within five years, to commence from December 30, 1785.

The money to be emitted was to be received in payment of all taxes already imposed and was to be considered legal tender in discharge of all debts and contracts.

b. Bills of Credit

The Treasurer was given the authority to exchange any of the bills of credit circulated by congress and now in circulation in the commonwealth with those wishing to do so. The legislature exempted the bills of credit already emitted (and to be called in) according to the March Congressional resolution.

The penalty for forgery or counterfeiting these bills was death, without benefit of clergy.

All certificates granted by public agents and commissioners for horses, provisions, or other articles furnished the public are to be receivable as payment of any tax or duty whatsoever.[58]

- **October 1780 Tax legislation to amend the act for giving further time for counties to pay their specific taxes**

    In the October 1780 legislative session the General Assembly dealt, once again with allowing counties more time to pay specific taxes.[59]

- **October 1780 legislation for more "effectual collection" of taxes and public duties**

    The same legislative session also dealt with coming up with ways to make the collection of taxes more efficient: The legislation provided for a Solicitor General to be responsible for the account books kept by the board of auditors of public accounts. The legislature lay out his duties to his office and the measures he could take to move against delinquent tax payers.[60]

- **Summary of the 1780 tax situation**

    In many instances, the 1780 tax legislation was just more of the same for Virginia residents. The commonwealth, like the rest of the independent states, was paying the price for being part of a loose confederacy of states rather than forming a union around a central government.

    Each state had the right to place their own import duties on trade coming into their jurisdiction. Virginia was no exception. Thus, any merchant or farmer who dealt with inter-state commerce realized that such trade was fraught with difficulties. Farmers, planters and merchants were all taxed on their goods, whether through a tax on their cattle, their brandy or their spirits distilled from grain, or a tax on tobacco or a tax on stock in trade. Merchants were taxed to export tobacco.

The tax payers of Virginia (that is, the free males over 21) were taxed for *each* riding vehicle they owned rather than by the number of wheels the vehicle had. Even wagons, if they were used to get from place to place, were taxed. Then, as tithables, they were taxed for each free male over the age of 21; they were taxed for each slave. If one of their family members wanted to marry, they paid a tax for a marriage license. Inn and tavern keepers also paid a hefty tax to operate an ordinary.

Finally there were taxes that affected even the wealthiest of Virginia's residents. Every proprietor of an inhabited house was to pay a tax for each glass window in his house. Virginia's office holders who were not salaried were expected to pay a tax on their salaries. Then there were the taxes on annuities, including quit rents owed to the proprietors of the northern neck. Finally, any one who purchased land or took out a mortgage had to pay a tax for recording their conveyance in the county court. In an attempt to stabilize land values, the General Assembly attempted to set the worth of acreage at a pre-Revolutionary 1774 levels.

Added to the already complex tax situation in which Virginians found themselves, were the difficulties associated with the disproportionate amount of paper money in circulation through out the commonwealth. There were already treasury notes issued by Congress and bills of credit offered by the commonwealth before the 1780 tax legislation. The General Assembly, in both their legislative sessions, passed laws to call in and redeem some of the previously issued notes and bills of credit. At the same time, however, they passed new laws to print even *more* money. Added to these notes was the paper money issued by Maryland and by the Carolinas, in general circulation, due to the import duties on liquor and tobacco. Inflation was rampant largely because of the excessive amount of paper in circulation whether legal tender or its forged or counterfeited counterparts.

What was all this paper worth? How do you deal with forgery of bank notes? Or counterfeiting? How do you deal with rampant inflation? How do you fund the war effort? How do you fund the civil infrastructure? What measures do you take to call in the largely worthless paper bills or credit and still be able to issue money to pay for the government's needs for 1780? These were the kinds of questions the General Assembly faced as they headed into a fourth year of war with Great Britain.

At the same time, they realized that more taxes would be needed to call in the paper bills now in circulation. Moreover, they realized that until the currency was tied to something of recognizable value, it would be all but worthless even if they did decree it to be legal tender. So, in both sessions, the legislators made laws tying the value of the new bills to Spanish milled dollars or their equivalent in gold or silver coins.

Virginia's tax and fiscal policy was no different than the other twelve independent states under the war time Articles of Confederation. It merely pointed up the flaws inherent in the United American States' individual efforts to coin money tied to their own standards of value without sufficient protection against forgery and counterfeiting and to lay taxes on both residents and on trade from other states. For example, when Virginia taxed liquor imported from Maryland, Maryland retaliated with a tax on liquor imported from Virginia. Legal tender in Virginia might or might not be accepted across the Potomac. Or the rate of exchange may have been disproportionate between Virginia bills and Maryland currency. Thrown into this wild mix of paper money were the United States Treasury notes, issued by the wartime Confederation Congress.

It is small wonder that, from a tax and fiscal standpoint alone, the Articles of Confederation were scuttled in favor of a government with a strong, centralized tax and fiscal system.

8. 1781 Taxes: Overview

Hostilities between the Americans and Great Britain ended in October 1781 when Cornwallis surrendered at Yorktown. In February 1782, the British House of Commons recognized the inevitable and voted against continuing the war. It would then take the British nearly eighteen months more before they would sign the Treaty of Paris in September 1783.[61]

In the interim between the end of hostilities in October 1781 and the signing of the Treaty of Paris in September 1783, the Virginia legislature met to move towards peace-time legislation and to deal with several challenges. One of the foremost was the task of producing tax legislation that would ensure the state's financial stability. This meant putting together a tax package that would not be overly cumbersome to its citizens. It also meant coming up with a way to collect the taxes in a fair and timely manner in the local jurisdictions.

In both sessions of the 1781 General Assembly, the legislature gave counties more time to pay their specific taxes (the tax payable in enumerated commodities). In the May session, the General Assembly dealt with the grain taxes in delinquent counties.[62]

The November session dealt with allowing more time for the collection of the 1781 taxes due to the distress caused Virginians by the invasion of British troops. More time was given for collecting, accounting for and paying the 1781 taxes.[63]

Barely a month after the end of the fighting the General Assembly met and passed one of its first pieces of tax legislation This legislation accomplished several goals. It set out the way the taxes were to be collected and it listed the rate of taxation for certain enumerated articles.

The legislature established the way the counties were to appoint commissioners of taxes, how the taxes were to be received, the penalties for non-collection, where the taxes were to be sent, how the accounts of the tax returns were to be made, and the powers of the sheriff in the collection of these taxes.[64]

- **November 1781 Taxes on Enumerated Commodities**

    The General Assembly made taxes, heretofore payable in paper or hard currency, payable in commodities. They issued the following taxes on tithables and slaves.

    a. **Poll Tax on Tithables and slaves**

    A tax of ½ bushel of wheat or a bushel of corn, rye or barley, or five pecks of oats was placed on each free man above the age of 21 and for each slave over the age of 16. A list of tithables and slaves was to be furnished by the tax commissioners to the clerk of the county court. The tithable person was then to deliver to the clerk of the county court the tax in form of one of the above commodities. Tax payers had the option to pay their taxes for each bushel of wheat, 3s specie in Spanish milled dollars at 6s each; or in other gold or silver coin at proportional value.

    b. **Tax on each person in household and slaves**

    In addition a tax of 2 lbs. of "good sound" bacon was assessed on each free *person* above the age of 21 and on each slave above the age of 16. Taxpayers could choose to pay this tax at 6d for each pound of bacon in Spanish milled dollars or in gold or silver coins.

- **November 1781 Act for ascertaining certain taxes and duties and for establishing a permanent revenue**

    Seven taxes were levied in this 1781 tax legislation:

    a. **The Tax on Lands**

    A tax of L10 for every L100 of the valuation of lands and lots, in proportion for greater or lesser sums, was levied on land in each county.

    The General Assembly set out guidelines for the appointment of three commissioners, any two of whom could act, to ascertain the value of all the lands, except their own, within their jurisdiction. Two of the justices appointed by the county court were to ascertain the value of land of any commissioner.

After setting out the oath the commissioners were to take, the General Assembly established their duties. The commissioners of the land tax were to account, in writing, for the name of the proprietor, his quantity of land and the value of his land by its acreage. Town lots were to be valued separately from other lands. The valuation was to be completed without regard to any buildings or other improvement on the land.

The legislature went on to establish the procedures to follow for vacancies in this post and dealt with the penalties that would accrue for the failure of proprietors to cooperate in the valuation.

Once the list of proprietors and number and value of their land had been computed in acreage, it was to be returned to the clerk of the county court on or before June 1st of each year. . The clerk was to make out three copies. One copy was to go to the sheriff or collector of taxes, each year, before June 10th. The clerk of the court was to deliver another copy to the auditors of public accounts by August 1st of each year. The clerk was to set up the last copy in the court house on the next court day following its delivery by the commissioners.

The legislature stipulated small monetary allowances to the commissioners, sheriff and clerks of the court for performing the duties required and established penalties for any of these official's refusal, or neglect in returning the list of proprietors and lands.

b. Tax on tithables and slaves

A poll tax of 10s was to be paid by every free male person over the age of 21 who is a citizen of Virginia. Likewise, slave holders were to paid the same tax on their slaves. This act did not apply to any free person or slave exempted by the county court because of age or bodily infirmity.

c. Taxes on horses, cattle and carriages

A new tax of 2s was laid upon every horse, mare, colt and mule while the legislature continued to tax neat cattle at 3d per head.

Riding vehicles went back to being taxed by the wheel rather than by the vehicle. The rate on all riding vehicles, whether coaches, chariots, phaetons, four-wheeled chaises, stage wagons for riding, chairs or two-wheeled chaises, was to be 5s per wheel.

d. Taxes on Billiard Tables and Ordinary Licenses

Another new tax was introduced at this session: a L50 tax for every billiard table to be found in the county. The tax on ordinary licenses was hiked to L5.[65]

The General Assembly then set out a procedure for the collection of these taxes. The county court was to divide the county into convenient precincts and, annually, before April 10th, appoint a justice for each precinct to take a list of these enumerated articles. After announcing his appointment, the Justice was to give public notice of where he intended to receive these lists and between April and June, 1782, deliver these tax lists to the clerk of the county court.

These lists were to contain the names of all free male persons over 21 who resided in his precinct along with the names of all slaves, specifying to whom they belong. The list was also to contain, besides the names of the free males over 21 and slaves, the number of cattle, horses, mares, colts and mules; wheels for riding carriages, billiard tables and ordinary licenses, each proprietor held.[66]

The clerk was to make out three copies from all the lists taken and delivered to him and deliver copies to the auditors of public accounts and sheriff or tax collector and post a copy in the county court house.

Penalties for non-payment of taxes or from refusal or neglect association with collecting the taxes were established and other measures for the collection of taxes were set down.[67]

The taxes on these enumerated articles could be paid in spanish milled dollars at the rate of 6s each, in other current gold or silver coin at a proportionate value, in bills of credit, or in produce in these proportions: 1/10, or 2s per pound of the land tax could be paid in bills of credit issued by Virginia or by the U.S.; Any of these bills of credit received by the treasurer were not t be reissued but to be eventually burned and destroyed.

All of the other taxes on enumerated articles could be paid for either in specie (i.e. gold or silver coins), tobacco or hemp at rates determined by the legislature. The legislators spent some time on detailing these arrangements and specify the particulars of the storage of tobacco, hemp and flour.[68]

The General Assembly also established a tax on land patents exceeding 1400 acres which specifically did *not* include bounty lands. Custom duties were to be collected on every gallon of rum, brandy and other distilled spirits and for each gallon of wine imported into the commonwealth by land or water. Other custom duties were placed on sugar, coffee and *all other goods* imported into Virginia.

The legislature made the captain or purser of the ship liable for the payment of this custom duty. The legislature went on to address the details for the collection and penalties for non-collection of these custom duties associated with any goods imported into Virginia from another state or country.[69]

- **Summary of the 1781 Tax Legislation**

The 1781 Tax package differed little from its predecessors. The poll taxes on tithables and slaves were continued. However, this legislation also required that the names of all slaves were to be recorded. Taxes were kept on cattle and carriages, although carriages went back to being taxed by the wheel rather than by the type of vehicle. New taxes, in the form of a tax on horses, mares and colts and a tax on billiard tables, were issued.

The land tax also continued with a detailed accounting as to the contents of the land lists and the methods of collection of the taxes owed by the proprietors.

This tax legislation concluded with several pages dealing with the promulgation of custom duties on any goods imported into the commonwealth. This customs duty legislation portended a shadow of things to come as other states soon followed suit and the United American States became battlegrounds for a different kind of war: one of retaliatory duties on any goods associated with inter-state commerce.

9. 1782 Tax Legislation

The General Assembly opened their May 1782 session determined to put the commonwealth on a sound tax and fiscal basis as it moved into a peacetime economy based on independence from Great Britain.

- **1782 Act granting further time for payment of taxes in enumerated commodities…**

The Assembly's first act of the May session was to give further time to Virginia's taxpayers to pay their taxes in the form of enumerated commodities (tax on tithables, slaves, cattle, horses, mares and colts, billiard tables and ordinary licenses) enacted in the last legislative session in 1781. They extended the deadline from May 1, 1782 to September 1, 1782.[70]

- **1782 Act for appropriating the public revenue**

This legislation was enacted so that a just appropriation of funds of the state could be made and so that the public faith in the state's fiscal policy could be preserved and the state's credit be supported. The legislature also wanted the amount of supplies furnished for use by the United States to be more certainly ascertained. This accounting would cause less inconvenience to the public.

The legislature decreed that the treasurer was to raise and state an account of all monies received for every species or subject of taxation specified in the act for ascertaining certain taxes and duties and for establishing a permanent revenue. One account was to be set up for the land taxes; another account was to be set up enumerated articles.

The land taxes, along with all other taxable articles, was to be used for the sole purpose of paying of and discharging debts due to officers of the civil government, including members of congress and of the General Assembly; L10,000 was to be applied to the use of the Governor. If there is a residue left, it was to be appropriated to the payment of interest coming due on the several emissions of paper money called in and funding under previous legislation for that purpose.

Money arising from taxes payable in certain specific articles was to be appropriated and applied to the credit of the commonwealth, on the requisitions of congress on October 4, 1781. The state was to retain only as much money or specific articles sufficient to discharge debts due from the state agent and to hold onto L15,000 for any necessary future expenditures due the states military department.

Money arising from taxes payable in certain specific articles, according to the enumerated articles enactment, were to be appropriated by the treasurer and put towards the credit of the state according to Congressional requisitions. The treasurer was to retain L5,000 to pay for pensions due wounded or disabled revolutionary war veterans or for pensions or allowance due wounded or disabled officers or to their widows or children.[71]

- **1782 Tax to amend the act [passed in 1781] for ascertaining certain taxes and duties and to establish a permanent revenue**
This piece of legislation was needed due to the destruction of Virginia's property by the British. The legislation granted further time for the collection of taxes required for the support of the late war against Great Britain. Half of those taxes could be paid July 1, 1783; the other half was to be due November 1, 1783.

Buck skins, fitted for breeches, were to be added to the specific taxes that could be paid in either Spanish milled dollars or in gold or silver coins.

Instead of a list of all tithable persons, now the list was to be drawn up as a list of all persons taxable by the act and the tax imposed upon cattle was to be paid on *all* cattle.[72]

The legislature also dealt with custom duties and other miscellaneous items.[73]

Finally, the legislature stated that no certificates, receipts or warrants for militia or military service, except for one for supplying the southern army with wagons and horses, were to be received in discharge of taxes imposed by the earlier 1781tax legislation on taxes and duties. The legislature also would not allow certificates granted for money, according to a requisition of the Governor in February 1782 for recruiting soldiers, to be paid in discharge of taxes.[74]

- **May 1782 Act for calling in and redeeming all military certificates, either for tobacco or for specie**
The General Assembly found that they needed a levy for additional taxes in order to pay for and redeem all the military certificates. The also needed money to pay for the claims for property either impressed for war service or taken for public service.
    a. **Tax on lands**
    The legislature placed a 1 % tax for every L100, in proportion for greater or lesser sums, on all lands and lots valued by the commissioners of the land tax.
    b. **Tax on Tithables and Slaves**
    A tax of 10s was to be paid by every free male, over the age of 21, who was a citizen of Virginia.

Likewise there was a 10 s tax on all slaves over the age of 16 which was to be paid by their owners. The legislation excluded free persons and slaves already exempt by the county court due to age or infirmity.

c. Tax on horses and cattle

Horses, mares, colts and mules were taxed at 2s per head. Cattle were taxed at 3d per head.

d. Tax on Billiard Tables and Ordinary Licenses

Coaches, chariots, phaetons, four-wheeled chaises, stage wagons used for riding, chairs and two wheel carriages were taxed at a rate of 5s per wheel.

A L15 tax on billiard tables and a L4 tax on ordinary licenses was levied *over and above* the taxes imposed by any of the previous acts of the General Assembly.

The sheriffs of the respective counties were to give bond in their county court in November 1782 to collect, pay and account for these taxes and send the same to the treasurer. The collection of the above taxes was to begin in March 1783.

Citizens of Virginia could pay these taxes in Spanish milled dollars, at the rate of 6s each; or in other current silver or gold coin at a proportionate value. They could also elect to pay in military audited certificates or in treasury tobacco notes, which had been paid enlisted soldiers, at the rate of 20s per hundred weight. They could also pay in warrants to be issued by the auditors of public accounts as the result of recent legislation authorizing the issuance of such warrants.[75]

- **October 1782 Act to amend and reduce the several acts of assembly for ascertaining certain taxes and duties and for establishing a permanent revenue, into one act**

In October 1782, the legislature passed tax legislation to amend and reduce all of the acts for ascertaining taxes and duties into one comprehensive act. Legislators were also concerned about land tax legislation; they felt that the sum produced by the land tax was disproportionate to the money resulting from other taxes. The General Assembly thought that property of every kind should be equally burdened for the defense and protection of the commonwealth.

These taxes were to be collected:

a. An additional tax on land

In addition to the land tax already imposed on land holders, the General Assembly levied an additional 10s on the pound of all sums payable for the tax on lands and lots.

b. Taxes on Tithables and Slaves

Every free male person, who was a citizen of Virginia and over the age of 21 was to pay a poll tax of 10s. The same 10s tax was to be paid by the owners of all slaves. Only free persons and slaves exempted by county courts because of age and infirmity were excused from paying these taxes.

c. Taxes on horses including covering horses and on cattle

A 2s tax on every horse, mare, colt and mule was to be paid by their owners. A new tax was added regarding covering horses. They were to be taxed at the amount charged by the owner for the horse to cover a mare in season; The owner was to turn in this rate when he delivered his list of property to the justice.

Cattle were taxed at 3d per head.

d. Taxes on Carriages

A 6s tax was imposed per wheel for all coaches, chariots, phaetons, four-wheeled chaises, stage wagons used for riding, chairs and two-wheeled chaises.

e. Taxes on Billiard Tables and Ordinary Licenses

Billiard tables were taxed at the rate of L15 per table. A L5 tax was levied on each ordinary license granted to those wishing to keep an ordinary.

The legislature then set up the administration to collect these taxes. They authorize the county court to divide the county into precincts and annually appoint a justice for each precinct before march 10th. The justice was to give the public notice of his appointment and set the time and place for the collection of the above enumerated taxes in form of written notice through out his precinct. The completed lists were to be returned to the county court on or before April 20, 1783.

The list was to be in alphabetical form, listing the names of all free male persons residing in his precinct and listing all the names of the slaves with their owners, distinquishing those who were over 16 in a separate column. Columns were also to delineate, for the same free males over 21, the number of cattle; the number of horses and number of covering horses along with the sum charged for covering horses by the owners; the number of wheels per riding carriage; the number of billiard tables; and ordinary licenses.

The clerk was to file this list in his office and make out three further lists from the original. One copy was to go to the auditors of public accounts before July 1st of each year; the second copy was to be set up in the court house of the county at the May Court; the third list was to go to the sheriff or collector of public taxes on or before May 1st annually.[76]

The legislature also spelled out how the taxable property lists were to be given in and what the penalties would be for not delivering these lists to the justice. The legislature also authorized the sheriff to collect these taxes between May 1st and June 1st of each year. If he has not receive the taxes by that time, the sheriff was authorized to distrain the land, slaves, goods or chattels found on the lands and, within five days, could sell the distrained property at public sale, for the amount of the owed taxes.

This legislation also dealt with other administrative manners concerning land and damages.[77]

The property taxes could be paid in a number of ways: they could be paid in Spanish milled dollars, at the rate of 6s each; they could be paid in other current silver or gold coin, at a proportionate value; they could be paid in bills of credit; they could be paid in produce.

A tenth part (or 2s per pound) of the land tax was to be payable in bills of credit emitted on funds of the commonwealth and the faith of the U.S according to a Congressional resolution of March 18, 1780. If these bills of credit are received in payment of taxes, they were to be paid to the treasury and not re-issued. Instead they were to be destroyed.

Forty percent of these property taxes could be paid in commutable articles as long as the gold coins paid into the treasury were received at the following rates: **Johannes**, weighing 18 pennyweight at L4 16s; **half Johannes**, weighing 9 pennyweight, at L2 8s; **guineas**, whether French or English, weighing 5 penny weight 6 grains, at L1 8s; **½ guineas**, weighing 2 penny weight 15 grains, at 14s; **Moidores**, weighing 6 penny weight, 18 grains at L1 16s; **doubloons**, weighing 17 pennyweight at L14 10 s; **pistoles**, weighing 4 pennyweight, 6 grains, at L1 2s 6d.

The rest of the taxes could be paid (except for the land tax), at the option of the payer, in the following ways: ½ could be paid in coin, tobacco or hemp; the other half in coin, tobacco, hemp or flour.[78]

The General Assembly then proceeded to spell out in detail the administrative measures necessary for the collection of these taxes and the provisions to be made for storage of the perishable produce along with penalties associated with non-collection.[79]

The legislators added deer skins as another way of paying taxes: these were to be skins "well dressed and fitted for the purpose of making breeches". The skins, payable as taxes, were to be paid at the rate of 8s per pound of deer-skin.[80]

The last tax to be imposed in this legislation was a tax on patents for every hundred acres over 1400 granted by patent.[81]

The General Assembly then turned their attention to the quit rents owed to the now deceased proprietor of the Northern Neck. Those who held land in the Northern Neck were to "retain sequestered in their hands, all quit-rents which are now due," until the right of descent to the property could be more fully determined. Then the General Assembly would determine what was to happen to these quit rents.

Quit rents which were to come due within the Northern Neck were to be paid to the public treasury and, as provided by previous legislation, the inhabitants of the Northern Neck were to be exonerated from any future claims to these rents by the any future proprietor of the Northern Neck.[82]

The final pages of this legislation are taken up with the administrative measures relating to the imposition of import duties on spirits, wine, sugar, coffee and other goods brought into the commonwealth by land or water from other countries or other states.[83]

- **October 1782 Act for equalizing the Land Tax**

The land tax, the General Assembly found, was "very unequal" and the legislators feared, from past experience, that the neither the tax nor the income, would "produce the equality so essentially necessary to the happiness of all the good citizens of this commonwealth."[84]

So. the General Assembly proceeded to divide the counties within the commonwealth into four classes or districts. Stafford, Prince William and Fairfax counties belonged to the first district. Fauquier, Loudoun, Culpeper, Orange and others comprised the second district.

Examiners were appointed to regulate the taxes and to ascertain the average price per acre of all the lands in each county within their District. The standard for the average used to compute the land tax base for the first District was to be 10s; for the second District, 7s 6d.[85]

Examiners were required by law to keep their accounts in books for each county. These books were to be transmitted to the commissioner of taxes in each county. The Commissioner was then to make a copy of the book and deliver it to the sheriff for collection of the land tax.

There was to be a separate book for each county, with the land holder's name and tax information listed in alphabetical order. The rest of the act dealt in great detail with how this new tax was to be administered.[86]

- **Summary of the 1782 Tax packages**

The 1782 Tax packages exhibited some marked differences from their predecessors. The General Assembly began to set up some long range goals for the collection of taxes and to establish a peacetime fiscal policy. It set out specific guidelines for the tax base. Land taxes and the other taxes known as enumerated articles or specific taxes were separated from one another. The legislature further divided the state into districts or classes for the collection of land taxes. They fixed the value of the land for each District in order to equalize the burden among the land holders.

In the fall legislative session, the General Assembly consolidated the earlier tax packages into one comprehensive act. They kept the tax on land, tithables and slaves (although slaves no longer were required to be identified by name), horses, cattle, carriages, billiard tables and ordinary licenses. They added a tax on stud horses. They also added an additional land tax, over and above the existing legislation.

They set out, in great administrative detail, the way in which the land taxes (see above) and enumerated or taxes, now known as property taxes, were to be handled. The General Assembly authorized the justices of the county court to divide the county into precincts, and to appoint a justice for each precinct to take the list of property. The person chargeable for the property tax brought in his list to the justice.

The justice then compiled the lists in alphabetical order, arranged by the name of the tax payer; he separated the enumerated property into columns. So there were separate columns for the numbers of tithables over 21 (for the poll tax); the numbers of slaves over 16, for the tax on slaves; number of horses, colts, mares and mules for the tax on horses; the number of cattle, for the tax on cattle; the number of stud horse and the rate charge for stud fees, for those taxes; the number of carriages, for the tax, computed per wheel; the number of billiard tables; and the number of ordinary licenses.

The lists were then filed with the clerk of court, who made out three more copies. One of the copies went to the state; one was published in the Court; one went to the Sheriff or tax collector for collection. The clerk of court kept the original compilation. Thus, there were back up copies of these tax lists.

The General Assembly also began the process to pay off war debts associated with the late war with Britain. They dealt with the thorny issues of public claims for property damage incurred during the war and with claims related to goods impressed by Continental forces and the state militia; they came up with ways to pay for the redemption of military certificates; finally, the legislature grappled with the development of a long term fiscal policy to rescue the state's paper currency and stabilize the bewildering array of foreign and domestic coins in circulation.

Paper currency and bills of credit, issued by the commonwealth and the Confederation Congress, had been already been tied to the rate of exchange established for the Spanish milled dollar and other gold coins, in proportionate value. The 1782 fiscal policy strove to formalize this de facto standard.

In addition, the General Assembly looked at new ways for the public to pay their taxes. They attempted to make it easier by adding options: taxes could be paid in spanish milled dollars, silver or gold coins, or in produce – tobacco, hemp, flour, and a new in-kind payment – deer skins.

Another thorny issue the General Assembly confronted was the issue over the forthcoming quit rents owed by land holders residing in the Northern Neck proprietary. Since the proprietor of the Northern Neck had died, the General Assembly decided that these rents should go into the public treasury until the estate and heirs could be settled to the state's satisfaction.

Finally, the legislature continued their administration of import duties on spirits, wine, sugar, coffee and other goods brought into the commonwealth by land or water from other countries or other states.

E. Conclusions

The tax and fiscal legislation passed by the Virginia legislature between 1759-1782 traces the evolution of a tax and fiscal package that started out simply as measures to provide for a militia to defend her frontier against Indian attacks. At the same time, the legislature continued the practice of collecting for the public levy used to fund the colonial county bureaucracy. Then, as the 1760s moved into the 1770s, the furor over additional British taxation on stamps resulted in successful boycotts. When the British added more taxes on imported goods like paper, paint, lead, glass and tea, the colonists simply boycotted the goods again and forced all the taxes except the one on tea to be withdrawn.

Virginia's vital interests were not touched by the worsening relations between the commonwealth of Massachusetts and the British crown during this period. However, a young firebrand named Patrick Henry did his best to fan the flames of rebellion by calling for the establishment of an army in 1775. Many Virginians came to agree with his sentiments when he passionately declared for independence with the words "Give me liberty or give me death!"

Still, Virginia's tax and fiscal legislation as late as 1775 was concerned with paying the militia for expeditions against the Indians rather than funding the recruitment of the militia to be used against the British. It was 1776 before the legislature seriously turned its attention to providing fortifications for the defense of the new commonwealth and setting up a militia establishment and a navy.

The budget for funding the militia and defense of the commonwealth came close to L4 million during the war. The ingenuity and inventiveness of the General Assembly approached that of modern day tax collection with the levying of new taxes on liquor, and land conveyances; innovative taxes in the form of a sales tax on goods, wares and merchandise, on the amount of money in your possession, and on windows.

As the war moved towards a stalemate in the late 1770s, the General Assembly had to become more innovative in their approaches for new funding to continue fighting. Virginia also had to contend with massive inflation and extensive, uncontrollable counterfeiting of paper money issued by both the state and the Continental congress. Fauquier county has four previously unknown tax lists taken between 1775-1778. These tax lists cover events from the heady days of 1775 through the dark days of 1778. They offer hitherto unknown insights into the county's tax base.

Virginia became a battleground during the late 1770s and early 1780s as fighting moved into the south. The successful conclusion at the final battle at Yorktown in 1781 marked the beginning of American independence. The march towards Yorktown and the skirmishes along the way were felt through out the commonwealth as citizens had cattle, sheep, guns, horses, saddles, and household articles requisitioned by the Continental troops for the final push toward victory. The legislature decided that Virginians could present claims to the county courts for their lost articles and receive payment for their value.

In 1782, with the fighting over, Virginia could at last begin to put together a peacetime tax package and work towards stabilizing their fiscal policy. The five 1782 tax lists that have survived for Fauquier County bring a greater understanding of the burdens undergone by the county's tax payers who managed to persevere through the struggle for independence.

END NOTES
1. Conlin, Joseph R. *The American Past* (New York: Harcourt, Brace Jovanovich, 1990) pages 100-101.
2. *Ibid.*
3. Hening's *Statutes At Large, Being a Collection of all the Laws of Virginia* (Richmond: George Cochran, 1822) Volume 7, pages 257-259.
4. *Ibid.*, v.7, page 259.
5. *Ibid.*, v.7, pages 290-291.
6. *Ibid.*, v. 7, pages 347-348.
7. *Ibid.*, v. 7, pages 348-351.
8. *Ibid.*, v. 7, page 895
9. *Ibid.*, v. 7, pages 495-496.
10. *Ibid.*, v. 7, page 540.

END NOTES (Continued)

11. *Ibid.*
12. *Ibid.*, v. 7, page 542.
13. Conlin, pages 101-103.
14. *Ibid.*, page 107.
15. Everton, George B. & Everton, Louise E. *The Handy Book for Genealogists* 8th Edition (Logan, Utah: Everton Publishers, 1991), pages 265-272.
16. Hening, v. 8, pages 39-41
17. *Ibid.*, v. 8, pages 47.
18. *Ibid.*, v. 8, pages 178-182.
19. *Ibid.*, v. 8, pages 201-202.
20. *Ibid.*, v. 8, pages 297-298.
21. See Hening, v. 8, pages 343-346 for details regarding the enforcement of these laws.
22. *Ibid.*, v. 8, page 393.
23. *Hening*, v. 9, pages 61-63.
24. *Ibid.*, v. 9, page 65.
25. *Ibid.*, v. 9, pages 66.
26. *Ibid.*, v. 9, pages 66-67.
27. *Ibid.*, v. 9, pages 143-145.
28. *Ibid.*, v. 9, pages 166-167. See Section VII through VIII for details concerning the legislation dealing with tithable lists.
29. *Ibid.*, v. 9, page 219-222.
30. *Ibid.*, v. 9, page 349.
31. *Ibid.*, v. 9, page 365.
32. *Ibid.*, v. 9, pages 349-365. This act addresses in great detail the method for election of tax commissioners and the ways they were to collect taxes. See these pages for details.
33. *Ibid.*, v. 9, pages 369-370.
34. *Ibid.*, v. 9, pages 551-552.
35. *Ibid.*, v. 9, pages 547-552.
36. Hening, v. 10, pages 10-14.
37. *Ibid.*, v. 10, pages 79-81.
38. *Ibid.*, v. 10, page 166.
39. *Ibid.*, v. 10, pages 168-169.
40. *Ibid.*, v. 10, pages 170-171.
41. *Ibid.*, v. 10, pages 168.
42. *Ibid.*, v. 10, pages 165-171.
43. *Ibid.*, v. 10, pages 171-172.
44. *Ibid.*, v. 10, pages 190-191.
45. *Ibid.*, v. 10, pages 189-190.
46. *Ibid.*, v. 10, pages 242-254.
47. *Ibid.*
48. *Ibid.*
49. *Ibid.*, v. 10, pages 279-286.
50. *Ibid.*, v. 10, pages 280-281.
51. *Ibid.*, v. 10, page 281.
52. *Ibid.*, v. 10, page 281-283.
53. *Ibid.*, v. 10, page 283.
54. *Ibid.*, v. 10, pages 284-285.
55. *Ibid.*, v. 10, pages 285-286.
56. *Ibid.*, v. 10, pages 292-293.
57. *Ibid.*, v. 10, pages 320-324.
58. *Ibid.*, v. 10, pages 347-350.
59. *Ibid.*, v. 10, pages 357-538.
60. *Ibid.*, v. 10, pages 358-361.
61. Conlin, pages 151-152.
62. Hening, v. 10, page 435.
63. *Ibid.*, v. 10, page 494-495.
64. *Ibid.*, v. 10, pages 490-492.

END NOTES (Continued)

65. *Ibid.*, v. 10, page 504.
66. *Ibid.*, v. 10, pages 504-505.
67. *Ibid.*, v. 10, pages 505-508.
68. *Ibid.*, v. 10, pages 509-510.
69. *Ibid.*, v. 10, pages 511-517.
70. Hening, v.11, pages 10-12
71. *Ibid.*, v. 11, pages 12-14
72. *Ibid.*, v. 11, pages 66-67.
73. *Ibid.*, v. 11, pages 67-71.
74. *Ibid.*, v. 11, page 68.
75. *Ibid.*, v. 11, pages 93-94.
76. *Ibid.*, v. 11, pages 113-114.
77. *Ibid.*, v. 11, pages 116-117.
78. *Ibid.*, v. 11, pages 117-118.
79. *Ibid.*, v. 11, pages 119-121.
80. *Ibid.*, v. 11, page 128.
81. *Ibid.*, v. 11, page 121.
82. *Ibid.*, v. 11, pages 128-129.
83. *Ibid.*, v. 11, pages 121-128.
84. *Ibid.*, v. 11, page 140.
85. *Ibid.*, v. 11, pages 140-141.
86. *Ibid.*, v. 11, pages 143-145.

ABBREVIATIONS COMMONLY USED IN TAX LISTS
1759-1782

ABBREVIATION	MEANING
Ab^r	Abraham
Agga	Aggy
Alex^r	Alexander
Ant^y	Anthony
Ben:/Benjn	Benjamin
Carr^d	Carried (Carr^d Over)
Chas/Ch^s	Charles
child^n	children
Christ^r	Christopher
C^l	Clerk (C^l of Court)
Col^o/Colo:	Colonel
Danl	Daniel
dec^d	deceased
d^o	ditto
Edwd	Edward
Elizth/ Elth	Elizabeth
Esqr	Esquire
Est.	Estate
Exempt^d	Exempted
Fra^s	Francis
Fred^k	Frederick
Gab^l	Gabriel
Geo:/G^o	George
g^t	gentleman
h^d	head (of cattle)
Hows:	Howson
H^y	Henry
Ja^s/J^s	James
Jerem^a	Jeremiah
Jno	John
Jos:	Joseph
J^r/Junr	Junior
Maj^r	Major
Marg^t	Margaret
Math^w	Mathew
Messrs	Messers
Moreh^d	Morehead
M^{rs}	Mrs.
Nathl	Nathaniel
N/N~/N^o/N^s/Neg$^{o(s)}$	Negro, Negroes
Ord^r	Order
Ov^r	Over
Ool^e	????
pat^r	patroller
p^d	paid
p^r	per
Q^r/Qt^r/Quart^r	Quarter
Rach^l	Rachel
Raw:	Rawleigh
Rev:/Rev^d	Reverend
R^d/Rich^d	Richard
R^t/Robt/Robt.	Robert
Sam:/Saml	Samuel
S^r/Senr	Senior
Servt	Servant
Sh^{dk}	Shadrack
Thos/Tho./Thom	Thomas
Tim^y	Timothy
Und^r	Under
W^m	William
y^e	the
y^t	that
Zach:/Zach^r	Zachariah
&/+	and

1759-001 Thomas Marshall's Tithable List

A List of the Tithables in Fauquier County in the Year 1759. Taken by Tho. Marshall.

[page 1 column 1]   [Tithes]

At Churchill's Quart^r
John Churchill
Henry Churchill
William Hunton
Pharnach George
John Ship, Edwd Hunton
Edward Fields
Alex^r Smith
Neg^s Ullises, Will, Boatswain, Nell, Guy, Tom, Dick, Punch,
Phillis, Moses, Warner, Lucy, Sarah, China, Harper, Jack,
Jeoffery, Peter, Charles, Jenny, Phillis, Cuttena, Ajax, Brister,
Cate, Margery, Bess, Guy, George, Doll, Cate, Diana, Hannah,
Andrew, Ratliff, Sawney, Nell, Nanny, Sarah, Persel, Joan
                            Total --------- 49

John Shumate Senr

Mary Settle
Newman Settle. Merryman Settle -------------- 2

Benj. Roberts Junr, Overseer
Neg^s Robin, Sawney, Moll, Kate ---------------- 5

At Carters Q^r at Ludwell Park
John Barns
Neg^s Bob, Harry, Humph^y, Gun, Moll,
Phillis, Nan, Dinah, Jenny -------------------- 10

Ben Morgan.   Neg. Nan ---------------------- 2
Moses Fletcher -------------------------------- 1

Robt Emry. Thos Embry. John Emry.
William Emry --------------------------------- 4

George Gest ---------------------------------- 1
William Bradford. Benj. Bradford. Neg. Nan   3
William Flowers ------------------------------ 1
William Butler ------------------------------- 1
                                        80

[page 1 column 2]   [Tithes]

At Hooe's Q^r
Steven Morris. Neg^s Harry, James, Ben, Roger,
James, Ben, Roger, Harry, James, Frank,
Sarah, Kate, Nell, Winney, Mime -------------- 13

John Corder Junr ----------------------------- 1
Henry Boatman. Neg. Charles ----------------- 2

Thos Mitchell.   Neg^s Jack & Hannah ------ 3
Thos Garner Senr.   Neg. George ----------- 2

At Skinkers Q^r
Michael Marr.   [Neg] Harry, Charles, Jeney,
Jude, Nan, Hack ------------------------------ 7

Chas Hogan ----------------------------------- 1
John James. Neg. Phillis, Winney ------------- 3
Thos Porter ---------------------------------- 1
Ja^s Cullins. Neg. Sarah --------------------- 2
John Bowdin --------------------------------- 1
Robert Hinson ------------------------------- 1
                                        66

[page 2 column 1]   [Tithes]

Henry Bramlet -------------------------------- 1

at Hedgmans Q^r
Steven McCormack. Neg^s Tomboy, Joe,
George, Dick, Aminy, Kitcher, Charles,
Tom, Kate, Hannah, Dinah -------------------- 12

William Turner. Alex^r Turner.
Edward Turner ------------------------------- 3

James Turner -------------------------------- 1

Thos McClanahan.   [Neg^s] Dick, Jack, Sarah   4
William Bragg -------------------------------- 1
George Herrin -------------------------------- 1
Thos Kirk ---------------------------------- 1
William Bramlet ------------------------------ 1

Joseph Bragg. Reuben Bragg.
Joseph Bragg -------------------------------- 3

Benj. Settle. John Spence.
Neg^s Tobey, Rose ---------------------------- 4

James Murrow. William Murrow ------------- 2

At Fitzhugh's Q^r
George Russel.   Neg. Brister, Tom, Ben,
Titas, Milley, Milley, Mureah, Jean ----------- 9

Danl Hogan, Willm Banester ----------------- 2
William Duling. Neg. Phillis ------------------ 2
Charles Jones -------------------------------- 1

1759-001 THOMAS MARSHALL'S TITHABLE LIST
A List of the Tithables in Fauquier County in the Year 1759. Taken by Tho. Marshall.

[page 2 column 2]   [Tithes]
[At Fitzhugh's Quarter (Cont.)]

Name	Tithes
Richd Hill	1
Nathl Dodd. Nathl Dodd. Neg. Bowson, Kate	4
John Auldin	1
Benj^a Snelling	1
John Butler	1
Eliz. Page. Neg. Hannah	1
Peter Beech	1
Nath Hickerson	1
Thos Hickerson	1
Danl Shumate	1
Thos Smith	1
Martin Hardin. Neg. Cambro, Ceasar, Betty, Kate, Phillis	6
	69

[page 2 column 2]   [Tithes]

Name	Tithes
Catherin Holtzclaw. Joseph Holtzclaw. Neg. Pegg	2
Howsin Kenner. Patrick McClawlin. Neg. Nick, Isaac, Anthony, Abraham, Lett, Caney	8
James Seaton. Neg. Iky, Job, Ben, James, Beck, Luce, Frank, Jude	9
Burdett Cliften	1
Eliz. Ambrose. William Obanion. Neg. Harry, London, Scipio, Luce	5
George J[illegible] Kenner. Neg. James, Hannah	3
Thos Withers, John Hewit. Neg. Jam, Jude, Flowra	5
Henry Utterback. John Utterback	2
John Carr Senr. John Carr Junr. Neg. Nan	3
John Morehead, Willm Morehead. Neg. James, Sarah, Jude	5

1759-001 THOMAS MARSHALL'S TITHABLE LIST
A List of the Tithables in Fauquier County in the Year 1759. Taken by Tho. Marshall.

[page 2 column 2]   [Tithes]

Name	Tithes
James Morgan, William Knowles	2
Joseph Oder, Const^b. John Hen^y	1

At Foots Q^r

Name	Tithes
William Foote. Thos Scags. Neg. Lewis, Peter, Brist., Dick, Aaron, Joe, Ned, Rose, Moll	11
James Duncan, P^t Routt. Neg. Will, Hannah	2
George Crump. [Neg] Ben, Bellender, Hannah	4
William Grant. Eli Griffin. Neg. Jack, Pompey, Harry, Frank, Grace, Dorcas, Nan, Betty	10
William Fletcher	1
Joseph Delaney. Joseph Delaney. Neg. Tom, Nan, Dinah	1
	80

[page 2 column 3]   [Tithes]

Name	Tithes
John Wright Junr. Francis Self	2
Joseph Duncan. Neg. Phill, Luce, Grace	4
Harman Rector. John Rector. Harman Rector Neg. Peter	4
Alex^r Snelling	1
Francis Day. Thos Bridges. Neg. Beck	3
William Jennings	1
John Edwards. James Edwards. Samuel Edwards	2
John Edge	1
Robt Southard. Neg. Charles	2
Ool^e [?] Bethel	1
John Woodside	1
Gerrard Edwards. Isaac Sparks	2

at Mrs Turner's Q^r

Name	Tithes
Danl Frazer. [James?] Parmer. [Name illegible]	3
John Kirk	1
Alex^r Sangster	1

1759-001 THOMAS MARSHALL'S TITHABLE LIST
A List of the Tithables in Fauquier County in the Year 1759. Taken by Tho. Marshall.

[page 2 column 2]   [Tithes]

at J. Skinkers Q^r
Willm Jones.
Neg. Scipio, Will, Flora, Winney --------------   5

John Combs. Neg. George, Judy, Winney -----   4

[page 2 column 3]   [Tithes]

Jacob Holtzclaw. Jacob Holtzclaw.
Joseph Holtzclaw.
Neg. Robin, Sarah, Nan, Judy -------------------   7

John Allen. John Colvin ------------------------   2
William Norman --------------------------------   1

Elias Edmonds.
Neg. Humphry, Simon, Tiney, Nan -----------   5

Gaydon Settle. Joseph Settle --------------------   2
Edward Ball. Wm Ball.   Neg. Harry -------- 3
Richard McPherson -----------------------------   1
                                                    59

[page 2 column 4]   [Tithes]

John Rictor. Jacob Rictor -------------------------   1
Joseph Morehead.   Neg. Kate ----------------   2
Benj. Bullett. [Neg.] Roger, London, Hager --   4

Thos Bullet's Q^r
Absolem Ramey.
Neg. Brister, Anthony, Nanney, Judy ---------   5

Absolem Ramey. Neg. Winney, Dab^y ---------   2
John Brown --------------------------------------   1
Thos Matthews ----------------------------------   1
John Betthell -------------------------------------   1
Lewis Prichett -----------------------------------   1
Clem^t Norman Junr -------------------------------   1
David Darnall.   Neg. Ceasar --------------------   2
Morgan Darnall Junr ----------------------------   1

at Downmans Q^r
William Humphry.
Neg. Toney, Tom, Betty, Mary, Will -----------   6

at Barnards Q^r
James P[name illegible; on fold]
Neg. Glasgow, James, Mack, Judy, Priss -----   6

1759-001 THOMAS MARSHALL'S TITHABLE LIST
A List of the Tithables in Fauquier County in the Year 1759. Taken by Tho. Marshall.

[page 2 column 4]   [Tithes]

Added by Ord^r of Court

Nine Tithes belonging to Armistead Churchill   9

Two tithes belonging to John Twentyman   2

John Robertson   1
                                                    49

1759-002 GEORGE LAMKIN'S TITHABLE LIST
A List of tithes for the yaer End of June ye 10ᵈ 1759

Robert ashbee tithes –	
James Davice &	
Joined in all ---	3
James Jones	1
Benjamon ashbee tithes	
John Harris ------------	
John followay in all	3
William Stokes in all	1
John williamson in all	1
John browns tithes -----	
Burr wallace in all ---	2
Thomas ashbees tithes –	
William ashbee	
Jessey ashbee	
Thomas Sayor	
James whitte in all -----	5
William Robards tiths	
James Selve in all --	1
John Routs tithes ------	
William hharris -- in all	2
Elious wood tithe -----	1
Michael Darmonts in all	1
John Grigbes tiths	
Andrew Davice in all	2
Thomas ealitts tiths --	2
William ealitt	2
Eanock Beary tiths	1

1759-002 GEORGE LAMKIN'S TITHABLE LIST
A List of tithes for the yaer End of June ye 10ᵈ 1759

Thomas for tiths in all --	1
Simon Commings tiths in all	1
Charles talers tithes	
William taler in all --------------	2
Jacob addams tiths in all -------	
Thomas williams tithes	
John Settle & Peter	
Joseph morriss & Subinate in all	
William Rice Tithes in all	
David Robinson tithes in all	
Thomas wats tithes --------------	
Nell & San in all --------------	
Mallakiar Cummings tithes	
Thomas Cumings ----------------	
Eeallakiar Cummings tiths	
Johnnathan Cummings in all	
John woods tithes --------------	
Robart Day in all	
Royly wood tithe in all –	
David bartons tithes	
William jones & Joe in all	
Francis Suttle tithes –	
Francis Suttel Jʳ in all ----	
Jacob Rictor tithe ------------	
Henry Rictor tithes -----------	
John Ricktor tithes	
Jack & Juda in all	
Thomas Glascock tithes	
John Glascock in all	
Geo: Glascock ᵗⁱᵗʰ in all ------	

COMPILIER'S NOTE: 2ⁿᵈ Column numbers are missing in original list except as specified above.

1759-003 JOHN MARSHALL'S TITHABLE LIST

A List of the Tithes in that part of Dittengen Parish in Fauquier County in the Year 1759 taken by Jno. Marshall

Thomas Harrison, William Harrison} Neg^r Peter, Jacob, Charles, Daniel, } Dinah, Phillis, Sarah Judy, Pegg, }	11
John Catlett Senr -------------------------	1
John Catlett Junr -------------------------	1
Willm Banester --------------------------	1
Isaac Murphey ---------------------------	1
	15

1759-004 ADDED TITHABLES TO EXISTING LISTS

To George Lamkin's List:

"August 28^d 1759 Mr Charles taler Came to me and Declared y^t he had omited Giving his Son Charles tithe through amistak & Desires he may Be Listed P^r G Lamkin."

To Thomas Marshall's List:

"I hope youll Excuse my neglect if possible on putting my tithable for I must own it was a great mistake and if you Will Redress it now Youll Very much oblige your hum Ser^t
   (signed) John Robertson

To Mr. Thos Marshell Sep^t 27th 1759
 [illegible word]
 John Robertson one tithable"

1759-004 ADDED LAND TAXES

"John Duncan Junr holds 150 Acres of Land in the County of Fauquier –

Rice Duncan To 189 Acres of Land

Henery Hardin holds 960 acres of Land in ye County of fauquier october ye 27 1759

John fishback 275 Land"

1765-001 TITHABLE LIST
[This list is a partial listing of Tithes and Land. It is tentatively identified as 1765 from the notation on second page that says "Deeds tc. recorded Sepr 1765."]
[page 1 column 1]

J (Cont.)	Tithes	Land
Jett, Francis	3	100
Jett, James	1	
Johnson, John	2	
Jefferies, Joseph		336
Jefferies, George	2	120
Johnson, Jeffery	5	130
Johnson, John	2	

K

	Tithes	Land
Kirk, John Constable		
Kerrs John	2	150
Kenner, Howson	5	750
Kenner, George	3	150
King, Joshua	1	
Kamper, Harman	2	132
Keirns, William	3	170
Kamper, Henry	1	187
Kamper, John	3	123
Kamper, Jacob	1	163
K[eith?] Mary Isham	5	1500
K[illegible – on fold] John	1	
Kelly, John	1	
Kitts, William	2	
Kincheloe, John	2	
Kincheloe, William	2	
Kibble, John	1	
Kerr, James	2	
Kesterson, William	1	

L

	Tithes	Land
Lambert, William	1	
Luttrell, James	1	70
Luttrell, Richard	2	314
Luttrell, Samuel	1	70
Laurance, Edward	9	317
Luttrell, Michael	1	70
Luttrell, John	1	70
Lawrance, Edward	1	
Lee, Joseph	1	
Laws, John	1	
Lee, Mary	16	750
Lee, Henry Richard Col°	15	1500

[page 1 column 2]

	Tithes	Land
Lewis, Zachariah	7	263
Lassfield, Moses	1	
Latham, George	2	
Leachman, John	3	

1765-001 TITHABLE LIST
[This list is a partial listing of Tithes and Land. It is tentatively identified as 1765 from the notation on second page that says "Deeds tc. recorded Sepr 1765."]
[page 1 column 2]

L [Cont.]	Tithes	Land
Legg, Fortunatus	1	
Latham, Anthony	2	
Littlejohn, Charles	2	
L[am?]kin, George	3	925
L[each?], George Senr	2	
Lawrance, Peter	2	
Leachman, Thomas	2	

M

	Tithes	Land
Matthews, Thomas	1	300
Morgan, Charles	1	108
McDaniel, William	3	
Marshall, Elizabeth	2	
Marshall, Markham	1	
McDaniel, James	1	
Morehead, Joseph	3	273
Mynatt, Richard, Const^a		
Morgan, Charles Senr	1	8[torn]
Morgan, John	--	23[torn]
Mauzy, Elizabeth	5	321
Morgan, John	2	
Matthews, John	2	
McConway, Robert	1	
Marshall, William	3	
Markham, John	3	
Miller, William	1	100
Murry, James	3	130
Murdoch, Joseph	7	362
Morgan, Simon	5	450
Morgan, William	6	382
Martin, Tilman	1	
Mauzy, Henry	8	200
Marr, Ann	3	1135
Miller, Simon	12	1289
Morehead, John	10	450
Morehead, Charles	5	181
McClanaham, William	3	184
Martin, Joseph	1	150
Macrae, Allan	--	490
Matthews, Robert	4	--
Martin, Charles	4	181
Martin, Henry	1	163
Martin, John	1	110
McKenzy, James	1	--

1765-001 Tithable List
[This list is a partial listing of Tithes and Land. It is tentatively identified as 1765 from the notation on second page that says "Deeds tc. recorded Sepr 1765."]
[page 1 column 1]

T	Tithes	Land
Turner, Henry	5	
Turner, James	2	
Tullos, Rodham	1	
Tullos, Rodham	1	200
Thornsbury, Samuel	0	286
Taylor, Benjamin	3	[torn]
Taylor, Richard	[torn]	[torn]
Taylor, Joseph	1	
Thornton, Francis	5	800
Tomlin, John	5	--
Taylor, Henry	2	87
Tennill, Francis	2	100
Toms [?], Thomas	1	70
Thornton, Francis Junr	4	
Taylor, Pater	2	
Turner, George	2	
Turner, Henry's Estate	6	1600
Towles, John	3	
Taylor, Charles	1	

U		
Utterback, Jacob	2	100
Underwood, William	1	100

V	[Tithes]	[Land]
Vanhufflen, Peter John	1	

W	[Tithes]	[Land]
Williams, Joseph	1	
Walker, William	1	
Waller, William	3	400
Wood, James	1	
Wood, Joshua	1	130
Wheatly, George	2	
Waite, William	5	350
Wilburn, Edward	--	134
Walker, Samuel	2	
Wood, Gidden	5	
Wood, Samuel	1	
Wood, Edward	1	
Waller, Charles Estate	8	400
Withers, Thomas	9	688
Waddle, John	--	60
Withers, James	12	600
Withers, William	8	600

1765-001 Tithable List
[This list is a partial listing of Tithes and Land. It is tentatively identified as 1765 from the notation on second page that says "Deeds tc. recorded Sepr 1765."]
[page 1 column 1]

W [Cont.]	Tithes	Land
Withers, Cain Estate	9	300
Winn, John	6	
Weaver, Tilman	5	596
Wilburn, Edward	2	170
Wright, John	2	
Wright, John	5	236
Williams, George	4	147
Williams, Jonas	1	
Williams, Joseph	1	
Woodsides, John	3	271
Williams, Thomas	5	
Wood, Benjamin	1	
Woodyard, Lewis	1	
Williams, Paul	4	590
Wilson, Jonathan	1	
White, Benjamin	1	
Wright, Charles	1	
Watts, Thomas	3	
Williams, Thomas (Const^a)	--	
Wheatley, John	2	
Weaver, Jacob	1	
Welch, David	1	
Williams, Nathaniel	--	[torn]
Williams, Jane		250
Williams, Pope John	--	250
Williams, Jessie	--	260
Whiting, Francis	--	534
Washington, Warner		

Y		
Young, Original	2	
Young, Sonnett	1	
Young, Christian	2	150
Young, James	6	159

On the side of this page:
"Deeds tc Recorded
Sepr 1765"

1766-001 GILSON FOOTE'S TITHABLE LIST
A List of the Tithables in Fauquier County for the Year 1766.

page 1 [column 1]	L	W	B	C
A				
Allen, Thos. Edward Turner. Will, Dick, Winney Will, Dick, Winney	178	2	3	
B				
Broke, Thos		1		
Bullett, Sarah. Wm. Bullett		1		
Roger, Will, Sarah			3	
Bullett, Cuthbert. Norman Drummond. Julia, Caesar, Sarah, Poll, Dunkan, Graham	700	1 2	4	
Bullett, Joseph. Samuel Newland. Phillis, Jane, Bess	272	2	3	
Bruton, Patrick		1		
Bethel, Valentine		1		
Brooke, W^m	200	1		
Brown, George. George Brown, Marmaduke Brown. Nell	150	3	1	
Burdett, John			1	
Bethel, John. John Embry		2		
Blackwell, Joseph. Brister, Toby, Jack, Jeffrey, Siller, Sue, Grace, Jane, Bett	1050	1	9	1
Butler, John. Wm Butler	423	2		
Beach, Peter. Thos Beach	200	2		
Bronaugh, W^m. John Brahan Bofon, Caesar, Coner, Bess	337	1	4	
Brahan, John. Tom, Harry			2	
Bullett, Thos. Thos Scaggs, Matthew Jones. Bristor, Will, Harry, James, Jude, Cate		3	6	
C				
Conway, W^m. George, Will, Joe Frank	300	1	4	
Coppage W^m. Daniel	800	1	1	
Catlett, John. L. Parrish	350	1		
Catlett, John Junr. [illegible abbreviation]		1		
Cummings, John. [illegible abbreviation]		1		
[page 1 column 2]				
Crosby George. John Gun. Daniel, James, Jude	226	1	4	
Coram, Champ, Richd Coram	227	2		
Crump, George. George Crump Junr Tony, Ben, Hanah, Sall, Sall	670	2	5	
Craford, Reuben		1		
Combs, John Junr. George	350	1	1	
Cummings, Moses. Moses Cummings Junr		2		
Conway, Thos. Thos Conway Junr. Peter Conway. George, James, Sarah, Lucy, Jane, Jude	649	3	6	
Churchill, Armstead. Wm. Petty. Jonathan Marsh. Tom, dick, Jack, sharper, Tony, Emanuel, Nell, Jane, Lett, Phillis, Tom, Sawney, Michai, Nell, Role, Moll. Joseph Broke. Wm Moore	1262	5	16	
Crump, Benj^a. Hannah, Nan, Sam, Bob, Harry	372	1	5	
E				
Embry, John P		1		
Ellis, John. Charles		1	1	
Ellis, John Junr Earlar, Reubin, Ben Richard Covington		2	1	

1766-001 GILSON FOOTE'S TITHABLE LIST

A List of the Tithables in Fauquier County for the Year 1766.

page 1 [column 2]	L	W	B	C
[F]				
Foote, Richd's Quarter				
John Wood. Ned, James, Joe				
Bristor, Dick, Aaron, Moll	1918	1	7	
Foote, Wm. Wm Fletcher. Peter,				
Lewis, Frank, Rofs, Milly, Hester		2	6	
Foote, George. Roger, Tom,				
Priss	365	1	3	
Foote, Gilson. Jack, Sam, Joe,				
Lucy, Sue, Sall	600	1	6	
Foote, Richd Junr. Jz{t} Foote.	555	1	1	Bole
Wm Junr. Infant	295		1	Adam

page 2 [column 1]	L	W	B	C
Fitzhugh, John's Quarter				
Ben, Titus, Maria, Poll, Nan		5		
Fitzhugh, Thos	800			
Fletcher, Wm. Thos Howle,				
Benja Fletcher		3		
Mofes Fletcher		1		
Thos Fletcher		1		
G				
Gibson, Jonathan. Harry, Joe,				
Charles, Charles, Dick, Bob, Lucy,				
Jude, Dennis	1050	1	9	
Grant, Wm. Braham, Colly, Jack,				
Pompey, Frank, Bett, Bett, Grace,				
Dorcas, Nan	1200	1	9	
George, Nicholas. Hotton,				
Hannah, Dick	180	1	3	
H				
Harwich, Aaron. Edwin Horton				
Jack, Neyls [?]		2	2	
Homes, Thos		1		
Hogan, Thos	181	1		
Harrel, Daniel	102	1		

1766-001 GILSON FOOTE'S TITHABLE LIST

A List of the Tithables in Fauquier County for the Year 1766.

page 2 [column 1]	L	W	B	C
Hambleton, Wm. Jane, Nan	282	1	2	
Hendring, John. Jack, Detter		1	2	
Hackley, Lott. Dinah, Jude	246	1	2	
Hopper, Joseph		1		
Hopper, Blagrove	325	1		
Harrison, Thos. D[ettingen] Parrish				
Wm. Harrison. Benja Harrison.				
Jacob, Peter, Charles, Caesar,				
Daniel, Frank, Phillis, Sarah,				
Alice, Sinah, Jude	2679	3	11	
Harrison, Thos. Hambleton P[arish]				
James, Toby, Roger, Cate, Phil, Hester		1	4	
Humston, Edward, Edward Humston.				
Tom, Patience, Frank, Hannah,				
Linny	234	2	5	

page 2 [column 2]	L	W	B	C
J				
Jones, Brereton. Wm Prim.				
Sarah, Cate	800	2	2	
K				
Kirk, Thomas P	1			
Kenner, Howsin. Isaac, Lett,				
Abram, Toney, Jonathan, Moses		1	6	1
Kenner, George. James, Hannah	150	1	2	
L				
Luttrell, Richd	38	1		
Laurance, Edward. Richd Laurance.				
Jane, Jude, Nan, Mym, Sarah,				
Mofes, Jacob, Sam	317	2	8	
Large, Josep. James W{ms}		2		
Luttrell, John	74	1		

1766-001   GILSON FOOTE'S TITHABLE LIST
A List of the Tithables in Fauquier County for the Year 1766.

page 2 [column 2]	L	W	B	C
M				
Moreh^d, John. Samuel Moreh^d James, Tony, Tom, Lett	450	2	4	
Moreh^d, Alexander, Geo Bethel Sarah		2	1	
Moreh^d, W^m. Jude		1	1	
Mauzy, Eliz^a Will, Bob, Sam	321		3	
Millard, W^m. Marthy	100	1	1	
Morgan, Charles. Joseph Morgan	108	2		
Mynatt, Rich^d, Constable				
N				
Nelson, John. Thos Nelson Wm Nelson	298	3		
Nelson, John	180	1		
Norman, Clement		1		
P				
Peters, James. Phill		1	1	
Peters, John. Will, Bob	800	1	2	
Priest, Thos. Thos Priest Junr Wm Priest	100	3		
R				
Rousau, William. Jude, Jane, Nell, Davy	250	1	4	

page 3 [column 1]	L	W	B	C
S				
Stuart, John. Reubin Bates. Toby, Hannah, Blunder, Daphne, Judy, Nell		1	6	
Shumate, John Junr d[ettingen] P[arish] Phillis		1	1	
Scagges, Isaac			1	

page 3 [column 1]	L	W	B	C
Simmons, Moses. Joseph Turner		2		
Smith, Thos. John Smith	200	2		
Snelling, Benjamin. Anthony, Ben		1	2	
Stuart, William. the Rev^ds Q^r Thomas Green. James, Mars, Phill, Nan, Dinah, Rose. Jeremiah Spiller. Ned, Jonathan, Tom, Nell, Joe, Davy	2352	2	12	
T				
Tullos, Joshua Pat^r [Patroller]		1		
Turner, Henrys Estate John Claytor. Obier, Phillis, Nan, Jane	500	1	4	
Threlkeld, George		1		
W				
Whitledge, Thos. Bob, Phillis		1	2	
Wallers Estate W^m. Tippet. James, Joe, Cyrus, Hannerboy, Winney, Phillis, Lettice & Dye	400	1	8	
Waller W^ms Tithes Charles Colvin. Isaac, Backus, John	400	1	3	
Wood, Jo^s. Levy free, Baley Wood, James Wood.		2		
Wood, Edward		1		
Wagener, Peter, Maj^r	800			
Watchway, John. Hannah		1	1	
Winn, James. John Rousau.		2		
Winn, Minor. W^m. Green. Tony, Fryday, Adam, Moll, Rachel		2	5	
Watts, Thomas. Thos Wats Junr. Nell		2	1	

1766-001 GILSON FOOTE'S TITHABLE LIST

A List of the Tithables in Fauquier County for the Year 1766.

page 3 [column 2]　　　　　L　　W　B　C

[Y]
Young, Original. John Twentyman.
Cupid　　　　　　　　　250　　1　2

M
Murry, James. Ja^s Murry Junr.
Wm Murry.　Prose　　　　　　3　1

Oliver, John　　　　　　　　　　1

Davis, John　　　　　　　　　　1

John Kirk　　　　　　　　　　　1

Benj^a Robinson. Isaac Curtiss.
Pegg, Moll, Jude　　　　　　　　2　3

Sarah Dodson.　George Dodson　100　1

Robert Munday.　Wm Munday.
John Munday.　Harry, Jude, Pegg　　3　3

James Mercer's Q^r
John Madclafe.　Jack, Barbadois,
H[illegible], Peter, Winney, Beauty,
Sephinia　　　　　　　　　　　1　7

Gilson Foote

Augt 23th 1766

Charles Obrion　　　　　　　　1
John Stamps　　　　　　　　　1
Elisha Dodson　　　　　　　　1
George Dodson　　　　　　　　1
Moses Seafield　　　　　　　　1

1767-001   John Kirk's Tithable List

[page 1 column 1]   [Tithes]

Name	Tithes
Joseph Williams	2
Thos. Skinker	16
Joshuay Wood	2
John Cortney	3
William Cortney	2
William Johnson	1
george Henery	1
Prew Banson	4
David partlow	2
Roley dolman q^r	7
John Cortney Jn^r	1
Charles Duncan	1
Morris Jacobs	1
george Jacobs	1
Lott Hackley	4
Jos Odor	2
Jos Emmons	1
William Emmons	3
William Butler	2
John Henary	1
garred Edwards	1
Coll^o Blackwell	7
William Kesterson	1
Majer Eustace	8
Robert Embrey	4
Thos Kirk	2
John Bethel	1
Thos Brooks	1
Thos Embrey	1
Rodham Tullos	4

[page 1 column 2]

Name	Tithes
george Crump	6
Martin Harden	8
John Mebe	1
Benjaman snalen	3
Bettey page	2
Maxm Barryman	14
John Debuty	1
John Jones	3
Marcy Bradford	2
Danl Bradford	5
Alex^r Bradford	5
William Alen	3
Banja^m Bradford	2
William McDaniel	3
John Edwards	2
Swanson Brown	1
John stewards q^r	7
garrad Fuxes q^r	5
Thos Newgan	7
Hunters q^r Great ^{Marsh}	8
John Barnie	2
Coll^o Carters q^r Tin ^{pot}	8
Normans Ford q^r	13
Thos Alen	7
Ursla Alen	14
Capten grant	10
peter grant	9
William Embrey	1

[page 1 column 3]

Name	Tithes
John Brown	1
John Woodsides	3
Alexander woodsides	4
John Embrey	1
Jos blackwell	10
Thos smith	3
Vollentyne Bethel	1
John Brown Jn^r	1
Thos Conway	13
George Thralkeld	1
Thos Hopper	1
Jos Hopper	1
Thos Mathews	1
John Barber	2
Peter Beach	1
Nathanal Hicker^{son}	1
Thos Jeames	7
Banja^m Crump	6
John Alen	5
John Knoxs q^r	8
William Dulaney	4
Jos Dulaney	1
John Twentyman	1
Nacy Curtis	1
Richard Coventon	3
Charles Morgan	3
John Butler	2
John Kirk	2
William flowers	1
George Henary	1

"I have vewed the sevril feilds of Tobaco with in My presinqts as I have bin shode acording to Law and the Tithes there in are 328.
Vewed for the [year] 1767
           (signed) John Kirk, Constable"

1768-001 Armistead Churchhill's Tithable List
A List of tithes for the Year 1768

[page 1 column 1] [Tithes]

William Withers Joseph Settle, Overseer. Jack, Peter, Dick, Sarah, Dinah	7
The Estate Cane Withers William Withers Overseer. Daniel Fortune. Ned, Nan, Sue, Phillis, Easter, Thompson	9
William Smith	1
John Smith	1
Elizabeth Bunbury's. John Smith, Overseer. Harry, Titus, David, Winnie	5
James Crocket	1
Henry Mauzey. Jn° Mauzey. Henry Mauzey. David, Dick, Sarah, Lettice	7
Reubin Brag	1
Ch^s Carter Corotoman Francis Settle, Overseer; Bryan Thornhill Overseer. Robin, Randolph, Bess, Doll, Frank, Alice, Tom, Adam, Ambrose, Charles, Will, Cesar, Lucy, Nell, Jenny, Hannah, Winnie, pallas, Easter, Hampton, Daniel, Ben, Dido	26
William Morgan. George Settles. Jn° Ryle. Jn° Night. Dick, Jude, Luce, Jude	6
Jn° Utterback & Timby	2
	68

[page 1 column 2]

William Robinson K^g G[e]orge James Duff, Overseer. Plato, Edinburg, Nancy, Roger, Nell, Alice, Mille, Winnie, Leannah	10
James Frazier	1
Edward Newgent. Thomas Bennet. James, Hannah	4

1768-001 Armistead Churchhill's Tithable List
A List of tithes for the Year 1768

[page 1 column 2] [Tithes]

Thomas Pope. Richard Dean. Jeffery	3
Ch^s Garner	1
Joseph Leavill. Bristol, Hannah, Phillis, Lions	5
Thomas Bronaugh. Ross, Daniel, Luce, Ben	5
James Fletcher	1
Benjamin Butler. Peg	2
Mrs Henets Quarter Eastham Roach, Overseer. James, Tom, Is, Sarah	4
William Edmonds. Willm Crawford, Overseer. James, Tony, Abraham, Grace, Jude, Jude, Belinda and 1 chair	9
Humphrey Brooke. Wm Scoggan, Overseer. Peter, Cupid, Oxford, Dinah, Hannah, Arrabella & 1 Chair	8
Eliz^a Moira's Estate. Jn° Long, Overseer. Quiver, Ayre, Amy, Jinny	5
Saml Thornberry. William Thornberry. Jack, Sauny, Winfred, James	6
	64

[page 1 column 3] [Tithes]

Joseph Brag	1
Thomas Brag	1
Dozier Brag	1
Champ Coram. Richard Coram	2
James Armstrong	1
James Withers Senr. James Withers Junr. Jn° Withers. Andrew, Prince, Parish, Dick Robin, Cupid, Jinny, Phebe, Jude	11

1768-001 ARMISTEAD CHURCHHILL'S TITHABLE LIST
A List of tithes for the year 1768

[page 1 column 3]	[Tithes]
Jere Owens	1
Joshua Lamton. Suck, Pegg	3
John Fishback	1
Charles Martin. Peter, Racheal, Sue	4
John Colvin. Cossom Day. John Sharp.	3
Richd Halls Quarter. Edward Hamton. Ned, Lundon, Dick, Dermont, James, Charles, Jack, Peter, Lett	10
John Burdett	1
James Burdett	1
Turners Quarter Jno Suthard, Overseer. Adam, James, Cook, Hannah, Sarah, Bess	7
John Suthard	1
George Leach Senr. Geo. Leach Junr	2
	51

[page 2 column 1]	
George Williams. John Williams. William Williams. Jack, Hannah	5
Roger Tolle. George Foley. Stephen Foley. Harry	4
Elizabeth Etherington. Benj^a Etherington. John Johnson. Henry, Thos., London, Henry, Luce, Jean, Bess, Sarah	11
John Churchhill. Parnach George. James Bogg. Punch, Jacob, Boatswain, Ned, Ulises, Harry, China, Bibby, Phillis, Prisilla, Dinah, Guy, George, Andrew, Harvey, James, Doll, Hannah, Sarah, & one Chair	22
Bushrod Dogget. Benj^a Dogget, George Doggett, Richd Dogget. Tom, Dick, George, Phillis, Lettice, Moreah	10

1768-001 ARMISTEAD CHURCHILL'S TITHABLE LIST
A List of tithes for the year 1768.

[page 2 column 1]	[Tithes]
Joseph Hudnal Gent. James Hudnal. Ben, Crop, Judah	5
Tilmon Martin	1
Zacharias Lewis. George Adams. George, Dick, Daffney, Winney	6
William Brents Q^r Fran^s James. Joshua, Lett, Saunah, Jean	5
	69

[page 2 column 3]	Tithes	Wheels
Randolph Spicer, Patroler. Phillip	1	
George Boswell. Thomas Bird. Jacob, James, James, Simon, Champion, Jacob, Lett, Winney, Milley, Cate	12	2
Fran^s Attwell. Lawrance Castle. James, Cate, Jeany, Pompey	6	
Bennett Price. Bennett Browne. Markham McGregor	3	
Jeremiah Darnall. Joseph Darnall. Peter, Robin, Jack, Judah	6	
James Blackwell. Winney	2	
John Riley Senr. John Riley Junr.	2	
William Boswell. Ben, Daniel, Doll	4	
James Duncan. Sam, Will, Doll, Britain	5	
Thos Porter. Angus Cameron. Sarah	3	
John Wright. Ja^s Wright. Will, Bray, Dinah, Judah	6	
Robert Duncan. Sam, Joshua, Venus	4	
John Sinclair. Ja^s Sinclair. Tom, Phillis	4	
Luke Holder. Cull	2	
John Riley Senr. John Riley Junr	2	

1768-001 Armistead Churchill's Tithable List

A List of tithes for the year 1768.

[page 2 column 3]

	Tithes	Wheels
Richd Chichester. Ja^s Hathaway. Peter, Harculus, Ned, Shederach, Peter, Harry, Peter, Duke, Tom, Solomon, Jack, Daniel, Solomon, Abraham, Phil, Cain, Prince, Nan, Betty, Hannah, Sarah, Judah, Jane, Mary, Martha, Peg, Frank, Hannah	30	2
	92	

[page 3 Column 1]

	Tithes	Wheels
Thomas Parker	1	
John Martin	1	
Peter Bolle	1	
Armstead Churchill. Samuel Reids. Gabriel Amiss. Sharper, Toney, Manuel, Jack, Nott, Thomas, Dick, Rose, Moll, Jenny, Venus, Lette, Micajah, Phill, Sawney, Tom, Nell	20	2
Saml Fox. James Arnold. Harry, Sam	4	
George Herring. Wm Herring	2	
	29	

1768-002 John Kirk's Tithable List

[page 1 column 1] [Tithes]

Thos Conway	8
John Barber	2
Peter Beach	2
Thos Mathis	1
Joseph Hoper	1
Thos Hoper	1
George Thralkeld	1
William Flowers	1
William Butler	2
George Henary	1
John Butler	2
Jos Blackwell	12
John Brown Jn^r	1
Thos Smith	3
Thos Brookes	1
John Bethel	1
John Henary	1
Edward West	3
Alex^r Woodsides	3

1768-002 John Kirk's Tithable List

[page 1 column 1] [Tithes]

John Woodsides	4
Benjaman Bradford	3
Danal Bradford	7
Alex^r Bradford	4
William Allen	3
Mary Bradford	3
John Jones	4
Bettey page	1
Benjaman snallen	4
John Burck	1
John Mebe	1
Morris Jacobs	1
George Jacobs	1

[page 1 column 2] [Tithes]

William Embrey	[illegible – on fold]
Lott Hackley	[illegible – on fold]
William Emmons	2
William Johnson	1
John Cortney Jn^r	1
George Henary	1
Richard Lais	2
William Cortney	1
John Cortney	3
George Henary Jn^r	1
Prew Banson	7
Joshuay Wood	2
Thos Skinker	10
Jos William	1
Thos Jeames	8
Nathanal Hickerson	2
Co^{ll} Blackwell	9
Majer Eustace	8
George Crump	6
William Kesterson	1
Rodaham Tulles	3
Robert Embrey	4
Thos Kirk	2
John Embrey	1
Thos Embrey	1
Banj^m Crump	7
John Alen	4
Charles Garner	1
John Knoxs qu^r	10
John Twentyman	1
Nacy Curtis	2
Roley Dolmans qu^r	6
David partlow	3

1768- 002   JOHN KIRK'S TITHABLE LIST

[page 2 column 1]   [Tithes]

Charles Wicklef	4
Max^m Barryman	12
William Norman	2
Richard Bryan	2
John Debuty	1
Charles Morgan	2
John Stewards qu^r	7
Swanson brown	1
John Edwards	2
William McDannal	3
garret Fuckses qu^r	5
Harry Bramblet	1
John Skinkers q^r	5
Mr Hunter qu^r Gr[e]at Ma[r]sh	8
Norman ford	18
Thos Allen	8

[page 2 column 2]   [Tithes]

Ursla Allen	9
Jeames Allen	2
Jos Allen	2
William Grant	10
Mrs Margret Grant	6
Thos Newgan	8
Charles Duncan	1
John Henary Jn^r	1
Jos Odor	2
John Brown	1
John Kirk	2
Gared Edwards	1
Richard Coventon	

"I have vewed the sevril feilds of tobaco with in My precinks as I have ben shoed and the and the Tithes there in are 324.
Vewed P^r Me John Kirk Constable."

1775-001 WILLIAM GRANT'S TITHABLE LIST
A List of Tithables taken by William Grant the 10th of June 1775.

[page 1 column 1]   [Tithes]

Geo. Crosby. Wm. Crosby.
John Crosby. John Gun.
N. Daniel, Harry, Ben, Jere   8

Cha. Waller.   N. Essea,
Jack, Bachus, Truelove   5

1775-001 WILLIAM GRANT'S TITHABLE LIST
A List of Tithables taken by William Grant the 10th of June 1775.

[page 1 column 1]   [Tithes]

Howsin Kenner. Geo. Seaton.
N. Isaac, Moses, Abram, Anthony,
Jonathan, Letty, Lucy   9
    1 chair

Lazarus Mattox   1

Jonathan Gibson   1 chair
N. Harry, Joe, Charles, Charles, Eugene,
Lucy, Judy, Kate, Venus, Sargo   11

James Gillison.   [N.] Robin, Frank,
Will, Bess, Jenny   6

Mrs Gillisons Tithes
[N.] Plato, Ben, York, Nanny, Milly   5

Pet. Wagener's Tithes
Jacob Morland.
[N.] Essex, Neptune, Sarah   4

Robt Berryman
[N.] Quitus, Aaron, Judy, Amy, Jenny   6

Saml Wood. Richard Wood.	2
John Midly	1
Peter Hodo. Nat Hodo	2
John Kerr. [N.] Joe, Nan, Lucy, Milly	5

Revd Rodham Kenner.
[N.] Ant^o, Manuel, Pegg, Hannah   5

Geo. Tur. Kenner [N.] James, Ned	3
Joseph Morgan	1
Stephen Pritchard [N.] Edinburg, Sarah	3

                                            77

[page 1 column 2]   [Tithes]

Nicholas George.
[N.] Holland, Dick, Judy, Hannah, Lucy   6

Wm Conway. [N.] George, Will, Joe,
Frank, Moll   6

Capt John James.
[N.] Charles, Phillis, Winny, Judy   5

Presly Morehead.
[N.] Tom, Danl, Tony, James   5

1775-001 WILLIAM GRANT'S TITHABLE LIST

A List of Tithables taken by William Grant the 10th of June 1775.

[page 1 column 2]	[Tithes]
Brereton Jones. Wm Jones [N.] Pompey, Sarah	4
John Blackwell. Sam Phillips. [N.] James, Dick, Harry, Lucy, Mary, Sarah, Lydia, Grace, Sue	11
John Shumate Junr [N.] Cato, Tim, Grace, Jane, Phillis	6
Nic.[?] Springs. [N] Bob	2
John Mauzy. [N.] Sarah, Dinah, Jane	4
Phil Spiller	1
Ben Crump. Travers Crump. [N.] Harry, Bob, Sam, Nan, Jane	7
Wm Hogain. John Hogan.	2
Dan. Shumate, Pat^r [N.] Bess	1
John Peters [N.] Robin, Will, Lucy	4
John Nelson, Planter. [N.] George	2
Edward Humston. [N.] Allen, Will, Charles, Tom, Linny, Frank, Mary	8
	74

[page 1 column 3]	[Tithes]
John Shumate Levy free	
Baly Shumate. [N.] Jenny	2
Wm Shumate. Spencer Shumate	2
Alexander Williamson. W^m McAndrew	2
Swanson Brown. Phil Lucas.	2
John Nelson Smith. John Wood. N. Arch & Belinda	4
John Ennis	1
Thomas Raily. Wm Raly. [N.] Kap	3
John Burk	1
John Brahan. [N.] Tom & Sarah	3
Stephen McCormick. Fran^s McCormick. [N.] Chas, Nick, Jem, Bett, Sarah	7
John Jones. [N.] Peter, Guy, Pender, Bett	5

1775-001 WILLIAM GRANT'S TITHABLE LIST

A List of Tithables taken by William Grant the 10th of June 1775.

[page 1 column 3]	[Tithes]
George Brown. Jon^a Brown. Wm Brown. N. Newman	4
Cha. Martin N. Peter, Rachel, Sue	4
Thos Conway. Thos Conway j^r. Geo. Conway. N. James, George, George, Warner, Davy, Sarah, Jane, Judy, Patience, Hannah, Lydia	14
Peter Conway	1
Ben Bradford. Joshua Butler. Cha. Duncan. N. Jeoffery, Cate	5
John Nelson Junr	1
Wm Sturdy. Danl Wheatley	2
Thos Shumate, Pat^rl	
Joseph Duncan (Marsh)	1
David Partlow	1
	65

[page 2 column 1]	[Tithes]
Thos Newgent. Jno. Jewel. N. Mingo, Harry, Will, Venus, Belinda, Mary, Doll, Pegg, Moll, Rachel	12
Mrs Ann Newgent tiths John Ballance Ov^r [N.] Sam, Hannah, Sal, Sal	5
Wm Brooks	1
Robt Emry j^r	1
Wm Butler [N.] Peg & Nell	3
John Butler. John Butler j^r [N.] Ned, Admiral	4
Col. W. Eustace. John Eustace Isaac Eustace. N. Robin, Cato, Ezekiel, Kent, Rose, Jane, Aggy, Mary, Harry, Ned, Tom, Moll	15
Marmaduke Brown	1
Wm Edmonds. Wm Edmonds j^r [N.] Joe	3
Geo. Pullen	1
Richard Covington [N.] Ben	2
Pat. Redman	1

1775-001 WILLIAM GRANT'S TITHABLE LIST

A List of Tithables taken by William Grant the 10th of June 1775.

[page 2 column 1] [Tithes]

Dan¹ Harrill. Sam. Harrel	2
Thoˢ Barber	1
Thomas Price	1
Wᵐ Kesterson	1
John Kirk	1
Robᵗ Knox's Qʳ	
Alexʳ MᶜChonkie.	
N. Whipster, Judy, Harry, Winny, Pompey, Frank, Moses, Jane	9
Alexʳ MᶜChonkie tiths N. Sarah	1
George Threlkeld N. Charles	2
Joˢ Emmonds. [N.] Ambrose, Arnold	2
Lott Hackley.	
[N.] Jude, Dinah, Pender, Judy	5
Greenham Dodson [N.] Adam	2
E David Thomas	1
	77

[page 2 column 2] [Tithes]

Ra. Downman tithes	
James Shumate.	
[N.] Plato, Nacy, Roger, Plato, Milley, Alice, Winny, Patt	9
Geo. Crump.	
[N.] Tony, Jaˢ, Hannah, Sarah	5
Cap. L. Helm's Qʳ	
Jesse Nelson.	
[N.] Sambo, Lucy, Richᵈ, Pitt, Flora	6
John Alexanders Estate	
John Bowen.	
[N.] James, James, James, Tom, Stephen, Peg, Juno, Phillis	9
Joˢ Allen. [N.] George, Dinah	3
James Allen [N.] Soloman, Judy	3
Thoˢ Allen's tithes	
Gab. Sullivan. [N.] Jack & Jem	3

[page 2 column 2] [Tithes]

Ursla Allen's tithes	
Robᵗ Kerns, Ovʳ.	
[N.] Danˡ, Harry, Lydia, Nan, Lucy	6
Thomas Shepard. John Shepard. Sam. Wright	3
Geo. Wright, Patʳ	
Joseph Honton	1
Landon Carter Esqʳ of Richmond County	
N. Sam, Will, Kitt & Bush	4
John Bethel	1
Thoˢ Kirk, Patʳ	
John Kirk. Thoˢ Kirk Junʳ	2
Geo. Henry	1
Danˡ Bradford. Wᵐ Bradford. Ben Bradford	
N. Dick & Sythe	6
Mary Bradford's tithes [N.] Peter, Lucy	2
	64

[page 2 column 3] [Tithes]

Margᵗ Grant's tithes	
[N.] Bob, Jack, Judy, Cloe	4
1 chair	
Wᵐ Hooes tithes	
Ben Hall. [N.] Charles, Rachel, Clara	4
Wm. Smith, shoemaker	1
John Henry, Patʳ	
Geo. Davis	1
Thoˢ Grinnan	1
Wᵐ Johnson. Wᵐ Johnson jʳ	2
Prue Benson. Enoch Benson.	
[N.] Bob, Nurrum, Cate, Winny	5
Joˢ Odor [N.] Judy	2
John Holden	1
Wᵐ Wright	1
Joshua Wood. [N.] Joe	2
Mor. Jacobs. Thoˢ Jacobs N. Easter	3
Joˢ Butler	1
Wᵐ Smith	1
Ben. Weeks	1

1775-001 WILLIAM GRANT'S TITHABLE LIST

A List of Tithables taken by William Grant the 10th of June 1775.

[page 2 column 3] [Tithes]

Jo^s Odor Junr	1
Wm Flowers	1
Ger. Edwards. Jo^s Edwards	2
Wm Embry	1
Jo^s Embry	1
Sam Edwards. James Edwards	2
Tho. Brooks	1
Jo^s Hopper	1
Wm Jones, Pat^r	
Tho. Kirk Jn^r, Pat^r	
Pet. Beach	1
Sam Baker	1
Wm Hickerson	1
Joshua Tullos, Pat^r	
Thos Smith [N.] Dublin	2
John Embry	1
	$\overline{47}$

[page 3 column 1] [Tithes]

Nat Hickerson	1
John Brown (Taylors son). Jere Brown	2
Wm Butler Senr. Spencer Butler. Chas Butler	3
Geo. Embry	1
Cha. Embry	1
Wm Grant. Wm Willis. N. Jack, Pompey, Frank, Betty, Betty, Grace, Darky, Hannah, Lett, Sylvia, Nan	13
James Peters N. George	2
John Crump	1
John Hellen	1
John Cortney Levy free Leonard Cortney	1
Ed. Lawrence, Richd Lawrence. N. Moses, Will, Richard, Jane, Judy, Nan, Mimy, Sarah, Rose, Moriar	12
Alex^r Morehead [N.] Sarah, Violet	3
Jo^s Wheatly. John Rogers. [N.] Sara, Judy	4
Zach. Lewis N. Sim	2

1775-001 WILLIAM GRANT'S TITHABLE LIST

A List of Tithables taken by William Grant the 10th of June 1775.

[page 3 column 1] [Tithes]

Herman Fishback. Jo^s Huffman	2
Wm Waite [N.] Bob, Jack, York, Lucy	5
John Bronaugh's tiths [N.] Bob & Sam	2
Moses Harril.	1
Thos Embry	1
Wm Bennet	1
James Duff [N.] Will	2
Revd Wm Stuarts tithes Thos Green. N. James, Mars, Robert, Nan, Rose, Sue	7
	$\overline{60}$

[page 3 column 2] [Tithes]

Jo^s Bullet. James Wood. N. Will, Davy, Phillis, Bess	6
Edmond Homes. Abra. Wigginton	2
Mrs Celia Foote's tiths N. Charles, Dick, Bashey, Bob, Poll, Lett, Judy	7
Thos. James. Jo^s James. Saml Bronaugh. N. Ti[t]hes Ben, Ben, Hannah, Pegg, eve, Rachel	10
Wm Poole	1
James Hunters Q^r John Quisenbury. N. Moco, Tom, Jacob, Betty, Judy, Phillis, Tenar	8
Ja^s Withers (son of Ja^s). John Askins. Wm Addinton Thos Coleman [N.] Harry, Robin, Sara, Phillis	7
John Woodside. Wm Woodside. Wm Addinton. [N.] Aaron, Nan.	5
John Duncan. [N.] Tony, Will, Patt	4
Jacob Crouch	1
John Stuarts Est. Q^r Ruebin Bates [N.] Tony, Tom, Hannah, Belinda, Daphney, Nell, Dinah, Judy	9

1775-001 WILLIAM GRANT'S TITHABLE LIST

A List of Tithables taken by William Grant the 10th of June 1775.

[page 3 column 2]	[Tithes]
Charles Day. Harry Day	2
John Fletcher. James Fletcher.	2
John Kelly. Jos Kelly. Jos Henry	3
John Twentyman.	1
Miss Betsy Footes tithes	
John Pinnel.	5
[N.] Bristow, James, Joe, Lucy	

[page 3 column 3]	[Tithes]
Mrs Eliz. Fowkes tithes	
Martin Hardin Ovr	
[N.] Toby, Tom, Burgen, Mahomet, Cate, Sue, Grace	8
Thos Fidlar	1
Alexr Cummins	1
John Cummins	1
Wm McDanl. Wm McDanl Junr.	
John McDanl. Spencer McDanl	4
John Brown	1
John Wilson. Henry Fewell	2
Land Carter Junr	
Simon Dodd. John Cantfield	
N. George, Tom, Sam, Harry, Sam, Isham, Joe, Harry, Will, Jacob, Martin, Sue, Cate, Judy, Cloe, Winny, Hanah, Nan, Bett, Harry, Truelove, Jenny, Betty	26
1 chariot & 1 chair	
Richard Foote Junr. Ben Gregory	
[N.] Bob, Pender, Patt	4
Wm Footes tithes. [N.] Adam, Sarah	3
Lau. Washington Qr	
Joshua Fletcher, Ovr [N.] Joe, George, Hannah, Sue, Winny, Jane	7
Henry Dade Hooe	
N. Laurence, Phill, Rachel	62
	62
Total Carrd over	607

1775-001 WILLIAM GRANT'S TITHABLE LIST

A List of Tithables taken by William Grant the 10th of June 1775.

[page 4 column 1]	[Tithes]
Tithables in Dittengen Par. Fauq. Coty	
Capt. Jona Gibson's Qr	
Ben Orear. N. David, Isaac, Danl, Tom, Dinah, Alice	7
Benja Harrison	
[N.] Caesar, Jacob, Peter, Sam, Sarah, Phillis, Pegg	8
1 chair	
Alderson Weeks [N.] Nell	2
	17
Brot over	607
Total amount	624

1777-001 JOHN MOFFETT'S LIST OF TITHES, LAND & WHEELED CARRIAGES IN LEEDS PARISH

A List of Tithables, Land & wheel Carriages taken by John Moffett for the Year 1777 in Leeds Parish Fauq' Co'y

[page 1 column 1]

	Land in Acres	Tithables
Thomas Williams		1
John Williams (son of Tho's)		1
George Williams (D°)		1
John Thompson		1
John Whitton		1
Lewis Woodyard		1
Robert Gall		1
William Lane		1
W'm Wheatley		1
Robert Sinclair. Negro Tim		2
Henry Asbury (Carters Run)		1
John Parker. Benj. Parker		2
Michael Flynn		1
Hezekiah Shacklett. Negro Abigal		2
John White		1
Benjamin Elliott		1
W'm Elliott. Negros Jem & Poll		3
W'm Ford. Geo. Wood & Wm. Ford Jun'		3
Henry Snyder		1
Thomas Watts. Bennett Watts & Neg. Caleb		3
Samuel Rust. Neg. Geo. Nan & Frank	220	4
Samuel OBannon	147	1
William Asbury Jun'	100	1
John Moffett's List Tithables. Sam'l Pepper Jun', Overseer. Negro Cate, Dick, Prince, Ben, Winney, Esther and Jerimiah. 1 Two wheel'd Riding Chair	409	9
Alexander Johnson		1
Abraham Goodwin		1
Benjamin Neale. Matt'w Neale.	80	2
Andrew Barbey. Negro Jack, Dick, Sarah, Hannah & Nan		6
Andrew Barbey Jun'		1
James Armstrong		1
Archibold Allen. Wm. Allin & Ja's Allin		3

[page 1 column 1]

	Land in Acres	Tithables
Thomas Foley. Bryant Foley. Negro Moll		3
Cap. John Marshall. Hump. Marshall. Negro Juba, Nan & Hannah		5
Menoah Crawley. Negro Thom		2
Samuel Harriss		1
Jonathan Ellis		1
Garner Burgess. Negro Luce, Dinah & Luce		4
Dickerson Wood. Negro Luke		2
		77

1777-001   JOHN MOFFETT'S LIST OF TITHES, LAND & WHEELED CARRIAGES IN LEEDS PARISH

A List of Tithables, Land & wheel Carriages taken by John Moffett for the Year 1777 in Leeds Parish Fauq^r Co^{ty}

[page 2 column 1]

	Land in Acres	Tithables
Benjamin Fletcher		1
Valentine Flynn		1
John Smith. John Thomas.		2
Ezekiel Haddux		1
Thomas James. Negro Lett	309	2
Archibald Campbell		1
Robert Thompson		1
Bryant McCarty. Dawson Burgess.		4
John Murphy & Negro Ned		
William Briggs. Negro Harry & Bob		3
Jesse Thompson. Negro Willm & Sim		3
Joseph Barbee. In. Edwards. N[egro] Cate		3
William Smith Senr I (Carters run)		1
William Smith Jn^r (D^o)		1
James McCabe		1
Frederick Rictor. Negro Jude	100	2
Daniel Rictor		1
Samuel Pepper. Roberts Allen. William Pepper. Negro Sam, Jack, Pompey, Esther & Venus	300	8
James Drummond		1
Moses Congrove		1
Peter Hitt. N. hone	276	2
Joseph Hitt		1
George Cordell. N. Sam		1
John Miller. W^m. Miller	150	2
Robert Sanders. George Walden. N[egro] Sam & Hannah	100	4
Joshua Kennard		1
George Chapman. Geo. Kennard. N[egro] Jesse, James, Peter, Nell, Frank, Deallear, Nanna		8
William Hawkins		1

[page 2 column 2]

	Land in Acres	Tithables
John James	350	1
Thomas Payne		1
Benjamin Stone		1
James Jeffries		1
Alexander Jeffries Junr		1
Henry Kamper. Jno Kamper. N[egro] James	187	3
William Carrill. Negro Jone		2
Alexander Jeffries. Negro James		2
John Harris		1
Charles Carter Esqr Corotomon. William Herndon. Negro Sam, Ralph, Margaret		5
Captn Aylett Buckner. Negro Caesar omitted		1
		78

[page 2 column 2]

	Land in Acres	Tithables
Robert Cleveland. N[egro] Jack & Chloe		3
John Rogers. Stephen Rogers. Timothy Gent & Edward Laurence		4
John Dearing & his man		2
James Foley Junr		1
Jesse Norman		1
William Dearing		1
Col^o Thomas Marshall. John Ritchie. Thomas Marshall Jn^r. Negro Juba, Jacob, Dixon, Jacob, Joe, Jenny, Caesar, Hannah, Esther & Old Hannah & Bett	1700	13
Capt. Edward Dixon Q^r Humphrey Burdett, Overseer. Negro Tim, Caesar, Tim, Will, Tom, Tom, Judy, Moll, Hannah, Peg, Sall, Mimah, Sall, Betty, Lucy, Judy, Joab & Jenny	4406	19
James Sanders	89	1

1777-001 JOHN MOFFETT'S LIST OF TITHES, LAND & WHEELED CARRIAGES IN LEEDS PARISH

A List of Tithables, Land & wheel Carriages taken by John Moffett for the Year 1777 in Leeds Parish Fauq[r] Co[ty]

[page 2 column 2]

	Land in Acres	Tithables
Thomas Evens		1
William Hunton.	400	
Negro Bob, Robin, Moll,		
Winney, Cate & Sarah		7
Parnach George. Gabriel	150	
George. N. Scipio, Jack,		
Rose & Winney		6
M[r] William Heale.	800	
Abraham Silvey, N. Daniel,		
Moses, Domini, Joseph,		
Adam, Fielding, Nan, Phillis,		
Abigail, Young Nan, Margery		14
1 Pleasure waggon, 4 wheels		
John Kemper. Jn[o] Kemper his son		
Tilman Kemper, & Negro Winney	161	4
Robert Turnbull		1
Jacob Kamper	161	1
Benjamin Ball. David Ball.	161	3
William Kitson		1
Thomas Edwards. Negro Joe	125	2
James Crockett. Jn[o] Crockett		
& N. Jane, [illegible]	124	3
John Healey. Negro Jane & Dick		3
George Randall		1
Capt. William Ball. Negro James,		
Mary, Hannah & Nancy		5
1 Riding chair, 2 wheels		
Roley Smith.		
N. Pris, Amey & Bab	103	4
John Waddell. N. Jack	300	2
Richard Green. N. David, Jane		
& Sall		4
William Donaldson		1
		107

[page 3 column 1]

	Land in Acres	Tithables
William Bernard Esq[r] Q[r]	575	
James Penny, overseer.		
N. Daniel, Peter, Frank,		
Glasgow, Sall, Grace,		
Lynna & Nan		9
Ezekiel Philips. Geo. Odam		2
Francis Payne. N. Grace		2
Capt. William Thornton's Q[r]		
Isaac Johnson, Overseer.		
N. Simon, Sambo, Jack, Tom,		10
Sarah, Cate, Milley, Luke		
& Nann		
Capt. Wharton Ransdell.	1245	
Wm. Ransdell. John Paint.		
N. Geo., Geo., Tom, Joe, Dick,		
Jere, Dick, Jere, Jenny, Sarah,		
Jessly, Peg.		15
1 Riding chair, 2 wheels		
Wharton Ransdell Jn[r]		
N. Frank & Zekiel		3
M[r] John Churchill	600	
John Layton. Rich[d] Layton.		
Samuel Pharis.		
N. ulyses, punch, Garry, Jude,		
James, Anth[y], Cha[s], Bob, phillis,		
China, Diana, Doll, Bibby,		30
Betty, Andrew, Geo, Jack, Peter,		
Thom, Sarah, Han[h], Guy, Jack,		
Jenney, Frank & Nanny		
1 Pleasure waggon, 4 wheels		
James Harris		1
James Weatherly		1
Benjamin Martin		1
Daniel Bennett		1
Joseph Martin		1
Lazarus Hitt		1
Charles Delany		1
Reuben Martin		1
Henry Martin	163	1
William Day. Jn[o] Day.		2
William Grimes by Leo[d] Smoote		2
William Jones		1
Anny Day. Wm. Bradley		2

1777-001 JOHN MOFFETT'S LIST OF TITHES, LAND & WHEELED CARRIAGES IN LEEDS PARISH

A List of Tithables, Land & wheel Carriages taken by John Moffett for the Year 1777 in Leeds Parish Fauqr Coty

[page 3 column 1]

	Land in Acres	Tithables
John Smoote		1
Charles Smith		1
John Crimm		1
Harman Crimm. N. Cyrus [?] & Menava		3
Joseph Crimm		1
Thomas Harriss		1
Chatharine Crimm. Pel. Crimm N. Easther		2
John Glover. James Glover		2
Jacob Crimm		1
Reuben Payne		1
William Smith (Hicory) Spencer Smith. N. Luce, Cate, Rose & Esther		6
John Hopper		1
Dixon Brown. John Brown. Dixon Brown Junr. Negro Luce		4
Henry Jones Junr		1
		113

[page 3 column 2]

	Land in Acres	Tithables
John Shumate		1
Benjamin Glover		1
Richard Glover		1
[entry scratched out]		0
James Corder. Wm Lindsey & Wm Corder Jnr		3
James Grant		1
Jacob Brisoning [?]		1
John Wine		1
Benjamin Piper. N. Sam, peg, patts, Mimah & Sall		6
Samuel Lutterall. Danl Lutterall		2
Charles Morgan N. Bob		2
William Thomas John Green. N. James, Harry, Sarah, Judey & Betty		7
Humphrey Hopper		1
John Jones		1
James Suddith		1
John Smoote Senr		1
Laurence Suddith		1
William Fletcher. James Fletcher & Bart Fletcher		3
Richard Murphey		1
Miles Murphey		1
John Dodd		1
[entry scratched out]		0
Mr Burr Harrison. Chas Haycock. N. Harry, Danl, Jeff, Moll, Bett, Sylva, Rose		9
Thomas Jackman Jnr. Saml Madden	150	2
Anderson Cockrell		1
James Neavill. Jos Neavill. Negro Dick, Venus, Phillis	300	5
Edward Ball. N. Chas, Robin & Sam		4
Thomas Doughty		1
George Ash. N. Ellis omitted	463	1
George Honestt		1
John Elliot N. Peter		2
Joseph Williams		1
Peter Hitt		1
John Turner. Saml Wood.		2
Mary Bayley. Joseph Bayley. N. Bole, Danl, Sall & Sarah		5
Mary Hill. N. Jude		1
John Hitt Negro Sarah		2
		75

1777-001 JOHN MOFFETT'S LIST OF TITHES, LAND & WHEELED CARRIAGES IN LEEDS PARISH

A List of Tithables, Land & wheel Carriages taken by John Moffett for the Year 1777 in Leeds Parish Fauq^r Co^{ty}

[page 4 column 1]

	Land in Acres	Tithables
William Grigsby.	475	
N. Harry, Sue, Sarah, Nell, Timby, Jude		7
Edward Humston Junr.	575	
Negro Geo., Patience, Hannah & Banner		5
Thomas Massey		1
William Hemmings		1
Jane Harrison. Jesse Nelson.	992	
Negros Roger, Dublin, Cate, Cate, Patt, Milley, Winney & Angeler		9
Josias Basye		1
William Barker. N. Adam	197	2
Charles Martin N. London	170	2
Francis Attwell.		
N. Jack, Dick, Pegg, Kiziah		5
Alexander Bradford	148	
N. Joe, Toney, Milley, Rose, Cate		6
Joseph Smith. John Smith.	395	
Negro Nero, Rofe, Scipio, Joe, Phillis		7
Joseph Taylor.	200	
N. Will, Joshua, Hannah & Sarah		5
Eli Thompson.	100	
N. Aaron, Kiza.		3
Thomas Stone Senr		1
Captn Charles Morehead.	600	
Turn^r Morehead. John Marr.		
Negro Danl, Aaron, Will, Jenny, Monday.		8
1 Two wheel'd Riding chair		
William Jones. James Jones. Wm Jones Jr.		
Negro Jack, Roswell, Sam, Let, Beniter		8
Leroy, Hughlett. John Hughlett		2

	Land in Acres	Tithables
Joseph Holtzclaw.	163	
Negro Gully & Esther		3
Peter Larrence. Jno Larrance & N. Jack		3
William Jett		1
John Hamrick		1
John Jett		1
William Groves		1
Caleb Browning		1
Samuel Porter. Angus Campbell.		5
N. Tom, Sarah & Esther		
James Jett. Wm Jett & N. Bett		3
Henry Rogers. James Rogers		2
John Randall		1
Jacob Wever. N. Peter & Nance		3
John Bolt [Belt?]		1
Clement Normon		1
William Robinson		1
	200	

[page 4 column 2]

	Land in Acres	Tithables
Joel Settle.		
N. Jack, Juba, Hampshire Newton, Adam & Fann		7
William Norman. Jno Norman		2
Isaac Norman		1
Anthony Garrard		1
Robert Hume		1
James Oldham		1
William Welch		1
Mary Oldham.		
Negro Geo. Jess, Jude, Lucy, & Hannah		5
Eppa Timberlake. N. Geo. & Isabell		3
John Garlington. N. Sinor		2
Henry Taylor	87	1
Nimrod Taylor		1
William Roach.		
N. Phillis, Sarah & Ned		4

1777-001 JOHN MOFFETT'S LIST OF TITHES, LAND & WHEELED CARRIAGES IN LEEDS PARISH

A List of Tithables, Land & wheel Carriages taken by John Moffett for the Year 1777 in Leeds Parish Fauqr Coty

[page 4 column 2]

	Land in Acres	Tithables
John Rosser. Geo. Rosser. Negro Ben, Yambo, Cate & Jane	450	6
John Coppedge. N. Frank, Jone, James & Sue	625	5
William Kirk. N. Dan, Denbo, Moses, Jacob, Nell, peg, Betty & Coadyer	555	9
William OBannon. Joseph OBannon. N. Jane & Winney	589	4
Sarah OBannon. Benjamin OBannon. N. Caesar, Nan & Jude	265	4
Bryant OBannon. N Luce		2
Thomas Maddux. Thomas Shaw. Negro, Sam, Ezek^l, & Nell	1657	5
Col^o William Edmonds. Negro James, Danl, Abram, Judah, Judah, Mary, Cate 1 Riding chair, 2 wheels.	817	8
Mrs Frankey Bell N. Peter & Dinah		2
James Cox		1
Jeffrey Johnson	464	1
Major Martin Pickett. J^{no} Porter. N. Jack, will, Pomp, Aaron, Jacob, Frank, Sall, Nan & Winney 1 Riding chair, 2 wheels		11
		88

1777-001 JOHN MOFFETT'S LIST OF TITHES, LAND & WHEELED CARRIAGES IN LEEDS PARISH

A List of Tithables, Land & wheel Carriages taken by John Moffett for the Year 1777 in Leeds Parish Fauqr Coty

[page 5 column 1]

	Land in Acres	Tithables
Capt. William Pickett. N. Jemmimiah, Michael, Jack, Mohomet, Jupiter, Anthony. Charles, Daphney, Jude, Caroline. 1 Riding chair, 2 wheels.	200	11
Mrs Mary Ransdall. Wharton Ransdell. Chilton Ransdell. N. Bob, Sue, Nan & Peg	335	6
Mrs Elizabeth Pickett. James Holmes. Negro James, Sam, Chloe & Suck		5
George Suter		1
Humphrey Brooke. Peter, Cupid, Daniel, Dann, Phill, Hannah, Dinah, Toby, Milly two Chairs, 2 Wheels each	300	10
		33

1778-001 THOMAS KEITH'S TITHABLE LIST

A List of Tithes Taken by Thomas Keith 1778

[page 1]

	[Tithes]
Francis Atwell Tiths Neg. Jack, Dick, Peg & Keg	5
Robt Ashby Tiths Neg. Anthoney, Jane, Kate & Silvia	5
George Asbury tith	1
William Asbury tiths [Neg] Phillis & King	3
Henry Asbury	1
John Allen	1
William Allen	1
Arch^d Allen	1
Henry Asbury	1
William Asbury Junr [Neg] Robt, Kell [?] & Jack	2
	27

1778-001 THOMAS KEITH'S TITHABLE LIST
A List of Tithes Taken by Thomas Keith 1778

[page 2] [Tithes]

Mychael Byrn tith.	1
William Barker. & Adam	2
John Barker Tiths.	
John & Winney	3
Daniel Barrons	1
Joseph Blackerby.	
Tom, George & Winney	4
Burr Barton	1
Joseph Blackwell Jn^r.	
James & Mymey	3
Jeremiah Boggess. Negro Nan	2
Peter Bryan	1
William Barkley.	
London, Bill & Hager	4
Mary Bland. Negro Will	1
Henry Berry Ben & George	3
John Burditt Tiths.	
Arjy Burditt.	2
Thomas Bartlett. Thos Bartlett Jn^r.	
Neg. Jack, Franky, Dick, Joe, Hannah,	
Feby & Judy	9
William Bartlett. Neg. Dimbo	2
John Baley Jn^r.	1
Joseph Baley. Charles Woodard.	2
	42

[page 3] [Tithes]

Kimber Barton Tith.	1
Saml Butler	1
Joseph Baley. Neg Daniel	2
Moses Baley Tiths.	
Neg. Bob, Sal & Sarah	4
Peter Beshaw. Neg. Chris	2
John Boden. James Boden	2
Ja^s Baley (Mary Son)	1
John Baley Senr	1
James Barton	1

[page 3] [Tithes]

Peter Carter Tiths.	
Neg. Bob & Harry	3
Chas Chaddox. Neg. Will	2
Anderson Cockrell	1
Stephen Conner	1
	22

[page 4] [Tithes]

Simon Cornwell Tith^s. Neg. Joseph	2
James Cornwell. C. Oneal.	
Neg. Mary	3
Edmond Collins. Neg. Frank	2
Thos Clark	1
Ben Clark	1
The Estate of Joh. Chilton.	
James Gafney. Neg. Joe, Jess, Lucy	
& Letty	5
John Combs.	
Neg. Cuffy, Sarah & David	4
Robt Combs. Neg. Bosen	2
William Carrell	1
Elizth Carrell Tith. John Bartlett	1
Isaac Cundiff	1
John Coppage. Neg. Frank, Jane,	
James, Sue & Cris	6
Collin Campbell Tiths.	
John Layton. Neg. James, Henry,	
Charles, & Esther	5
Joseph Cartor	1
Geo Cartor [of] Stafford	
Neg. dick, Sesor & Diner	3
George Chapman Q^t	
George Kennard. Neg. Peter, Joe,	
James, Frank, Nel, Delia & Nan	8
	45

1778-001 Thomas Keith's Tithable List
A List of Tithes Taken by Thomas Keith 1778

[page 5]   [Tithes]

John Davis Tiths. Ely Davis	2
Cap. Wm Downing Tiths. Samuel Jones Ovr^s. Neg. Isaacs, Joe, Peter, Sam, Will, Ellen, Manuel, Nelson, Judy, Rachel, Grace, Let, Bet, Patience & Milley	16
Thomas Doly [Doty?]. Neg. Nan	2
Col. William Edmonds. Neg. James, Daniel, Jude, Jude, Moll, Kate & Viner [?]	8
Thomas Edwards. Neg. Joe	2
Rubin Eliott. Neg. Troop & Bet	3
Elias Edmonds Jn^r. Neg. Jack, Jack, Tine, Stephen, Jude & Margret	6
Ben Elliott.	1
John Elliott.	1
Wm Elliott. [Neg.] James	2
	43

[page 6]   [Tithes]

William Fitzgarrell. John Fitzgarrell.	2
John Fields Tith. Neg. Jemime	2
John Flynn	1
Josiah Fishback. Neg. Joe, Nan & Monica	4
Phil Fishback. John Fishback	2
Jacob Fryer	1
John Fishback. Neg. London & James	3
Henry Feagen	1
William Foley	1
James Foley. Bryan Foley Neg. Luis, Fanny & Hannah	5
William Flowereree	1
	23

[page 7]   [Tithes]

Edward Feagon Tiths. John Feagon. Edward Feagon. [Neg.] George, Harry, Will, Kate, and Sarah	8
John Feagen Tith. Daniel Commens	1
William Ford. W^m [Ford] & George Ford	3
George Glascock Tiths. Nan, Bet & Jack	4
Even Griffith	1
Peter Grant. Neg. Will, Jack, Hannah, Peg	5
Mrs Ann Green Tiths Willis Green. Henry Green. Neg. Toby, Jack, Sam, Jane and Milly	7
	29

[page 8]   [Tithes]

George Gibson	1
Saml Grigsby Tith. Neg. Kooper, James, Jack, Jane & Winney	6
Thomas Glascock	1
Richard Green	1
Parnich George. Gabriel George. Sipoe, Jack, Rose and Winney	6
Benaga Grubs	1
William Grigsby Tiths. Neg. Henry, Nell, Sarah and Timby	5
	21

1778-001 Thomas Keith's Tithable List
A List of Tithes Taken by Thomas Keith 1778

[page 9] [Tithes]

John Hathaway Tiths. Neg. Winney & Jude	3
James Harriss	1
Ephraim Hubbard. Anthony, Sarah, Jane and Kate	5
William Hambrick	1
John Peyton Harrison. William Priest. Buck, Dick, Lid & Jane	5
Thomas Hogen Tiths. Neg. Ralph	2
William Hamilton. John Mason. Davy, Jane & Sall	4
Honour Haley. Michael Leonard.	2
William Hunton Tiths. Ben Robison. Thos Evins. Daniel, Moll, Winney, Kate, Sarah & Ismer	9
William Holton	1
Robt Hall	1
Burr Harrison. Neg. Harry, Jeffry, Daniel, Chas, Ha[n]cock, Moll, Bett, Sylva & Rose	9
	43

[page 10] [Tithes]

John Johnson Tith	1
George Johnson	1
Peter Jones	1
John James	1
Joseph Jeffris. Thomas Jeffris. Henry Jeffris. [Neg.] Bess & Jenny	5
Alex^r Johnson. (Neg.) Lett	2
Moses Johnson. [Neg] Ralph	2
	13

[page 11] [Tithes]

Thomas Keith Tiths. Neg. Harry, George, Ned, Jupiter, Peg, Nan, Morier & Beck	9
John Keith. Joseph Doniphan. [Neg.] Moroco, Bob, Peter, Peter, Nan, Moll	8
Robt Kerns	1
John Kibbell. James Kibbell	2
Alex^r Keith. [Neg.] Will, Bill, Sarah and Hannah	4
Isham Keith. Neg. Toby, Sarah & Nell	4
William Kenton. John Doniphan. James Waller. John Smith. [Neg.] Nan	5
William Kidwell. John Kidwell	2
William Kirk. Geo. Baley. [Neg.] Daniel, Dimbo, Moses, Jacob, Nell, Peg, Bet & Coader	10
	46

[page 12] [Tithes]

Thomas Leachman	1
Benjamin Levill. Neg. Will, Sam, Suse an[d] Hester	5
William Leachman	1
James Lewis. William Begs. [Neg.] Cloe	3
James Leach. James Leach Jn^r.	2
William Leak	1
Vincent Leak	1
James Lamkin Neg. Charles & Isable	3
Thomas Laws	1
George Leach. Patrick Whaeling	2
John Leachman	1
	24

1778-001 Thomas Keith's Tithable List
A List of Tithes Taken by Thomas Keith 1778

[page 13]	[Tithes]
Augustine Love Tith Pr Wm C^t Neg. Phil, Robt, Roley, Suck & Jone	5
Murthy M^{c}aboy	1
William McCafrey	1
Edward Mathews	1
Nathan Mathews	1
Ben Mathew. Joanna Mathew. Ben Mathews	3
John Francis Mercer. William Moore. Alex^r Lain. Neg. Sipio, Captain, George, Ben, Sauney, Moccow, Lida, Phillis, Mary, julia, Sarah, Truelove, Amia, Jenney, Loudon, Will, Cliffen, George, Millard, Andrew, Bristol, David, Captain, Peter, Cupid, Philis, Sall, Grace	29
John Morey	1
John Murphey	1
	38

[page 14]	[Tithes]
John Monday. [Neg.] Jude, Peg, Harry & Frank	5
Robt Monday. Neg. Rose & Luce	3
William Morehead. Neg. Judy	2
Simon Morgen. Benj^a Morgan. [Neg] Will, Soloman, Sam & Jane	6
John Metcalf	1
Charles Marton. [Neg] London	2
William Matthews. John Robison. [Neg] Fill & Winney	4
Jonathan Mathew	1
Turner Morehead. John Marr. [Neg] Aaron	3
Cap. Chas Morehead. Daniel Monday. [Neg] Will and Jennay	5

[page 14]	[Tithes]
Joseph Mintor Tiths. Neg. Net & Barton	3
The Estate John Mintor. Neg. Baccus, Jacob, Sarah & Rachel	4
Henry Moffett. Son Jesse	2
	41

[page 15]	[Tithes]
Jonathin Newhouse	1
William Norris. John Norris. John Dean. [Neg] Let, Vilet & Kate	6
William Nall	1
John OBannon. W^m OBannon. Joseph OBannon. William Birdit. [Neg] Gabril, Dick, Solomon, Peter, Jesse, Sarah, Kate & Jude	12
Andrew OBannon. Neg. Frank & Mimey	3
Edward Oneal. John Owens. [Neg.] Suck	2
William Owens. John Owens. Neg. Cane	3
Sarah OBannon. Bryan OBannon. [Neg] Casor, Nan, Lucy & Judy	5
John Otterback. [Neg] Timpy, Joe & Liz	4
John Owine ~~Christopher Oneal~~	1
Ben Orear. Neg. Tom & Ann	3
Saml OBannon	1
	35

1778-001 THOMAS KEITH'S TITHABLE LIST
A List of Tithes Taken by Thomas Keith 1778

[page 16]　　　　　　　　　　[Tithes]

Henry Peyton.　Thos Leach.
[Neg] Ned, Mountain, Moses,
Spencer, Hannah & Milley　　　7

Samuel Perl.　John Hazeldon.
[Neg] Lucy　　　　　　　　　　3

Martin Pickett.　[Neg] Jack,
Will, Aaron, Pompy, Jacob, Frank,　10
Nan, Winney and Frank

Peter Priest　　　　　　　　　1
Henry Pinkstone　　　　　　　1

Rust, Samuel
Neg. George, Frank & Nan　　　4

William Roach
Neg. Philis & Ned　　　　　　　3

George Rhuther　　　　　　　　1
Cornelius Ranes　　　　　　　　1

Mrs Mary Ransdell.
Whorten Ransdell.
Edward Ransdell.
Clifton Ransdell.
[Neg] Jeries, Bet, Nan, Peg & Sue　8
　　　　　　　　　　　　　　　39

[page 17]　　　　　　　　　　[Tithes]

Richard Rixy.　Wills: Leach.
John Pirkins.　[Neg] Ton, Aaron,
Hager & Hannah　　　　　　　7

Cap Wharton Ransdell.
Wharton Ransdell.　Wm. Ransdell.
Thos Ransdell.　Thos Parent.　22
Neg. Geo., Geo:, Geo:, Dick, Dick,
Jonathan, Tom, Joe, Moses, Jeremy,
Frank, Jesse, Sis, Pegg, Jean, Sarah
& Sue

William Strange　　　　　　　1

William Steward.
Neg. Winney, Sue & Bess　　　4

1778-001 THOMAS KEITH'S TITHABLE LIST
A List of Tithes Taken by Thomas Keith 1778

[page 17]　　　　　　　　　　[Tithes]

William Skinker.
William Cortney.　[Neg] Guy,
Isaac, Luis, Hannah, Hester
& Winney　　　　　　　　　　7

James Scott.　Wm Congrove.
[Neg] Will, Sawney, Frank, Elger,
James, Hannah, Pegg, Jean,　　12
Charlotte & Bet

William Pickett Sanford.
[Neg] Frank, Winney & Gib　　4

Anne Stephens.　Neg. Harry & Hager　2

The Estate Geo. Sullivin.
Thos Whitledge.　[Neg] Siser, Joe,
Philis & Dine　　　　　　　　5
　　　　　　　　　　　　　　64

[page 18]　　　　　　　　　　[Tithes]

The Revd William Stuard.
William Prim.　[Neg] Dick,
Jonathan, Tom, Harry, Rose, Pegg,　11
Nell, Flowrey, Diner, Winney

Robert Scott.　John Whaling　　2
John Sires.　Neg. Sam & Frank　3

James Shard　　　　　　　　　1

The Revd James Scott.　Patrick Hambrick.
[Neg] James, Ceasor, Titus, Ben, Davy,
George, Beck, Nan, Bet and Judy　11

James Sanders　　　　　　　　1
Robt Sanders.　Neg. Sam & Hannah　3
Thomas Shaw　　　　　　　　1
　　　　　　　　　　　　　　33

[page 19]　　　　　　　　　　[Tithes]

Aaron Thomas　　　　　　　　1

Joseph Taylor.　Neg. Will, Josuas,
Sarah, Hannah　　　　　　　　5

1778-001 THOMAS KEITH'S TITHABLE LIST
A List of Tithes Taken by Thomas Keith 1778

[page 19]   [Tithes]

Judith Taylor.   Richd Basey.
[Neg] Adam, George, Kate, Nan,
Bett & Tabb   7

Nimrod Taylor   1

Epy Timberlake.
Neg. George & Isbel   3

David Thomas Tiths.
Neg. ~~Philis~~, Patience   2

Ben: Thomas   1
                                           ——
                                           20

[page 20]   [Tithes]

William Van   1
Joseph Vanpelt   1

Thomas Wats   1
John Willowby Jn^r 1
John Willowby   1

Silvester Welch.
Neg. Winney, Salley & Moses   4

Cap. Ja^s Winn.   Richd Dennison.
William Constabel.   [Neg] Moses,
James, Harry & Sarah   7

The Estate Mynor Winn.
Charles West.   [Neg] Tony, Sawny,
Paul, Jean & Grace   6

Luke Woodyard   1

Alderson Weeks. Neg. Daniel & Nel 3
John Waddell.   Neg. Jack   2

John Wake.   Neg. Lot, James, Judas
and Judas   5
                                           ——
                                           31

[page 21]   [Tithes]

Lewis Woodyard   1

Francis Wats.   Neg. James & Nell   3

1778-001 THOMAS KEITH'S TITHABLE LIST
A List of Tithes Taken by Thomas Keith 1778

[page 21]   [Tithes]

John Young   1

William Young
[Neg] Henly & Harry   3

William Yates   1

Bryan Young Tiths.
William Reddings.   Geo. Owens.   4
(Neg) Ned
                                           ——
                                           13

   Forw^d
   Samuel Boyd   5
[Note On line above the number 4 is scratched
through and replaced by the number 5]

[page 22]   [Tithes]

Added by Order of Court

Elizabeth Ash   4
Henry Rector   5
William Ball   3
Alex^r Sangster   1
~~Samuel Boyd~~   ~~5~~
John Monroe   3
John Cornwell   2

1778-002 WILLIAM PICKETT'S TITHABLE LIST
A List of Tiths for the year 1778 William Pickett

[page 1]   [Tithes]

John Healy.   N. Aron, Jene, Dick   3

John Smith Junr. son to Admoral   1

William Morgan for Manner Quarter.
Wm Harris, overseer.
Negros Phill, Edwards, Ore, Dick,   6
Tom, James, Jenney

Joseph Holtzclaw. [N.] Nearoe,
Gulley, Ester   3

Peter Hitt.   Negroe Monney   2

John Riley Senr 1

William Welch   1

1778-002 WILLIAM PICKETT'S TITHABLE LIST
A List of Tiths for the year 1778 William Pickett

[page 1]   [Tithes]

Henry Kemper. N. James	2
Andrew Barby Junr	1
John McCormack. N. Jude	2
Nathanel Fewell	1
Peter Greenlees. N. Jone	2
Benjamin Ball	1
John Robinson Junr	1
Andrew Anderson	1
Thos James. N. Lettice	2
John Michel	1
Wm Dulin Junr. Phillip Duling. Negroe Jude	3
Henry Martin. Joseph Martin. Benjamine Martin	3
Reubin Martin	1
Alexander Welsh	1
Wm Bernard Tyths. James Spenny, Overseer. N. Daniel, Peter, Frank, Glasgow, Sal, Grace, Linney, Nan	9
John Lathey	1
James Weatherly	1
William Smith, Carters Run	1
George Howell	1
John Davis	
John Harris	1
William Feltins	1
	54

[page 2]   [Tithes]

William Smith Senr [N.] Nim	1
Nicholas Lawler	1
John Moffett. Sam Pepper Ov^r Negroe Cato, Dick, Ben, Joe, Prince, Winney, Esther, Jemima 1 Riding Chair, 2 wheels	10
Alex^r Higgins	1
Scoldfield Maddux	1
John Kemper. N. Winney & Nancy	3
Jacob Kemper	1
Robert Turnbull	1

1778-002 WILLIAM PICKETT'S TITHABLE LIST
A List of Tiths for the year 1778 William Pickett

[page 2]   [Tithes]

Alexander Jeffres. Neg^o James	2
John Miller William Millar	2
James Ball. N^o Grace	2
Wm Smith, Great Run. Neg. Tom, Lundon	3
James Crocket. John Crocket. Neg^r Jenney	3
Nathanel Rector	1
Aylet Buckner. Negroes Toby, Bob, Charles, Peter, Seaser, Vilet, Cuttenarl [?], Patience, Beck, Milly, Phillis, Sarah	13
Uriel Crosby	1
Joseph Jackson. George Jackson. Neg^r Jenney	3
George Tolle	1
Roger Tolle Junr	1
Siers Hamrick	1
James White	1
William Heale tythes. Abraham Silvey. Neg^{ro} Daniel, Moses, Dameny, Joe, Adam, Mancelle, Fielding, Nan, young Nan, Abigal, Margery, Phillise	14
	67

[page 3]   [Tithes]

Thomas Priest. Wm Stansgray	2
Edward Turner. Negroe Luce, Betty, and Nell	4
Ships Tyths. Richard Vilet. Neg^{ro} Luce	2
George Heale tyths. George Brent. Negroe Nat, Harry, Andrew, Will, Mathew, Peter, Sue, Jenney, Hannah, Margret	11
George Brent Tyth. Negroe Mary	1

1778-002 WILLIAM PICKETT'S TITHABLE LIST
A List of Tiths for the year 1778 William Pickett

[page 3]   [Tithes]

John Smith. [N.] Bumbry Charles Christy.	2
Edward Ball. Jessey Ball. Negroes Charles, Robin, Sam	5
Joseph Smith. Neg^r Nero, Scipio, Joseph, Rose, Phillis	6
Thomas Underwood. Wm Underwood Neg^r Harry	3
Reubin Smith	1
Benjamine Ball	1
Thomas Smith Scarlet Smith	2
Thomas Stone Senr. James Stone	2
Thomas Stone Junr	1
Spencer Stone	1
William Corder jun^r	1
Francis Witherall	1
John Dodd	1
Isaac King	1
John Ellis	1
Edward Dulin	1
Alexander Bradford. Negroe Joe, Toney, Milly, Rose, Cate	6
Thomas Jackman Senr. Joseph Jackman. Negroe Jack, Ralph, Cate	5
Henry Cannon	1
Ezekel Haddox	1
	63

[page 4]   [Tithes]

James McCabe	1
Lazarus Hitt	1
George Creswell	1
Elizabeth Pickett Tyths Wm Cannon Ov^r. Negr^o James, Sam, Cloe, Suck	5

1778-002 WILLIAM PICKETT'S TITHABLE LIST
A List of Tiths for the year 1778 William Pickett

[page 4]   [Tithes]

William Pickett. John Askins. N. Emanul, Jack, Homaden, Jupiter, Antony, Charles, Judy, Daphney, Caroline, David 1 Riding Chair, 2 wheals	12
John Rosser. Richard Rosser. George Rosser. John Rosser jun^r. Negroe Ben, Yambon, Cate, Jinn, Lucy	9
James Adkins	1
Leroy Hughlet. Wm Hughlet. John Hughlet	3
Reubin Bramlet. Reubin Bramlet Junr. Hugh Bramlet	3
Charles Pinkard. Negroe Dick, Kit, Lucy	4
Charles Smith	1
James Ball	1
John Watts. N. Mol	1
Peter Kemper jun^r	1
James Wevell	1
Thomas Watts. Negroe Calup	2
Benjamine Stone	1
Addom Finch	1
Wm Jackman Neg^r Roze	2
John Turner	1
Rolley Fegan. Negroe Boson, Judey	3
James Beredit	1
Michal Jerman	1
Joseph Jones alias Bassham	1
Jeffrey Johnson	1
John M^cbee	1
David Darnall. John Darnall. Negroe Seasor	3
Ely Thompson. Negro Aaron, Roz	3
John Randol	1
	67

Done 251

1782-001 WILLIAM BLACKWELL'S PROPERTY LIST
[page 1]

Person's Names and all Names of Negroes	White Tithes	White Tithes Under 21	Negro Tithes	# Negroes	# Horses	Cattle	Billiard Tables	Ordinary Licenses
James Wood	James Wood			Lidia 1				
Elias Clark	Elias Clark		Peter, Sarah	Peter, Sarah, Henry, David, Jenny, Milly 6	5	9		
James Thomson	James Thomson		Solomon Jenney Nagt. Chil^d	Solomon, Jenney Nag^t, Dick, Grace, Limass 6	4	10		
George Kenner	George Kenner	Robert Kenner	James, Catena	James, Catena 2	5	9		
~~Wm. Jones~~	~~Wm. Jones~~		~~Abner Lucy~~	~~Abner Lucy~~	~~2~~	~~2~~		
Wm Seaton	Wm Seaton		Sam, Keziah	Sam Isaac Keziah Jeffery Cary 5	4	15		
Stephen Lee	Stephen Lee		1		4	10		
Elizabeth Peters	Elizabeth Peters	John Peters	Lucy Frank Cate 3	Lucy, Frank, Cate Isac, Ben, George, Winney, Will, Hethey 9	11	17		
James Horner	James Horner		1		3	21		
Original Young	Original Young		Will, Bell Fortain, Sarah, Lucy 5	Will, Bell, Fortain, Sarah, Lucy Nag^t, Jerry, Patience, Peter Jett, Peter Chinn 10	10	30		

1782-001 WILLIAM BLACKWELL'S PROPERTY LIST
[page 2]

Person's Names and all Names of Negroes	White Tithes	White Tithes Under 21	Negro Tithes	# Negroes	# Horses	Cattle	Billiard Tables	Ordinary Licenses
John Wood	John Wood				2	6		
Wm Blackwell	Wm Blackwell		James, Bash, Bob, David, Pegg, Sarah, Pegg, Mary, Nell, Will — 10	James, Bash, Bob, David, Pegg, Sarah, Pegg, Mary, Nell, Will, Jack, John, Bartley, John, Tom, Henry, Celia, Winney, Luis, Jenney, Dinah — 21	9	50		
Geo. Foote Estate			Charles, Dick, Tom, Moll, Luis, Judah	Charles, Duke, Tom, Moll, Luce Judah, Dick, Hannah, Nance, Denbe, Moll, Denbe, Linney, Sherlett — 12	77	25		

1782-001 WILLIAM BLACKWELL'S PROPERTY LIST
[page 3]

Person's Names and all Names of Negroes	White Tithes	White Tithes Under 21	Negro Tithes	# Negroes	# Horses	Cattle	Billiard Tables	Ordinary Licenses
John Mauzey	John Mauzey		Sarah, Dinah Jean	Sarah, Dinah Jean, Cate Patience, Ben Will, Jerrard, Jerimiah 9	5	19		
John Nelson	John Nelson		Arch, Dick, David	Arch, Dick, David, Sam 4	3	11		
Gerrard Gray	Gerrard Gray, Gerrard Gray Jn^r				3	7		
John Hogan	John Hogan, James Hogan				3	2		
John Hume	John Hume				3	7		

1782-001 WILLIAM BLACKWELL'S PROPERTY LIST
[page 3]

Person's Names and all Names of Negroes	White Tithes	White Tithes Under 21	Negro Tithes	# Negroes	# Horses	Cattle	Billiard Tables	Ordinary Licenses
Edward Luttrell	Edward Luttrell				3	3		
James Stark	James Stark		Beck, George, Cate	Beck, George, Cate, Daniel, Lize, Lyda 6	3	10		
William Coppage	William Coppage	Land 862 Ac^s	Sepio, Jeney 2	Sepio, Jeney				
Charles Coppage	Charles Coppage		Dinah & child	Dinah & child 2	1			
Jeremiah Stark	Jeremiah Stark				1	6		
Jeremiah Northcutt	Jeremiah Northcutt				1	2		
William Bishop	William Bishop				1			
Peter Hodo	Peter Hod[o] Peter Hodo Junr				3	10		
Lett[i]se Brohon	Lettise Brohon	Thomas Brohon		Tom, Sarah, Frank 3	2	12		

1782-001 WILLIAM BLACKWELL'S PROPERTY LIST
[page 4]

Person's Names and all Names of Negroes	White Tithes	White Tithes Under 21	Negro Tithes	# Negroes	# Horses	Cattle	Billiard Tables	Ordinary Licenses
John McCoy	John McCoy		Sam, Mary, Ciss, Alex^r	Sam, Mary, Ciss, Alex^r 4	4	10		
James Dowdell Banner Dowdell	James Dowdell Banner Dowdell		Abraham, Charles, Nan, Jin, Patt	Abraham, Charles, Nan, Jin, Patt, Patt Abe, Dol, Plat, Suck 10	10	10		

1782-001 WILLIAM BLACKWELL'S PROPERTY LIST
[page 4]

Person's Names and all Names of Negroes	White Tithes	White Tithes Under 21	Negro Tithes	# Negroes	# Horses	Cattle	Billiard Tables	Ordinary Licenses
Edward Waller Tolliver Shumate	Edward Waller Tolliver Shumate		James, Will, Dy, Cloe, Lett Lid 6	James, Dy, Cloe, Lett, Lid, Jack, Isaac, Bet, Dinah, Celia, Ben, James, Johua, Jack 11	4	7		
Henry Jones	Henry Jones		Joshua, Fanney 2	Joshua, Fanney, Jude, Lett 7	3	9		

1782-001 WILLIAM BLACKWELL'S PROPERTY LIST
[page 5]

Person's Names and all Names of Negroes	White Tithes	White Tithes Under 21	Negro Tithes	# Negroes	# Horses	Cattle	Billiard Tables	Ordinary Licenses
Harman Rictor	Harman Rictor		Peter, Ben	Peter, Ben	8	11		
Agnes Utterback	Agnes Utterback, Chaˢ Utterback				3	6		
James Roach	James Roach		Jude	Jude 1	2	2		
Dinah James	Dinah James		Charles, Moses, Ezable, Will, Winnie, Jude, Luce, Charlot, Cato, Jack, Philis, Tab, Mary, Nan, Vilet, Jude, Joe, Clary	Charles, Moses, Ezable, Philis, Will, Winney, Jude, Luce, Charlot, Cato, Jack, Philis, Tab, Mary, Nan, Vilet, Jude, Joe, Clary 19	11	24		
Duke Brown	Duke Brown				1	6		

1782-001 William Blackwell's Property List
[page 6]

Person's Names and all Names of Negroes	White Tithes	White Tithes Under 21	Negro Tithes	# Negroes	# Horses	Cattle	Billiard Tables	Ordinary Licenses
Reverend Wm Stewart Q^r	Revd Wm Stewart Edward Luttrell, Ov^r		James, Moses, Robin, Aron, Nan, Rose, John, Nell, Will	James, Moses, Robin, Aron, Nan, Rose, John, Nell, Will, Nib 10	4	36		
Mrs Kenner	Mrs Kenner Spencer Morgan		~~Spencer Morgan~~ Antony, Moses, John, Isac, Hannah, Jaive, Fortin, Cate, Suck	~~Spencer Morgan~~ Antony, Moses John, Isac, Hannah, Lucy, Jaive, Fortin, Cate, Suck 12	6	19		
Phill Spiller Sn^r	Phill Spiller Sn^r		Sam	Sam	4	13		
James Miller	James Miller				4	6		
Wm Jones	Wm Jones			Lucy, Abner	2	2		
John Medley	John Medley				1	3		
James Horton	James Horton				3	2		
John Singer	John Singer Jn^r George Singer				5	8		
George Cosby	George Cosby William Cosby John Cosby ~~Uriah Cosby~~	Uriah Cosby	Daniel, Jerry, Henry, Ben	Daniel, Jerry, Henry, Ben 4	11	26		
Joseph Bullitt	Joseph Bullitt		Will, Peter, Philis, Bess, Jean	Ned, Will, Peter, Philis Bess, Jean, Ned, Lewis, Geo., Cate, Lett, Nell 11	3	15		

1782-001 William Blackwell's Property List
[page 7]

Person's Names and all Names of Negroes	White Tithes	White Tithes Under 21	Negro Tithes	# Negroes	# Horses	Cattle	Billiard Tables	Ordinary Licenses
Cuth. Bullitt Qr	Cuth. Bullitt Walter Stalard, Overseer		Jubey, Tom, Peter, Sarah, Cloe	Jubey, Tom, Peter, Sarah, Cloe, Jeary, Adam, Sue, Moses, Brister, Nell 11	6	24		
Walter Stalard	Walter Stalard		Hannah		1	4		
Baley Shumake	Baley Shumake		Brister, Harry, Nell, Peter	Brister, Harry, Nell, Peter 4	2			
John Shumake Snr	John Shumake				3	4		
Cpt John Ashby Snr	Cpt John Ashby Snr		Will, Daniel, Jean, Milly, Spencer, Daniel, Will, Sucky, Lydia, Sall, Teanah, Judith, Lucy	Will, Daniel, Jeany, Milly, Spencer, Daniel, Will, Sucky, Lydia, Sall, Teanah, Judith, Lucy 13	4	16		
Tilman Weaver	Tilman Weaver		Luse, Hannah, Siner, Dinah, Hannah	Luse, Hannah, Siner, Dinah, Hannah 5	10	33		
Margarett George	Margarett George		Hollan, Dick, Hannah, Jude, Lucy, Alex, Arch, Agatha	Hollan, Dick, Hannah, Jude, Lucy, Alex, Arch, Agatha 8	7	16		

1782-001 William Blackwell's Property List
[page 8]

Person's Names and all Names of Negroes	White Tithes	White Tithes Under 21	Negro Tithes	# Negroes	# Horses	Cattle	Billiard Tables	Ordinary Licenses
Mary Crook	Mary Crook		Nan	Nan, Harry, & Enoch	1	4		
David Wheatly	David Wheatly David Wheatly Charles Wheatly		Jenny, Ben, Ned, Peg 4	Jenny, Ben, Ned, Peg 4	5	11		

1782-001 WILLIAM BLACKWELL'S PROPERTY LIST
[page 8]

Person's Names and all Names of Negroes	White Tithes	White Tithes Under 21	Negro Tithes	# Negroes	# Horses	Cattle	Billiard Tables	Ordinary Licenses
Thos Conway Jn^r	Thos Conway Jn^r		George, David, Sal, Jen	George, David, Sall, Jen, Ben, Henry, Lucy, Patt, James, Will, Tom, Peter	4	17		
Daniel Harrill	Daniel Harrill				4	10		
William Rose	William Rose Jesse Rose				3	4		
Richard Luttrell	Richard Luttrell				1			
John Markhams Q^r John Medley, Overseer	John Medley		Will, Joe, Winney, Esther, Jude, Bett, Poll, Patience, Lucy	Will, Joe, Winney, Esther, Jude, Bett, Poll, Patience, Lucy 9	5	8		
John Edge	John Edge	Simon Edge			2	8		
Jeremiah Spiller	Jeremiah Spiller	Phill. Spiller			4	10		
Elijah Thailkill Q^r	Elijah Thrailkill		Aron, Dinah	Aron, Dinah, Lis, Frank	1	4		

1782-001 WILLIAM BLACKWELL'S PROPERTY LIST
[page 9]

Person's Names and all Names of Negroes	White Tithes	White Tithes Under 21	Negro Tithes	# Negroes	# Horses	Cattle	Billiard Tables	Ordinary Licenses
John Smith	John Smith				2	4		
John Nelson [of] Elk Run, George Dofany	John Nelson, [Name illegible]	William Nelson.	George	2	4	20		
Thomas Shumate Dinah	Thos Shumate			1	2	8		
Alexander Morehead Timatha, Sarah, Vilat, Bob	Alexand^r Morehead		Timatha, Sarah, Vilat	5	6	27		
Henry Utterback, Levey free Jack			Jack	1	4	12		

1782-001 William Blackwell's Property List
[page 9]

Person's Names and all Names of Negroes	White Tithes	White Tithes Under 21	Negro Tithes	# Negroes	# Horses	Cattle	Billiard Tables	Ordinary Licenses
John Rector	John Rector				7	21		
Samuel Morehead Lil, Suck, Jean, Dick, Nan, Daniel, Frank	Saml Morehead		Lil, Suck	7	7	18		
Robert Luttrell	Robt Luttrell			1	five	seven		
Charles Colvin	Charles Colvin				3	12		
John Person	John Person				1	2		
William Conaway	William Conaway		Geo., Will, Joe, Frank, Moll 5	Nell, Amy, Lewis 8	7	19		
Chattin Lamkin	Chattin Lamkin				1			

1782-001 William Blackwell's Property List
[page 9]

Person's Names and all Names of Negroes	White Tithes	White Tithes Under 21	Negro Tithes	# Negroes	# Horses	Cattle	Billiard Tables	Ordinary Licenses
Cudberth Bullett Jinkins, George, Cate, Jude, Winny, Loudon, Toney, Cloey, Hannah, Rachel, Hannah, Philis, Luce, Nan, Joe, James, Winny, Mimy, Nance, Cate, Charles, Mimy, Nance, Antony, Jack	William Porter		Jenkins, George, Cate, Jude, Winny, Loudon, Toney, Cloey, Hannah, Rachel, Hannah, Phillis	Jenkins, George, Jude, Winny, Loudon, Toney, Cloey, Hannah, Rachel, Hannah, Phillis, Luce, Nan, Joe, James, Winny, Mimey, Nance, Cate, Charles, Mimy, Nance, Antony, Jack 25	14	58		
Hack Eustace David, Mol, Weaver, Mary, Winny	Hack Eustace		David, Mol, Weaver 3	5	3	6		
James Peters George, Nelly, Sarah	Ja^s Peters		George, Nelly	3	2	10		

1782-001 WILLIAM BLACKWELL'S PROPERTY LIST
[page 10]

Person's Names and all Names of Negroes	White Tithes	White Tithes Under 21	Negro Tithes	# Negroes	# Horses	Cattle	Billiard Tables	Ordinary Licenses
Richard Littrell Beck, Peter, Harry	Richard Littrell	Francis Littrell John Littrell Ja^s Littrell	Beck	3	5	8		
John Littrell		Joshua Littrell			3	8		
Edward Humston Alin, Wil, Charles, Frank, Liney, Betty, Paul, Davey, Wil, Winey, Jude, Joe, Luce	Edward Humston		Alin, Wil, Charles, Frank, Liney	13	4	10		
Thos Fidlar	Thos Fidlar				2	4		

1782-001 WILLIAM BLACKWELL'S PROPERTY LIST
[page 11]

Person's Names and all Names of Negroes	White Tithes	White Tithes Under 21	Negro Tithes	# Negroes	# Horses	Cattle	Billiard Tables	Ordinary Licenses
Benjamin Harrison George, George, Tom, Phil, Peter, Murf, Loudon, Mary, Amey, Nancy, Grace, Beck, Nancy, Jeney, Cloe, Nel, Mol, Josh, Sen, Sanco, Rachel, Ben, John, Hannah, Lucy, Toney, Miney, Sarah, Amey, Wil, Rose, Peter, Ned, Dol, Jesse, Frank, Jeany, Haver, Jenny, John, Wil, Haley, Haley, Hannah, Philis, Isham, Loudon, Jean, Bob, Sancco, Dick, Bellow, Cloe	Geo Grant Wm Russell		George, George, Tom, Phil, Peter, Murf, Loudon, Mary, Amey, Nancy, Grace, Beck, Nancy, Jeaney, Cloe, Nel, Mol, Josh, Sen, Sancco, Rachel	53	6	27		
James Lewis Britian Lewis Ned, Larke	James Lewis	Britain Lewis	Ned	2	5	12		

1782-001 William Blackwell's Property List
[page 11]

Person's Names and all Names of Negroes	White Tithes	White Tithes Under 21	Negro Tithes	# Negroes	# Horses	Cattle	Billiard Tables	Ordinary Licenses
Margret Hufman Peter Hufman Benjamin Hufman	Peter Hufman Benjamin Hufman				5	11		
John Martin Peter, Nance	John Martin John Parker		Peter	2	7	15		
John Hufman					1			
John Kearns					2	3		
Captn Zacariah Lewis George, Tom, Winey, Bett, Peter, Jude, Jack, Suck, Stephen			George, Tom, Winey, Bett	9	6	17		
Mr John Norton Charles Pain Charles, Grimige, Pompy, Frank, Antony, Sam, Jacob, Betty, Hannah, Hannah, Jeny	Charles Pain		Charles, Grimige Pompy, Betty	11	3	7		
Charles Pain Enter^d before					2	2		

1782-001 William Blackwell's Property List
[page 12]

Person's Names and all Names of Negroes	White Tithes	White Tithes Under 21	Negro Tithes	# Negroes	# Horses	Cattle	Billiard Tables	Ordinary Licenses
Maryan Bronaugh	Maryan Bronaugh		Daniel, Sam	Daniel, Sam 2	2	1		
Charles Waller	Charles Waller		Essex, Jack, Trulove	Essex, Jack, Trulove, Sam, Sarah 5	7	17		
Enniss Combs	Enniss Combs		Harry, Lett	Hary, Lett Esther, Viney Charlott 5	3	9		
Sarah Combs	Sarah Combs		George, James, Hagner	George, James, Hagner, Daniel 4	2	7		

1782-001 WILLIAM BLACKWELL'S PROPERTY LIST
[page 12]

Person's Names and all Names of Negroes	White Tithes	White Tithes Under 21	Negro Tithes	# Negroes	# Horses	Cattle	Billiard Tables	Ordinary Licenses
George Putir Sn^r	George Putir Joseph Putir				4	9		
Bettey Mauzey	Bettey Mauzey		Jeanny	Jeanny, Hannah, Will, Sall 4				
Mary Peters	Mary Peters					3		
Richard Cooper	Richard Cooper				2	8		
William Pickard	Wm Pickard				2	3		
Elaxander Cumings	Elaxd^r Cumings				2	3		
Daniel Shumake	Daniel Shumake		Tom, Bess	Tom, Bess 2	3	9		
James Shumake	James Shumake		Platoe, Esther, Brister, Mimy, Sela, Cate, Sarah	Platoe, Esther, Brister, Mimy, Sela, Cate, Sarah 7	4	7		
Rodam Tuellas	Rodam Tuellas		Will, Bess, Antony, Esther, Silva	Will, Bess, Antony, Esther Silva 5	5	17		

1782-001 WILLIAM BLACKWELL'S PROPERTY LIST
[page 13]

Person's Names and all Names of Negroes	White Tithes	White Tithes Under 21	Negro Tithes	# Negroes	# Horses	Cattle	Billiard Tables	Ordinary Licenses
James Markham	James Markham			Abraham, Scipeo, Milly, Rachel, Clarey 5	2	6		
Abraham Cox	Abraham Cox	Zachariah Cox	Nell, Harry	Nell, Harry, Charles 3	3	8		

1782-001 William Blackwell's Property List
[page 13]

Person's Names and all Names of Negroes	White Tithes	White Tithes Under 21	Negro Tithes	# Negroes	# Horses	Cattle	Billiard Tables	Ordinary Licenses
William Rusaw	Wm Rusaw		George, Peter, Nell, Judah	George, Peter Nell, Judah James, Milly Anthony, Ben 8	5	17		
Champ Corum	Champ Corum				3	12		
Richard Corum	Richard Corum				2	4		
Thos Cumings	Thos Cumings			Moll	2	4		
Mrs Elizabeth Miller	Elizabeth Miller				2	6		
John Cumings	John Cumings	George Cumings Willis Cumings			2	7		
Thomas Doudall	Thos Doudall		Charles, Bett, Hannah	Charles, Bett Hanah, Milley, Isaac, Bett 6	2	7		
George Brown	George Brown William Brown		Newman, Silva	Newman, Silva, Nell 3	4	12		
Thos Priest	Thos Priest [Levy] Free		Will	Will, Priss, Nimro 3	3	12		
Edward Lawrence	Edward Lawrance, Richard Lawrence, Rodham Lawrence		Mosses, Dick, Adam, Nan, Jude, Jude, Mime, Sarah, Mary 9	Mosses, Dick Adam, Nan, Jude, Jude, Mime, Mime, Sarah, Mary, Sam, Jack, Ridge, Dark, Sue, Sary, Seth, Virgin, Hath 18	6	18		

1782-001 WILLIAM BLACKWELL'S PROPERTY LIST
[page 14]

Person's Names and all Names of Negroes	White Tithes	White Tithes Under 21	Negro Tithes	# Negroes	# Horses	Cattle	Billiard Tables	Ordinary Licenses
Thomas Realy	Thos Realy	Thos Realy Jnr	Cate, James, Jack	Cate, James, Jack, Robin 4	5	12		
Brerinton Jones	Brerinton Jones	John Warner Jones one horse	Pompie	Pompie, Phillis	5	19		
Jonathan Gibson [1 wheel carriage] Henry Bowin	Jonathan Gibson Thos Gibson Henry Bowin	John Gibson	Henry, Joe, Charles, Ugene, David, Ben, Lucy, Lidia, Cate, Virgin, Clary, Rose, Polly, Daniel, Isaac, Thos, Dinah, Alis	Henry, Joe, Charles, Ugene, David, Ben, Lucy, Lidia, Cate, Virgin, Clary, Rose, Polly, Ben, Will, Rubin, James, Zachariah, Celey, Charlotte, Milly, Hettey, Vicey, Robin, Daniel, Isaac, Thos, Dinah, Alis, Adam 30	17	35		
Mrs Mary Gillison	Mary Gillison		Ben, Nanny, Lucy, Milly	Ben, Nanny, Lucy, Milly, Rose, Buckery, Harry, George, Lucinda	3	6		

1782-002 CHARLES CHILTON'S PROPERTY LIST
[page 1]

Person's Names and all Names of Negroes	White Tithes Above 21	White Tithes Under 21	Negro Tithes	# Negroes	# Horses	Cattle	Wheels	Billiard Tables	Ordinary Licenses
Barnett, Ambrose Negroes Aaron, Bett, Molley, Claris, Sarah, Silvey, Dick, Will, Glasgow, Bob, Violet, Janey, Tom, Lewis, George.	1		Aaron, Bett, Molley, Claris, Sarah. 5	15	11	26			1
Boyd, Samuel (Dr.) Negroes Matt, Lucy, Cate, Tom, Cupid, Dick, June, Adam, Frank.	1		Matt, Lucy, Cate. 3	9	7	16			
Boswell, Elizabeth Negroes Dolly, Esther, Grace, James, Bailey, Eve, James, Ben, Simon, Jane.			Dolly, Esther, Grace, James. 4	10	2	8			
Bailey, Simon	1				1	3			
			4	34	21	55			

1782-002 CHARLES CHILTON'S PROPERTY LIST
[page 2]

Person's Names and all Names of Negroes	White Tithes Above 21	White Tithes Under 21	Negro Tithes	# Negroes	# Horses	Cattle	Wheels	Billiard Tables	Ordinary Licenses
Bryan, John. Isachar Pawling John Agar Negroes Robert, Gilbert, Toney, Bristol, Will, Jane.	3		Robert, Gilbert, Toney, Bristol Will. 5	6	9	16	4		
Brooke, Humphrey Negroes Peter, Cupid, Daniel, Harry, Betty, Hannah, Dinah, Milley, Jane, Lucy, Will, Nedd, Phillis, Rose, Moll.	1		Peter, Cupid, Daniel, Harry, Betty, Hannah, Dinah, Milley, Jane, Lucy, Will. 11	15	9	18	2		

1782-002 CHARLES CHILTON'S PROPERTY LIST
[page 2]

Person's Names and all Names of Negroes	White Tithes Above 21	White Tithes Under 21	Negro Tithes	# Negroes	# Horses	Cattle	Wheels	Billiard Tables	Ordinary Licenses
Blackwell, Samuel Negroes Toby, Frank, Tom, Cyrus, Jane, Bill, Kate, Toby, Amos, Bill, Jane, Lett, Muter, Dinah, Cynar, Will.	1		Toby, Frank, Tom, Cyrus Jane, Bill, Kate. 7	16	4	11			
Barber, Thomas	1				4	11			
Chichester, Richard John Stone, Overseer Negroes Tom, Abram, Cain, Peter, George, Ned, Solomon, Betty, Nan, Martha, Peg, Kate, Darcus, Jack, Phill, Joshua, Shadrach, Jane, Sarah, Moses, Milley, Lett, Amy, Davy, Phillis, Hannah, Lewis, Judah, James, Frank, Emanuel, Suky, Liddy, Daphney, Jacob, Jesse, Rachel, Esther, Jacob, Beck, Charles, Hannah, Winney, Lucy, Levina.	1		Tom, Abram, Cain, Peter, George, Ned, Solomon, Betty, Nan, Martha, Peg, Kate, Darcus, Jack, Phill, Joshua, Shadrach, Jane, Sarah. 19	45	16	100			
Cooke, John Negroes Harry, Betty, Abel, George, Mary.	1 — 9		Harry 2 44	5 87	6 52	13 134			

1782-002 CHARLES CHILTON'S PROPERTY LIST
[page 3]

Person's Names and all Names of Negroes	White Tithes Above 21	White Tithes Under 21	Negro Tithes	# Negroes	# Horses	Cattle	Wheels	Billiard Tables	Ordinary Licenses
Carter, Charles L. Esq. Catesby Woodford, William Suttle, Gabriel, George, Francis Suttle, James Collins Negroes Joe, Adam, Harry, Harry, John, Peter, Daniel, Will, Peter, Daniel, Dick, Will, Tom, Manuel, James, Patt, Nan, Peg, Betty, Judy, Nan, Molley, Sue, Criss, Jallace, Lucy, Ben, James, Dick, Jonco, Kate, Beck,									

1782-002 CHARLES CHILTON'S PROPERTY LIST
[page 3]

Person's Names and all Names of Negroes	White Tithes Above 21	White Tithes Under 21	Negro Tithes	# Negroes	# Horses	Cattle Wheels	Billiard Tables	Ordinary Licenses
Carter, Charles L. Esq. (Cont) 5 [Negroes] Patt, Sarah, Winney, Doss, Hampton, Robin, Ambrose, Daniel, Dick, Gumby, Single, Joe, Sall, Dido, Doll, Frank, Aggay, Jane, Alice, Frank, Jack, Amos, Frank, Robin, Anthony, Sam, Ralph, James, Margaret, Nann, Sarah, Joanna, Dinah, Hannah, Pegg, Betty, Esther, David, John, Jacob, Stephen, Jane, Bathsheba, Suky, Sebre, Lett, Jane, Alice, Jenny, Adam, Gabriel, Ezekiel, Joseph, Nelson, Lemon, John, Isaac, Nott, Sawney, Moses, Strother, Edward, Will, Wilson, Dinah, Martha, Martha, Lucy, Rose, Isabell, Dido, Charity, Lett, Betty, Mirian, Betty, Joan, Eddie, Keziah, Eve, Patience, Jemima, Phillis, Rachel, Silla, Amy, Winney, Susannah, Lucy, Ned, Sam, Jacob, George, Jane, Nell, Fanny, Lizza, Kate, Charlotte, Betty, Betty, Judy, Sylva, Rachel, Sall, Hannah, James, Roger, James, Windsor, Caesar, Harry, John, Philander, Tolbert, Ned, Sam, Dosse, Shurley, Judy, Doll, Delila, Lucy, Abram, Billey, Tom, Abram, Manuel, George, Jerry, Peter, Harry, Jacob, Ralph, Charity, Scelia, Letty, Scelia, Lilly, Winney, Abram, Aaron, Isaac, Mima, Betty, Rachel, Hannah, Scelia, Nelson, Gabriel, Jerry, Tom, Scelia, Sukey, Harry, Billey Jacob.			81	188	40	193		

1782-002 CHARLES CHILTON'S PROPERTY LIST
[page 3]

Person's Names and all Names of Negroes	White Tithes Above 21	White Tithes Under 21	Negro Tithes	# Negroes	# Horses	Cattle Wheels	Billiard Tables	Ordinary Licenses
Collins, James					1			
Chilton, Charles Negroes Charles, Tony, Sam, Harry, Sarah, Patience, Dinah, Jane, Sarah, Penny, Lucy, Celia Celia, Bett, Mima, Nancy Lett, Jane, Moses, Milley.	1 6 9 15 30	Charles, Tony, Sam, Harry, Sarah, Patience, Dinah, Jane, Sarah, Sarah, Penny, Lucy. 11 92 44 136	19 207 87 34 328	8 49 52 21 122	23 216 184 55 455			

1782-002 CHARLES CHILTON'S PROPERTY LIST
[page 4]

Person's Names and all Names of Negroes	White Tithes Above 21	White Tithes Under 21	Negro Tithes	# Negroes	# Horses	Cattle	Wheels	Billiard Tables	Ordinary Licenses
Dale, William Negroes Ned, Hannah, Nann, Sarah.	1		Ned, Hannah. 2	4	4	9			
Deane, John	1				1	3			
Donephan, Joseph	1				1	3			
	3			4	6	15			

1782-002 CHARLES CHILTON'S PROPERTY LIST
[page 5]

Person's Names and all Names of Negroes	White Tithes Above 21	White Tithes Under 21	Negro Tithes	# Negroes	# Horses	Cattle	Wheels	Billiard Tables	Ordinary Licenses
Fitzhugh, George Negroes Frank, Captain, Mack, Dan, Jeffery, Rachel, Nan, Harry, Betty, John, Anthony, Alice, Lucy, Sally, Frank, Jack, James, Molly, Beck, Sukey & two small children.	1		Frank, Captain, Mack, Dan, Jeffery, Rachel, Nan, Harry, Harry, Betty, John, Anthony, Alice. 12	22	7	25			
Fitzhugh, William John Kennedey, Overseer. Negroes Tom, Phill, Bryan, Dick, Anthony, Joe, Charles, Harry, Anthony, Ben, Bett, Joan, Nell, Judith, Jane, Chany, Jude, Lucy, Nancy, Sue, Kate, Willis, Lucy, Godfrey, Dennis, James, Simon, Joe, Dick, Rose, Nell, Mary, Nell, Kate, Patt, Mary, Sue.	1		Tom, Phill, Bryan, Dick, Anthony, Joe, Charles, Harry, Anthony, Ben, Bett, Joan, Nell, Judith, Jane, Chany, Jude, Lucy, Nancy, Sue, Kate. 20	36	11	36	4		
Foster, Thomas Negroes Nell, Amos, Jacob, Braddock, Suck, Dick.	1		Nell 1	6	3	8			
Foote, William Richard Luttrell, Overseer Negroes Adam, Joe, Peter, Bob, Sarah, Judy, Patt, Daniel, Priss, Selia, Jane, Ann, Dick.	2		Adam, Joe, Peter, Bob, Sarah, Judy, Patt 7	13	10	26			

1782-002 CHARLES CHILTON'S PROPERTY LIST
[page 5]

Person's Names and all Names of Negroes	White Tithes Above 21	White Tithes Under 21	Negro Tithes	# Negroes	# Horses	Cattle	Wheels	Billiard Tables	Ordinary Licenses
Fitzhugh, Henry Corn¹ Bussy Negroes Bob, Will, Sarah, Nanny, Easter, Beck, Alexander, Scilla, Tamer, Judy, Major, Dennis, Billy.	1 ——— 7		Bob, Will, Sarah, Nanny, Easter, 6 46	14 ——— 91	5 ——— 36	16 ——— 111	4		

1782-002 CHARLES CHILTON'S PROPERTY LIST
[page 6]

Person's Names and all Names of Negroes	White Tithes Above 21	White Tithes Under 21	Negro Tithes	# Negroes	# Horses	Cattle	Wheels	Billiard Tables	Ordinary Licenses
George, Parnack Negroes Scipio, Jack, Rose, Bob, Peter, Winny, Ned, Bob, Peter	1		Scipio, Jack, Rose, Bob. 4	7	8	28			
Green, Ann William Green Negroes Toby, Sam, Jane, Lucy, Betty, Alice, Dick, Winney, Mima, Fanny.	1		Toby, Sam, Jane, Lucy. 4	3	7	17			
Griffin, Henry James Tayloe, Overseer Negroes Andrew, Tenor, Solomon.	1		Andrew, Tenor. 2	3	3	8			
Green, Thomas Negro Limas	1		Limas 1	1	3	8			
Genn, James Negroes Scillar, Dick, Jerry, Charles, Solomon	1		Scillar 1	5	2	7			
Guy, Samuel	1				3	9			
Gibson, Robert	1 ——— 6		12	1 ——— 26 ——— 95 60 ——— 181	25 42 21 ——— 88	77 127 92 ——— 296			

1782-002 Charles Chilton's Property List
[page 7]

Person's Names and all Names of Negroes	White Tithes Above 21	White Tithes Under 21	Negro Tithes	# Negroes	# Horses	Cattle	Wheels	Billiard Tables	Ordinary Licenses
Heale, George John Hopper, Car Bailey, Overseers Smith Heale Negroes James, Spencer, Dennis John, Shadrack, Hagar, Synar, Milley, Stephen, Anthony, Dick, Winney, Nanny, Beck, Charles, Solomon, Nelson, Daniel, Abram, Abel, Scilla, Rachel, Alice, Winney, Hannah, Lucy, Darcus, Bally, Grace, Darcus, James, Hannah, Peter, Lucy, Scilla, Robin, Fortune, Anne, Esther, Tiller, John, Phill, Letty, Ralph, Jacob, Charles, Aaron, Adam, Nedd, Peggy, Kate, Letty, Frank, Betty.	3		James, Spencer, Dennis, James, John, Shadrack, Hagar, Synar, Milley, Stephen, Anthony, Dick, Winney, Nanny, Beck, Charles, Solomon, Nelson, Daniel, Abram, Abel, Scilla, Rachel, Alice, Winney, Hannah, Lucy, Darcus, Bally, Grace. 30	55	13	70	4		
Hoagan, John Negroes George, Lett	1	2	George, Lett. 2	4	9				
Hoagan, Rawleigh	1				2	5			
Hardwick, William Negroes Sarah, Bett, Rachel.	1 ——— 6		Sarah 1 ——— 33	3 ——— 60	2 ——— 21	8 ——— 8	——— 4		

1782-002 Charles Chilton's Property List
[page 8]

Person's Names and all Names of Negroes	White Tithes Above 21	White Tithes Under 21	Negro Tithes	# Negroes	# Horses	Cattle	Wheels	Billiard Tables	Ordinary Licenses
Hunton, William James Hunton Negroes Bob, Robin, Tom, Moll, Winney, Kate, Sarah, Ismuth, Harry, Lemon, Orange, Mary, Sarah, Peter, Isaac, Jack, Charlotte.	1	1	Bob, Robin, Tom, Moll, Winney, Kate, Sarah, Ismuth 8	19	9	34			
Hooe, Housin Phill Lucas, Overseer Negroes Edmund, Lett, Nace, Sook, Jack, Patt, Hannah, Edmond.	2		Edmond, Lett, Nace. 3	8	5	24			

1782-002 CHARLES CHILTON'S PROPERTY LIST
[page 8]

Person's Names and all Names of Negroes	White Tithes Above 21	White Tithes Under 21	Negro Tithes	# Negroes	# Horses	Cattle	Wheels	Billiard Tables	Ordinary Licenses
Holtzclaw, Benjamin Negro Murray	1		Murray 1	1	4	8			
Heale, Philip Negroes Robin, Ned, Charles, James, Rhoda, Betty, Sarah, Martha, Letty, Frank, Amy, Aggaitha, Luke, George, Ned, George, Ned, Robin, George, Aaron, Isaac, Manual, James, Abel, Polly, Ruth	1		Robin, Ned, Charles, James, Rhoda, Betty, Sarah, Martha, Letty. 12	26	7	22			
Hathaway, James Neg^r Jack, Lemon, Will, Jenny, Hanah, Patt, Frank, Mary, Mary, Joshua, Winny, Pegg, Sarah, Hannah, Tom.	1		Jack, Lemon, Will, Jenny, Hanah, Patt, Frank, Mary. 8	15	12	46			
Hopper, Joseph	1				4	13			
	7			109	41	147			

1782-002 CHARLES CHILTON'S PROPERTY LIST
[page 9]

Person's Names and all Names of Negroes	White Tithes Above 21	White Tithes Under 21	Negro Tithes	# Negroes	# Horses	Cattle	Wheels	Billiard Tables	Ordinary Licenses
Kendall, Thomas					2	2			
Keith, John Negroes Moracco, Bob, Peter, Peter, Mary, Nann, Jane, Tom, Lucy, Sam, Tilly, Nelly.	1 2		Moracco, Bob, Bob, Peter, Peter, Mary, Nann. 6	12 12	7 9	10 12			

1782-002 CHARLES CHILTON'S PROPERTY LIST
[page 10]

Person's Names and all Names of Negroes	White Tithes Above 21	White Tithes Under 21	Negro Tithes	# Negroes	# Horses	Cattle	Wheels	Billiard Tables	Ordinary Licenses
Lowry, George Negroes Venus, Dinah, Bess, Tom, Bob, Ben, Hannah, Truley, Scipio, Isaac, Phill, Jack, Anthony.	1		Venus, Dinah, Bess. 3	13	6	26			
Luttrell, Richard					2				

1782-002 Charles Chilton's Property List
[page 10]

Person's Names and all Names of Negroes	White Tithes Above 21	White Tithes Under 21	Negro Tithes	# Negroes	# Horses	Cattle	Wheels	Billiard Tables	Ordinary Licenses
Layton, Robert Negroes Augustin, George	1		Augustin 1	2	4	13			
Love, Augustine Negroes Phill, Joel, Nell, Ellen, Jude, Daniel, Samuel.	1 — 3		Phill, Joel, Nell. 3	17 — 32	6 — 18	8 — 47			

1782-002 Charles Chilton's Property List
[page 11]

Person's Names and all Names of Negroes	White Tithes Above 21	White Tithes Under 21	Negro Tithes	# Negroes	# Horses	Cattle	Wheels	Billiard Tables	Ordinary Licenses
Mooney, Nicholas	1				3	5			
McLanahame, James Negroes Ned, Sampson, Lydda, Robin, Aggai, Winney, Ned, Sam, Davy, Hannah.	1		Ned, Sampson, Lydda. 3	10	5	17			
~~James McLanahame~~		~~6~~							
Muschett, James Neg. Nero, Luis, Jacob, Winny, Cloe, Judy, Nan, Rose, Letty, Judy, Abraham, Hanah, Quacko, Hanah, Peter, Nelson, Henry, Aaron, Jesse.	1		Nero, Luis, Jacob, Winny, Cloe, Judy, Nan, Rose, Letty, Judy. 10	19	8	33			
Mullikan, Burton Negroes Sampson, Bett.	1		Sampson, Bett. 2	2	1	2			
McClanahame, Moore	1								
Metcalfe, William	1				1				
Minter, Mary Negroes Baccus, Sarah, James, Lucy & baby.			Baccus, Sarah. 2	5	1	6			
Metcalfe, John Negroes Sall, Guy, Mary, Kate, Dick, Kate.	1 — 6 3 2		Sall 1	6 — 42 22 12	2 — 21 18 09	6 — 68 47 12			

1782-002 CHARLES CHILTON'S PROPERTY LIST
[page 12]

Person's Names and all Names of Negroes	White Tithes Above 21	White Tithes Under 21	Negro Tithes	# Negroes	# Horses	Cattle	Wheels	Billiard Tables	Ordinary Licenses
Martin, Charles Negro Jerremy	1		Jerremy 1	1	5	12			
Minter, Joseph Negroes Ned, Barton, Lett, Rachel, Harry, Ned, Winney, Dick.	1		Ned, Barton, Lett, Rachel. 4	8	5	12			
Nash, Traverse James Bailey, Overseer Negroes Tom, Frank, Jacob, Richmond, Judy, Hannah, Sam, Pegg, Nell, Lucy, Ned, James, Elijah.	2		Tom, Frank, Jacob, Bob, Richmond, Judy, Hannah. 7	14	7	37			
Neale, Benjamin Thomas Neale, James Neale Negroes Abram, Sarah, Winney, Daniel, Lucy, Rachel.	2	1	Abram, Sarah. 2	6	7	17			
Newby, Betty					3	3			
	5			29	27	81			

1782-002 CHARLES CHILTON'S PROPERTY LIST
[page 13]

Person's Names and all Names of Negroes	White Tithes Above 21	White Tithes Under 21	Negro Tithes	# Negroes	# Horses	Cattle	Wheels	Billiard Tables	Ordinary Licenses
Organ, Samuel Negroes Beck, Jane.	1		Beck 1	2	2	5			
Pettit, Obadiah Samuel Pettit Thomas Pettit	3				4	13			
Pettit, Nathaniel	1				1	1			
Parker, Richard Negroes Jupiter, Esther, Isaac.	1		Jupiter, Esther. 2	3	4	13			
Porter, Samuel Martin Porter Negroes Tom, Ben, James, Winney, Dinah, Nance, Winney.	1	1	Tom, Ben, James, Winney, Dinah. 5	7	11	34			

1782-002 CHARLES CHILTON'S PROPERTY LIST
[page 13]

Person's Names and all Names of Negroes	White Tithes Above 21	White Tithes Under 21	Negro Tithes	# Negroes	# Horses	Cattle	Wheels	Billiard Tables	Ordinary Licenses
Porter, Thomas Thomas Porter Jun[r] Charles Porter Negroes Will, Ned.	1	2	Will 1	2	8	26			
Parker, Alexander Negroes Sarah, Bett, Peter, H~~~, Hannah, Harry, Lett, Sall, Dakey, Charles, Simon, Jack.	1 — 9		Sarah, Bett, Peter. 3	11 — 25	9 — 37	22 — 114			

1782-002 CHARLES CHILTON'S PROPERTY LIST
[page 14]

Person's Names and all Names of Negroes	White Tithes Above 21	White Tithes Under 21	Negro Tithes	# Negroes	# Horses	Cattle	Wheels	Billiard Tables	Ordinary Licenses
Ransdell, John Negroes Harry, Daniel, Charles, Judy.	1		Harry, Daniel. 2	4	3	9			
Rooch, William Robert Rooch Negroes Ned, Phillis.	1	1	Ned, Phillis 2	2	3	9			
Robison, Stephen	1								
Rogers, George George Rogers Jun[r] Edward Rogers Negroes Kate, Lett, Kate, Prince, Duke, Adam, Charles.	2	1	Kate, Lett, Kate. 3	7	6	11			
Roe, Alexander	1				1	3			
Red, Allan Neg. Abram, Moses, Mary.	1		Abram, Moses. 2	3	2	24			
Robison, Benjamin Negroes Peg, Molley, Lucy Sen[r], Simon, Harry, Charles, Adam, Violet, Joe, Moses, Aggai, Hannah, Nelly, Solomon, Rachel, James.	1		Peg, Molley, Lucy Sen[r]. 3	16	5	24			

1782-002 Charles Chilton's Property List
[page 14]

Person's Names and all Names of Negroes	White Tithes Above 21	White Tithes Under 21	Negro Tithes	# Negroes	# Horses	Cattle	Wheels	Billiard Tables	Ordinary Licenses
Roach, John	1					1			
~~Robert Smith~~	~~1~~					~~1~~	~~2~~		
	9			36	21	60			

1782-002 Charles Chilton's Property List
[page 15]

Person's Names and all Names of Negroes	White Tithes Above 21	White Tithes Under 21	Negro Tithes	# Negroes	# Horses	Cattle	Wheels	Billiard Tables	Ordinary Licenses
Stewart, William (Rev^d) Thomas Green, Overseer Negroes Ben, Moses, David, Sam, Jack, Peter, Giles, Judith, Bess, Sarah, Hannah, Nancy, Nan, Milly, Simon, George, Alice, Kate, Jacob, Daniel, Charles, Frank, Tom, Celia.	1		Ben, Moses, David, Sam, Jack, Peter, Giles, Judith, Bess, Sarah, Hannah, Nancy. 12	24	3	27			
Shackleford, James James Shackelford Junr George Shackelford Negroes Joe, Fortune, Scipio, Delf, Harry, Fanny, Violet, Winney, Frank, Peter, Joe, Isaac, Charlotte, Jane, Rachel, Grace, Judy, Lett, Sall, Mima, Adam, Dinah, George, Guilford, Harry, Lucy, Hannah.	1	2	Joe, Fortune, Scipio, Delf, Harry, Fanny, Violet, Winney, Frank. 9	27	11	44			
Siddall, John Job Siddall	1	1			2	8			
Shirley, John Benjamin Shirley Negro Prince.	1	1	Prince 1	1	4	13			
Sanders, Robert John Sanders, William Sanders Negroes Jesse, Sam, Hannah, Lucy, Peter & a child.	1	2	Jesse, Sam. 3	6	4	15			

Person's Names and all Names of Negroes	White Tithes Above 21	White Tithes Under 21	Negro Tithes	# Negroes	# Horses	Cattle	Wheels	Billiard Tables	Ordinary Licenses
Suttle, Francis						4			

1782-002 CHARLES CHILTON'S PROPERTY LIST
[page 15]

Person's Names and all Names of Negroes	White Tithes Above 21	White Tithes Under 21	Negro Tithes	# Negroes	# Horses	Cattle	Wheels	Billiard Tables	Ordinary Licenses
Stewart, Allan Neg. Tom, Solomon, Joan, Nan, Lucy.	1		Tom, Solomon, Joan. 3	5	2	11			
Stewart, William Negroes James, Winney, Sue, Rachel, Mass.	1		James, Winney, Sue. 3	5	4	5			
Suttle, William						2			
Steele, Samuel George Steele Negroes Jack, James, James, Charlotte, Jane, Abel.	1	1	Jack, James, James, Charlotte. 4	6	5	21			
Stone, John Negroes Rachel, Sarah, Lett.	1			3	3	1			
	9			77	45	147			

1782-002 CHARLES CHILTON'S PROPERTY LIST
[page 16]

Person's Names and all Names of Negroes	White Tithes Above 21	White Tithes Under 21	Negro Tithes	# Negroes	# Horses	Cattle	Wheels	Billiard Tables	Ordinary Licenses
Thornberry, John John Reveley, William Thornberry, Thomas Thornberry, Francis Thornberry Negroes Tom, Daniel, Jude, Milley, Tom.	3	2	Tom, Daniel, Jude. 3	5	10	34			
Thornberry, Henry	1				1				
Thornberry, Samuel Junr	1				3				
Thornberry, Samuel Senr Negroes Jack, Humpprey, Ralph, Jacob, Jeter, Phill, Winney, Letty, Milley, Kate, Nan, Sarah, Chloe, Hannah, Nelly, Joe, Sciah, Duddley, Harry.	1		Jack, Humpprey, Ralph, Jacob, Jeter, Phill, Winney, Letty, Milley. 9	19	9	58			

1782-002 CHARLES CHILTON'S PROPERTY LIST
[page 16]

Person's Names and all Names of Negroes	White Tithes Above 21	White Tithes Under 21	Negro Tithes	# Negroes	# Horses	Cattle	Wheels	Billiard Tables	Ordinary Licenses
Tomlin, John Senr Wm. Tomlin, Samuel Tomlin Negroes Fortune, Joc, Kate, Jack, Charles, Ned, Bett, James, Fortune, Jane, Joe, Lucy.	2	1	Fortune, Joc, Kate, Jack, Charles. 5	12	8	16			
Tomlin, John Junr Negro Tom.	1		Tom	1	3	6			
Taylor, Nimrod	1				2	5			
Taylor, Henry	1				3	7			
	11			37	39	126			

1782-002 CHARLES CHILTON'S PROPERTY LIST
[page 17]

Person's Names and all Names of Negroes	White Tithes Above 21	White Tithes Under 21	Negro Tithes	# Negroes	# Horses	Cattle	Wheels	Billiard Tables	Ordinary Licenses
Whiting, Francis Negroes Oliver, Tom, Frank, James, Will, Cesar, Tony, Sam, Charles, Sie, Lewis, Rose, Nanny, Kate, Sarah, Daniel, Chloe, Harry, Willis, Joshua, Oliver, Aaron, Jonathan, George, Carter, Hannibal, Sam, Daniel, Mary, Nanny, Judy, Lucy, Grace, Siller.	1		Oliver, Tom, Frank, James, Will, Cesar, Tony, Sam, Charles, Sie, Lewis, Rose, Nanny, Kate, Sarah, Daniel, Chloe. 17	34	18	61	4		
White, William Negroes Tom, Jack, Aaron, Betty, Bob, Jane.	1		Tom, Jack, Aaron. 3	6	6	24			
Wattson, Thomas	1				1				
Woodford, Catesby Negroes James, Harry, Jack, Ally, James, Harry, Milley, Fanny, Edmond, Celia, Joan, Judy.			James, Harry, Jack, Ally, Harry, Milley. 7	12	3	2			
	3			53	27	87	4		

1782-002 CHARLES CHILTON'S PROPERTY LIST
[page 18]

Person's Names and all Names of Negroes	White Tithes Above 21	White Tithes Under 21	Negro Tithes	# Negroes	# Horses	Cattle	Wheels	Billiard Tables	Ordinary Licenses
Young, James Negroes Will, Tom, Toney, Ben, Rose, Venus.	1		Will, Tom, Toney Ben, Rose, Venus. 6	6	8	18			

1782-003 John Blackwell's Property List
[page 1]

Person's Names and all Names of Negroes	White Tithes Above 21	White Tithes Under 21	Negro Tithes	# Negroes	# Horses	Cattle	Wheels	Billiard Tables	Ordinary Licenses
Alexander, Phillip Quarter James Bowen Oseer. 1 Neg^os Sam, James, Tom, James, Stephen, James, Ben, James, Pegg, Phillis, Tuner				11	16				
Sall, Pegg, Sambo, Rose, Phillis				[illegible]	7	36			
Armstrong, James William Armstrong	1	1			3	16			

1782-003 John Blackwell's Property List
[page 2]

Person's Names and all Names of Negroes	White Tithes Above 21	White Tithes Under 21	Negro Tithes	# Negroes	# Horses	Cattle	Wheels	Billiard Tables	Ordinary Licenses
Bowmer, Peter	~~1~~	~~1~~	~~1~~		1				
Blackwell, Thomas Negroes James, Peter, Grace, Vilet, Bob, George, Mima Laz^a rus, Dick, Daniel	1		5	10	4	2			
Bryan, John. Neg^ro Hary.		1	1	1	1	2			
Bramblett, Peggy Reubin Bramblett, John Bramblett	2				3	14			
Ball, John John Hammons Negroes Daniel, George, Winney, Nance Jin, Charles, Luce, Jude, Phillis, Rachel.	2		4	10	6	17			
Berryman, Benjamin Neg. Jean, Mason	1		1	2	3	9			
Berryman, Maximilion James, Moses, George, Sarah, Nan, Hanah,	1				6	15			

Rachal, Susanah — 8

1782-003 John Blackwell's Property List
[page 2]

Person's Names and all Names of Negroes	White Tithes Above 21	White Tithes Under 21	Negro Tithes	# Negroes	# Horses	Cattle	Wheels	Billiard Tables	Ordinary Licenses
Berryman, Maximilion (Cont.) Daniel, Joshua, Vinson, Ben, Zachariah, Winny, Sarah, Milley				17					
Bower, Peter Charles, Tim, Phillis, Sarah, Hanah, Mary, Charles Winney, Juda, Tom	1		7	10	7	41			
Battaley, Bryan Neg^r Cate	1		1	1	3	6			
Blackwell, John John Hermon, Overseer Neg^{ro} James, Will, Harry, Jacob, George, Lucy, Winney, Susanah, Grace, Lidy Robin, Judy, Hanah, Mary, Nan, Sealey, Fanny	2		10	17	7	41			
Brown, John Neg. Rose	1		1	1	3	1			
Brent, William Thos Gore Neg^{roes} Sam, Sharper, Isaac, Cate, Lett, Sall, Jenney, Fran Sall, Luce, Hanah, Nick, Charles, David, Tom, Jaffrey, Easter, Beck, Jack, James, Dick	2		9	22	7	16			

1782-003 John Blackwell's Property List
[page 3]

Person's Names and all Names of Negroes	White Tithes Above 21	White Tithes Under 21	Negro Tithes	# Negroes	# Horses	Cattle	Wheels	Billiard Tables	Ordinary Licenses
Bowen, James Levy charged to Mr Alexander Negroes Judy, Hannah				2	3	2			

1782-003 JOHN BLACKWELL'S PROPERTY LIST
[page 3]

Person's Names and all Names of Negroes	White Tithes Above 21	White Tithes Under 21	Negro Tithes	# Negroes	# Horses	Cattle	Wheels	Billiard Tables	Ordinary Licenses
Bradford, John					3				
Bryant, James	3				2	[illegible]			
William Bryant,									
Thomas Millon									
[Negroes] Abram & Prince			2						
Abram				1					
Thos Bronaugh – at the end of the book	1			6	9				
Negroes Daniel, Ross, Ben, Lucie, Rachel, Nell, Kate			7						
Will, Judy, Harry				10					
Churchill, Armisteads	1				11	20			
Negroes Sharper, Joshua, Lewis, James, Tom, Tom, Emanuel, Dick, Natt, James, Cager, Sawney, Phill, Jane, Lilly, Lucy, Venus, Bett, Billy, Molley, Cate			21						
Will, Phill, Harry, Charles, Punch, Sall, Sookey, Mary, David, Woner, Siller, Aggy, Jess, Shadrick, Anney, Spencer, Leevinah				38					
Craig, John	1				3	1			
Craig, James Rev^d					7	20			
Neg^{ro} Tom, Bob, Winny			3						
Young Neg^s Billey, Tom, Harry, Scipio, Moses, Amy, Suky				10					
Cussenberry, John	1				3	16			
Zachariah Vann		1							

1782-003 John Blackwell's Property List
[page 4]

Person's Names and all Names of Negroes	White Tithes Above 21	White Tithes Under 21	Negro Tithes	# Negroes	# Horses	Cattle	Wheels	Billiard Tables	Ordinary Licenses
Duncan, Charles Neg. Sam, Briton, Daniel, Prince. Doll, Primos, Sam, Lucy, Sarah, Frank, Bell, Suck.	1		4	11		12	22		
John Duncan Sen[r] Joseph Duncan [Negroes] Toney, Will, Tom, Patt Temp	2		4	6		7	17		
Jeremiah Darnall [Negroes] Peter, Bett, Moses, Hanah, Milley, Jack. Toney, David, Judy	1		6	10		7	96		
Duncan, Joseph Sen[r] [Negroes] Dick, Tom, Phill, Grace, Jane, Pat Peter, Win, Tong, Lewis, Tom, Nan, Ephraim, Phillis, Cloe	1		6	14		6	5		
Duncan, Joseph Jun[r] [Negroes] Harry, Charles, Cain	1		1	2		1	3		

1782-003 John Blackwell's Property List
[page 5]

Person's Names and all Names of Negroes	White Tithes Above 21	White Tithes Under 21	Negro Tithes	# Negroes	# Horses	Cattle	Wheels	Billiard Tables	Ordinary Licenses
Duncan, Houson [Negroes] Ben, Pegg	1			2		3	6		
Darnall, Joseph Neg[rs] Tom Franny, Will, Lucy	1		1	4		9	9		
Dodd, Nath[l] Sen[r] James Dodd [Negroes] Bosen, Cate, Moses Lucy, Dinah, Jaley, Will, Jeffery	2		3	8		5	19		

1782-003 John Blackwell's Property List
[page 5]

Person's Names and all Names of Negroes	White Tithes Above 21	White Tithes Under 21	Negro Tithes	# Negroes	# Horses	Cattle	Wheels	Billiard Tables	Ordinary Licenses
Dodd, Nathl Junr Neg^s Rose, Venus.	1		1	2	3	5			
Duff, James John Duff James Duff Senr Neg. Will.	2	2	1	1	4	16			
~~Rawleigh Downman~~ Downman, Rawleigh Q^{ur} Charly Ficklin, Oseer [Negroes] Kate, Nance, Will, Kitty, Alce, Winney, Sall, Ross, Meligan, Dick, Ren, Frank, Easter, John, Lee, Moses, Jeffrey, David, Mimey, Venes, Nall.	1		9	9	4	32			
Dodd, Benjamin Neg^{ro} Jenny	1		1	1	4	8			

1782-003 John Blackwell's Property List
[page 6]

Person's Names and all Names of Negroes	White Tithes Above 21	White Tithes Under 21	Negro Tithes	# Negroes	# Horses	Cattle	Wheels	Billiard Tables	Ordinary Licenses
Ellis, James	1				1				
English, Robert Robt English	1	1			3	4			
Elliott, Samuel	1				1	4			

1782-003 John Blackwell's Property List
[page 7]

Person's Names and all Names of Negroes	White Tithes Above 21	White Tithes Under 21	Negro Tithes	# Negroes	# Horses	Cattle	Wheels	Billiard Tables	Ordinary Licenses
Fox, Samuel [Negroes] Sam, James, Jacob, Judy, Jean Peter, Charity.	1		5	7	6	16			

1782-003 JOHN BLACKWELL'S PROPERTY LIST
[page 7]

Person's Names and all Names of Negroes	White Tithes Above 21	White Tithes Under 21	Negro Tithes	# Negroes	# Horses	Cattle	Wheels	Billiard Tables	Ordinary Licenses
Ficklin, Charles his tiths Charged to Downman [Negroes] Levinah, Pallace				2	1				

1782-003 JOHN BLACKWELL'S PROPERTY LIST
[page 8]

Person's Names and all Names of Negroes	White Tithes Above 21	White Tithes Under 21	Negro Tithes	# Negroes	# Horses	Cattle	Wheels	Billiard Tables	Ordinary Licenses
Garner, Charles	1				2	13			
Garner, Charles Junr	1				1	2			
Greenwood, Daniel [Negroes] Sam, Sarah	1		2	2	1	5			
Goff, Joshua	1				3	4			
Grasty, George [Negroes] Miller, Hannah, Patt, Frank, Rose. Toba, Mill, Barbra, Judah, Luce, Dick, Toney, Lidy, Charles	1		5	14	9	26			

1782-003 JOHN BLACKWELL'S PROPERTY LIST
[page 9]

Person's Names and all Names of Negroes	White Tithes Above 21	White Tithes Under 21	Negro Tithes	# Negroes	# Horses	Cattle	Wheels	Billiard Tables	Ordinary Licenses
Hinson, Robert	1				5	12			
Hovell Williams Quarter Peter Taylor, Overseer Neg^r James, Cato, Prince, Dick	1		1 4	4	3	16			
Hume, William	1				3	7			
Holiday Samuel	1								

1782-003 John Blackwell's Property List
[page 9]

Person's Names and all Names of Negroes	White Tithes Above 21	White Tithes Under 21	Negro Tithes	# Negroes	# Horses	Cattle	Wheels	Billiard Tables	Ordinary Licenses
Helm, Thomas Cap^tn [Negroes] Plato, Sambo, Peter, Will, Luce, Pinder, Grace. Aaron, Titus, Solomon, Lewis, Enoch, Nance, Phillis	1		7	14	7	20			
Holtzclaw, Josiah	1				4	13			
~~Miller, John~~	~~1~~				~~2~~	~~4~~			
John Hedgman's Quarter, James Tharp overseer. [Negroes] Ship, Robin, Ben, Harry, Jack, Whip, Will, Grace, Winney, Sook, Frank, Jean. Sam, Hanah, Alic, Lucy, Judy, Hanah, Tom, Joe, Judy, Siss.	~~1~~ 1	~~1~~	~~1~~ 12	~~1~~ ~~10~~ 22	7	32			
Hume, John	1				3	7			
Hundon, John Neg. Susanah. Gabriel, Peter, Sarah, Tom, Charlot, Edmond.	1	1		7	5	16			
Hunter, James Quarter Reuben Wright, Overseer [Negroes] Beecher, Phillis, Tener, Margus, Tom, Judy, Jacob, Betsy, Milley, Sithy, Ben, Alexander. Aggy, Daniel, Ned, Charrity, Milley, Aaron, Will, Margues, Caskus, Will, Emanuel, Jenny, Sall, Will.	1		10	26	7	35			

1782-003 JOHN BLACKWELL'S PROPERTY LIST
[page 10]

Person's Names and all Names of Negroes	White Tithes Above 21	White Tithes Under 21	Negro Tithes	# Negroes	# Horses	Cattle	Wheels	Billiard Tables	Ordinary Licenses
Johnson, Tunis Tunis Johnson [Negroes] Mary, Harry, George	1	1	2	3	4	11			
Johnson, Yellis [Negroes] James, Nell.	1			2	4	6			
Jennings, Lewis Geo. Jennings [Negroes] ~~George,~~ Bray, Winny, Sall, Frank. Joe, Rachel, Lucy, Tom, Spencer, Charity.	1	1	4 6 10		5	21			
Jefferson, William	1				1	4			
Jennings, Augustain Negroes Ben, Bett, Aggy, Bell, Moses, Sall, Lett.	1		2	7	3	13			
Jennings, Balis [Negroes] Sam, Willoughby, Alec, Toney	1		3	4	2	7			
Jones, John [Negroes] Guy, Peter, Pen, Bett, Nanny, Jane. Gerrard, Ruth, Charlotte	1		6	9	3	21			

1782-003 JOHN BLACKWELL'S PROPERTY LIST
[page 11]

Person's Names and all Names of Negroes	White Tithes Above 21	White Tithes Under 21	Negro Tithes	# Negroes	# Horses	Cattle	Wheels	Billiard Tables	Ordinary Licenses
Knox, William's Quarter Peter Bowman, Overseer [Negroes] Tom, London, Peter, Anthony, Ammy, Cate, Sarah, Milley, Dinah, Luce. Charity, Will, Sarah, Elijah, Nan, Bett, Winney, Patt, Jack.	1		10	10 9	8	66			
Keirnes, Daniel	1				1	4			

1782-003 John Blackwell's Property List
[page 12]

Person's Names and all Names of Negroes	White Tithes Above 21	White Tithes Under 21	Negro Tithes	# Negroes	# Horses	Cattle	Wheels	Billiard Tables	Ordinary Licenses
Lunsford, Jemima William Lunsford Negro Chloey	1		1	1	3	10			
Lawson, Gavin's Quarter [Negroes] Sam, Aker, Bill, Moll. Peter, Blandford, Daniel, Lucy.			4	4 8	3	11			
~~Fran James Neg'. Milley~~	~~1~~		~~1~~	~~2~~	~~2~~				
Lee, Hancock Negroes George, Ben, James, Natt, Grace, Nan, Alce, Rose, Levinah, Fanney. Henry, Abram, Lewis, Shadrick, Scipio, Zachariah, Amey, Amey.	1		11	19	9	24			
Lynn, William William Linn, Alex' Linn, James Linn	2 0 0	2		0	5	5			

1782-003 John Blackwell's Property List
[page 13]

Person's Names and all Names of Negroes	White Tithes Above 21	White Tithes Under 21	Negro Tithes	# Negroes	# Horses	Cattle	Wheels	Billiard Tables	Ordinary Licenses
Maddox, Thomas Sen' Levy free					2	6			
Maddox, George, Horses only					2				
Marr, Daniel	1				1				
Matthews, Richard, Levy free					2	3			

1782-003 JOHN BLACKWELL'S PROPERTY LIST
[page 13]

Person's Names and all Names of Negroes	White Tithes Above 21	White Tithes Under 21	Negro Tithes	# Negroes	# Horses	Cattle	Wheels	Billiard Tables	Ordinary Licenses
Martin, Charles [Negroes] Peter, Charles, Rachel, Sue, hanah, Charrity. George, Bob, Bob, Sipio, Lott, Aggy.	1		6	6- 12	8	27			
McCormack, Stephen John McCormack [Negroes] Charles, Nick, James, Bett, Sarah. Jenney, Lucy, Hanah, Moses, Will, Joe, Adam, Eve, Suck, Dinah, Aggy, Daniel, Isaac.	1	1	5	18	7	21			
Miller, John	1				2	4			

1782-003 JOHN BLACKWELL'S PROPERTY LIST
[page 14]

Person's Names and all Names of Negroes	White Tithes Above 21	White Tithes Under 21	Negro Tithes	# Negroes	# Horses	Cattle	Wheels	Billiard Tables	Ordinary Licenses
Nelson, John Blacksmith	1				2	4			
[No names listed under "O"]									

1782-003 JOHN BLACKWELL'S PROPERTY LIST
[page 15]

Person's Names and all Names of Negroes	White Tithes Above 21	White Tithes Under 21	Negro Tithes	# Negroes	# Horses	Cattle	Wheels	Billiard Tables	Ordinary Licenses
Preston, William J^r [Negro] Peter	1		1	1	2	11			
Phillips, Abner [Negro] Lewis	1		1	1	3	13			
Phillips, Elias Neg^r Jack Amay, Winney, Jenny.	1		1	4	1	8			

1782-003 John Blackwell's Property List
[page 15]

Person's Names and all Names of Negroes	White Tithes Above 21	White Tithes Under 21	Negro Tithes	# Negroes	# Horses	Cattle	Wheels	Billiard Tables	Ordinary Licenses
Preston, William Senr Jeremiah Preston	2̶ 1	1			3	8			
Preston, John	1				3	5			
Preston, Joshua	1				3	5			
Preston, Jacob	1				3	5			
Pearce, John	1				1				
Parr, James Neg^r Milly	1		1	1	3	2			

1782-003 John Blackwell's Property List
[page 16]

Person's Names and all Names of Negroes	White Tithes Above 21	White Tithes Under 21	Negro Tithes	# Negroes	# Horses	Cattle	Wheels	Billiard Tables	Ordinary Licenses
Russell, William Negroes Lucy, Nann				2					
Routt, James Negroes Daniel, Lucy.	1		2	2	2	8			
Routt, Peter Negroes Tom, Chloey, Tom.	1		2	2 1	3	10			

1782-003 John Blackwell's Property List
[page 17]

Person's Names and all Names of Negroes	White Tithes Above 21	White Tithes Under 21	Negro Tithes	# Negroes	# Horses	Cattle	Wheels	Billiard Tables	Ordinary Licenses
Sharp, Ann Horses & Cattle	1	1	1		2	5			
Stevenson, James John Swenson	2				3	7			
Sinclair, James	1				3	4			

1782-003 JOHN BLACKWELL'S PROPERTY LIST
[page 17]

Person's Names and all Names of Negroes	White Tithes Above 21	White Tithes Under 21	Negro Tithes	# Negroes	# Horses	Cattle	Wheels	Billiard Tables	Ordinary Licenses
Shoemate, John	1					7	12		
Benj^a Shoemate		1							
Negroes Cato, Jenney, Grace.			3						
Sam, Peter, Dick, Milley, Lucy, Dinah, Alley				17					
Shoemate, William	1								
John Shoemate		1				1	11		
Shoemate, James						2	5		
Negroe Ceni			1						
Shanks, John	1					1	9		
Sinclair, William	2					7	14		
Geo. Latham									
[Negroes] Tom, Harry, Gillis, Bett, Nan, Suck.			[illegible]						
Peter, Jacob, Phillis, Charlott, Dick				11					

1782-003 JOHN BLACKWELL'S PROPERTY LIST
[page 18]

Person's Names and all Names of Negroes	White Tithes Above 21	White Tithes Under 21	Negro Tithes	# Negroes	# Horses	Cattle	Wheels	Billiard Tables	Ordinary Licenses
Turbervill, George's Quarter									
George Maddox, OvSeer	1					3	23		
Negs Dimont, Dick, Dick, Hagor, Cate, Cate, Prue.			7						
James, Derende, Suck, Tom, Rachel, Solomon, Seppi, Peter, Chloey, Hannah.				10̶ 17					
Taylor, Peters Cattle,									
Neg. Jack			1			3			
Turner, John	1					5	14		
Taylor, Elizabeth									
Nimrod Taylor		1				3	12		

1782-003 JOHN BLACKWELL'S PROPERTY LIST
[page 19]

Person's Names and all Names of Negroes	White Tithes Above 21	White Tithes Under 21	Negro Tithes	# Negroes	# Horses	Cattle	Wheels	Billiard Tables	Ordinary Licenses
Vowls, Richard	1								
Negroes Zachariah, Nell		2	2	2	8				

1782-003 JOHN BLACKWELL'S PROPERTY LIST
[page 20]

Person's Names and all Names of Negroes	White Tithes Above 21	White Tithes Under 21	Negro Tithes	# Negroes	# Horses	Cattle	Wheels	Billiard Tables	Ordinary Licenses
Withers, Thomas Sen[r] George Creswell, Overseer	2					8	28		
[Negroes] Ceaser, George, Moses, Cate, Hanah, Jess, Bess.			7	7					
Tom, Aaron, Phillis, Dick, Roger, Will, Dinah, Bett, Winny, Clarey, Harry, Solomon.				12					
Withers, James (Cains son)	1					4	19		
[Negroes] Tom, Brook, Ben, Nann, Judy, Sarah.			6	6					
Lucy, Joe, Cain, Simon, Jenny, Isaac.				6					
Wheatley, James	1					11	22		
[Negroes] George, Harry, Rose, Ester, Sall.			5						
Glasgo, Daniel, Judy, Winny, Mimey, Nell.				11					
Williams, Paul	1					10	19		
Neg[r] Ovid, Ben, James, Florah, Pendar, Phillis, Milley, Tamer.			7						
Moses, Charles, Lule, Abraham, Delphia, Will, Toliver, George, Ephraim, Dorithy	1[?]		7	11 18					

1782-003 JOHN BLACKWELL'S PROPERTY LIST
[page 20]

Person's Names and all Names of Negroes	White Tithes Above 21	White Tithes Under 21	Negro Tithes	# Negroes	# Horses	Cattle	Wheels	Billiard Tables	Ordinary Licenses
Wilkins, William Sen. Lewis Withers Negroes Jack, Peter, Briton, Sam, Sarah, Samuel, Nan j^r, Priss. Jeffrey, Samson, Amey, Easter, Adam, Winney, Bess, Hanah, Abraham, George.	2		8	8					
Willis, Ursley (Tomlett Quarter) Jesse Withers, Overseer [Negroes] Dick, Dinah, Phillis. Ben, Ralph, Ursley, Isaac, Sisser.	1		3	13 3 5	7	48			
Watson, William Neg^r Nell	1		1	1		2			
Wright, John Capt Neg. Bob, Will, Dinah, Jude, Lidy, Easter, Lucy. Jean, Will, Tom, Troy, Ann, Moses, Milley.	1		6	6 8	5	20			
Wheatley, John [Negroes] Henry, Nathl [?], Will, Lucy.	1 1 [?]		2	~~2~~ 4	4	8			

1782-003 JOHN BLACKWELL'S PROPERTY LIST
[page 21]

Person's Names and all Names of Negroes	White Tithes Above 21	White Tithes Under 21	Negro Tithes	# Negroes	# Horses	Cattle	Wheels	Billiard Tables	Ordinary Licenses
Wheatley, Joseph Neg. Stephen, Sarah, Judy. Shadrack.	1		3	4	6	31			
Williams, Jonas	1				3	9			

1782-003 JOHN BLACKWELL'S PROPERTY LIST
[page 2]

Person's Names and all Names of Negroes	White Tithes Above 21	White Tithes Under 21	Negro Tithes	# Negroes	# Horses	Cattle	Wheels	Billiard Tables	Ordinary Licenses
Weaver, John	1	[illegible]			5	11			
Weathers, Cain Negroes Will & Ester	1		2	2	3	11			
Thomas Bronaugh Neg' Daniel, Ross, Ben, Lucie, Rachel, Nell, Cate. Will, Judy, Harry.	1		7	10	6	9			

List of P[r]operty
Taken by John Blackwell.

1782-004 William Heale's Property list
A List of Property taken by Wm Heale
[page 1]

Person's Names and all Names of Negroes	White Tithes Above 21	White Tithes Under 21	Negro Tithes	# Negroes	# Horses	Cattle	Wheels	Billiard Tables	Ordinary Licenses
Asbury, Wm Thomas Asbury Under 21 N. King, Phillis, Lin 5 horses, 11 Cattle	1	1	3	3	5	11			
Anderson, David 1 horse 5 cattle	1				1	5			
Asbury, George N 1) 1 horse 1 cow	1			1	1	1			
Asbury W^m 2 horses, 4 Cattle	1				2	4			
Asbury, Henry 1 horse, 4 Cattle	1				1	4			
Allison, W^m Ex^r to Kirk Abraham Silvey, Overseer. N. Dimbo, Cogger, Daniel, Moses, Peg, Currier, Bet, D°[Bet] young, Tener, Esther, Ben, Beck, Charles. 6 horses, 14 Cattle.		1	7	12	6	14			

1782-004 William Heale's Property list
A List of Property taken by Wm Heale
[page 2]

Person's Names and all Names of Negroes	White Tithes Above 21	White Tithes Under 21	Negro Tithes	# Negroes	# Horses	Cattle	Wheels	Billiard Tables	Ordinary Licenses
Bartlett, Thomas Richard Bartlett Und^r 21 N. Jack, Humphrey, Frank, Joe, Dinah, Judah, Hannah, Abigail, D° [Abigail] young, Phoebe, Let, Pat, Humphrey, Parker, Gill. 9 horses 24 cattle.	1	1	8	14	9	24			
Berry, Henry N. Ben, Sam, D° [Sam] young, Tom, Beck. 6 horses, 7 cattle	1		2	4	6	7			

1782-004 WILLIAM HEALE'S PROPERTY LIST
A List of Property taken by Wm Heale
[page 2]

Person's Names and all Names of Negroes	White Tithes Above 21	White Tithes Under 21	Negro Tithes	# Negroes	# Horses	Cattle	Wheels	Billiard Tables	Ordinary Licenses
Barker, Charles 2 horses, 4 cattle	1				2	4			
Bryan, Enoch 2 Cattle	1					2			
Barton, James 3 horses, 3 Cattle	1				3	3			
Barton, Cuthbert clear Levy 3 horses, 3 cattle	0				3	3			
Brady, Peregin 1 horse	1				1				
Bartlett, W^m N dimbo. 2 horses, 5 Cattle	1		1	1	2	5			
Bartlett, John 1 horse, 4 Cattle	1				1	4			
Banister, Augustine 3 horses, 1 cow	1				3	1			
Berry, George N. Gloucester, Dick, Jarrard, Bess, Moll, D° [Moll] young, Frank, Joe, Tom, Patrick. 7 horses 10 Cattle	1		5	9	7	10			
Berry, W^m N Harry, Phillis, D°[Phillis] young, Charles, Elizabeth, Polley. 3 horses, 2 Cattle	1	0	2	5	3	2			
Berkley, Wm N. Harry, London, Agor, Agor, D° [Agor] young, Aaron, Moses, hannah, Bet. 7 horses, 21 Cattle	1		4	8	7	21			

Carried forward [to page 4]

1782-004 William Heale's Property List
A List of Property taken by Wm Heale
[page 3]

Person's Names and all Names of Negroes	White Tithes Above 21	White Tithes Under 21	Negro Tithes	# Negroes	# Horses	Cattle	Wheels	Billiard Tables	Ordinary Licenses
Clerk, Benjamin Negroe Jud young. 4 horses, 12 Cattle	1			1	4	12			
Chaddox, Charles N. James 2 horses, 7 Cattle	1		1	1	2	7			
Cantwell, John N. Cato, Cate, D° [Cate] young, Solomon.	1		2	3	2	9			
Cornwell, John young N. Will. 3 horses, 5 Cattle	1			1	3	5			
Chick, John George Stewart, over 21 N. Grinage, Hester, Mary. 4 horses, 17 Cattle.	2		3	3	4	17			
Cochrum, Richens 1 horse					1				
Carrell, Elizabeth Robert Bartlett un^r 21 N Lid. N young Mill, Harry. 2 horses, 4 Cattle.		1	1	3	2	4			
Carter, Peter Dale Carter N. Bob, Harry. 1 horse, 7 Cattle.	1	1	2	2	1	7			
Covender, John 1 horse, 2 Cattle	1				1	2			
Courtney, W^m W^m D° [Courtney] un^r 21 N. Anthony, Polly, D° [Poll] young, Tom, Aggy. 5 horses, 5 Cattle	1	1	2	5	5	5			
Cornwell, Jervis N. Tom. 2 horses, 5 Cattle	1		1	1	2	5			

Carried forward

1782-004 William Heale's Property list
A List of Property taken by Wm Heale
[page 4]

Person's Names and all Names of Negroes	White Tithes Above 21	White Tithes Under 21	Negro Tithes	# Negroes	# Horses	Cattle	Wheels	Billiard Tables	Ordinary Licenses
Bruin, Michael Tom Bruin un{r} 21 3 horses, 4 Cattle.	1	1			3	4			
Barton, Kinber 4 horses, 8 Cattle	1				4	8			
Barton, Levy N. Williby young. 3 horses, 2 Cows	1			1	3	2			
Barker, Wm Wm Barker J{r} un{r} 21 N. Adam 6 horses, 6 Cattle	1	1	1	1	6	6			
Baley, Rite [Wright] un{r} 21 2 horses, 3 Cattle		1			2	3			
Baley, Moses N. Sal, Sarah, D{o} [Sarah] young, Baccus, Mill, hannah, George, Sepio, Dick. 8 horses, 11 Cattle	1		2	8	8	11			
Bashaw, Peter un{r} 21 N Bet, D{o} [Bet] young, Beck. 3 horses, 7 Cattle		1	1	2	3	7			
Baley, Wm 1 horse	1				1				
Bartlett, Robert 1 horse					1				
Ball, Nicholas 1 horse	1				1				
Brent, George proporty N. Harry, D{o} [Harry] young, Antony, Sam, Solomon 4 horses, 3 Cattle	1		1	4	4	3			
Bland, Mary Charles Bland un{r} 21 N. Will 4 horses, 9 Cattle		1	1	1	4	9			

1782-004 WILLIAM HEALE'S PROPERTY LIST
A List of Property taken by Wm Heale
[page 4]

Person's Names and all Names of Negroes	White Tithes Above 21	White Tithes Under 21	Negro Tithes	# Negroes	# Horses	Cattle	Wheels	Billiard Tables	Ordinary Licenses
Brady, Hezekiah N. Sawney. 2 horses, 3 Cattle	1		1	1	2	3			
Bryant, Peter 4 horses, 4 Cattle	1				4	3			

1782-004 WILLIAM HEALE'S PROPERTY LIST
A List of Property taken by Wm Heale
[page 5]

Person's Names and all Names of Negroes	White Tithes Above 21	White Tithes Under 21	Negro Tithes	# Negroes	# Horses	Cattle	Wheels	Billiard Tables	Ordinary Licenses
Carter, George N. Dick, Dinah, Priscilla, D° [Priscilla] young, Suck, Dark, Judah, Jude, Jack, Let, Harry, Charles. 5 horses, 13 cattle	1		3	11	5	13			
Case, Samuel ovr 21	1								
Chinn, Christopher N. Ralf, Sam, Daniel, Dick, Bet, Sal, D° [Sal]young, Malbrough, Adam, Sam, Bet, Caiff, Nell, Henry, Isaac, Jane. 8 horses, 14 Cattle.	1		6	15	8	14			
Craine, John N. Adam, Martha, D° [Martha]-young, Lidda, darca. 5 horses, 9 Cattle	1		2	4	5	9			
Chinn, Thomas of Loudoun N. Stiephan, James, Dinah. 2 horses, 7 Cattle			3	3	2	7			
Cundiff, Isaac N. Robin. 3 horses, 7 Cattle	1		3̶ 1	1	3	7			
Crosby, Uriell 4 horses, 12 Cattle	1				4	12			

1782-004 WILLIAM HEALE'S PROPERTY LIST
A List of Property taken by Wm Heale
[page 5]

Person's Names and all Names of Negroes	White Tithes Above 21	White Tithes Under 21	Negro Tithes	# Negroes	# Horses	Cattle	Wheels	Billiard Tables	Ordinary Licenses
Combs, Robert Joshua Owens, Overseer N. Boatswain. 3 horses, 1 cow.	1		1	1	3	1			
Constable, W^m 2 horses, 3 Cattle	1				2	3			
Combs, Catharine Ben. Athel, Overseer N. Cuffey, David, Sarah. 3 horses, 7 Cattle	1		3	3	3	7			
Coats, Thomas 2 horses, 4 Cattle	1				2	4			
Collins, Edmond N. Nan, Frank, D° [Frank]young, Henry, Jude, Ben, Sampson, Sarah. 4 horses, 9 Cattle	1		2	7	4	9			
Cundiff, James 1 horses 2 Cattle	1				1	2			

1782-004 WILLIAM HEALE'S PROPERTY LIST
A List of Property taken by Wm Heale
[page 6]

Person's Names and all Names of Negroes	White Tithes Above 21	White Tithes Under 21	Negro Tithes	# Negroes	# Horses	Cattle	Wheels	Billiard Tables	Ordinary Licenses
Downing, Wm N. Isaac, Joe, Peter, Will, Manuel, Rachel, Grace, Milley, Milley, Let, patience, Mimey, Bet, Betty, D° [Betty]young, Leanna, Silvy, Rose, Tab, Gabriel, Eli, Levy. 4 horses, 24 Cattle Given by Sam Jones			14	21	4	24			
~~Samuel James 1 horse~~	1				1				
Donaldson, John 1 young Negroe. 2 horses, 4 Cattle	1			1	2	4			

1782-004 WILLIAM HEALE'S PROPERTY LIST
A List of Property taken by Wm Heale
[page 6]

Person's Names and all Names of Negroes	White Tithes Above 21	White Tithes Under 21	Negro Tithes	# Negroes	# Horses	Cattle	Wheels	Billiard Tables	Ordinary Licenses
Drummond, Aaron 2 horses, 5 Cattle	1				2	5			

1782-004 WILLIAM HEALE'S PROPERTY LIST
A List of Property taken by Wm Heale
[page 7]

Person's Names and all Names of Negroes	White Tithes Above 21	White Tithes Under 21	Negro Tithes	# Negroes	# Horses	Cattle	Wheels	Billiard Tables	Ordinary Licenses
Edwards, Thomas Martin Edwards un^r 21 N. Joe. 3 horses, 8 Cattle	1	1	1	1	3	8			

1782-004 WILLIAM HEALE'S PROPERTY LIST
A List of Property taken by Wm Heale
[page 8]

Person's Names and all Names of Negroes	White Tithes Above 21	White Tithes Under 21	Negro Tithes	# Negroes	# Horses	Cattle	Wheels	Billiard Tables	Ordinary Licenses
Fields, John N. Mimey. 3 horses, 7 Cattle	1		1	1	3	7			
Fishback, Josiah N. Joe, Winney, Monico, D° [Monico]young, Daniel, Peg, Ben, Harry, Tom, Mill. 5 horses, 12 Cattle	1		3	9	5	12			
Fling, John 1 horse, 4 Cattle	1				1	4			
Flowrance Wm N. Adam, Nan, D° [Nan]-young, Patty. 3 horses, 10 Cattle	1		2	3	3	10			

1782-004 WILLIAM HEALE'S PROPERTY LIST
A List of Property taken by Wm Heale
[page 8]

Person's Names and all Names of Negroes	White Tithes Above 21	White Tithes Under 21	Negro Tithes	# Negroes	# Horses	Cattle	Wheels	Billiard Tables	Ordinary Licenses
Fishback, Philip John Fishback ovr 21 James Fishback unr 21 N. Jarrard. 5 horses, 11 Cattle	2	1	1	1	5	11			
Fishback, John Wm Fishback un^r 21 N. London, James, D° [James]young, Mary. 5 horses, 12 Cattle	1	1	2	3	5	12			
Flowers, Andrew 2 horses, 8 Cattle	1				2	8			
Feagins, Edward N. Harry, Cate. 2 horses, 5 Cattle	1		2	2	2	5			
Flathers, Edward N. David, Jane, Sal, D° [Sal] young, Jane, hannah 4[x'ed out] 5 horses, 4 Cattle	1		3	5	5	4			
Fielding, Edward N. Daniel, Nan, Mary, D° [Mary] young, Sue, Dick, John, Let. 2 horses, 7 Cattle	1		2	6̶ 7	2	7			
		Carried to Q.							
Feagins, Rawleigh 1 horse, 4 Cattle	1				1	4			

1782-004 WILLIAM HEALE'S PROPERTY LIST
A List of Property taken by Wm Heale
[page 9]

Person's Names and all Names of Negroes	White Tithes Above 21	White Tithes Under 21	Negro Tithes	# Negroes	# Horses	Cattle	Wheels	Billiard Tables	Ordinary Licenses
Griffiths, John 2 horses, 2 Cattle	1				2	2			
Glascock, Thomas N. Stepan, D° [Stepan]young, Orange. 3 horses, 12 Cattle	1		1	2	3	12			

1782-004 WILLIAM HEALE'S PROPERTY LIST
A List of Property taken by Wm Heale
[page 9]

Person's Names and all Names of Negroes	White Tithes Above 21	White Tithes Under 21	Negro Tithes	# Negroes	# Horses	Cattle	Wheels	Billiard Tables	Ordinary Licenses
Grigsby, Ann Taliaferro Grigsby un^r 21 Aaron Grigsby un^r 21 N. Cooper, Frank, James, Jack, dimby, Winney, Jane, Hester, Mill, D° [Mill] young, Amey, Alice, Clary, Ben. 9 horses, 19 Cattle		2	9	13	9	19			
Grigsby, Betsey George Leach, ovr 21 Permenes Bullett, un^r 21 N. Harry, Charles, Sarah, Luce, D° [Luce] young, Hester, Doll, Mary, Jarrard, Reuben, Leir, Rose, Sue. 8 horses, 15 Cattle	1	1	3	12	8	15			
Gibson, Abraham N. Jude. 4 horses, 13 Cattle	1		1	1	4	13			
Glascock, George N. Jack, Nan, Bet, D° [Bet] young, Bob, Jude, will, Sarah. 3 horses, 18 Cattle	1		3	7	3	18			
Griffiths, Evan Elijah Griffiths un^r 21 N. George, Sarah. 5 horses, 6 Cattle	1	1	2	2	5	6			

1782-004 WILLIAM HEALE'S PROPERTY LIST
A List of Property taken by Wm Heale
[page 10]

Person's Names and all Names of Negroes	White Tithes Above 21	White Tithes Under 21	Negro Tithes	# Negroes	# Horses	Cattle	Wheels	Billiard Tables	Ordinary Licenses
Hitt, Harmon Martin Hitt un^r 21 N. Tom, Sareh, winney, D° [winney] young, Dinah, Jude, hannah, Sam. 5 horses, 17 Cattle	1	1	3	7	5	17			
Heagins, John 1 horse, 1 Cow	1				1	1			

1782-004 WILLIAM HEALE'S PROPERTY LIST
A List of Property taken by Wm Heale
[page 10]

Person's Names and all Names of Negroes	White Tithes Above 21	White Tithes Under 21	Negro Tithes	# Negroes	# Horses	Cattle	Wheels	Billiard Tables	Ordinary Licenses
Hawkins, John 2 horses, 1 Cow	1				2	1			
Hathaway, John John Hathaway un^r 21 N. winney, Phillis, D^o [Phillis] young, Sam, Rose, Stephan, Rachel, Tom. 4 horses, 8 Cattle	1	1	2	7	4	8			
Heale, Wm George French N. Daniel, Moses, Dominy, Joe, Adam, Manuel, Charles, Fielding, Nan, phillis, Abigail, Margery, Nan, Mirtiller, Jane, D^o [Jane] young, Pat, Hannah, Sarah, Cate, Eve, Aaron, Stephan, Daniel, John, Donnice, Moses, Ned, Abel, Jacob. 10 horses, 19 Cattle	2		15	29	10	19			
Hogans, Thomas N. Ralf, Jane, Let, D^o [Let] young, Tom, Rose. 5 horses, 3 Cattle	1		3	5	5	3			
Hegins, W^m 2 horses	1				2				
Hegins, Alexander 2 horses, 3 Cattle	1				2	3			
Holtzclaw, Jacob 1 horse	1				1				
Harrison, John Peyton N. Brick, Dick. 4 horses, 6 Cattle	1	~~2~~	2	2	4	6			

   Carried to J

1782-004 WILLIAM HEALE'S PROPERTY LIST
A List of Property taken by Wm Heale
[page 11]

Person's Names and all Names of Negroes	White Tithes Above 21	White Tithes Under 21	Negro Tithes	# Negroes	# Horses	Cattle	Wheels	Billiard Tables	Ordinary Licenses
Johnson, Moses N. Rachel, D° [Rachel] young, Joe, Isaac, Aaron. 3 horses, 7 Cattle	1		1	4	3	7			
Hamrick, W^m 2 horses, 2 Cattle	1				2	2			
Heale, George George Brent N. Nat, Harry, Andrew, will, Peter, Matthew, Sue, Jane, Hannah, Margaret, Sifley, D° [Sifley] young, James, Cuff, Mary, John, Lucy, Fanney, Polley, Peter, Leanna, Cate, Jacob. 9 Horses, 24 Cattle	1		11	22	9	24			
Harrison, George N. Tom, Nace, Jerry, Judah, Violett, Henny, D° [Henny] young, Jo, Charles, Will, Frank, Jack, Mary, Jock, Nancy. 11 horses, 21 Cattle	1		6	14	11	21			

1782-004 WILLIAM HEALE'S PROPERTY LIST
A List of Property taken by Wm Heale
[page 12]

Person's Names and all Names of Negroes	White Tithes Above 21	White Tithes Under 21	Negro Tithes	# Negroes	# Horses	Cattle	Wheels	Billiard Tables	Ordinary Licenses
Jones, Peter James Jones ovr 21 Francis Jones & Wm Jones, un^r 21 3 horses, 8 Cattle	2	2			3	8			
~~Hogan, Thomas~~ ~~N. Ralf, Jane, Let,~~ ~~D° [Let] young, Tom, Rose.~~ ~~5 horses, 3 Cattle~~	~~1~~		~~2~~	~~5~~	~~5~~	~~13~~			
Jenkins, Thomas 1 horse	1				1				

1782-004 WILLIAM HEALE'S PROPERTY LIST
A List of Property taken by Wm Heale
[page 12]

Person's Names and all Names of Negroes	White Tithes Above 21	White Tithes Under 21	Negro Tithes	# Negroes	# Horses	Cattle	Wheels	Billiard Tables	Ordinary Licenses
Jones, Samuel 1 horse	1				1				
Johnson, George 2 horses, 2 Cattle	1				2	2			
James, John N. hannah, D° [hannah] young, Bet, Manuel. 3 horses, 9 Cattle	1		1	3	3	9			
Jackson, Joseph George Jackson Dempsey Jackson un^r 21 N. Jane, D° [Jane] young, Amey. 7 horses, 19 Cattle	1	2	1	2	7	19			

1782-004 WILLIAM HEALE'S PROPERTY LIST
A List of Property taken by Wm Heale
[page 13]

Person's Names and all Names of Negroes	White Tithes Above 21	White Tithes Under 21	Negro Tithes	# Negroes	# Horses	Cattle	Wheels	Billiard Tables	Ordinary Licenses
Kidwell, John Joseph Markwell ovr 21 4 horses, 5 Cattle	2				4	2			
Kenton, Mark Clear Levy 0 2 horses, 9 Cattle					2	9			
Keith, Isham N. Tobe, Baeris, Jane, Nel; Milley, D° [Milley] young, Eppa, Charlotte, Aaron, James, Harry. 4 horses, 13 Cattle	1		5	10	4	13			
Keith, Alexander N. will, Bill, Sarah, Jane, D° [Jane] young, James, hannah, Daphney, Leak, Tom. 3 horses, 15 Cattle	1		4	9	3	15			

1782-004 WILLIAM HEALE'S PROPERTY LIST
A List of Property taken by Wm Heale
[page 13]

Person's Names and all Names of Negroes	White Tithes Above 21	White Tithes Under 21	Negro Tithes	# Negroes	# Horses	Cattle	Wheels	Billiard Tables	Ordinary Licenses
Kibble, John Anderson Kibble, un^r 21	1	1			2	6			
Kibble, Wm N. Sarah, D^o [Sarah] young. 1 horse, 1 Cow	1			1	1	1			

1782-004 WILLIAM HEALE'S PROPERTY LIST
A List of Property taken by Wm Heale
[page 14]

Person's Names and all Names of Negroes	White Tithes Above 21	White Tithes Under 21	Negro Tithes	# Negroes	# Horses	Cattle	Wheels	Billiard Tables	Ordinary Licenses
Leachman, W^m 3 horses, 4 Cattle	1				3	4			
Leachman, Thomas 3 horses, 8 Cattle	1				3	8			
Leach, George Burdett Leach un^r 21 2 horses, 7 Cattle	1	1			2	7			
Lake, W^m 4 horses, 7 Cattle	1				4	7			
Laws, Thomas 3 horses, 8 Cattle	1				3	8			
Leach, W^m 1 horse, 4 Cattle	1				1	4			
Leach, James James Leach, un^r 21 Thomas Leach, un^r 21 4 horses, 9 Cattle	1	2			4	9			
Loller, James 1 horse, 3 Cattle	1				1	3			
Lake, Vinson 2 horses, 4 Cattle	1				2	4			

1782-004 WILLIAM HEALE'S PROPERTY LIST
A List of Property taken by Wm Heale
[page 14]

Person's Names and all Names of Negroes	White Tithes Above 21	White Tithes Under 21	Negro Tithes	# Negroes	# Horses	Cattle	Wheels	Billiard Tables	Ordinary Licenses
Lee, Henry's Estate Nat Robertson. N. Tom, Baley, Jack, Dick, Sarah, Peg, Dinah, D° [Dinah] young, Bet, Darca, will, Gabriel, Alexander, west, Sal. 5 horses, 18 Cattle	1		7	14	5	18			
Lamkin, James N. Isbell, Nan, D° [Nan] young, Reuben, Sarah. 3 horses, 7 Cattle	1		2	4	3	7			
Linton, W^m 2 horses, 2 Cattle	1				2	2			
Laing, Alexander Property 1 horse, 3 Cows					1	3			

1782-004 WILLIAM HEALE'S PROPERTY LIST
A List of Property taken by Wm Heale
[page 15]

Person's Names and all Names of Negroes	White Tithes Above 21	White Tithes Under 21	Negro Tithes	# Negroes	# Horses	Cattle	Wheels	Billiard Tables	Ordinary Licenses
McClenachan, Andrew 3 horses, 8 Cattle	1				3	8			
McClenachan, David 3 horses, 9 Cattle	1				3	9			
McMillian, John Joseph McMillian un^r 21 5 horses, 10 Cattle	1	1			5	10			
Matthew, Edward Simon Matthew un^r 21 3 horses, 5 Cattle	1	1			3	5			
Morehead, Presley John Baley N. Tom, Sall, James, Toney, Rose, D° [Rose] young, Ned, hannah, Judah, David, Aga, Tom. 8 horses, 17 Cattle	2		5	11	8	17			

1782-004 William Heale's Property List
A List of Property taken by Wm Heale
[page 15]

Person's Names and all Names of Negroes	White Tithes Above 21	White Tithes Under 21	Negro Tithes	# Negroes	# Horses	Cattle	Wheels	Billiard Tables	Ordinary Licenses
Matthew, Benjamin Isaac Benjamin 3 horses, 3 Cattle	2				3	3			
Morgan, John 1 horse, 4 Cattle	1				1	4			
Matthew, Nathan 4 horses, 3 Cattle	1				4	3			
Morehead, Charles N. Monday, will, James, Dinah, D° [Dinah] young, Peter. 9 horses, 16 Cattle	1		4	5	9	16			
Morgan, Simon James Morgan un^r 21 N. william, Jane, D° [Jane] young, Cyonis, Esther. 6 horses, 19 Cattle	1	1	2	4	6	19			
Morehead, Wm N. Toney, Jude, D° [Jude] young, George. 3 horses, 3 Cattle	1		2	3	3	3			
Monday, Robert N. Rose, Lucy, D° [Lucy] young, Elizabeth, Jeffery, Ben. 6 Cattle, 1 horse	1		2	5	1	6			
		Carried to V							
Monday, John N. Henry, Frank, Gibby, Judah, Peg, D° [Peg] young, Tom, Adam, Aaron, Judah, Rose, Rachel. 4 horses 5 Cattle	1		5	11	4	5			

1782-004 WILLIAM HEALE'S PROPERTY LIST
A List of Property taken by Wm Heale
[page 16]

Person's Names and all Names of Negroes	White Tithes Above 21	White Tithes Under 21	Negro Tithes	# Negroes	# Horses	Cattle	Wheels	Billiard Tables	Ordinary Licenses
Neilson, Thomas John Proudfoot, ovr 21 N. Daniel, Jude, D° [Jude] young, Rose, Aaron, Daniel, Harry. 2 horses, 5 Cattle	1		2	6	2	5			
Nawls, Wm Wm Nawls ^{unr 21} Qr 6 horses, 4 Cattle	1	1			6	4			
Newhouse, Jonathan 3 horses, 6 Cattle	1				3	6			
Norriss, Wm N. Let, Violett, Solomon, D° [Solomon] young, norah, Vina, Harry, Kit. 5 horses, 10 Cattle	1		3	7	5	10			
Norriss, John 1 horse	1				1				
Neal, Christopher 1 horse, 2 cattle	1				1	2			

1782-004 WILLIAM HEALE'S PROPERTY LIST
A List of Property taken by Wm Heale
[page 17]

Person's Names and all Names of Negroes	White Tithes Above 21	White Tithes Under 21	Negro Tithes	# Negroes	# Horses	Cattle	Wheels	Billiard Tables	Ordinary Licenses
Owens, John [of] Pignut 2 horses, ten Cattle	1				2	10			
Orsborn, Wm N. Tom, James, David 1)^{young}. 3 horses, 2 Cattle	1		3	3	2				
Obannon, Samuel N. hannah,^{young}. 4 horses, 10 Cattle	1			1	4	10			
Obannon, Benjamin N. Nan young. 2 horses, 3 Cattle	1			1	2	3			

1782-004 WILLIAM HEALE'S PROPERTY LIST
A List of Property taken by Wm Heale
[page 17]

Person's Names and all Names of Negroes	White Tithes Above 21	White Tithes Under 21	Negro Tithes	# Negroes	# Horses	Cattle	Wheels	Billiard Tables	Ordinary Licenses
Obannon, John Will Obannon, Joseph Obannon, Phil Linor, James Obannon un^r 21 N. Gabriel, Dick, Solomon, Jes, Sarah, Cate, Judah, D° [Judah] young, will, Tom, David, Amey, Phil. 9 horses, 25 Cattle	4	1	7	12	9	25			
Owens, John Bethell Owens un^r 21 N. Robin, Suck, D° [Suck] young, Milley, Agga, Moses, Suckey. 6 horses, 9 Cattle	1	1	2	6	6	9			
Owens, Joshua 3 Cattle	1				0	3			
Owens, Wm Wm Owens un^r 21 N. Cain, Edmond, D° [Edmond] young, David. 3 horses, 7 Cattle	1	1	2	3	3	7			

1782-004 WILLIAM HEALE'S PROPERTY LIST
A List of Property taken by Wm Heale
[page 18]

Person's Names and all Names of Negroes	White Tithes Above 21	White Tithes Under 21	Negro Tithes	# Negroes	# Horses	Cattle	Wheels	Billiard Tables	Ordinary Licenses
Pearle, Charity, wife of Wm Pearle 3 Horses, 7 Cattle					3	7			
Pinkstone, Henry 3 horses, 4 Cattle	1				3	4			
Prim, Wm John Williams ovr 21 4 horses, 10 Cattle	2				4	10			
Peyton, Henry N. Mountain, Moses, Spencer, Ned, Hannah, Milley, Will, D° [Will] young, Ned, Jane, Solomon, Bet, Cate, Priss, Hannah. 7 Horses, 17 Cattle	1		7	14	7	17			

1782-004 WILLIAM HEALE'S PROPERTY LIST
A List of Property taken by Wm Heale
[page 18]

Person's Names and all Names of Negroes	White Tithes Above 21	White Tithes Under 21	Negro Tithes	# Negroes	# Horses	Cattle	Wheels	Billiard Tables	Ordinary Licenses
Pidge, John N. John, James, Sue, D° [Sue] young, Jes, Jone. 2 horses, 7 Cattle	1		3	5	2	7			
Preaile, John Wm Baley N. Jacob, James, Mimey, Cumber, Nell, D° [Nell] young, Gabriel, Harry, John, Judah, Pris, Luce, Randolph, Val, Daniel, Minor. 7 horses, 7 Cattle	2		5	15	7	7			
Pearle, Samuel N. Charles, Lucy, Mary, D° [Mary] young, Jack, Charles, Nan. 4 horses, 17 Cattle	1		3	6	4	17			
Wm Pearle N. Will, Cuffey, Moll, Jone, Winney, D° [Winney] young, Milley, Tom, Jack, Sam, Nan, Ned, George, Sall, Hendley, Milley. 2 horses 20 Cattle	1		5 Carried to Q	15	2	20			
Pinckard, James N. Stephan. 1 horse, 2 Cattle	1		1	1	1	2			

1782-004 WILLIAM HEALE'S PROPERTY LIST
A List of Property taken by Wm Heale
[page 19]

Person's Names and all Names of Negroes	White Tithes Above 21	White Tithes Under 21	Negro Tithes	# Negroes	# Horses	Cattle	Wheels	Billiard Tables	Ordinary Licenses
Peak, W^m 3 horses, 9 Cattle	1				3	9			

1782-004 WILLIAM HEALE'S PROPERTY LIST
A List of Property taken by Wm Heale
[page 19]

Person's Names and all Names of Negroes	White Tithes Above 21	White Tithes Under 21	Negro Tithes	# Negroes	# Horses	Cattle	Wheels	Billiard Tables	Ordinary Licenses
F									
Floweree, Daniel Wm Flowerree Daniel Flowerree un^r 21 N. Nat, Jane, Cloe, Rachel, D° [Rachel] young, Jack, London, henny, hannah, Dinah, Lid, Arch, Sinah, Henry, Patty. 14 horses, 13 Cattle	1	2	4	14	14	13			
Foley, James Enoch Foley N. Lucy, Fenny, Hannah, Gloucester, D° [Gloucester] young, Doctor, Peg, Newton, Daniel, Emanuel, Bet, Armistead, Simon, Judah. 6 horses, 7 Cattle	2		4	16	6	7			
Feagins, Elizabeth George Leach ovrseer N. will, Lucy, D° [Lucy] young, Winney. 3 horses, 6 Cattle	1		2	3	3	6			
Feagins, John N. Joseph. 2 horses, 5 Cattle	1		1	1	3	5			
Fletcher, Joshua N. Sib. 2 horses, 9 Cattle	1		1	1	2	9			
French, John Daniel French John French un^r 21 N. Frank, D° [Frank] young, James, George, Grace, Spencer. 4 horses, 10 Cattle	2	1	1 Carried to Y	5	4	10			
Fitzgiarrald, Wm Tom Fitzgiarrald un^r 21 N. D° [Tom?] young, Harry, Sarah. 4 horses, 10 Cattle	1	1		2	4	10			

1782-004 WILLIAM HEALE'S PROPERTY LIST
A List of Property taken by Wm Heale
[page 20]

Person's Names and all Names of Negroes	White Tithes Above 21	White Tithes Under 21	Negro Tithes	# Negroes	# Horses	Cattle	Wheels	Billiard Tables	Ordinary Licenses
Robertson, Joseph John Muchett, John Robertson un^r 21 N. Ned, Jone, D° [Jone] young, Bryant, Val. 6 horses, 13 Cattle	2	1	2	4	6	13			
Robertson, Nathaniel 2 horses	1				2				
Rust, Samuel N. George, Fill, Lewis, D° [Lewis] young, Mary, Alice. 7 horses, 8 Cattle	1		3	5	7	8			
Rust, Matthew all young Negroes. Let, Rose, Abrener. 2 horses	1			3	2				
Rice, W^m 1 horse, 4 Cattle	1				1	4			
Ransdell, Whorton Q^r N. Frank, Tom, Jane. 2 horses	1		3	3	2				
Ransdell, Whorton Capt Wm Ransdell Thomas Ransdell un^r 21 N. George, Dick, George, Tom, Joe, Jeremy, Moses, Sue, Sisley, Jane, Moll, Peg, D° [Peg] young, edom, James, Sisley, Sinah. 13 horses, 26 Cattle	2	1	12	16	13	26			
Rust, John N. Frank, Moll, D° [Moll] young, Hannah, Jacob. 4 horses, 2 Cattle	1		2	4	4	2			
Rector, Charles 3 horses, 2 Cattle	1				3	2			

1782-004 WILLIAM HEALE'S PROPERTY LIST
A List of Property taken by Wm Heale
[page 21]

Person's Names and all Names of Negroes	White Tithes Above 21	White Tithes Under 21	Negro Tithes	# Negroes	# Horses	Cattle	Wheels	Billiard Tables	Ordinary Licenses
Smith, Mary Richd Smith un^r 21 N. Tom, Williby, Balley, Mirreah, D^o [Mirreah] young, Boron, Jane, Betsy, Henry, Bob, Violett. 4 horses, 7 Cattle		1	4	10	4	7			
				207 [written very lightly]					
Stewart, Wm Revd N. Dick, Jonathan, Tom, Harry, Jarrard, Florah, peg, Rose, winney, Dinah, Nell, D^o [Nell] young, Phil, Sal, Pompy, John, Jone, Mary, Jerry, Milley, Amey, Peggy, winney, Lizah, Judith, Reuben. 5 horses, 28 Cattle Given by Richard Cockrum, overseer	1		11	25	5	28			
Sinclair, John N. Ben, Jacob, Manuel, Grii, Dick, Sam, hannah, Agg, Nell, Hannah, D^o [Hannah] young, Dinah, Bet, Mimey, Amey, Sarah, Tom, George, Solomon, James. 4 horses, 13 Cattle	1		10	19	4	13			
Scott, Robert 3 horses	1				3				
Sanford P[ickett?] Wm John [Pickett?] un^r 21 Sanford [Pickett?] N. London, Gilbert, winney, D^o [winney] young, Tom. 9 horses, 24 Cattle	1	2	3	4	9	24			
Singleton, Standley Tonshend Singleton Wm Singleton un^r 21 N. Tom, Harry, Frank, hannah, D^o [hannah] young, Milley, Hannah, winn, Mason, Dinah, Stephan. 6 horses, 7 Cattle	2	1	4	10	6	7			

1782-004 WILLIAM HEALE'S PROPERTY LIST
A List of Property taken by Wm Heale
[page 22]

Person's Names and all Names of Negroes	White Tithes Above 21	White Tithes Under 21	Negro Tithes	# Negroes	# Horses	Cattle	Wheels	Billiard Tables	Ordinary Licenses
Stone, Menoah N. Sarah, D° [Sarah] young, Squire. 2 horses, 6 Cattle	1		1	2	2	7			
Scott, James Prince William County Harmon Utterback Over^{seer} N. Cesar, Elgan, Titus, Ben, Joe, James, Beck, Nan, Cloe, Bet, D° [Bet] young, Daniel, Stephan, Mary, Pris, Poll, Mol, Daphney, Murriah. 6 horses, 15 Cattle	1		10	18	6	15			
Skinker, W^m, Prince William County N. Grii, Isaac, Jerry, Sue, Esther, winney, hannah, D° [hannah] young, Robin, Ned, Sealey, Subbinia, Fanney, Peter, Harry, Stephan, Pressley, Jane. 4 horses, 9 Cattle			7	17	4	9			
Scott, John Revd John White, overseer N. John, Jack, Robin, George, James, Phil, Joe, Rose, Mirta, Judah, D° [Judah] young, David, Harry, Ned, Ephraim, Ben, Lucinda, Pris, Bridget, Nancy, Nelley, Thomas. 37 Cattle, 1 Riding Chair	2		10	20	7	37	2		
Seaton, John 2 horses, 4 Cattle in Turner's district.	1				2	4			

1782-004 WILLIAM HEALE'S PROPERTY LIST
A List of Property taken by Wm Heale
[page 23]

Person's Names and all Names of Negroes	White Tithes Above 21	White Tithes Under 21	Negro Tithes	# Negroes	# Horses	Cattle	Wheels	Billiard Tables	Ordinary Licenses
Smith, Joseph N. Lid, Rose, Charlotte, hannah, D° [hannah] young, Mary, Lewis, Ann, Charlotte. 6 horses, 7 Cattle	1		4	8	6	7			
Sarah Sullivan John Coppedge un^r 21 N. Cesar, Joe, Dinah, Phillis, D° [Phillis] young, Mimey, Dick, Elijah, winney. 4 horses, 16 Cattle		1	4	8	4	16			
Stage, Richard 2 horses, 2 Cattle	1				2	2			
Saunders, James N. Sepio, Sal. 2 horses 8 Cattle	1		2	2	2	8			
Sinclair, Wm N. Pat, D° [Pat] young, Nat, hannah, Rachel, Cas, Tom. 4 horses, 1 Cow	1		1	6	4	1			
Silvey, Abraham' Property N Milley, young. 2 horses, 8 Cattle				1	2	8			
Scott, Elizabeth Alexander Scott un^r 21 N. will, James, Jane, Bet, Jude, Beck, Frank, hannah, Charlotte, Jane, D° [Jane] young, Sal, Lucy, Jane, Charles, Daniel, mason, Sauney, Harry, London, Lewis, Cela, Jemima, Dianna, Ady, Amy, hannah, Tone, Rose, winney. 12 horses, 19 Cattle, 1 Riding Chair		1	10	29	12	19	2		
Saunders, W^m 1 horse, 2 Cattle	1				1	2			
Strother, Reuben N. Sambo, Henry, Dinah, Luce, D° [Luce] young, Rose, Jack, Frank, Charles. 15 Cattle	1		4	7	6	15			

1782-004 WILLIAM HEALE'S PROPERTY LIST
A List of Property taken by Wm Heale
[page 24]

Person's Names and all Names of Negroes	White Tithes Above 21	White Tithes Under 21	Negro Tithes	# Negroes	# Horses	Cattle	Wheels	Billiard Tables	Ordinary Licenses
Taylor, Charles 1 horse, 2 Cattle	1				1	2			
Tate, Peter N. Moses, Let, D° [Let] young, Sue, moll, minta, Peter. 4 horses, 5 Cattle	1		2	6	4	5			
Thompson, James Revd Vall Leach N. Tab, Let, D° [Let] young, hannah, Ishham, Bet, Moses. 4 horses, 7 Cattle	2̶ 1		2	6	4	7			
Thomas, David N. Dick, Patience, D° [Patience] young, Lott, orson, Prue, Tom. 5 horses, 3 Cattle	1		2	6	5	3			
Turner, John 3 horses, 3 Cattle	1				3	3			
Taylor, Benjamin 1 horse, 2 Cattle	1				1	2			
Taylor, Joseph N. Joshua, Neilson, Sarah, Bet, D° [Bet] young, Simon, Arguile, Sal, Sha^d, Mesheck. 4 horses, 14 Cattle	1		4	9	4	14			
Taylor, Isaac 6 Cattle	1					6			
Taylor, Judith N. George, Adam, Isaac, Tobe, bet, Cate, D° [Cate] young, hannah, Solomon, Charles, Esther, Mary, Alice, wilkins, Jerry, Peter, Luce. 4 horses, 17 Cattle			6	16	4	17			
Thomas, Elisha Carried forward	1				1				

1782-004 WILLIAM HEALE'S PROPERTY LIST
A List of Property taken by Wm Heale
[page 25]

Person's Names and all Names of Negroes	White Tithes Above 21	White Tithes Under 21	Negro Tithes	# Negroes	# Horses	Cattle	Wheels	Billiard Tables	Ordinary Licenses
Utterback, John N. Joe, Tibby, Elizabeth, D° [Elizabeth] young, George. 4 horses, 8 Cattle	1		3	4	4	8			
Utesler, Christian 2 horses, 7 Cattle	1				2	7			
Utterback, Harmon N. Cate 1 Horse, 2 Cattle			1	1	1	2			

1782-004 WILLIAM HEALE'S PROPERTY LIST
A List of Property taken by Wm Heale
[page 26]

Person's Names and all Names of Negroes	White Tithes Above 21	White Tithes Under 21	Negro Tithes	# Negroes	# Horses	Cattle	Wheels	Billiard Tables	Ordinary Licenses
Vaughan, Wm John Vaughan un^r 21 2 horses, 4 Cattle	1	1			2	4			
M Murrey, Enoch 3 horses	1				3				
Morrison, Hugh Daniel Morrison 3 horses, 10 Cattle	2				3	10			
Mercer, John F. Estate under the direction of Battle Muse, Wm Moore. N. Andrew, Cupid, Minard, Brister, Peter, Captain, George, George, Philis, Sal, Truelove, D° [Truelove] young, Neriate, Boatswain, Catena, Lynn, Cloe, Milley, Sarah. **Laings Quarter** N. London, will, David, George, Captain, Sauney, Mollo, Sepio, Liddy, Sarah, Amey, Phillis, Selah, D° [Selah] young, Toney, Ben, Dinah, Tom, will, Sepio, hannah, Phill, Isbell, 9 horses, 50 Cattle by Battaile Muse	3		24	40	9	50			

1782-004 WILLIAM HEALE'S PROPERTY LIST
A List of Property taken by Wm Heale
[page 26]

Person's Names and all Names of Negroes	White Tithes Above 21	White Tithes Under 21	Negro Tithes	# Negroes	# Horses	Cattle	Wheels	Billiard Tables	Ordinary Licenses
Monday, Wm N. Ben, Cate, D° [Cate] young, Sal, Jane. 2 horses, 2 Cattle	1		2	4	2	2			
Moore, John 1 horse, 2 Cattle	1				1	2			
Murrey, James Reuben Murrey [N.] Peter, Rose, winney, hannah, D° [hannah] young, Phillis. 4 horses, 14 Cattle	1	1	4	5	4	14			

1782-004 WILLIAM HEALE'S PROPERTY LIST
A List of Property taken by Wm Heale
[page 27]

Person's Names and all Names of Negroes	White Tithes Above 21	White Tithes Under 21	Negro Tithes	# Negroes	# Horses	Cattle	Wheels	Billiard Tables	Ordinary Licenses
Welch, Cilvester Cilvester Welch un^r 21 N. Winney, Alley, Moses, D° [Moses] young, Hannah, Jerry. 4 horses, 18 Cattle	1	1	3	5	4	18			
Whailin, Patrick 1 horse, 2 Cattle	1				1	2			
Williby, John 2 horses, 3 Cattle	1				2	3			
Winn, James John Smith ov^r 21 N. James, Harry, Abraham, Sarah, Venus, D° [Venus] young, Lewis, Solomon, Berkey. 9 horses, 12 Cattle	2		5	8	9	12			
West, Charles un^r 21 3 horses		1			3				

1782-004 WILLIAM HEALE'S PROPERTY LIST
A List of Property taken by Wm Heale
[page 27]

Person's Names and all Names of Negroes	White Tithes Above 21	White Tithes Under 21	Negro Tithes	# Negroes	# Horses	Cattle	Wheels	Billiard Tables	Ordinary Licenses
Winn, Minor N. Frank. Lewis Force N. Rewben, Harry, King, Moses, Peter, Rose, D° [Rose] young, Philip, Frank, James, Sall, Jane. 9 horses, 28 Cattle	2		7	11	9	28			
Winn, Margaret N. Sauney, Jane, Grace, Poll, D° [Poll] young, Jack, Hester. 5 horses, 17 Cattle			4	6	5	17			
Watts, John N. Mary, D° [Mary] young, Bet, Kelley, will. 5 horses, 4 Cattle	1		1	4	5	4			
Waddle, John Wm Waddle, over 21 James Waddle un^r 21 N. Jack, winney, D° [winney] young, Ben, hannah. -4 5 horses, 9 Cattle	2	1	2	4	5	9			
White, W^m 2 horses, 1 Cow	1				2	1			
Woodard, Charles	1								
Wake, John N. Lot, James, Lucy, Jude, D° [Jude] young, Milley, Sarah, Lid, Daniel, Harry, Pris, Jane, Chris. 8 horses, 10 Cattle	1		4	12	8	10			

Carried forward

1782-004 WILLIAM HEALE'S PROPERTY LIST
A List of Property taken by Wm Heale
[page 28]

Person's Names and all Names of Negroes	White Tithes Above 21	White Tithes Under 21	Negro Tithes	# Negroes	# Horses	Cattle	Wheels	Billiard Tables	Ordinary Licenses
Woodard, Luke 1 horse, 5 Cattle	1				1	5			

1782-004 WILLIAM HEALE'S PROPERTY LIST
A List of Property taken by Wm Heale
[page 29]

Person's Names and all Names of Negroes	White Tithes Above 21	White Tithes Under 21	Negro Tithes	# Negroes	# Horses	Cattle	Wheels	Billiard Tables	Ordinary Licenses
Young, William Willm Young J^r ov^r 21 N. Hendley, George, Rose, D^o [Rose] young, Jane, Amey, Daniel. 4 horses, 23 Cattle	1	1	3	6	4	23			
F Foley, Wm N. George. 2 horses, 8 Cattle	1		1	1	2	8			
French, George 1 horse	1				1				

1782-004 WILLIAM HEALE'S PROPERTY LIST
A List of Property taken by Wm Heale
[page 30]

Person's Names and all Names of Negroes	White Tithes Above 21	White Tithes Under 21	Negro Tithes	# Negroes	# Horses	Cattle	Wheels	Billiard Tables	Ordinary Licenses

[There are no names on page 30]

1782-004 WILLIAM HEALE'S PROPERTY LIST
A List of Property taken by Wm Heale
[page 31]

Person's Names and all Names of Negroes	White Tithes Above 21	White Tithes Under 21	Negro Tithes	# Negroes	# Horses	Cattle	Wheels	Billiard Tables	Ordinary Licenses
B Brown, Jehu 4 horses, 2 Cattle	1				4	2			
Barker, John N. Phillis, John, Winney, Peg, D^o [Peg] young, Agga, Grii, winney. 6 horses, 8 Cattle	1		4	7	6	8			
Baley, Stephan 1 horse	1				1				
Barton, Prue 3 horses, 4 Cattle	1				3	4			

1782-004 WILLIAM HEALE'S PROPERTY LIST
A List of Property taken by Wm Heale
[page 31]

Person's Names and all Names of Negroes	White Tithes Above 21	White Tithes Under 21	Negro Tithes	# Negroes	# Horses	Cattle	Wheels	Billiard Tables	Ordinary Licenses
Butler, Samuel 3 horses, 2 Cattle	1				3	2			
Baley Joseph Q^r Martin Bayley unr 21 N. Daniel, D° [Daniel] young, will. 4 horses, 6 Cattle	1	1	1	2	4	6			
Baley, Joseph Green Baley un^r 21 2 horses, 5 Cattle	1	1			2	5			
Baden, John James Baden 1 horse, 3 Cattle	2				1	3			
Baley, John 1 horse, 5 cattle	1				1	5			
Baley, Rice [?] un^r 21 1 horse, 2 Cattle	1				1	2			
Bradley, Hugh Peter Bashaw un^r 21 N. Adam, Cris, D° [Cris] young, David. 4 horses, 13 Cattle	1	1	2	3	4	13			
Blythe, James 2 horses, 3 Cattle	1				2	3			
Basey, Richard N. Pris, Livy, Isham. 1 horse	1		3	3	1				
Brooks, James 5 horses, 5 Cattle in Chiltons District	1				5	5			

1782-004 WILLIAM HEALE'S PROPERTY LIST
A List of Property taken by Wm Heale
[page 32]

Person's Names and all Names of Negroes	White Tithes Above 21	White Tithes Under 21	Negro Tithes	# Negroes	# Horses	Cattle	Wheels	Billiard Tables	Ordinary Licenses
Thomas, Benjamin 2 horses, 5 Cattle	1				2	5			
Turner, Samuel 1 horse, 5 Cattle	1				1	5			
Turner, Edward John Turner un^r 21 N. James, Will, Isaac, Lucy, Betty, Sillar, Alice, D^o [Alice] young, George, David, Reuben, Sauney, Dinah, Winna, Milley. 7 horses, 16 Cattle	1	1	7	~~12~~ 14	7	16			
Thomas, Aaron 5 horses, 4 Cattle	1				5	4			
Tolle, Sarah Roger Tolle N. Harry 6 horses, 9 Cattle	1		1	1	6	9			
Tolle, George 3 horses, 8 Cattle	1				3	8			
Taylor, W^m 3 horses, 2 Cattle	1				3	2			

1782-005 Personal Property Tax List
page 1

Person's Names and all Names of Negroes	White Tithes Above 21	White Tithes Under 21	Negro Tithes	# Negroes	# Horses	Cattle	Wheels	Billiard Tables	Ordinary Licenses
Arnal, Jack	1								
Negro Nead, Diner, Bob			3	3	6	11			
Allen, Robert	1				2	3			
Armstrong, James	1				1	2			
Allen, John	1				3	2			
Allen, James	1			1	1	1			
Negro Vilet									
Anderson, Cornealus	1				1	2			
Back, Harmon	1				1	1			
Calup Browning	1		1	1	2	3			
Negro Daffiney									
Bridwell, William	1				2	2			
Burgis, Garnar	1	1			5	16			
Edward Burgis									
Negroes Dinah, Lucy, Patt, Sam, Harry, Milly, Winny			3	07					
Browning, Jacob	2				1	3			
George Browning									
Basye, Josias	1				3	14			
Blackaby, Joseph	1								
Negroes George, Winea, Will, Moll, Cate, Jenny, Jude, Lucey, Amelia, Rhoda			2	10					
Brown, Mary			1	2		6			
Negro Luce, Negro Child Tramp									
Brown, John	1				1				
Brown, Dixson	1				1				
Briggs, William	1				8	9			
Negros Sam, Daniel, Hannah, Rose, Bob, Charrity			1	6					
Barbee, Joseph	3				4	7			
Wm Harril.									
Jesse Harris.									
Negroes Rose, Charrity, Jacob, Cate.			4	4					
Burk, John	1				3	3			

1782-005 PERSONAL PROPERTY TAX LIST
page 1 (Cont.)

Person's Names and all Names of Negroes	White Tithes Above 21	White Tithes Under 21	Negro Tithes	# Negroes	# Horses	Cattle	Wheels	Billiard Tables	Ordinary Licenses
Bowling, Francis	1				2	3			
Bennett, Daniel	2				2	6			
Bramblet, Ruben Jn^r	1				2	2			
Barbey, Andrew Se^r	1				5	7			
[Negroes] Dick, Hanah, Nancy Rose.			4						
Willam, Lucy, Joseph, Jessee, Eve, Liza				10					
Barbee, Andrew Jn^r	1				3	2			
Negro Mima			1						
Bailey, James	1				2	2			
Blackerby, Goduthern	1				4	4			
Negro Cook, Moll, Fran, Titus			4	4					
Barbey, Joseph	1				3	7			
Negro Lever			1	1					

1782-005 PERSONAL PROPERTY TAX LIST
page 2

Person's Names and all Names of Negroes	White Tithes Above 21	White Tithes Under 21	Negro Tithes	# Negroes	# Horses	Cattle	Wheels	Billiard Tables	Ordinary Licenses
Clarkson, Henry	1	0			7	5	2		
Negroes Abe, Dick, Sanda, Cate, Jane, Vick, Selea, Jack, Abe, Ben, Diner				11					
Crim, John	1				1				
Chadwell, John	1				3	3			
Crafford, William	1				3	3			
Cammoron, Anquish	1				3 1	2			
Cook, John	1				3				
Clemdenea, John	1				2	4			
Negroes Robert, Frank			2	2					
Crim, Joseph	1				1	4			
Crim, Peter	1				1	2			
Caunna, Stephen	1				1	1			

1782-005 Personal Property Tax List
page 2 (Cont.)

Person's Names and all Names of Negroes	White Tithes Above 21	White Tithes Under 21	Negro Tithes	# Negroes	# Horses	Cattle	Wheels	Billiard Tables	Ordinary Licenses
Curtis, John	1				1	1			
Crimm, Harmon	1				3	1			
Crim, Cattron			1	4	2	6			
Negroes Easter, Charles, George, Hannah									
Crim, Jacob	1				3	4			
Cristi, Charles	1				1	1			
Corder, James	1				2	5			
Collins, John			0	0	1				
Negroes Peter, Henna			1	2					
Day, Leonard	1				2	1			
Dennerson, James	1				3	3			
Dodd, John	1				3	5			
Negro Fillis, Rose			1	3					
Dearing, John	1				4	4			
Negro Clares			1	1					
Dearing, Jeremiah	1				2	2			
Drummond, James	1				2	2			
Evins, Sammuel	1				2	3			
Ellis, Jonathan	1				2	3			
Edwards, John	1								
Ellis, Nathaniel	1				1	3			
Fletcher, Moses	1				1	4			
Felkings, John	1				2	2			
Flecher [?], Benjamin	1				3	3			
Felkings, William	1				1	2			
Flynn, Michail	1				2	1			

1782-005 PERSONAL PROPERTY TAX LIST
page 3

Person's Names and all Names of Negroes	White Tithes Above 21	White Tithes Under 21	Negro Tithes	# Negroes	# Horses	Cattle	Wheels	Billiard Tables	Ordinary Licenses
Foley, Briant	1				2	1			
Foley, James	1		1	3	2	5			
[Negroes] Will, bob, Charity									
Fuel, Nathaniel	1				1	1			
Valentine Flynn	1				3	5			
Flecher, Mosses	1				1	1			
Fle[c]her, William	1	1			3	4			
Ford, William	1				2	4			
Foley, Thomas	1				4	4			
Negroes Moll, Mill, George, Charity			1	4					
Grant, James	1				2	3			
Glover, Thomas	1				1	1			
Groves, William	1				1	2			
Guttridge, Allen	1				3	3			
Negro Winney			1	1					
Grimsley, William	1				4	8			
Negro Winney			1	1					
Goodwin, Abraham	1				2	2			
Garrard, Anthony	1	1			1	2			
Greenlees, Peter	1				2	6			
Negroes Jone, Jane, Dick, Clare			2	4					
Heflin, Simon	1				2	4			
Hitt, Charles	1				2	3			
Harris, Thomas	1				3	7			
Harris, James	1				2	3			
Hopper, John Sen'					3	3			
Hopper, John	1				1	6			
Humes, Andrew	1				2	3			
Hitt, Lazarus	1				1	2			
Hitch, Cristopher	1				4	4			
Negroes Paul, George			1	2					
Hambrick, John	1				3	5			

1782-005 PERSONAL PROPERTY TAX LIST
page 3 (Cont.)

Person's Names and all Names of Negroes	White Tithes Above 21	White Tithes Under 21	Negro Tithes	# Negroes	# Horses	Cattle	Wheels	Billiard Tables	Ordinary Licenses
Hume, Robert	1				5	9			
Haddox, Zekel	1				1	2			
Hopper, Mary					2	4			
Harris, Richard	1				2	5			
Negro Fanny			1	1					
Hilliary, William	1				2	2			
Hefferlins, William	1				1	3			
Harris, Sammuel	1				5	7			
Negro Doll, Easter, Easter, Child [unnamed]			1	4					
Humemody, Henry	1				2	2			
Harris, Elisha	1				2	4			
Negro Hannah			1						
Hill, John	1				2	1			

1782-005 PERSONAL PROPERTY TAX LIST
page 4

Person's Names and all Names of Negroes	White Tithes Above 21	White Tithes Under 21	Negro Tithes	# Negroes	# Horses	Cattle	Wheels	Billiard Tables	Ordinary Licenses
Heaton, William	1				2	2			
Hust, [Hurst] Henry	1				2	2			
Hust [Hurst], Rosannah					1				
Hulet, William	1				4	6			
Johnson, Beede	1	1			1	2			
Charles Shaw									
Negroes Ginn, Ann, Leet [?]			1	3					
Jones, John	1				3	3			
Jett, John	1								
Jarrard, William	1				3	2			
Negroes Sesor, Julen, Mary, Elige			2	4					
Jones, Henry	1	1			3	2			
Jett, William	1				2	3			
Jett, Francis	1				2	2			
Negro Pegg			1	1					

1782-005 PERSONAL PROPERTY TAX LIST
page 4 (Cont.)

Person's Names and all Names of Negroes	White Tithes Above 21	White Tithes Under 21	Negro Tithes	# Negroes	# Horses	Cattle	Wheels	Billiard Tables	Ordinary Licenses
Johnson, Isaac	1				1	3			
Jett, William	1				1	2			
King, William	1				2	2			
King, Robert	1					3			
Kerns, Robert	1				2	1			
Larrance, Edward	1	1			8	8			
Negroes Henry, Sary, Rose. Jeane, Mason, Ennis, Hannah			3	4					
Larrance, Peter	1	2			3	5			
Negroes George, Jack, Bettey			3	3					
Lane, William	1				4	2			
Maccade, James	1				1	1			
Martin, John	1				2	2			
Massey, Thomas	1				3				
Negroes Winea, Luce, Amelia			1	3					
McQueen, Charles	1				4	8			
Negro Will			1	1					
Martin, Maryan					1				
McCormick, John	1				2	3			
Negroes Jude, James			1	2					
Morgan, William Par^h [of] Leeds	1								
Picket, W^m					6	20			
[Negroes] Dick, Tom, James, Pegg, Mill			5	5					
Morgan, Charles	1				3	7			
Negroes Bob, Ben, Winea, Adam, Allen			3	5					
Morehead, John Senr	1	1			12	12			
John Morehead J^r Negroes Ben, Will, Suck, Bett, Hannah, Dinah, Luce, Fanna, Mary, Sarah, Lyd, Daniel, Charles, Easter, Linney, Isaac, Bet, Charles			8	18					

1782-005 PERSONAL PROPERTY TAX LIST
page 4 (Cont.)

Person's Names and all Names of Negroes	White Tithes Above 21	White Tithes Under 21	Negro Tithes	# Negroes	# Horses	Cattle	Wheels	Billiard Tables	Ordinary Licenses
Monroe, John	2				2	5			
Joseph Barton									
Negro Jane			1	1					
McBee [?], John					1	1			

1782-005 PERSONAL PROPERTY TAX LIST
page 5

Person's Names and all Names of Negroes	White Tithes Above 21	White Tithes Under 21	Negro Tithes	# Negroes	# Horses	Cattle	Wheels	Billiard Tables	Ordinary Licenses
Norman, Isack	1				1	2			
Norman, Clem	1				4	2			
Norman, Martin	1	1							
Norman, John	1				2	2			
Norman, William	1				2	4			
Norman, Ezekel	1				1	2			
Norman, Jesse	1				3	3			
Nickols, Samuel	1				2	2			
Negro George			1	1					
Newton, Abraham	1				1	5			
Negroes (1) [space left blank]			3	5					
Payne, Ann	1				5	5			
Negroes Glascow, Hannah, Heath, Nan, Samson, Jenney, Sall, Susanah, Dianah, Sillar,			3	10					
Pearle, Edward	1				3				
Piper, Benjamin	1				3	4			
Negroes Sam, Peg, Patt, Mime, Sall, Mille, Charles, Isaac, Jack, Luce, Sharlet, Manuel, Jane			5	13					
Payne, William	1				1	1			
Preast, John	2	1			4	7			
Mason Preast									
Rodam Preast									
Payne, Thomas	1				2	2			
Negro Lizzy, Jack			1	2					

1782-005 PERSONAL PROPERTY TAX LIST
page 5 (Cont.)

Person's Names and all Names of Negroes	White Tithes Above 21	White Tithes Under 21	Negro Tithes	# Negroes	# Horses	Cattle	Wheels	Billiard Tables	Ordinary Licenses
Francis Payne	1	1				3	6		
Wm. Payne Negroes Grace, James, Moses, Daniel, Winney			1	5					
Qussenbery, James	1					2	2		
Rixsey, Richard Negroes Tom, Aron, Hager, Hannar, Joseph, Sarah, Violet, Danial, William	1		5	9		7	6 7		
Randell, William	1					3	3 7		
Randoll, John	1					3	3		
Rogers, Henry James Rogers	2	2				6	6		
Righley, John						2	4		
Robertson, John	1	0				2	2		
Rogers, Steaven Henry Rogers	2								
Righley, Thomas	1					1	3		
Robertson, William	1					2	4		
Riddle, William	1						2		
Riley, Charles						2	6 [?] 2		

1782-005 PERSONAL PROPERTY TAX LIST
page 6

Person's Names and all Names of Negroes	White Tithes Above 21	White Tithes Under 21	Negro Tithes	# Negroes	# Horses	Cattle	Wheels	Billiard Tables	Ordinary Licenses
Rogers, John Negro [unnamed]	1		1	1		6	5		
Robertson, James	1					2	5		
Shackelford, Benjamin Negroes Minny, Ned, Lewis, Harry, Peter, Daniel, Harry, Robin, Nelson, Phill, Kate, Judath, Dinah, Hannah, Kate, Molly, Beck	1		8	17		7	9		

1782-005 Personal Property Tax List
page 6

Person's Names and all Names of Negroes	White Tithes Above 21	White Tithes Under 21	Negro Tithes	# Negroes	# Horses	Cattle	Wheels	Billiard Tables	Ordinary Licenses
Stone, Benjamin	1				1	2			
Smoote, John	1				2				
Smoot, Leonard	1								
Selman, Ann					3	4			
Settle, Joel Neg^s Jack, James	1		2	2	1				
Smoot, John	1	1			3	3			
Smoot, James		1			1				
Snyder, Jacob	1				3	4			
Shumate, John Negro Girl [unnamed]	1		1	1	3	6			
Smith, William	1					2			
Suddoth, Larrance	1				2	3			
Strothers William Neg^r Daniel	1		1	1	2	3			
Smith, William Senr [of] Hickry Ne[groes] Luce, Rose, Cate, Easter, Diner, Seaser, James, Hannah, Bet, Jacob, Moses	2		5	11	4	4			
Sinkler, Robert Negroes Jim, Mimey, Guss, Lidd	1		1	4	4	2			
Suddoth, James	1				4	5			
Samuel Shumate Negro Luce	1			1	2	2			
Smith, John Berryman Smith Negroes Jefry, Ben, Jude, Grace, John, George, Luce, Mary	1	1	4	8	4	9			
Smith, John Junr Neg: Nan	1		0	1	6	4			
Smith, William [of] Carter's Run	1				2	3			

1782-005 Personal Property Tax List
page 6

Person's Names and all Names of Negroes	White Tithes Above 21	White Tithes Under 21	Negro Tithes	# Negroes	# Horses	Cattle	Wheels	Billiard Tables	Ordinary Licenses
Smith, John	1				4	5			
Smith, William [of] Carter's Run Negro Mille	1			1	2	3			
Thomson, Eli Negroes Aaron, Cis, Tiers, Jo, Ned	1		5	5	6	9			
Thomson, Jesse Negroes William, Sip	1		2	2	4	8			
Triplett, Francis Negroes Harry, John, Cate, Charles, Clo, James	1		5	6	7	9			
Triplett, William					3				

1782-005 Personal Property Tax List
page 7

Person's Names and all Names of Negroes	White Tithes Above 21	White Tithes Under 21	Negro Tithes	# Negroes	# Horses	Cattle	Wheels	Billiard Tables	Ordinary Licenses
Way, John	1				2	6			
Wood, Dickerson Negroes Alce, Jeremiah	1		1	2	4	5			
Wynne, John	1				2	2			
Withers, James Negroes Jobe, Winny, Hester, Sam, Joy, Danel, George	1		[obscured by flap]	7	4	3			
Weatherly, James	1				2	2			
Welch, William	1				1	1			
Lewis Woodyard	1				5	2			
Willson, Richard	1				1				
~~Weaver, Jacob Negᵃ Bett, Nann~~	~~1~~		~~0~~	~~0~~					
Whitley, William Negroes Jeffrey, Charles, Jean, Harry	1			4	3	2			

1782-005 PERSONAL PROPERTY TAX LIST
page 7 (Cont.)

Person's Names and all Names of Negroes	White Tithes Above 21	White Tithes Under 21	Negro Tithes	# Negroes	# Horses	Cattle	Wheels	Billiard Tables	Ordinary Licenses
Weaver, Jacob Negroes Peter, Nann, Robin, John, Henry, Ben, Jes, Hannah	1		2	8	6	5			
Left out by Mystak Crawley, Minoah Neg^r Tom	1		1	1	3	5			
Cammel, Anguish	1				1	2	ent^d		
Jett, James Negroes Bett, David, Tab, Lott	1		1	4	2	3			
Jett, William	1				1				
Neale, Benjamin					2	2			
Neale, Mathew	1				3	5			
Hall, Robert	1				2	3			
Bray, John	1				2	2			
Bragg, Dozzer Negroes Jane, Mimy	1		1	2	1	2			

Index "A" Tithables 1759-001 to 1778-002

Surname, Given Name	page(s)
ADAMS	
George	14
ADDAMS	
Jacob	4
ADDINGTON	
W^m	19
ADKINS	
James	34
ALEN	
John	12
Thos.	12
Ursla	12
ALEXANDER	
John's Estate	18
ALLEN	
Archd, Archibold	21, 26
James, Jeames	16, 18
John	3, 26
Jos.	16, 18
Roberts	22
Thomas, Thos.	8, 16
Ursla	16
William	15, 26
ALLIN	
Jas.	21
Wm.	21
AMBROSE	
Eliz.	15
AMISS	
Gabriel	15
ANDERSON	
Andrew	33
ARMSTRONG	
Andrew	33
James	13, 21
ARNOLD	
James	15
ASBURY	
Henry	26
William	26
William Jr.	21, 26
ASH	
Elizabeth	32
George	24
ASHBEE	
Benjamon	4
Jesse	4
Robert	4
Thomas	4
William	4

Surname, Given Name	page(s)
ASHBURY	
George	26
Henry	21
ASKINS	
John	19, 34
ATTWELL	
Francis, Fran^s	2, 14, 26
AULDIN	
John	19
BAKER	
Sam	19
BALEY	
Ja^s (Mary's son)	27
John Jr.	27
John Sr.	27
Joseph	27, 27
Moses	27
BALL	
Benjamin, Benjamine	23, 33, 34
David	23
Edward	3, 24, 34
James	33, 34
Jessey	34
William, Wm.	3, 32
William (Capt.)	23
BALLANCE	
John (Overseer)	17
BANESTER	
Willm	1, 5
BANSON	
Prue	15
BARBEE	
Joseph	22
BARBER	
John	12, 15
Thos	18
BARBEY, BARBY	
Andrew	21
Andrew Jr.	21, 33
BARKER	
John	27
William	25, 27
BARKLEY	
William	27
BARNIE	
John	12
BARNS	
John	1
BARRONS	
Daniel	27

Index "A" Tithables 1759-001 to 1778-002

Surname, Given Name	page(s)
BARRYMAN	
Max^m	16
BARTLETT	
John	27
Thomas	27
Thomas Jr.	27
William	27
BARTON	
Burr	4
David	27
James	27
Kimber	32
BASEY	
Richard	34
BASSHAM (a.k.a. JONES)	
Joseph	25
BASYE	
Josias	25
BATES	
Reubin	10, 19
BAYLEY	
Joseph	24
Mary	24
BEACH	
Peter	8, 12, 15
Thomas	8
BEARY	
Enock	4
BEECH	
Peter	2
BEGS	
William	29
BELL	
Franky (Mrs.)	26
BELT	
John	25
BENNET	
Thomas	13
W^m	19
BENNETT	
Daniel	23
BENSON	
Enoch	18
Prue	18
BEREDICT	
James	34
BERNARD	
William	23, 33
BERRY	
Henry	27
BERRYMAN	
Robt	16
BESHAW	
Peter	27
BETHEL	
George	10
John	8, 12, 15, 18
Valentine	8
Vollentyne	12
BETHELL	
John	3
BIRD	
Thomas	14
BIRDIT	
William	30
BLACKERBY	
Joseph	27
BLACKWELL	
Coll^o	12, 15
James	14
John	17
Jo^s	12, 15
Joseph	8
Joseph Jr.	27
BLAND	
Mary	27
BOATMAN	
Henry	1
BODEN	
James	27
John	27
BOGG	
James	14
BOGGESS	
Jeremiah	27
BOLLE	
Peter	15
BOSWELL	
George	14
William	14
BOWDIN	
John	1
BOWEN	
John	18
BOYD	
Samuel	32
Bradford	
Alexander	25, 34
Alex^r	12, 15
Benj^a	12
Ben	17, 18
Benjamin	1, 15
Danal	15
Danl	12, 18
Marcy	12

Index "A" Tithables 1759-001 to 1778-002

Surname, Given Name	page(s)	Surname, Given Name	page(s)
BRADFORD (Cont.)		BROWN (Cont.)	
Mary	15, 18	Dixon Jr.	24
William	1	George	8, 17
W^m	18	Jere	19
BRADLEY		John	3, 4, 12, 16, 20, 24
W^m	23	John ("Taylor's son")	19
BRAG		John Jr.	12, 15
Dozier	13	Jon^a	17
Joseph	13	Marmaduke	8, 17
Reubin	13	Swanson	12, 16, 17
Thomas	13	W^m	17
BRAGG		BROWNE	
Joseph	1	Bennet	14
Reuben	1	BROWNING	
William	1	Caleb	25
BRAHAN		BRUTON	
John	8, 17	Patrick	8
BRAMBLET		BRYAN	
Harry	16	Peter	27
BRAMLET		Richard	16
Henry	1	BUCKNER	
Hugh	34	Aylet	33
Reubin	34	Aylett (Capt.)	22
Reubin Jr.	34	BULLET	
William	1	Joseph	19
BRENT		BULLETT	
George	33	Benj.	3
William	14	Cuthbert	8
BRIDGES		Joseph	8
Thos	2	Sarah	8
BRIGGS		Thos	8
William	22	William	8
BRISONING		BUNBURY	
Jacob	24	Elizabeth	13
BROKE		BURCK	
Joseph	8	John	15
Thos	8	BURDETT	
BRONAUGH		Cliften	2
John	19	Humphrey (Overseer)	22
Saml	19	James	14
Thomas	13	John	8, 14
W^m	8	BURDITT	
BROOKE		Arjy	27
Humphrey	13, 26	John	27
W^m	8	BURGESS	
BROOKES		Dawson	22
Thos	15	Garner	21
BROOKS		BURK	
Tho.	19	John	17
Thos	12	BUTLER	
W^m	17	Benjamin	13
BROWN		Chas	19
Dixon	24	John	2, 8, 12, 15, 17

Index "A" Tithables 1759-001 to 1778-002

Surname, Given Name	page(s)	Surname, Given Name	page(s)
BUTLER (Cont.)		CHILTON	
John Jr.	17	John's Estate	27
Jo^s	18	CHRISTY	
Joshua	17	Charles	34
Saml	27	CHURCHHILL	
Spencer	19	John	14
William	1, 12, 15	CHURCHILL	
W^m	8, 17	Armistead	3, 8, 15
W^m Sr.	19	Henry	1
BYRN		John	1, 23
Mychael	27	CLARK	
CAMERON		Ben	27
Angus	14	Thos	27
CAMPBELL		CLAYTON	
Angus	25	John	10
Archibald	22	CLEVELAND	
Collin	27	Robert	22
CANNON		COCKERELL	
Henly	34	Anderson	27
W^m (overseer)	34	COCKRELL	
CANTFIELD		Anderson	24
John	20	COLEMAN	
CARR		Thos	19
John Jr.	2	COLLINS	
John Sr.	2	Edmond	27
CARRELL		COLVIN	
Elizth	27	Charles	10
William	27	John	3, 14
CARRILL		COMBS	
William	22	John	3, 27
CARTER		John Jr.	8
Charles (Corotoman)	13, 22	Robt	27
Coll^o (Tin Pot)	12	COMMENS	
Land Jr.	20	Daniel	28
Landon (Richmond Co.)	18	COMMINGS	
Peter	27	Simon	4
CARTOR		CONGROVE	
George (Stafford)	27	Moses	22
Joseph	27	W^m	31
CASTLE		CONNER	
Lawrence	14	Stephen	27
CATLETT		CONSTABEL	
John	8	William	32
John Jr. (Dettingen Parish)	5	CONWAY	
John Sr. (Dettingen Parish)	5	Geo.	8
CATTLETT		Peter	8, 17
John Jr.	8	Thos	8, 12, 15, 17
CHADDOX		Thos Jr.	8, 17
Charles	27	W^m	8, 16
CHAPMAN		COPPAGE	
George	22, 27	John	27
CHICHESTER		W^m	8
Richard	15		

Index "A" Tithables 1759-001 to 1778-002

Surname, Given Name	page(s)
COPPEDGE	
John	26
CORAM	
Champ	8, 13
Richard	8, 13
CORDELL	
George	22
CORDER	
James	24
John Jr.	1
William Jr.	24, 34
CORNWELL	
James	27
John	32
Simon	27
CORTNEY	
John	12
John (Levy Free)	15
John Jr.	12, 15
Leonard	19
William	12, 15, 31
COVENTON	
Richard	12, 16
COVINGTON	
Richard	8, 17
COX	
James	8
CRAFORD	
Reuben	8
CRAWFORD	
Willm (overseer)	13
CRAWLEY	
Menoah	21
CRESWELL	
George	34
CRIMM	
Chatharine	24
Harman	24
Jacob	24
John	24
Joseph	24
Pel.	24
CROCKET	
James	13, 33
John	33
CROCKETT	
James	23
Jno	23
CROSBY	
Geo., George	16, 8
John	16
Uriel	33
W^m	16

Surname, Given Name	page(s)
CROUCH	
Jacob	19
CRUMP	
Ben, Benj^a, Benj^m	17, 8, 12, 15
Geo., George	18, 2, 8, 12, 15
George Jr.	8
Travers	17
CULLINS	
Ja^s	1
CUMINGS	
Thomas	4
CUMMINGS	
Eeallakiar	4
John	8
Johnnathan	4
Mallakiar	4
Moses	8
Moses Jr.	8
CUMMINS	
Alex^r	20
John	20
CUNDIFF	
Isaac	27
CURTIS, CURTISS	
Nacy	12, 15
DARMONT	
Michael	4
DARNALL	
David	3, 34
Jeremiah	14
John	34
Joseph	14
Morgan Jr.	3
DAVICE	
Andrew	4
James	4
DAVIS	
Ely	28
Geo.	18
John	23, 28, 33
DAY	
Anny	23
Charles	20
Cossom	14
Francis	2
Harry	20
Jno	23
Robart	4
William	23
DEAN	
John	30
Richard	13

Index "A" Tithables 1759-001 to 1778-002

Surname, Given Name	page(s)	Surname, Given Name	page(s)
DEARING		**DULIN**	
John	22	Edward	34
William	22	W^m Jr.	33
DEBUTY		**DULING**	
John	12, 16	Phillip	33
DELANEY		William	1
Joseph	2, 2	**DUNCAN**	
DELANY		Cha., Charles	12, 16, 17
Charles	23	James	2, 14
DENNISON		John	19
Rich^d	32	John Jr.	5
DIXON		Joseph	2, 17
Edward (Capt.)	22	Rice	5
DODD		Robert	14
John	24, 34	**EALITT**	
Nathl [1st]	2, 2	Thomas	4
Simon	20	**EALLIT**	
DODSON		William	4
Elisha	11	**EARLAR**	
George	11, 11	Reubin	8
Greenham	18	**EDGE**	
DOGGET		John	2
Benj^a	14	**EDMONDS**	
Bushrod	14	Elias	3
George	14	Elias Jr.	28
Rich^d	14	William	13, 17
DOLMAN		William (Col^o)	26, 28
Roley	12, 15	W^m Jr.	17
DOLY [DOTY?]		**EDWARDS**	
Thomas	28	Gared, Garred, Gerrard	2, 12, 16, 19
DONALDSON		In.	22
William	23	James	19
DONIPHAN		John	12, 16
John	29	Jo^s	19
Joseph	24	Sam, Samuel	2, 23
DOUGHTY		Thomas	23, 28
Thomas	24	**ELIOTT**	
DOWNING		Rubin	28
W^m (Capt.)	28	**ELLIOT**	
DOWNMAN		John	24
Ra[leigh]	18	**ELLIOTT**	
DRUMMOND		Ben, Benjamin	21, 28
James	22	John	28
Norman	8	W^m	21, 28
DUFF		**ELLIS**	
James	19	John	8, 34
James (overseer)	13	John Jr.	8
Will	19	Jonathan	21
DULANEY		**EMBREY**	
Jo^s	12	John	12, 15
William	12	Robert	12, 15

Index "A" Tithables 1759-001 to 1778-002

Surname, Given Name	page(s)	Surname, Given Name	page(s)
EMBREY (Cont.)		**FINCH**	
Thos	12, 15	Adom	34
William	12, 15	**FISHBACK**	
EMBRY		Herman	19
Cha.	19	John	5, 14
Geo.	19	John	28, 28
John	8, 8, 19, 19	Josiah	28
Thos	1, 19	Phil	28
W^m	19	**FITZGARRELL**	
EMMONDS		John	28
Jo^s	18	William	28
EMMONS		**FITZHUGH**	
Jo^s	12	John	9
William	12, 15	Thomas	9
EMRY		**FLETCHER**	
John	1	Bart	24
Robt	1, 17	Benj^a, Benjamin	9, 22
Robt Jr.	17	James	13, 20, 24
William	1	John	20
ENNIS		Joshua (overseer)	20
John	17	Moses	1, 9
ETHERINGTON		Thos	9
Benj^a	14	William	2, 24
Elizabeth	14	W^m	9, 9
EUSTACE			
Isaac	17	**FLOWERS**	
John	17	William	1, 12, 15
Major	12, 15	W^m	19
W. (Col.)	17	**FLYNN**	
EVENS		John	28
Thomas	23	Michael	21
EVINS		Valentine	22
Thos	29	**FOLEY**	
FEAGEN		Bryan	28
Henry	28	Bryant	21
John	28	George	14
FEAGON		James	28
Edward	28, 28	James Jr.	22
John	28	Stephen	14
FEGAN		Thomas	21
Rolley	34	William	28
FELTINS		**FOLLOWAY**	
William	33	John	4
FEWELL		**FOOTE**	
Nathaniel	33	Betsey (Miss)	20
FIDLAR		Celia (Mrs.)	19
Thos	20	George	9
FIELD		Gilson	9
John	28	Jzt.	9
FIELDS		Richard	9
Edward	1	Richard Jr.	9, 20
		William	2

124

Index "A" Tithables 1759-001 to 1778-002

Surname, Given Name	page(s)
FOOTE (Cont.)	
W^m	9, 20
W^m Jr. ("infant")	9
FORD	
George	28
William	28
W^m	21, 28
W^m Jr.	21
FORTUNE	
Daniel	13
FOWKE	
Eliz. (Mrs.)	20
FOX	
Saml	15
FRAZER	
Danl	2
FRAZIER	
James	13
FRYER	
John	28
FUCKS [FOX?]	
Garret	12, 16
GALL	
Robert	21
GARLINGTON	
John	25
GARNER	
Charles, Chs.	13, 15
Thos Sr.	1
GARRARD	
Anthony	25
GASNEY	
James	27
GENT	
Timothy	22
GEORGE	
Gabriel	23, 28
Nicholas	9, 16
Parnach, Parnich, Pharnach	1, 14, 23, 28
GEST	
George	1, 28
GIBSON	
George	28
Jonathan	9, 16
Jon^a (Capt.)	20
GILLISON	
James	16
Mrs.	16
GLASCOCK	
Geo.	4, 28
John	4
Thomas	4, 28

Surname, Given Name	page(s)
GLOVER	
Benjamin	24
James	24
John	24
Richard	24
GOODWIN	
Abraham	21
GRANT	
Captain	12
James	24
Margaret (Mrs.)	16, 18
Peter	12, 28
William	2, 16
W^m	9, 19
GREEN	
Ann (Mrs.)	28
Henry	28
John	24
Richard	23, 28
Thomas, Thos	10, 19
Willis	28
W^m	10
GREENLEES	
Peter	33
GREGORY	
Ben	2
GRIFFIN	
Eli	2
GRIFFITH	
Even	28
GRIGBE	
John	4
GRIGSBY	
Saml	28
William	28
GRIMES	
William	23
GRINNAH [GRINNAN?]	
Thos	18
GROVES	
William	25
GRUBS	
Benaga	28
GUN	
John	8, 16
HACKLEY	
Lott	9, 12, 15, 18
HADDOX	
Ezekel, Ezekiel	22, 34
HALEY	
Honour	29

Index "A" Tithables 1759-001 to 1778-002

Surname, Given Name	page(s)
HALL	
Ben	18
Richard	14
Robt	29
HAMBLETON	
W^m	9
HAMBRICK	
Patrick	31
William	29
HAMILTON	
William	29, 29
HAMRICK	
John	25
Silas	33
HAMTON	
Edward	14
HARDEN	
Martin	12
HARDIN	
Henery	5
Martin	2
Martin (overseer)	20
HARREL	
John	9
Sam	18
HARRIL	
Moses	19
HARRILL	
Danl	18
HARRIS	
James	23
John	4, 22, 33
W^m (overseer)	32
HARRISON	
Benj^a	9, 20
Burr	24, 29
Jane	25
John Peyton	29
Thomas	5
Thos	9, 9
William	5
W^m	9
HARRISS	
James	29
Samuel	21
Thomas	24
HARWICH	
Aaron	9
HATHAWAY	
Ja^s	15
John	29
HAWKINS	
William	22
HAYCOCK	
Chas	24
HAZELDON	
John	31
HEALE	
George	33
William	23, 33
HEALEY	
John	23
HEALY	
John	32
HELLEN	
John	19
HELM	
L. (Capt.)	18
HEMMINGS	
William	25
HENARY	
George	12, 15
George	15
George Jr.	15
John	12, 15
John Jr.	15
HENDRING	
John	9
HENERY	
George	12
HENRY	
Fewell	20
Geo.	18
John	2, 18
Jo^s	20
HERNDON	
William	1
HERRIN	
George	1
HERRING	
George	15
W^m	15
HEWIT	
John	2
Hharris	
William	4
HICKERSON	
Nat, Nath. Nathaniel	2, 12, 15, 19
Thos	2
W^m	19
HIGGINS	
Alex^r	33
HILL	
Mary	24

Index "A" Tithables 1759-001 to 1778-002

Surname, Given Name	page(s)	Surname, Given Name	page(s)
HILL (Cont.)		HOWELL	
Rich^d	2	George	33
HINSON		HOWLE	
Robert	24	Thomas	9
HITT		HUBBARD	
John	24	Ephraim	29
Joseph	22	HUDNAL	
Lazarus	23, 34	James	14
Peter	22, 24, 32	Joseph (Gent.)	14
HODO		HUFFMAN	
Nat	16	Jo^s	19
Peter	16	HUGHLET	
HOGAIN		John	34
John	17	Leroy	34
W^m	17	W^m	34
HOGAN		HUGHLETT	
Chas	1	John	25
Danl	1	Leroy	25
Thos	9	HUME	
Thomas	29	Robert	25
HOLDEN		HUMPHRY	
John	18	William	3
HOLDER		HUMSTON	
Luke	14	Edward	17
HOLMES		Edward	9, 9
James	26	Edward Jr.	25
HOLTON		HUNTER	
William	29	James	19
HOLTZCLAW		Mr. (Great Marsh)	12, 16
Catherin	2	HUNTON	
Jacob	3, 3	Edwd	1
Joseph	2, 3, 25, 32	William	1, 23, 29
HOMES		JACKMAN	
Edmond	19	Joseph	34
HONESTT		Thomas Jr.	24
George	24	Thomas Sr.	34
HONTON [HUNTON?]		W^m	34
Joseph	18	JACKSON	
HOOE		George	33
Henry Dade	20	Joseph	33
W^m	18	JACOBS	
HOPER		George	12, 15
Joseph	15	Morris	12, 15, 18
Thos	15	Thos	18
HOPPER		JAMES	
Blagrove	9	Fran^s	14
Humphrey	24	John	1, 22, 29
John	24	John (Capt.)	16
Jo^s, Joseph	9, 12, 19	Jo^s	19
Thos	12	Thomas, Thos	12, 19, 22, 33
HORTON		JEAMES	
Edwin	9	Thos	15

Index "A" Tithables 1759-001 to 1778-002

Surname, Given Name	page(s)	Surname, Given Name	page(s)
JEFFERIES		KAMPER	
George	6	Harman	6, 6
Joseph	6	Henry	22
JEFFRES		Jacob	6, 23
Alexander	33	Jn°, John	6, 22
JEFFRIES		KEIRNS	
Alexander	22	William	6
Alexander Jr.	22	KEITH	
James	22	Alex^r	29
JEFFRIS		Isham	29
Henry	29	John	6, 29
Joseph	29	Mary Isham	6
Thomas	29	Thomas	29
JENNINGS		KELLY	
William	2	John	6, 20
JERMAN		Jo^s	20
Michal	34	KEMPER	
JETT		Henry	33
Francis	6	Jacob	33
James	6, 25	Jn° (son of John)	23
John	25	John	23, 33
William	25	Peter Jr.	34
W^m	25	Tilman	23
JEWEL		KENNARD	
Jn°	17	George	22, 27
JOHNSON		Joshua	22
Alexander, Alex^r	21, 29	KENNER	
George	29	George	2, 6, 9
Isaac (overseer)	23	George Tur.	16
Jeffery	6, 26, 34	Howsin	2, 9, 16
John	6, 6, 14, 29	Howson	6
Moses	29	Rodham (Rev^d)	16
William, W^m	12, 15, 18	KENTON	
W^m Jr.	18	William	29
JONES		KERN	
Brereton	9, 17	Robt (overseer)	18
Charles	1	KERNS	
Henry Jr.	24	Robt	29
James	4, 25	KERR	
John	12, 15, 17, 24	James	6
Matthew	8	John	16
Peter	29	KERRS	
Samuel (overseer)	28	John	6
William	4, 23, 25	KESTERSON	
Willm	3	William	6, 12, 15
W^m	17, 19	W^m	18
W^m Jr.	25	KIBBELL	
JONES (alias BASSHAM)		James	29
Joseph	34	John	29, 29

Index "A" Tithables 1759-001 to 1778-002

Surname, Given Name	page(s)	Surname, Given Name	page(s)
KIBBLE		LAURANCE	
John	6	Edward	6, 9
KIDWELL		Rich^d	9
John	29	LAURENCE	
William	29	Edward	22
KINCHELOE		LAWLER	
John	6	Nicholas	33
William	6	LAWRANCE	
KING		Edward	6
Isaac	34	Peter	6
Joshua	6	LAWRENCE	
John	2, 11, 12, 16, 18	Ed	19
KIRK		Rich^d	19
John (Constable)	6	LAWS	
Tho. Jr.	18, 19	John	6
Thomas, Thos	1, 9, 12, 15, 18	Thomas	29
William	26, 29	LAYTON	
KITSON		John	23, 27
William	23	Rich^d	23
KITTS		LEACH	
William	6	George	29
KNOWLES		George Jr.	14
William	2	George Sr.	6, 14
KNOX		James	29
John	12, 15	James Jr.	29
Robert	18	Thos	31
LAIN		Wills	31
Alex^r	30	LEACHMAN	
LAIS		John	6, 29
Richard	15	William	29
LAMBERT		LEAK	
William	6	Vincent	29
LAMKIN		William	29
George	6	LEAVILL	
James	29	Joseph	13
LAMTON		LEE	
Joshua	14	Richard Henry (Col°)	6
LANE		Joseph	6
William	21	Mary	6
LARGE		LEGG	
Joseph	9	Fortunatus	6
LARRANCE		LEONARD	
Jn°	25	Michael	29
LARRENCE		LEVILL	
Peter	25	Benjamin	29
LASSFIELD		LEWIS	
Moses	6	James	29
LATHAM		Zach., Zachariah, Zacharias	6, 14, 19
Anthony	6	LINDSEY	
George	33	W^m	24
LATHEY		LITTLEJOHN	
John	6	Charles	6

Index "A" Tithables 1759-001 to 1778-002

Surname, Given Name	page(s)	Surname, Given Name	page(s)
LONG		**MASSEY**	
John (overseer)	13	Thomas	25
LOVE		**MATHEW**	
Augustine (Prince William)	30	Ben	30
LUCAS		Joanna	30
Phil	17	Jonathan	30
LUTTERALL		**MATHEWS**	
Dan[l]	24	Ben	30
Samuel	24	Edward	30
LUTTRELL		Nathan	30
James	6	Tho[s]	12
John	6, 9	**MATHIS**	
Michael	6	Tho[s]	15
Richard, Rich[d]	6, 9	**MATTHEWS**	
Samuel	6	Robert	6
MACRAE		Thomas	6
Allan	6	William	30
MADCLAFE		**MATTOX**	
John	11	Lazarus	16
MADDEN		**MAUZEY**	
Sam[l]	24	Henry	13, 13
MADDUX		Eliza	10
Scoldfield	33	Elizabeth	6
Thomas	26	Henry	6
MARGRET		John	17
Hannah	33	**McABOY**	
MARKHAM		Murthy	30
John	6	**McANDREW**	
MARR		W[m]	17
Ann	6	**McBEE**	
John	25, 30	John	34
Michael	1	**McCABE**	
MARSH		James	22, 34
Jonathan	8	**McCAFFREY**	
MARSHALL		William	30
Elizabeth	6	**McCARTY**	
Hump[hrey]	21	Bryant	22
John (Captain)	21	**McCHONKIE**	
Thomas (Col[o])	22	Alex[r]	18
Thomas Jr.	22	**McCLANAHAM**	
William	6	Tho[s]	1
MARTIN		William	6
Benjamin	23, 33	**McCLAWLIN**	
Cha., Charles	6, 14, 17, 25	Patrick	2
Henry	6, 23, 33	**McCONWAY**	
John	6, 15	Robert	6
Joseph	6, 23, 33	**McCORMACK**	
Reubin	23, 33	John	33
Tilman, Tilmon	6, 14	Steven	1
MARTON		**McCORMICK**	
Charles	30	Fran[s]	17
MASON		Stephen	17
John	29		

Index "A" Tithables 1759-001 to 1778-002

Surname, Given Name	page(s)	Surname, Given Name	page(s)
McDANIEL		MOREHEAD	
James	6	Alexander, Alex^r	10, 19
William	6, 12	Charles	6
McDAN^L		Charles (Captain)	25, 30
John	20	John	2, 6, 10
Spencer	20	Joseph	3, 6
W^m	20	Presly	16
W^m Jr.	20	Samuel	10
McDANNAL		Turner, Turn^r	25, 30
William	16	William, Willm, Wm	2, 10, 30
McGREGOR		MOREY	
Markham	14	John	30
McKENZY		MORGAN	
James	6	Ben	1
McPHERSON		Charles	6, 10, 12, 16, 24
Richard	3	Charles Sr.	6
MEBE		James	2
John	12, 15	John	6, 6
MERCER		Joseph	10, 16
John Francis	30	Simon	6
James	11	William	6, 13, 32
METCALF		MORGEN	
John	30	Benj^a	30
MICHEL		Simon	30
John	33	MORLAND	
MIDLY		Jacob	16
John	16	MORRIS	
MILLARD		Steven	1
W^m	10	MORRISS	
MILLER		Joseph	4
John	22, 33	MUNDAY	
Simon	6	John	11
William	6, 33	Robert	11
W^m	22	W^m	11
MINTOR		MURDOCH	
John's Estate	30	Joseph	6
Joseph	30	MURPHEY	
MITCHELL		Isaac	5
Thos	1	John	30
MOFFETT		Miles	24
Henry	30	Richard	24
Jesse (son of Henry)	30	MURPHY	
John	33	John	22
MOIRA		MURROW	
Elizabeth's Estate	13	James	1
MONDAY		William	1
Daniel	30	MURRY	
John	30	James	6, 11
Robt	30	James Jr.	11
MONROE		Wm	11
John	32	MYNATT	
MOORE		Richard	10
William, W^m	8, 30		

Index "A" Tithables 1759-001 to 1778-002

Surname, Given Name	page(s)
MYNATT (Cont.)	
Richard (Const^a)	6
NALL	
William	30
NEALE	
Benjamin	21
Matt^w	21
NEAVILL	
James	24
Jo^s	24
NEGROES (Slaves)	
Aaron	2, 9, 16, 19, 25, 25, 26, 30, 31, 31, 34
Abigail	23
Abigal	21
Abraham	2, 13, 15, 23
Abram	9, 16, 26
Adam	10, 13, 14, 18, 20, 23, 25, 25, 27, 32, 33
Admiral	17
Aggy	17
Ajax	1
Alice	9, 13, 13, 18, 20
Allen	17
Ambrose	13, 18
Amey	23
Amia	30
Aminy	1
Amy	13, 16
Andrew	1, 13, 14, 30, 33
Angeler	25
Ann	30
Anthoney	26
Anthony	1, 3, 16, 26, 29
Anth^y	23
Ant^o	16
Antony	34
Arch	17
Arnold	18
Aron	32
Arrabella	13
Ayre	13
Bab	23
Baccus	30
Bachus	16
Backus	10
Banner	25
Barbadois	11
Barton	30
Bashey	19
Beauty	11
Beck	2, 2, 29, 31, 33
Belinda	13, 17, 17, 19

Surname, Given Name	page(s)
NEGROES (Slaves) (Cont.)	
Bellender	2
Ben	1, 1, 1, 2, 2, 8, 8, 9, 13, 13, 14, 14, 16, 16, 17, 19, 19, 21, 26, 27, 30, 31, 33, 34
Bess	1, 8, 8, 13, 14, 14, 16, 17, 19, 29, 31
Bet	28, 28, 28, 29, 31, 31, 31
Bett	8, 9, 9, 17, 17, 20, 22, 24, 25, 29, 32
Betty	2, 2, 3, 15, 19, 19, 19, 20, 22, 23, 24, 26, 33
Bibby	14, 23
Bill	27, 29
Blunder	10
Boatswain	1, 14
Bob	1, 8, 9, 10, 10, 10, 17, 17, 18, 18, 19, 19, 20, 23, 23, 24, 26, 27, 27, 29, 33
Bole	24
Bosen	27
Boson	8
Boston	34
Bowson	2
Braham	9
Bray	14
Brist.	2
Brister	1, 1, 3, 8
Bristol	13, 20, 30
Bristor	8, 9
Britain	14
Buck	29
Bumbry	34
Burgen	20
Bush	18
Caesar	8, 8, 9, 20, 22, 22, 22, 26
Cain	15
Caleb	21
Calup	34
Cambro	2
Cane	30
Caney	2
Captain	30, 30
Caroline	26, 34
Casor	30
Cate	1, 1, 8, 9, 9, 14, 14, 17, 18, 20, 20, 21, 22, 23, 23, 24, 25, 25, 25, 26, 26, 34, 34, 34
Cato	17, 17, 33
Ceasar	2, 3, 31

Index "A" Tithables 1759-001 to 1778-002

Surname, Given Name	page(s)
NEGROES (Slaves) (Cont.)	
Cesar	13
Champion	14
Charles	1, 1, 1, 1, 2, 5, 8, 9, 9, 9, 13, 14, 16, 16, 16, 17, 18, 18, 19, 26, 27, 29, 33, 34 34
Charlotte	31
Chas	17, 23, 24, 29
China	1, 14, 23
Chloe	22, 26
Clara	18
Cliffen	30
Cloe	18, 20, 29, 34
Coader	29
Coadyer	26
Colly	9
Coner	8
Cook	14
Cris	27
Crop	14
Cuffy	27
Cull	14
Cupid	11, 13, 13, 26, 30
Cuttena	1
Cutternarl [?]	33
Cyrus	10, 24
Dab^y	3
Daffney	14
Dameny	33
Dan	26
Daniel	4, 8, 8, 9, 13, 13, 14, 15 16, 23, 26, 27, 28, 29, 29, 29, 32, 33, 33
Danl	16, 18, 20, 24, 24, 25, 26
Dann	26
Daphne	10
Daphney	19, 26, 34
Darky	19
David	13, 13, 20, 23, 27, 30, 34
Davy	10, 10, 17, 19, 29, 31
Deallear	22
Delia	27
Denbo	26
Dennis	9
Dermont	14
Detter	9
Diana	1, 23
Dick	1, 1, 1, 2, 8, 8, 8, 9, 9, 9, 13, 13, 13, 13, 14, 14, 14, 15, 16, 17, 18, 21, 23, 23, 23, 24, 26, 27, 27, 29, 30, 31, 31, 31, 32, 32, 33, 34

Surname, Given Name	page(s)
NEGROES (Slaves) (Cont.)	
Dido	13
Dimbo	27, 29
Dinah	1, 1, 2, 5, 9, 19, 13, 13, 14, 14, 17, 18, 19, 20, 21, 26, 26
Dine	31
Diner	27, 31
Dixon	22
Doll	1, 13, 14, 14, 14, 17, 23
Domini	23
Dorcas	2, 9
Dublin	19, 25
Duke	15
Dunkan	8
Dye	10
Easter	13, 13, 18
Easther	24
Edinburg	13, 16
Edwards	32
Elger	31
Ellen	28
Ellis	24
Emanuel	8
Emanul	34
Essea	16
Essex	16
Ester	32
Esther	21, 22, 22, 24, 25, 25, 27, 33
Eugene	16
Eve	19
Ezekiel	17
Ezek^l	25
Fann	25
Fanny	28
Feby	27
Fielding	23, 33
Fill	30
Flora	3, 18
Flowra	2
Flowrey	31
Frank	1, 2, 2, 8, 9, 9, 9, 9, 13, 15, 16, 17, 18, 19, 21, 22, 23, 23, 23, 26, 26, 27, 27, 27, 30, 30, 31, 31, 31, 31, 31, 31, 31, 33
Franky	27
Fryday	10
Gabril	30
Garry	23
Geo.	21, 23, 23, 23, 23, 25, 25, 25, 31, 31, 31
George	1, 1, 1, 3, 8, 8, 8, 14, 14, 14, 16, 17, 17, 17, 18, 19, 20, 20, 27, 27, 28, 29, 30, 30, 30, 31, 32, 32

Index "A" Tithables 1759-001 to 1778-002

Surname, Given Name	page(s)	Surname, Given Name	page(s)
NEGROES (Slaves) (Cont.)		NEGROES (Slaves) (Cont.)	
Gib	31	Jack	1, 1, 1, 2, 4, 9, 9, 9, 9, 11, 13, 13, 14, 14, 14, 15, 15, 16, 18, 18, 19, 19, 21, 22, 22, 23, 23, 23, 23, 25, 25, 25, 26, 26, 26, 27, 28, 28, 28, 28, 28, 28, 31, 32, 34, 34
Glasgow	3, 23, 33		
Grace	1, 1, 8, 9, 13, 17, 17, 19, 20, 23, 23, 28, 30, 32, 33, 33		
Graham	8		
Gulley	32		
Gully	25	Jacob	5, 9, 9 14, 14, 14, 19, 20, 20, 22, 22, 26, 29, 30, 31
Gun	1		
Guy	1, 1, 14, 17, 23, 31	Jam	2
H[illegible]	11	James	1, 1, 1, 2, 2, 2, 3, 8, 8, 8, 9, 9, 9, 10, 10, 10, 13, 13, 13, 14, 14, 14, 14, 14, 14, 16, 16, 17, 17, 18, 18, 19, 20, 22, 22, 22, 23, 23, 24, 26, 26, 26, 27, 27, 27, 27, 28, 28, 28, 28, 31, 31, 32, 32, 32, 32, 33, 33, 34
Ha[n]cock	29		
Hack	1		
Hager	3, 27, 31, 31		
Hampshire	25		
Hampton	13		
Hanah	8, 20		
Han^h	23		
Hannah	1, 1, 1, 2, 2, 2, 2, 8, 9, 9, 9, 10, 10, 13, 13, 13, 13, 14, 14, 14, 15, 15, 16, 16, 17, 17, 18, 19, 19, 19, 20, 21, 21, 22, 22, 23, 25, 25, 26, 27, 28, 29, 31, 31, 31, 31, 31, 31, 33	Jane	8, 8, 8, 8, 9, 9, 10, 10, 15, 17, 17, 17, 17, 17, 18, 19, 20, 23, 23, 23, 26, 26, 26, 27, 28, 28, 29, 29, 29, 30
		Ja^s	18
		Jean	1, 14, 14, 31, 31, 32
		Jeany	14
Hannerboy	10	Jeff	24
Harculus	15	Jeffery	8, 13, 29
Harper	1	Jem	17, 18, 21
Harry	1, 1, 1, 2, 2, 3, 8, 8, 8, 9, 11, 14, 14, 15, 15, 16, 16, 17, 17, 17, 17, 18, 18, 19, 20, 20, 20, 22, 24, 24, 25, 27, 28, 29, 29, 30, 31, 31, 32, 32, 33, 34	Jemima	33
		Jemime	28
		Jemmimiah	26
		Jene	32
		Jeney	1
		Jennay	30
Harvey	14	Jenney	23, 30, 32, 33, 33, 33
Henly	32	Jenny	1, 1, 13, 15, 16, 16, 17, 20, 22, 22, 23, 25, 29
Henry	14, 14, 27, 28		
Hester	9, 9, 29, 31	Jeoffery	1, 17
Holland	16	Jere	16, 23, 23
Homaden	34	Jeremy	31
Hone	22	Jeries	31
Hotton	9	Jerimiah	21
Humphrey	1	Jess	25, 27
Humphry	3	Jesse	22, 30, 31
Iky	2	Jessey	23
Isaac	2, 9, 10, 16, 20, 31	Jinn	34
Isaacs	28	Jinny	13, 13
Isabell	25	Joab	22
Isable	29	Joan	1
Isbel	32	Job	2
Isham	20		
Ismer	29		

Index "A" Tithables 1759-001 to 1778-002

Surname, Given Name	**page(s)**	**Surname, Given Name**	**page(s)**
NEGROES (Slaves) (Cont.)		NEGROES (Slaves) (Cont.)	
Joe	1, 2, 4, 8, 9, 9, 9, 10, 16, 16, 16, 17, 18, 20, 20, 20, 22, 23, 23, 25, 25, 27, 27, 27, 28, 28, 28, 30, 31, 31, 33, 33, 34	Linney	33
		Linny	9, 17
		Lions	13
		Liz	30
		London	2, 3, 14, 25, 27, 28, 30
John	10, 27	Lot	32
Jonathan	9, 10, 16, 31, 31	Loudon	30
Jone	22, 26, 30, 33	Luce	2, 2, 2, 13, 13, 14, 21, 21, 24, 24, 26, 30, 33, 33
Joseph	23, 27, 34		
Joshua	14, 14, 25	Lucy	1, 8, 9, 9, 13, 16, 16, 16, 16, 17, 17, 18, 18, 19, 20, 22, 25, 27, 30, 31, 34, 34
Josuas	31		
Juba	21, 22, 25		
Juda	4	Luis	28, 31
Judah	4, 14, 14, 14, 15, 26, 26	Lundon	14, 33
Judas	32, 32	Lydia	17, 17, 18
Jude	1, 2, 2, 2, 8, 8, 8, 9, 9, 9, 9, 10, 10, 11, 11, 13, 13, 13, 13, 13, 18, 22, 23, 24, 25, 25, 26, 26, 28, 28, 28, 29, 30, 30, 33, 33	Lynna	23
		Mack	3
		Mahomet	20
		Mancelle	33
		Manuel	15, 16 28
Judey	24, 34	Margaret	22, 28
Judy	3, 3, 3, 3, 5, 10, 16, 16, 16, 16, 17, 18, 18, 18, 18, 18, 19, 19, 19, 19, 19, 20, 22, 22, 27, 28, 30, 30, 31, 34,	Margery	1, 23, 33
		Maria	9
		Mars	10, 19
		Martha	15
Julia	8, 30	Marthy	10
Juno	30	Martin	20
Jupiter	26, 29, 34	Mary	3, 15, 17, 17, 17, 17, 23, 26, 27, 30, 33
Kap	17		
Kate	1, 1, 1, 2, 2, 3, 16, 26, 28, 28, 29, 29, 30, 30, 32	Mathew	33
		Menava	24
Keg	26	Micajah	15
Kell	26	Michael	26
Kent	17	Michai	8
King	26	Millard	30
Kit	34	Mille	13
Kitcher	1	Milley	1, 1, 14, 18, 23, 25, 25, 28, 31
Kitt	18		
Kiza	25	Milly	9, 16, 16, 26, 28, 33, 34
Kiziah	25	Mimah	22, 24
Kooper	28	Mime	1
Laurence	20	Mimey	30
Leannah	13	Mimy	19
Let	28, 30	Mingo	17
Lett	2, 8, 9, 10, 14, 14, 14, 19, 19, 22, 29	Moccow	30
		Moco	19
Lette	15	Mohomet	26
Lettice	10, 13, 14, 33	Mol	34
Letty	16, 27	Moll	1, 1, 2, 8, 9, 10, 11, 15, 16, 17, 21, 22, 23, 24, 28, 29, 29, 29
Lewis	2, 9		
Lid	29		
Lida	30		

Index "A" Tithables 1759-001 to 1778-002

Surname, Given Name	page(s)	Surname, Given Name	page(s)
NEGROES (Slaves) (Cont.)		NEGROES (Slaves) (Cont.)	
Monday	25	Patience	9, 17, 25, 28, 32
Monica	28	Patt	18, 19, 20, 25
Monney	32	Patts	24
Moreah	14	Paul	32
Moriar	19	Peg	13, 15, 17, 18, 22, 23, 24
Morier	29		26, 26, 26, 28, 29, 29, 30, 31
Moroco	29	Pegg	1, 5, 11, 11, 14, 16, 17, 19, 20,
Moses	1, 9, 9, 16, 18, 19, 23, 26		25, 31, 31, 31
	26, 29, 31, 31, 32, 32, 33	Pegro	26
Mountain	31	Pender	17, 18, 20
Mureah	1	Persel	1
Mym	9	Peter	1, 2, 2, 4, 5, 9, 9, 11, 13, 13,
Mymey	27		14, 14, 14, 15, 15, 15, 17, 17,
Nacy	18		20, 22, 23, 23, 24, 25, 26, 26,
Nan	1, 1, 1, 1, 2, 2, 2, 3, 3, 8,		27, 27, 28, 29, 29, 30, 30, 33,
	9, 9, 9, 9, 10, 10, 13, 15,		33
	16, 17, 18, 19, 19, 19, 19,	Phebe	13
	20, 21, 21, 23, 23, 26, 26,	Phil	9, 15, 30
	26, 27, 27, 28, 28, 29, 29,	Philis	30, 31, 31
	29, 30, 31, 31, 32, 33, 33	Phill	2, 10, 15, 20, 26, 32
Nance	25	Phillip	14
Nancy	13, 23, 33	Phillis	1, 1, 1, 1, 1, 2, 5, 8, 8, 9, 10,
Nann	23		10, 10, 10, 13, 13, 14, 14, 14,
Nanna	22		16, 17, 18, 19, 19, 19, 20, 23,
Nanney	3		23, 24, 25, 25, 26, 30, 33, 34
Nat	33	Phillise	33
Nearoe	32	Pitt	18
Ned	2, 9, 10, 13, 14, 14, 15, 16	Plato	13, 16, 18, 18
	17, 17, 22, 25, 29, 31, 31,	Poll	8, 9, 19, 21
	32	Pomp	26
Nel	27, 32	Pompey	2, 9, 14, 17, 18, 19, 22
Nell	1, 1, 1, 4, 8, 8, 8, 10, 10,	Pompy	31
	10, 10, 13, 13, 15, 17, 19,	Prince	13, 15, 31, 33
	20, 22, 25, 26, 26, 28, 29,	Pris	23
	29, 31, 32, 33	Prisilla	14
Nelson	28	Priss	3, 9
Neptune	16	Prose	11
Nero	25, 34	Punch	1, 14, 23
Net	30	Quitus	16
Newman	17	Quiver	13
Neyls	9	Racheal	14
Nick	2, 17	Rachel	10, 17, 17, 18, 19, 20, 28, 30
Nim	33	Ralph	22, 29, 29, 34
Nott	15	Randolph	13
Nurrum	18	Ratliff	1
Obier	10	Richard	19
Old Hannah	22	Rich^d	18
Ore	32	Robert	19
Oxford	13	Robin	1, 3, 13, 13, 14, 16, 17, 17,
Pallas	13		19, 23, 24, 34
Parish	13	Robt	26, 30
Patiance	33	Roger	1, 1, 3, 8, 9, 9, 13, 18

Index "A" Tithables 1759-001 to 1778-002

Surname, Given Name	page(s)	Surname, Given Name	page(s)
NEGROES (Slaves) (Cont.)		NEGROES (Slaves) (Cont.)	
Role	8	Solomon	15, 15, 30
Roley	30	Spencer	31
Rose	1, 2, 10, 15, 17, 19, 19, 23, 24, 24, 25, 25, 28, 29, 30, 31, 34, 34	Stephen	18, 28
		Suanah	14
		Subinate	4
Ross	9, 13	Suck	14, 26, 30, 30, 34
Roz	34	Sue	8, 9, 13, 14, 17, 17, 19, 20, 20, 25, 26, 26, 27, 31, 31, 31, 33
Roze	34		
Sal	17, 17, 27, 33		
Sall	8, 8, 9, 22, 22, 23, 24, 24, 26, 29, 30	Suse	29
		Sylva	24, 29
Salley	32	Sylvia	19
Sam	8, 9, 9, 10, 14, 14, 15, 17, 17, 18, 19, 20, 20, 20, 22, 22, 22, 22, 24, 24, 26, 26, 28, 28, 29, 30, 31, 31, 34, 34	Sythe	18
		Tabb	32
		Tenar	19
		Thom	21, 23
		Thomas	15
Sambo	18, 23	Thompson	13
San	4	Thos	14
Sara	19, 19	Tim	17, 21, 22, 22
Sarah	1, 1, 1, 1, 1, 2, 3, 5, 8, 8, 8, 9, 9, 9, 10, 13, 13, 14, 14, 14, 14, 15, 16, 16, 17, 17, 17, 17, 17, 17, 18, 18, 19, 20, 20, 21, 23, 23, 23, 23, 24, 24, 24, 25, 25, 25, 25, 27, 27, 28, 28, 29, 29, 29, 29, 30, 30, 31, 31, 32, 33	Timby	13, 25, 28
		Timpy	30
		Tine	28
		Tiney	3
		Titas	1
		Titus	9, 13, 31
		Tobey	1
		Toby	8, 9, 10, 20, 26, 28, 29, 33
Sargo	16	Tom	1, 1, 1, 2, 3, 8, 8, 8, 9, 9, 10, 10, 13, 14, 14, 15, 15, 16, 17, 17, 17, 18, 19, 19, 20, 20, 20, 22, 22, 23, 23, 25, 27, 30, 31, 32, 33
Sauney	30		
Sauny	13		
Sawney	1, 1, 8, 15, 31		
Sawny	32		
Scipio	2, 3, 23, 25, 34	Tomboy	1
Seaser	33	Ton	31
Seasor	34	Toney	3, 9, 15, 25, 34
Sephina	11	Toney	8, 8, 10, 10, 13, 16, 18, 19, 19, 32
Sesor	27		
Sharper	8, 15	Troop	28
Shederach	15	Truelove	16, 20, 30
Siller	8	Ulises	14
Silvey	23	Ullises	1
Silvia	26	Ulyses	23
Sim	19, 22	Venus	14, 15, 16, 17, 22, 24
Simon	3, 14, 23	Vilet	30, 33
Sinah	9	Viner	28
Sinor	25	Violet	19
Sipio	30	Warner	1, 17
Sipoe	28	Whipster	18
Sis	31	Will	1, 2, 3, 3, 8, 8, 8, 8, 8, 10, 10, 13, 14, 14, 16, 16, 17, 17, 17, 18, 19, 19, 19, 20,
Siser	31		
Soloman	18, 30		

Index "A" Tithables 1759-001 to 1778-002

Surname, Given Name	page(s)
NEGROES (Slaves) (Cont.)	
Will	22, 22, 25, 25, 26, 27, 28, 28, 28, 29, 29, 30, 30, 30, 31, 31, 31, 33
Winifred	13
Winney	1, 1, 3, 3, 3, 8, 8, 10, 11, 14, 14, 14, 21, 23, 23, 23, 25, 26, 26, 27, 27, 28, 28, 29, 29, 30, 31, 31, 31, 31, 31, 32, 33, 33
Winnie	13, 13, 13
Winny	16, 18,m 18, 18, 20, 20
Yambo	26
Yambon	34
York	16, 19
Young Nan	23, 33
Zekiel	23
NELSON	
Jesse	18, 25
John	10, 10, 17
John Jr.	17
Thos	10
W^m	10
NEWGAN	
Thos	12, 16
NEWGENT	
Ann (Mrs.)	17
Edward	13
Thos	17
NEWHOUSE	
Jonathin	30
NEWLAND	
Samuel	8
NIGHT	
Jno	13
NORMAN	
Clement	10
Clement Jr.	3
Isaac	25
Jesse	22
Jno	25
William	3, 16, 25
NORMON	
Clement	25
NORRIS	
John	30
William	30
OBANION	
William	2
OBANNON	
Andrew	30
Benjamin	26
Bryan	30

Surname, Given Name	page(s)
OBANNON	
Bryant	26
John	30
Joseph	26, 30
Saml, Samuel	21, 30
Sarah	21, 26
William, W^m	26, 30
OBRION	
Charles	11
ODAM	
Geo.	23
ODER	
Joseph	2
ODOR	
Jos.	12, 16, 18
Jos. Jr.	19
OLDHAM	
James	25
Mary	25
OLIVER	
John	11
ONEAL	
C.	27
Edward	30
OOLE [?]	
Bethel	2
OREAR	
Ben	20, 30
OTTERBACK	
John	30
Owens	
Geo.	32
Jere	14
John	30, 30
William	30
OWINE	
John	30
P[illegible; on fold}	
James	3
PAGE	
Bettey	12, 15
Eliz.	2
PAINT	
John	23
PARENT	
Thos	31
PARKER	
Benj.	21
John	21
Thomas	21
PARMER	
James	2

Index "A" Tithables 1759-001 to 1778-002

Surname, Given Name	page(s)
PARRISH	
L.	8
PARTLOW	
David	12, 15, 17
PAYNE	
Francis	23
Reuben	24
Thomas	22
PENNY	
James (overseer)	23
PEPPER	
Saml Jr. (overseer)	21
Samuel	22
Samuel (overseer)	33
William	22
PERL	
Samuel	31
PETERS	
James	10, 19
John	10, 17
PETTY	
W^m	8
PEYTON	
Henry	31
PHARIS	
Samuel	23
PHILIPS	
Ezekiel	23
PHILLIPS	
Sam	17
PICKETT	
Elizabeth (Mrs.)	26, 34
Martin	31
Martin (Major)	26
William	34
William (Captain)	26
PINKARD	
Charles	34
PINKSTONE	
Henry	31
PINNEL	
John	20
PIPER	
Benjamin	24
PIRKINS	
John	31
POOLE	
W^m	19
POPE	
Thomas	13
PORTER	
Jno	26
Samuel	25
PORTER	
Thos	1, 14
PRICE	
Bennett	14
Thomas	18
PRICHETT	
Lewis	3
PRIEST	
Peter	31
Thomas	33
Thos	10
Thos Jr.	10
William, W^m	9, 31
PRIM	
William, W^m	9, 31
PRITCHARD	
Stephen	16
PULLEN	
Geo.	17
QUISENBURY	
John	19
RAILY	
Thomas	17
William	17
RAMEY	
Absolem	3, 3
RANDALL	
George	23
John	25
RANDOL	
John	31
RANES	
Cornelius	31
RANSDALL	
Chilton	26
Mary (Mrs.)	26
Wharton	26
RANSDELL	
Clifton	31
Edward	31
Mary (Mrs.)	31
Thos	31
Wharton	31
Wharton (Captain)	23, 31
Wharton Jr.	23
Whorten	31
W^m	23, 31
RECTOR	
Harman	2, 2
Henry	32
John	2
Nathanel	33

Index "A" Tithables 1759-001 to 1778-002

Surname, Given Name	page(s)	Surname, Given Name	page(s)
REDDINGS		**ROUT**	
William	32	John	4
REDMAN		**ROUTT**	
Pat	17	P[e]t[er]	2
REIDS		**RUSSEL**	
Samuel	15	George	1
RHUTHER		**RUST**	
George	31	Samuel	21, 31
RICE		**RYLE**	
William	4	John	13
RICTOR		**SANDERS**	
Daniel	22	James	22, 31
Frederick	22	Robert, Robt	22, 31
Henry	4	**SANFORD**	
Jacob	3, 4	William Pickett	31
John	3, 4	**SANGSTER**	
RILEY		Alex^r	2, 32
John Jr.	14, 14	**SAYOR**	
John Sr.	14, 14, 32	Thomas	4
RITCHIE		**SCAGGES**	
John	22	Isaac	10
RIXY		**SCAGGS**	
Richard	31	Thos	8
ROACH		**SCAGS**	
William	25, 31	Thos	2
ROBARDS		**SCOGGAN**	
William	4	W^m (overseer)	13
ROBERTS		**SCOTT**	
Benjamin Jr.	1	James	31
ROBERTSON		James (Rev^d)	31
John	3, 5	Robert	31
ROBINSON		**SEAFIELD**	
Benj^a	11	Moses	11
David	4	**SEATON**	
John Jr.	33	Geo.	16
William	25	James	2
William (King George)	13	**SELF**	
ROBISON		Francis	2
Ben	29	**SELVE**	
John	30	James	4
ROGERS		**SETTLE**	
Henry	25	Benj.	1
James	25	Francis (overseer)	13
John	19, 22	Gaydon	3
Stephen	22	Joel	25
ROSSER		John	4
Geo., George	26, 34	Joseph	3
John	26, 34	Joseph (overseer)	13
John Jr.	34	Mary	1
Richard	34	Merryman	1
ROUSAU		Newman	1
John	10	**SETTLES**	
William	10	George	13

Index "A" Tithables 1759-001 to 1778-002

Surname, Given Name	page(s)
SHACKLETT	
Hezekiah	21
SHARD	
James	31
SHARP	
John	14
SHAW	
Thomas	26, 31
SHEPARD	
John	18
Thomas	18
SHIP	
John	1
Name Not Given	33
SHUMATE	
Baly	17
Dan., Danl	2, 17
James	18
John	24
John (levy free)	17
John Jr.	10, 17
John Sr.	1
Spencer	17
Thos	17
W^m	17
SILVEY	
Abraham	33
SIMMONS	
Moses	10
SINCLAIR	
John	14
Ja^s	14
Robert	21
SIRES	
John	31
SKINKER	
John	16
Thos	12, 15
William	31
SLAVE (John Dearing's unnamed)	22
SMITH	
Alex^r	24
Charles	24, 34
John	10, 13, 22, 25, 29, 34
John (overseer)	13
John Jr. (son of Admoral)	32
John Nelson	17
Joseph	25, 34
Reubin	34
Roley	23
Scarlet	34
Spencer	24
Thomas, Thos	2, 10, 12, 15, 19, 34
SMITH	
William	13, 24, 33
William Jr.	22
William Sr.	33
W^m	18, 33
W^m (shoemaker)	18
SMOOTE	
John	24
John Sr.	24
SNALEN	
Benjamin	12
SNALLEN	
Benjamin	15
SNELLING	
Alex^r	2
Benj^a	2
Benjamin	10
SNYDER	
Henry	21
SOUTHARD	
Robt	2
SPARKS	
Isaac	2
SPENCE	
John	1
SPENNY	
James (overseer)	33
SPICER	
Randolph	14
SPILLER	
Jeremiah	10
Phil	17
SPRINGS	
Nic	17
STAMPS	
John	11
STANSGRAY	
W^m	33
STEPHENS	
Anne	31
STEWARD	
John	12, 16
William	31
STOKES	
William	4
STONE	
Benjamin (e)	22, 34
James	34
Spencer	34
Thomas Jr.	34
Thomas Sr.	25, 34
STRANGE	
William	31

Index "A" Tithables 1759-001 to 1778-002

Surname, Given Name	page(s)
STUARD	
William (Rev^d)	31
STUART	
John	10
John's Estate	19
William (the Revd Qtr.)	10
W^m (Rev^d)	19
STURDY	
W^m	17
SUDDITH	
James	24
Laurence	24
SULLIVAN	
Gab	18
George's Estate	31
SUTER	
George	26
SUTHARD	
Jno (overseer)	14
SUTTLE	
Francis	4
Francis Jr.	4
TALER	
Charles	4, 5
Charles (son of Charles)	5
William	4
TAYLOR	
Benjamin	7
Charles	7
Henry	7, 25
Joseph	25, 31
Judith	32
Nimrod	25, 32
Pater	7
Richard	7
TENNILL	
Francis	7
THOMAS	
Aaron	31
Ben	32
David	32
E. David	18
John	22
Not Given	4
William	24
THOMPSON	
Eli, Ely	25, 34
Jesse	22
John	21
Robert	22
THORNBERRY	
Saml	13
William	13
THORNHILL	
Bryan (overseer)	13
THORNSBURY	
Samuel	7
THORNTON	
Francis	7
Francis Jr.	7
William (Captain)	23
THRALKELD	
George	12, 15
THRELKELD	
George	10, 18
TIMBERLAKE	
Eppa	25
Epy	32
TIPPET	
W^m	10
TOLLE	
George	33
Roger	14
Roger Jr.	33
TOMLIN	
John	7
TOMS	
Thomas	7
TOWLES	
John	7
TULLES	
Rodham	15
TULLOS	
Joshua	10, 19
Rodham	7, 7, 12
TURNBULL	
Robert	23, 33
TURNER	
Alex^r	1
Edward	1, 1, 8
George	7
Henry	7
Henry's Estate	7, 10
James	1, 7
John	24, 34
William	1
TWENTYMAN	
John	3, 11, 12, 15, 20,
UNDERWOOD	
Thomas	34
William, W^m	7, 34
UTTERBACK	
Henry	2
Jacob	7
Jno, John	2, 13

Index "A" Tithables 1759-001 to 1778-002

Surname, Given Name	page(s)
VAN	
William	32
VANHUFFLEN	
Peter John	7
VANPELT	
Joseph	32
VILET	
Richard	33
WADDELL	
John	23, 32
WADDLE	
John	7
WAGENER	
Peter	16
Peter (Major)	10
WAITE	
William, W^m	7, 19
WAKE	
John	32
WALDEN	
George	22
WALKER	
Samuel	7
William	7
WALLACE	
Burr	4
WALLER	
Cha[rles]	16
Charles' Estate	7, 10
James	29
William, W^m	10
WASHINGTON	
Warner	7
Lau[rence]	20
WATCHWAY	
John	10
WATS	
Francis	32
Thomas	4, 32
Thos Jr.	10
WATTS	
Bennett	21
John	7
Thomas	7, 10, 21, 34
WEATHERLY	
James	23, 33
WEAVER	
Jacob	7
Tilman	7
WEEKS	
Alderson	20, 32
Ben	18

Surname, Given Name	page(s)
WELCH	
David	7
Silvester	32
William	25, 32
WELSH	
Alexander	33
WEST	
Charles	32
Edward	15
WEVELL	
James	34
WEVER	
Jacob	25
WHAELING	
Patrick	29
WHALING	
John	31
WHEATLEY	
Danl	17
John	7
W^m	21
WHEATLY	
George	7
Jos.	19
WHITE	
Benjamin	7
James	33
WHITING	
Francis	7
WHITLEDGE	
Thomas	10, 31
WHITTE	
James	4
WHITTON	
John	21
WICKLEF	
Charles	16
WIGGINTON	
Abr^a	19
WILBURN	
Edward	7, 7
WILLIAM	
Jos.	15
WILLIAMS	
George	7, 15
George (son of Thomas)	14
Jane	7
Jessie	7
John	14
John (son of Thomas)	21
Jonas	7
Joseph	7, 7, 12, 24
Nathaniel	7

Index "A" Tithables 1759-001 to 1778-002

Surname, Given Name	page(s)
WILLIAMS (Cont.)	
Paul	7
John Pope	7
Thomas	4, 7, 21
Thomas (Const^a)	7
William	14
WILLIAMSON	
Alexander	17
John	4
WILLIS	
W^m	19
WILLOWBY	
John	32
John Jr.	32
WILSON	
John	20
Jonathan	7
WINE	
John	24
WINN	
James	10
Ja^s (Captain)	32
John	7
Minor	10
Mynor's Estate	32
WITHERALL	
Francis	34
WITHERS	
Cain's Estate	7
Cane's Estate	13
James	7
James Jr.	13
James Sr.	13
Ja^s (son of James)	19
Jno	13
Thomas, Thos	2, 7
William	7, 13
William (overseer)	13
WMS	
James	9
WOOD	
Baley	10
Benjamin	7
Dickerson	21
Edward	7, 10
Elious	4
Geo.	21
Gidden	7
James	7, 10, 19
John	4, 9, 17
Jos. (Levy Free)	10
Joshua	7, 18
Joshuay	12, 15

Surname, Given Name	page(s)
WOOD (Cont.)	
Richard	16
Royly	4
Saml, Samuel	4, 7, 16, 24
WOODARD	
Charles	27
WOODSIDE	
John	2, 19
W^m	19
WOODSIDES	
Alexander, Alex^r	12, 15
John	7, 12, 15
WOODYARD	
Lewis	7, 21, 32, 32
Luke	32
WRIGHT	
Charles	7
Geo.	18
John	7, 7, 14
John Jr.	2
Sam	18
W^m	18
YATES	
William	32
YOUNG	
Bryan	32
Christian	7
James	7
John	32
Original	7, 11
Sonnett	7
William	32

Index "B" Slaves & Slaveholders 1759-001 to 1778-002 Tithable Lists

Surname, Given Name	page(s)	Surname, Given Name	page(s)
ADDINTON, William (2 negroes)		ATTWELL, Francis (Cont.)	
Aaron	19	Kiziah	25
Nan	19	Pegg	25
ALEXANDER, John's Estate (8 negroes)		Pompey	14
James	18, 18, 18,	Dick	26
Juno	18	Jack	26
Peg	18	Keg	26
Phillis	18	Peg	26
Stephen	18	BALEY, Joseph (1 negro)	
Tom	18	Daniel	27
ALLEN, James (2 negroes)		BALEY, Moses (3 negroes)	
Judy	18	Bob	27
Solomon	18	Sal	27
ALLEN, Joseph (2 negroes)		Sarah	27
Dinah	18	BALL, Edward (4 negroes)	
George	18	Charles, Chas	24, 34
ALLEN, Thomas (8 negroes)		Harry	3
Dick (2)	8	Robin	24, 34
Jack	18	Sam	24, 34
Jem	18	BALL, James (1 negro)	
Will (2)	8	Grace	33
Winney (2)	8	BALL, William (Captain) (4 negroes)	
ALLEN, Ursla (5 negroes)		Hannah	23
Danl	18	James	23
Harry	18	Mary	23
Lucy	18	Nancy	23
Lydia	18	BARBEE, Joseph (1 negro)	
Nan	18	Cate	22
AMBROSE, Eliz. (4 negroes)		BARBEY, Andrew (5 negroes)	
Harry	2	Dick	21
London	2	Hannah	21
Luce	2	Jack	21
Scipio	2	Nan	21
ASBURY, William (2 negroes)		Sarah	21
King	26	BARKER, John (2 negroes)	
Phillis	26	John	27
ASBURY, William Jr. (3 negroes)		Winey	27
Jack	26	BARKER, Willam (1 negro)	
Kell	26	Adam	25, 27
Robt	26	BARKLEY, William (3 negroes)	
ASH, George (1 negro)		Bill	27
Ellis ("omitted")	24	Hager	27
ASHBY, Robt (4 negroes)		London	27
Anthoney	26	BARNARD'S Quarter, P. (1 negro)	
Jane	26	James	3
Kate	26	BARNS, John (8 negroes)	
Silvia	26	Bob	1
ATTWELL, Francis (11 negroes)		Dinah	1
Cate	14	Gun	1
Jack	25	Humphrey	1
James	14	Jenny	1
Jeany	14	Moll	1

Index "B" Slaves & Slaveholders 1759-001 to 1778-002 Tithable Lists

Surname, Given Name	page(s)	Surname, Given Name	page(s)
BARNS, John (cont.)		BLACKWELL, John (9 negroes)	
Nan	1	Dick	17
Phillis	1	Grace	17
BARTLETT, Thomas Jr. (7 negroes)		Harry	17
Dick	27	James	17
Feby	27	Lucy	17
Franky	27	Lydia	17
Hannah	27	Mary	17
Jack	27	Sarah	17
Joe	27	Sue	17
Judy	27	BLACKWELL, Joseph (9 negroes)	
BARTLETT, William (1 negro)		Bett	8
Dimbo	27	Brister	8
BAYLEY, Mary (4 negroes)		Grace	8
Bole	24	Jack	8
Dan[1]	24	Jane	8
Sall	24	Jeffrey	8
Sarah	24	Siller	8
BELL, Frankey (Mrs.) (2 negroes)		Sue	8
Dinah	26	Toby	8
Peter	26	BLACKWELL, Joseph Jr. (2 negroes)	
BENSON, Prue (4 negroes)		James	27
Bob	18	Mymey	27
Cate	18	BLAND, Mary (1 negro)	
Nurrum	18	Will	27
Winny	18	BOATMAN, Henry (1 negro)	
BERNARD, William (8 negroes)		Charles	1
Daniel	23, 33	BOGGESS, Jeremiah (1 negro)	
Frank	23, 33	Nan	27
Glasgow	23, 33	BOSWELL, George (10 negroes)	
Grace	23, 33	Cate	14
Lynna/Lynney	23, 33	Champion	14
Nan	23, 33	Jacob (2)	14, 14
Peter	23, 33	James (2)	14, 14
Sall/Sal	23, 33	Lett	14
BERRY, Henry (2 negroes)		Milley	14
Ben	27	Simon	14
George	27	Winney	14
BERRYMAN, Robert (5 negroes)		BOSWELL, William (3 negroes)	
Aaron	16	Ben	14
Amy	16	Daniel	14
Jenny	16	Doll	14
Judy	16	BRADFORD, Alexander (6 negroes)	
Quitus	16	Cate	25, 34
BESHAW, Peter (1 negro)		Joe	25, 34
Peter	27	Milley/Milly	25, 34
BLACKERBY, Joseph (3 negroes)		Rose	25, 34
George	27	Toney	25, 34
Tom	27	BRADFORD, Ben (2 negroes)	
Winney	27	Cate	17
BLACKWELL, James (2 negro)		Jeoffery	17
Winney	14		

Index "B" Slaves & Slaveholders 1759-001 to 1778-002 Tithable Lists

Surname, Given Name	page(s)
BRADFORD, Daniel (2 negroes)	
Dick	18
Sythe	18
BRADFORD, William (1 negro)	
Nan	1
BRAHAN, John (3 negroes)	
Harry	8
Sarah	17
Tom	8, 17
BRENT'S QUARTER (4 negroes)	
Jean	14
Joshua	14
Lett	14
Suannah	14
BRENT, George (1 negro)	
Mary	33
BRIGGS, William (2 negroes)	
Bob	22
Harry	22
BRONAUGH, John (2 negroes)	
Bob	19
Sam	19
BRONAUGH, Sam¹ (6 negroes)	
Ben (2)	19, 19
Eve	19
Hannah	19
Pegg	19
Rachel	19
BRONAUGH, Thomas (4 negroes)	
Ben	13
Daniel	13
Luce	13
Ross	13
BRONAUGH, Wᵐ (4 negroes)	
Bess	8
Boson	8
Caesar	8
Coner	8
BROOKE, Humphrey (11 negroes)	
Arrabella	13
Cupid	13, 26
Daniel	26
Dann	26
Dinah	13, 26
Hannah	13, 26
Milly	26
Oxford	13
Peter	13, 26
Phill	26
Toby	26
BROWN, Dixon Jr. (1 negro)	
Luce	24

Surname, Given Name	page(s)
BROWN, George (2 negroes)	
Nell	8
Newman	17
BUCKNER, Aylet (12 negroes)	
Beck	33
Bob	33
Charles	33
Cuttenarl [?]	33
Milly	33
Patiance	33
Phillis	33
Sarah	33
Seaser	33
Toby	33
Vilet	33
BULLET, Jos. (4 negroes)	
Bess	19
Davy	19
Phillis	19
Will	19
BULLETT, Benj. (3 negroes)	
Hager	3
London	3
Roger	3
BULLETT, Cuthbert (6 negroes)	
Caesar	8
Dunkan	8
Graham	8
Julia	8
Poll	8
Sarah	8
BULLETT, Joseph (3 negroes)	
Bess	8
Jane	8
Phillis	8
BULLETT, Sarah (3 negroes)	
Roger	8
Sarah	8
Will	8
BULLETT, Thoˢ (6 negroes)	
Bristor	8
Cate	8
Harry	8
James	8
Jude	8
Will	8
BUNBURY, Elizabeth (4 negroes)	
David	13
Harry	13
Titus	13
Winnie	13

Index "B" Slaves & Slaveholders 1759-001 to 1778-002 Tithable Lists

Surname, Given Name	page(s)
BURGESS, Garner (3 negroes)	
Dinah	21
Luce (2)	21, 21
BUTLER, Benjamin (1 negro)	
Peg	13
BUTLER, John (2 negroes)	
Admiral	17
Ned	17
BUTLER, W^m (2 negroes)	
Nell	17
Peg	17
CAMPBELL, Collin (4 negroes)	
Charles	27
Esther	27
Henry	27
James	27
CARR, John Sr. (1 negro)	
Nan	2
CARRILL, William (1 negro)	
Jone	22
CARTER, Charles (Corotoman) (25 negroes)	
Adam	13
Alice	13
Ambrose	13
Ben	13
Bess	13
Cesar	13
Charles	13
Daniel	13
Dido	13
Doll	13
Easter	13
Frank	13
Hampton	13
Hannah	13
Jenny	13
Lucy	13
Margaret	22
Nell	13
Pallas	13
Ralph	22
Randolph	13
Robin	13
Sam	22
Tom	13
Will	13
Winnie	13
CARTER, Landon (Richmond Co.) (4 negroes)	
Bush	18
Kitt	18
Sam	18
Will	18

Surname, Given Name	page(s)
CARTER, Landon Jr. (23 negroes)	
Bett	20
Betty	20
Cate	20
Cloe	20
George	20
Hanah	20
Harry (3)	20, 20, 20
Isham	20
Jacob	20
Jenny	20
Joe	20
Judy	20
Martin	20
Nan	20
Sam (2)	20, 20
Tom	20
Truelove	20
Will	20
Winny	20
CARTER, Peter (2 negroes)	
Bob	27
Harry	27
CARTOR, George (Stafford) (3 negroes)	
Dick	27
Diner	27
Sesor	27
CHADDOX, Charles (1 negro)	
Will	27
CHAPMAN, George (8 negroes)	
Deallear/Delia	22, 27
Frank	22, 27
James	22, 27
Jesse	22
Joe	27
Nan/Nanna	22, 27
Nel/Nell	22, 27
Peter	22, 27
CHICHESTER, Richard (28 negroes)	
Abraham	15
Betty	15
Cain	15
Daniel	15
Duke	15
Frank	15
Hannah (3)	15, 15, 15
Harculus	15
Harry	15
Jack	15
Jane	15
Judah	15
Martha	15
Mary	15

Index "B" Slaves & Slaveholders 1759-001 to 1778-002 Tithable Lists

Surname, Given Name	page(s)	Surname, Given Name	page(s)
CHICHESTER, Richard (cont.)		CHURCHILL'S QUARTER (Cont.)	
Nan	15	Jenny	1
Ned	15	Jeoffery	1
Peg	15	Joan	1
Peter (3)	15, 15, 15	Kate	1
Phil	15	Lucy	1
Prince	15	Margery	1
Shederach	15	Moll	1
Solomon (2)	15, 15	Moses	1
Tom	15	Nanny	1
CHILTON, John's Estate (4 negroes)		Nell (2)	1, 1
Jess	27	Persel	1
Joe	27	Peter	1
Letty	27	Phillis (2)	1, 1
Luce	27	Punch	1
CHURCHHILL, John (19 negroes)		Ratliff	1
Andrew	14	Robin	1
Bibby	14	Sarah (2)	1, 1
Boatswain	14	Sawney (2)	1, 1
China	14	Tom	1
Dinah	14	Ullises	1
Doll	14	Warner	1
George	14	Will	1
Guy	14	CHURCHILL, Armstead (22 negroes)	
Hannah	14	Dick	8, 15
Harry	14	Emanuel	8
Harvey	14	Jack	8, 15
Jacob	14	Jane	8
James	14	Jenny	15
Ned	14	Lett/Lette	8, 15
Phillis	14	Manuel	15
Prisilla	14	Michai	8
Punch	14	Moll	8, 15
Sarah	14	Nell	8, 15
Ulises	14	Nell	8
CHURCHILL'S QUARTER (45 negroes)		Nott	15
Ajax	1	Phill	15
Andrew	1	Phillis	8
Bess	1	Role	8
Boatswain	1	Rose	15
Brister	1	Sawney	8, 15
Cate (2)	1, 1	Sharper	8, 15
Charles	1	Tom (2)	8, 15
China	1	Toney/Tony	8, 15
Cuttena	1	Venus	15
Diana	1	CHURCHILL, John (Mr.) (26 negroes)	
Dick	1	Andrew	23
Doll	1	Anth^y	23
George	1	Betty	23
Guy (2)	1	Bibby	23
Hannah	1	Bob	23
Harper	1	Chas	23
Jack	1	China	23

Index "B" Slaves & Slaveholders 1759-001 to 1778-002 Tithable Lists

Surname, Given Name	page(s)
CHURCHILL, John (Mr.) (cont.)	
Diana	23
Doll	23
Frank	23
Garry	23
Geo.	23
Guy	23
Han[h]	23
Jack (2)	23, 23
James	23
Jenny	23
Jude	23
Nanny	23
Peter	23
Phillis	23
Punch	23
Sarah	23
Thom	23
Ulyses	23
CLEVELAND, Robert (2 negroes)	
Chloe	22
Jack	22
COLLINS, Edmond (1 negro)	
Frank	27
COMBS, John (6 negroes)	
Cuffy	27
David	27
George	3
Judy	3
Sarah	27
Winney	3
COMBS, John Jr. (1 negro)	
George	8
COMBS, Robert (1 negro)	
Bosen	27
CONWAY, Tho[s] (12 negroes)	
Davy	17
George	8
George (2)	17
Hannah	17
James	8, 17
Jane	8, 17
Jude/Judy	8, 17
Lucy	8
Lydia	17
Patience	17
Sarah	8, 17
Warner	17
CONWAY, W[m] (5 negroes)	
Frank	8, 16
George	8, 16
Joe	8, 16
Moll	16

Surname, Given Name	page(s)
CONWAY, W[m] (cont.)	
Will	8, 16
COPPAGE/COPPEDGE, John (6 negroes)	
Cris	27
Frank	26, 27
James	26, 27
Jane	27
Jone	26
Sue	26, 27
COPPAGE, W[m] (1 negro)	
Daniel	8
CORDELL, George (1 negro)	
Sam	22
CORNWELL, James (1 negro)	
Mary	27
COVINGTON, Richard (1 negro)	
Ben	17
CRAWLEY, Menoah (1 negro)	
Thom	21
CRIMM, Chatharine (1 negro)	
Easther	24
CRIMM, Harman (2 negroes)	
Cyrus	24
Menava	24
CROCKET, James (2 negroes)	
Jenney	33
Jane	23
CROSBY, George (6 negroes)	
Ben	16
Daniel	8, 16
Harry	16
James	8
Jere	16
Jude	8
CRUMP, Ben./Benj[a] (6 negroes)	
Bob	8, 17
Hannah	8
Harry	8, 17
Jane	17
Nan	8, 17
Sam	17
CRUMP, Geo./George (8 negroes)	
Bellender	2
Ben	2, 8
Hanah	8
Hannah	2, 18
Ja[s]	18
Sall (2)	8, 8
Sarah	18
Tony	8, 18
CULLINS, Ja[s] (1 negro)	
Sarah	1

Index "B" Slaves & Slaveholders 1759-001 to 1778-002 Tithable Lists

Surname, Given Name	page(s)
DARNALL, David (1 negro)	
Ceasar/Seasor	3, 34
DARNALL, Jeremiah (4 negroes)	
Jack	14
Judah	14
Peter	14
Robin	14
DEARING, John (1 negro)	
"his man" (name not given)	22
DELANEY, Joseph (3 negroes)	
Dinah	2
Nan	2
Tom	2
DIXON, Edward (Captain) (18 negroes)	
Betty	22
Caesar	22
Hannah	22
Jenny	22
Joab	22
Judy (2)	22, 22
Lucy	22
Mimah	22
Moll	22
Peg	22
Sall (2)	22, 22
Tim (2)	22, 22
Tom (2)	22, 22
Will	22
DODD, Nathl (2 negroes)	
Bowson	2
Kate	2
DODSON, Greenham (1 negro)	
Adam	18
DOGGETT, Bushrod (6 negroes)	
Dick	14
George	14
Lettice	14
Moreah	14
Phillis	14
Tom	14
DOLY [DOTY?], Thomas (1 negro)	
Nan	28
DOWNING, W^m (Captain) (15 negroes)	
Bet	28
Ellen	28
Grace	28
Isaacs	28
Joe	28
Judy	28
Let	28
Manuel	28
Milley	28
Nelson	28

Surname, Given Name	page(s)
DOWNING, W^m (Captain) (cont.)	
Patience	28
Peter	28
Rachel	28
Sam	28
Will	28
DOWNMAN, Rawleigh (8 negroes)	
Alice	18
Milley	18
Nacy	18
Patt	18
Plato (2)	18, 18
Roger	18
Winny	18
DULIN, W^m Jr. (1 negro)	
Jude	33
DULING, William (1 negro)	
Phillis	1
DUNCAN, James (5 negroes)	
Britain	14
Doll	14
Hannah	2
Sam	14
Will	2, 14
DUNCAN, John (3 negroes)	
Patt	19
Tony	19
Will	19
DUNCAN, Robert (3 negroes)	
Joshua	14
Sam	14
Venus	14
EDMONDS, Elias (4 negroes)	
Humphry	3
Nan	3
Simon	3
Tiney [Toney?]	3
EDMONDS, Elias Jr. (6 negroes)	
Jack (2)	28, 28
Jude	28
Margaret	28
Stephen	28
Tine	28
EDMONDS, William (7 negroes)	
Abraham	13
Belinda	13
Grace	13
James	13
Jude (2)	13, 13
Tony	13

Index "B" Slaves & Slaveholders 1759-001 to 1778-002 Tithable Lists

Surname, Given Name	page(s)	Surname, Given Name	page(s)
EDMONDS, William (Col.) (10 negroes)		FEAGON, Edward (cont.)	
Abram	26	Kate	28
Cate/Kate	26, 28	Sarah	28
Daniel	26, 28	Will	28
James	26, 28	FIELD, John (1 negro)	
Jude (2)	26, 28	Jemime	28
Mary	26	FISHBACK, John (2 negroes)	
Moll	28	James	28
Viner	28	London	28
EDMONDS, W^m (1 negro)		FISHBACK, Josiah (3 negroes)	
Joe	17	Joe	28
EDWARDS, Thomas (1 negro)		Monica	28
Joe	23, 28	Nan	28
ELLIOTT, Rubin (2 negroes)		FITZHUGH'S QUARTER (5 negroes)	
Bet	28	Ben	9
Troop	28	Maria	9
ELIOT, John (1 negro)		Nan	9
Peter	24	Poll	9
ELLIOTT, W^m (3 negroes)		Titus	9
James	28	FOLEY, James (3 negroes)	
Jem	21	Fanny	28
Poll	21	Hannah	28
ELLIS, John (1 negro)		Luis	28
Charles	8	FOLEY, Thomas (1 negro)	
ELLIS, John Jr. (1 negro)		Moll	21
Ben	8	FOOTE, W^m (6 negroes)	
EMMONDS, Joseph (2 negroes)		Frank	9
Ambrose	18	Hester	9
Arnold	18	Lewis	9
ETHERINGTON, Elizabeth (8 negroes)		Milly	9
Bess	14	Peter	9
Henry (2)	14, 14	Ross	9
Jean	14	FOOTE, Betsy (Miss) (4 negroes)	
London	14	Bristol	20
Luce	14	James	20
Sarah	14	Joe	20
Thos	14	Lucy	20
EUSTACE, W[illiam] (Col.) (12 negroes)		FOOTE, Celia (Mrs.) (6 negroes)	
Aggy	17	Bashey	19
Cato	17	Bob	19
Ezekiel	17	Charles	19
Harry	17	Judy	19
Jane	17	Lett	19
Kent	17	Poll	19
Mary	17	FOOTE, George (3 negroes)	
Moll	17	Priss	9
Ned	17	Roger	9
Robin	17	Tom	9
Rose	17	FOOTE, Gilson (6 negroes)	
Tom	17	Jack	9
FEAGON, Edward (5 negroes)		Joe	9
George	28	Lucy	9
Harry	28	Sall	9

Index "B" Slaves & Slaveholders 1759-001 to 1778-002 Tithable Lists

Surname, Given Name	page(s)	Surname, Given Name	page(s)
FOOTE, Gilson (cont.)		GIBSON, Jonathan (cont.)	
Sam	9	Joe	9, 16
Sue	9	Jude/Judy	9, 16
FOOTE, Richard Jr. (3 negroes)		Kate	16
Bob	20	Lucy	9, 16
Patt	20	Sargo	16
Pender	20	Venus	16
FOOTE, William/ W^m (11 negroes)		GILLISON, James (7 negroes)	
Aaron	2	Bess	16
Adam	20	Frank	16
Brist.	2	Jenny	16
Dick	2	Robin	16
Joe	2	Will	16
Lewis	2	GILLISON, Mrs. (5 negroes)	
Moll	2	Ben	16
Ned	2	Milly	16
Peter	2	Nanny	16
Rose	2	Plato	16
Sarah	20	York	16
FOWKE, Eliz. (Mrs.) (7 negroes)		GLASCOCK, George (2 negroes)	
Burgen	20	Bet	28
Cate	20	Jack	28
Grace	20	GRANT, Margaret (4 negroes)	
Mahomet	20	Bob	18
Sue	20	Cloe	18
Toby	20	Jack	18
Tom	20	Judy	18
FOX, Samuel (2 negroes)		GRANT, Peter (4 negroes)	
Harry	15	Hannah	28
Sam	15	Jack	28
GARLINGTON, John (1 negro)		Peg	28
Sinor	25	Will	28
GARNER, Thos Sr. (1 negro)		GRANT, William/ W^m (18 negroes)	
George	1	Bet (2)	9
GEORGE, Nicholas (6 slaves)		Betty	2
Dick	9, 16	Betty (2)	9, 19
Hannah	9, 16	Braham	9
Holland	16	Colly	9
Hotton	9	Darky	19
Judy	16	Dorcas	2, 9
Lucy	16	Frank	2, 9, 19
GEORGE, Parnach/Parnich (4 negroes)		Grace	2, 9, 19
Jack	23, 28	Hannah	19
Rose	23, 28	Harry	2
Scipio/Sipoe	23, 28	Jack	2, 9, 19
Winney	23, 28	Lett	19
GIBSON, Jonathan (13 negroes)		Nan	2, 9
Bob		Pompey	2, 9 19
Charles (2)	9, 16	Sylvia	19
Dennis	9	GREEN, Ann (Mrs.) (5 negroes)	
Dick	9	Jack	28
Eugene	16	Jane	28
Harry	9, 16	Milly	28

Index "B" Slaves & Slaveholders 1759-001 to 1778-002 Tithable Lists

Surname, Given Name	page(s)
GREEN, Ann (Mrs.) (cont.)	
Sam	28
Toby	28
GREEN, Richard (3 negroes)	
David	23
Jane	23
Sall	23
GREENLEES, Peter (1 negro)	
Jone	33
GRIGSBY, Sam[1] (5 negroes)	
Jack	28
James	28
Jane	28
Kooper	28
Winney	28
GRIGSBY, William (6 negroes)	
Harry/Henry	25, 28
Jude	25
Nell	25, 28
Sarah	25, 28
Sue	25
Timby	25, 28
HACKLEY, Lott (4 negroes)	
Dinah	9, 18
Jude	9, 18
Judy	18
Pender	18
HAMBLETON/HAMILTON, William/W^m (4 negroes)	
Jane	9, 29
Nan	9
Davy	29
Sall	29
HAMTON, Edward (9 negroes)	
Charles	14
Dermont	14
Dick	14
Jack	14
James	14
Lett	14
Lundon	14
Ned	14
Peter	14
HARDIN, Martin (5 negroes)	
Betty	2
Cambro	2
Ceasar	2
Kate	2
Phillis	2

Surname, Given Name	page(s)
HARRISON, Benj[a] (7 negroes)	
Caesar	20
Jacob	20
Pegg	20
Peter	20
Phillis	20
Sam	20
Sarah	20
HARRISON, Burr (9 negroes)	
Bet	24, 29
Cha[s]	29
Daniel	24, 29
Ha[n]cock	29
Harry	24, 29
Jeff/ Jeffry	24, 29
Moll	24, 29
Rose	24, 29
Sylva	24, 29
HARRISON, Jane (8 negroes)	
Angeler	25
Cate (2)	25, 25
Dublin	25
Milley	25
Patt	25
Roger	25
Winney	25
HARRISON, John Peyton (4 negroes)	
Buck	29
Dick	29
Jane	29
Lid	29
HARRISON, Thomas (8 negroes)	
Charles	5
Daniel	5
Dinah	5
Jacob	5
Judy	5
Pegg	5
Peter	5
Phillis	5
Sarah	5
HARRISON, Thomas (Dettingen Parish) (11 negroes)	
Alice	9
Caesar	9
Charles	9
Daniel	9
Frank	9
Jacob	9
Jude	9
Peter	9
Phillis	9
Sarah	9
Sinah	9

Index "B" Slaves & Slaveholders 1759-001 to 1778-002 Tithable Lists

Surname, Given Name	page(s)	Surname, Given Name	page(s)
HARRISON, Thomas (Hamilton Parish) (6 negroes)		HITT, John (1 negro)	
Cate	9	Sarah	24
Hester	9	HITT, Peter (2 negroes)	
James	9	Hone	22
Phil	9	Monney	32
Roger	9	HOGEN, Thomas (1 negro)	
Toby	9	Ralph	29
HARWICH, Aaron (2 negroes)		HOLDER, Luke (1 negro)	
Jack	9	Cull	14
Neyls	9	HOLTZCLAW, Catherin (1 negro)	
HATHAWAY, John (2 negroes)		Pegg	2
Jude	29	HOLTZCLAW, Jacob (4 negroes)	
Winney	29	Judy	3
HEALE, George (10 negroes)		Nan	3
Andrew	33	Robin	3
Hannah	33	Sarah	3
Harry	33	HOLTZCLAW, Joseph (3 negroes)	
Jenney	33	Esther/Ester	25, 32
Mathew	33	Gully/Gulley	25, 32
Nat	33	Nearoe	32
Peter	33	HOOE, Henry Dade (3 negroes)	
Sue	33	Laurance	20
Will	33	Phill	20
HEALE, William (15 negroes)		Rachel	20
Abigail/Abigal	23, 33	HOOE, W[m] (3 negroes)	
Abraham	23	Charles	18
Adam	23, 33	Clara	18
Daniel	23, 33	Rachel	18
Domini/Dameny	23, 33	HUBBARD, Ephraim (4 negroes)	
Fielding	23, 33	Anthony	29
Joseph/Joe	23, 33	Jane	29
Mancelle	33	Kate	29
Margery	23, 33	Sarah	29
Moses	23, 33	HUDNAL, Joseph (3 negroes)	
Nan	23, 33	Ben	14
Phillis/Phillise	23, 33	Crop	14
Silvey	23	Judah	14
Young Nan	23, 33	HUMPHRY, William (5 negroes)	
HEALEY/HEALY, John (3 negroes)		Betty	3
Dick	23, 32	Mary	3
Jane/Jene	23, 32	Tom	3
Aron	32	Toney	3
HELM, L. (Captain) (5 negroes)		Will	3
Flora	18	HUMSTON, Edward (9 negroes)	
Lucy	18	Allen	17
Pitt	18	Charles	17
Rich[d]	18	Frank	9, 17
Sambo	18	Hannah	9
HENDRING, John (2 negroes)		Linny	9, 17
Detter	9	Mary	17
Jack	9	Patience	9
HILL, Mary (1 negro)		Tom	9, 17
Jude	24	Will	17

Index "B" Slaves & Slaveholders 1759-001 to 1778-002 Tithable Lists

Surname, Given Name	page(s)
HUMSTON, Edward Jr. (4 negroes)	
Banner	25
George	25
Hannah	25
Patience	25
HUNTON, William (8 negroes)	
Bob	23
Cate/Kate	23, 29
Daniel	29
Ismer	29
Moll	23, 29
Robin	23
Sarah	23, 29
Winney	23, 29
JACKMAN, Thomas Sr. (3 negroes)	
Cate	34
Jack	34
Ralph	34
JACKMAN, W^m (1 negro)	
Roze	34
JACKSON, Joseph (1 negro)	
Jenney	33
JACOBS, Mor[r]is (1 negro)	
Easter	18
JAMES, John (2 negroes)	
Phillis	1
Winney	1
JAMES, John (Captain) (4 negroes)	
Charles	16
Judy	16
Phillis	16
Winney	16
JAMES, Thomas/Thos (1 negro)	
Lett/Lettice	22, 33
JEFFRES/JEFFRIES, Alexander (1 negro)	
James	22, 33
JEFFRIS, Joseph (2 negroes)	
Bess	29
Jenny	29
JETT, James (1 negro)	
Bett	25
JOHNSON, Alex^r (1 negro)	
Lett	29
JOHNSON, Moses (1 negro)	
Ralph	29
JONES, Brereton (3 negroes)	
Cate	9
Pompey	17
Sarah	9, 17
JONES, John	
Bett	17
Guy	17
Pender	17

Surname, Given Name	page(s)
JONES, John (cont.)	
Peter	17
JONES, William/Willm (4 negroes)	
Joe	4
Scipio	3
Will	3
Winney	3
KAMPER/KEMPER, Henry (1 negro)	
James	22, 33
KEITH, Alex^r (4 negroes)	
Bill	29
Hannah	29
Sarah	29
Will	29
KEITH, Isham	
Nell	29
Sarah	29
Toby	29
KEITH, John (6 negroes)	
Bob	29
Moll	29
Moroco	29
Nan	29
Peter (2)	29, 29
KEITH, Thomas (8 negroes)	
Beck	29
George	29
Harry	29
Jupiter	29
Morier	29
Nan	29
Ned	29
Peg	29
KEMPER, John (2 negroes)	
Nancy	33
Winney	23, 33
KENNER, George (2 negroes)	
Hannah	2, 9
James	2, 9
KENNER, George Tur. (2 negroes)	
James	16
Ned	16
KENNER, Howsin (9 negroes)	
Abraham/Abram	2, 9, 16
Anthony/Toney	2, 9, 16
Caney	2
Isaac	2, 9, 16
Jonathan	9, 16
Lett	2, 9, 16
Lucy	16
Moses	9, 16
Nick	2

Index "B" Slaves & Slaveholders 1759-001 to 1778-002 Tithable Lists

Surname, Given Name	page(s)
KENNER, Rodham (Rev^d) (4 negroes)	
Ant°	16
Hannah	16
Manuel	16
Pegg	16
KENTON, William (1 negro)	
Nan	29
KIRK, William (8 negroes)	
Betty/Bet	26, 29
Coadyer/Coader	26, 29
Dan/Daniel	26, 29
Denbo/Dimbo	26, 29
Jacob	26, 29
Moses	26, 29
Nell	26, 29
Peg	26, 29
LAMKIN, James (2 negroes)	
Charles	29
Isable	29
LAMTON, Joshua (2 negroes)	
Pegg	14
Suck	14
LARRANCE, Peter (1 negro)	
Jack	25
LAURANCE/LAWRENCE, Edward/Ed (12 negroes)	
Jacob	9
Jane	9, 19
Jude/Judy	9, 19
Mimy/Mym	9, 19
Moriar	19
Moses	9, 19
Nan	9, 19
Richard	19
Rose	19
Sam	9
Sarah	9, 19
Will	19
LEAVILL, Joseph (4 negroes)	
Bristol	13
Hannah	13
Lions	13
Phillis	13
LEVILL, Benjamin (4 negroes)	
Hester	29
Sam	29
Suse	29
Will	29
LEWIS, Zach./Zacharias (5 negroes)	
Sim	19
Daffney	14
Dick	14
George	14
LEWIS, Zach/Zacharias (cont.)	
Winney	14
LOVE, Augustine (Prince William Co.) (5 negroes)	
Jone	30
Phil	30
Robt	30
Roley	30
Suck	30
MADCALFE, John (7 negroes)	
Barbadois	11
Beauty	11
H[illegible]	11
Jack	11
Peter	11
Sephina	11
Winney	11
MADDUX, Thomas (4 negroes)	
Ezek^l	26
Nell	26
Pegro	26
Sam	26
MARR, Michael (6 negroes)	
Charles	1
Hack	1
Harry	1
Jeney	1
Jude	1
Nan	1
MARSHALL, John (Captain) (3 negroes)	
Hannah	21
Juba	21
Nan	21
MARSHALL, Thomas (Col°) (9 negroes)	
Bett	22
Caesar	22
Esther	22
Hannah	22
Jacob (2)	22, 22
Jenny	22
Joe	22
Juba	22
Old Hannah	22
MARTIN/MARTON, Charles (4 negroes)	
London	25, 30
Peter	14, 17
Racheal/Rachel	14, 17
Sue	14, 17
MATTHEWS, William (2 negroes)	
Fill	30
Winney	30

Index "B" Slaves & Slaveholders 1759-001 to 1778-002 Tithable Lists

Surname, Given Name	page(s)
MAUZEY, Henry (4 negroes)	
David	13
Dick	13
Lettice	13
Sarah	13
MAUZY, Elizabeth (3 negroes)	
Bob	10
Sam	10
Will	10
McCHONKIE, Alexander (9 negroes)	
Frank	18
Harry	18
Jane	18
Judy	18
Moses	18
Pompey	18
Sarah	18
Whipster	18
Winny	18
McCLANAHAM, Thomas (3 negroes)	
Dick	1
Jack	1
Sarah	1
McCORMACK/McCORMICK, Steven/Stephen (15 negroes)	
Aminy	1
Bett	17
Charles/Chas	1, 17
Dick	1
Dinah	1
George	1
Hannah	1
Jem	17
Joe	1
Kate	1
Kitcher	1
Nick	17
Sarah	17
Tom	1
Tomboy	1
MERCER, John Francis (28 negroes)	
Amia	30
Andrew	30
Ben	30
Bristol	30
Captain (2)	30, 30
Cliffen	30
Cupid	30
David	30
George (2)	30
Grace	30
Jenney	30
Julia	30

Surname, Given Name	page(s)
MERCER, John Francis (cont.)	
Lida	30
Loudon	30
Mary	30
Millard	30
Moccow	30
Peter	30
Phillis (2)	30, 30
Sall	30
Sarah	30
Sauney	30
Sipio	30
Truelove	30
Will	30
MILLARD, W^m (1 negro)	
Marthy	10
MINTOR, John's Estate (4 negroes)	
Baccus	30
Jacob	30
Rachel	30
Sarah	30
MINTOR, Joseph (2 Negroes)	
Barton	30
Net	30
MITCHELL, Thos (2 negroes)	
Hannah	1
Jack	1
MOFFETT, John (10 negroes)	
Ben	21, 33
Cate	21
Cato	33
Dick	21, 33
Esther	21, 33
Jemima	33
Jerimiah	21
Joe	33
Prince	21, 33
Winney	21, 33
MOIRA, Elizabeth's Estate (4 negroes)	
Amy	13
Ayre	13
Jinny	13
Quiver	13
MONDAY, John (4 negroes)	
Frank	30
Harry	30
Jude	30
Peg	30
MONDAY/MUNDAY, Robt (5 negroes)	
Harry	11
Jude	11
Luce	30
Pegg	11

Index "B" Slaves & Slaveholders 1759-001 to 1778-002 Tithable Lists

Surname, Given Name	page(s)
MONDAY/MUNDAY, Robt (cont.)	
Rose	30
MOREHEAD, Alexander/Alex^r (2 negroes)	
Sarah	10, 19
Violet	19
MOREHEAD, Charles/Chas (Captain) (5 negroes)	
Aaron	25
Danl	25
Jenny/ Jennay	25, 30
Monday	25
Will	25, 30
MOREHEAD, John (6 negroes)	
James	2, 10
Jude	2
Lett	10
Sarah	2
Tom	10
Tony	10
MOREHEAD, Joseph (1 negro)	
Kate	3
MOREHEAD, Presly (4 negroes)	
Danl	16
James	16
Tom	16
Tony	16
MOREHEAD, Turner (1 negro)	
Aaron	30
MOREHEAD, William/W^m (1 negro)	
Jude/Judy	10, 30
MORGAN, Ben (1 negro)	
Nan	1
MORGAN, Charles (1 negro)	
Bob	24
MORGAN, William (10 negroes)	
Dick	13, 32
Edwards	32
James	32
Jenney	32
Jude (2)	13, 13
Luce	13
Ore	32
Phill	32
Tom	32
MORGEN, Simon (4 negroes)	
Jane	30
Sam	30
Soloman	30
Will	30
MORRIS, Steven (15 negroes)	
Ben (2)	1, 1
Frank	1
Harry (2)	1, 1

Surname, Given Name	page(s)
MORRIS, Steven (cont.)	
James (3)	1, 1, 1
Kate	1
Mime	1
Nell	1
Roger (2)	1, 1
Sarah	1
Winney	1
MORRISS, Joseph (1 negro)	
Subinate	4
MURPHY, John (1 negro)	
Ned	22
NEAVILL, James (3 negroes)	
Dick	24
Phillis	24
Venus	24
NELSON, John (1 negro)	
George	17
NEWGENT, Ann (Mrs.) (4 negroes)	
Hannah	17
Sall (2)	17, 17
Sam	17
NEWGENT, Edward (2 negroes)	
Hannah	13
James	13
NEWGENT, Thos (10 negroes)	
Belinda	17
Doll	17
Harry	17
Mary	17
Mingo	17
Moll	17
Pegg	17
Rachel	17
Venus	17
Will	17
NORRIS, William (3 negroes)	
Kate	30
Let	30
Vilet	30
OBANNON, Andrew (2 negroes)	
Frank	30
Mimey	30
OBANNON, Bryant (1 negro)	
Luce	26
OBANNON, John (8 negroes)	
Dick	30
Gabril	30
Jesse	30
Jude	30
Kate	30
Peter	30
Sarah	30

Index "B" Slaves & Slaveholders 1759-001 to 1778-002 Tithable Lists

Surname, Given Name	page(s)
OBANNON, John (cont.)	
Solomon	30
OBANNON, Sarah (4 negroes)	
Caesar/Casor	26, 30
Jude/Judy	26, 30
Lucy	30
Nan	26, 30
OBANNON, William (2 negroes)	
Jane	26
Winney	26
ODOR, Joseph (1 negro)	
Judy	18
OLDHAM, Mary (5 negroes)	
Geo.	25
Hannah	25
Jess	25
Jude	25
Lucy	25
ONEAL, Edward (1 negro)	
Suck	30
OREAR, Ben (7 negroes)	
Alice	20
Ann	30
Danl	20
David	20
Dinah	20
Isaac	20
Tom	20, 30
OWENS, William (1 negro)	
Cane	30
P[illegible, on fold; possibly PAYNE?], James (5 negroes)	
Glasgow	3
James	3
Judy	3
Mack	3
Priss	3
PAGE, Eliz. (1 negro)	
Hannah	2
PAYNE, Francis (1 negro)	
Grace	23
PEPPER, Samuel (5 negroes)	
Esther	22
Jack	22
Pompey	22
Sam	22
Venus	22
PERL, Samuel (1 negro)	
Lucy	31
PETERS, James (2 negroes)	
George	19
Phill	10

Surname, Given Name	page(s)
PETERS, John (4 negroes)	
Bob	10
Lucy	17
Robin	17
Will	10, 17
PEYTON, Henry (6 negroes)	
Hannah	31
Milley	31
Moses	31
Mountain	31
Ned	31
Spencer	31
PICKETT, Elizabeth/Elizabeth (Mrs.) (4 negroes)	
Chloe/Cloe	26, 34
James	26, 34
Sam	26, 34
Suck	26, 34
PICKETT, Martin/ Martin (Major) (9 negroes)	
Aaron	26, 31
Frank	26
Frank (2)	31
Jack	26, 31
Jacob	26, 31
Nan	26, 31
Pomp/Pompy	26, 31
Will	26, 31
Winney	26, 31
PICKETT, William/ William (Captain) (13 negroes)	
Anthony/Antony	26, 34
Caroline	26, 34
Charles	26, 34
Daphney	26, 34
David	34
Emanul	34
Homaden	34
Jack	26, 34
Jemmimiah	26
Jude/Judy	26, 34
Jupiter	26, 34
Michael	26
Mohomet	26
PINKARD, Charles (3 negroes)	
Dick	34
Kit	34
Lucy	34
PIPER, Benjamin (5 negroes)	
Mimah	24
Patts	24
Pegg	24
Sall	24
Sam	24

Index "B" Slaves & Slaveholders 1759-001 to 1778-002 Tithable Lists

Surname, Given Name	page(s)
POPE, Thomas (1 negro)	
Jeffery	13
PORTER, Samuel (3 negroes)	
Esther	25
Sarah	25
Tom	25
PORTER, Thomas (1 negro)	
Sarah	14
PRITCHARD, Stephen (2 negroes)	
Edinburg	16
Sarah	16
QUISENBURY, John (7 negroes)	
Betty	19
Jacob	19
Judy	19
Moco	19
Phillis	19
Tenar	19
Tom	19
RAILY, Thomas (1 negro)	
Kap	17
RAMEY, Absolem (4 negroes)	
Anthony	3
Brister	3
Judy	3
Nanney	3
RAMEY, Absolem (2 negroes)	
Dab^y	3
Winney	3
RANSDALL, Mary (Mrs) (6 negroes)	
Bet	31
Bob	26
Jeries	31
Nan	26
Peg	26, 31
Sue	26, 31
RANSDELL, Wharton (Captain) (20 negroes)	
Dick (2)	23, 23, 31, 31
Frank	31
Geo. (2)	23, 23, 31, 31
George	31
Jean	31
Jenny	23
Jere (2)	23
Jeremy	31
Jessey	23, 31
Joe	23, 31
Jonathan	31
Moses	31
Peg /Pegg	23, 31
Sarah	23, 31
Sis	31
Sue	31
RANSDELL, Wharton (Captain) (cont.)	
Tom	23
RANSDELL, Wharton Jr. (2 negroes)	
Frank	23
Zekiel	23
RECTOR, Frederick (1 negro)	
Jude	22
RECTOR, Harman (1 negro)	
Peter	2
REGAN, Rolley (2 negroes)	
Boston	34
Judey	34
RICTOR, John (2 negroes)	
Jack	4
Juda	4
RIXY, Richard (4 negroes)	
Aaron	31
Hager	31
Hannah	31
Ton	31
ROACH, William (3 negroes)	
Ned	25, 31
Phillis/Philis	25, 31
Sarah	25
ROBINSON, Benjamin (3 negroes)	
Jude	11
Moll	11
Pegg	11
ROBINSON, William (9 negroes)	
Alice	13
Edinburg	13
Leannah	13
Mille	13
Nancy	13
Nell	13
Plato	13
Roger	13
Winnie	13
ROSSER, John (6 negroes)	
Ben	26, 34
Cate	26, 34
Jane	26
Jinn	34
Lucy	34
Yambo/Yambon	26, 34
ROUSAU, William (4 negroes)	
Davy	10
Jane	10
Jude	10
Nell	10
RUSSEL, George (8 negroes)	
Ben	1
Brister	1

Index "B" Slaves & Slaveholders 1759-001 to 1778-002 Tithable Lists

Surname, Given Name	page(s)
RUSSEL, George (cont.)	
Jean	1
Milley (2)	1, 1
Mureah	1
Titas	1
Tom	1
RUST, Samuel (3 negroes)	
Frank	21, 31
Geo./George	21, 31
Nan	21, 31
SANDERS, Robert/Robt (2 negroes)	
Hannah	22, 31
Sam	22, 31
SANFORD, William Pickett (3 negroes)	
Frank	31
Gib	31
Winney	31
SCOTT, James (10 negroes)	
Bet	31
Charlotte	31
Elger	31
Frank	31
Hannah	31
James	31
Jean	31
Pegg	31
Sawney	31
Will	
SCOTT, James (Rev^d) (10 negroes)	
Beck	31
Ben	31
Bet	31
Ceasor	31
Davy	31
George	31
James	31
Judy	31
Nan	31
Titus	31
SEATON, James (8 negroes)	
Beck	2
Ben	2
Frank	2
Iky	2
James	2
Job	2
Jude	2
Luce	2
SETTLE, Benj. (2 negroes)	
Rose	1
Tobey	1
SETTLE, Joel (5 negroes)	
Adam	25
Fann	25
Hampshire	25
Jack	25
Juba	25
SETTLE, John (1 negro)	
Peter	4
SHACKLETT, Hezekiah (1 negro)	
Abigal	21
SHIP, (First name not given) (1 negro)	
Luce	33
SHUMATE, Baly (1 negro)	
Jenny	17
SHUMATE, Dan (1 negro)	
Bess	17
SHUMATE, John Jr. (5 negroes)	
Cato	17
Grace	17
Jane	17
Phillis	10, 17
Tim	17
SINCLAIR, John (2 negroes)	
Phillis	14
Tom	14
SIRES, John (2 negroes)	
Frank	31
Sam	31
SKINKER, William (6 negroes)	
Guy	31
Hannah	31
Hester	31
Isaac	31
Luis	31
Winney	31
SMITH, John (1 negro)	
Bumbry	34
SMITH, John Nelson (2 negroes)	
Arch	17
Belinda	17
SMITH, Joseph (5 negroes)	
Joe/Joseph	25, 34
Nero	25, 34
Phillis	25, 34
Rose	25, 34
Scipio	25, 34
SMITH, Roley (5 negroes)	
Amey	23
Bab	23
Jack	23
Pris	23
John	23

Index "B" Slaves & Slaveholders 1759-001 to 1778-002 Tithable Lists

Surname, Given Name	page(s)
SMITH, Thomas (1 negro)	
Dublin	19
SMITH, William (Hicory) (4 negroes)	
Cate	24
Esther	24
Luce	24
Rose	24
SMITH, William Sr. (1 negro)	
Nim	33
SMITH, W^m (Great Run) (2 negroes)	
Lundon	33
Tom	33
SNELLING, Alex^r (1 negro)	
Beck	2
SOUTHARD, Robert (1 negro)	
Charles	2
SPICER, Randolph (1 negro)	
Phillip	14
SPILLER, Jeremiah (6 negroes)	
Davy	10
Joe	10
Jonathan	10
Ned	10
Nell	10
Tom	10
SPRINGS, Nic. (1 negro)	
Bob	17
STEPHENS, Anne (2 negroes)	
Hager	31
Harry	31
STEWART, William (3 negroes)	
Bess	31
Sue	31
Winney	31
STUARD/STUART, William/W^m (Rev^d) (16 negroes)	
Dick	31
Dinah/Diner	10, 31
Flowrey	31
Harry	31
Jonathan	31
James	10, 19
Mars	10, 19
Nan	10, 19
Nell	31
Pegg	31
Phill	19
Robert	19
Rose	10, 19, 31
Sue	19
Tom	31
Winney	31
STUART, John (6 negroes)	
Blunder	10
Daphne	10
Hannah	10
Judy	10
Nell	10
Toby	10
STUART, John's Estate (8 negroes)	
Belinda	19
Daphney	19
Dinah	19
Hannah	19
Judy	19
Nell	19
Tom	19
Tony	19
SULLIVIN, Geo.'s Estate (4 negroes)	
Dine	31
Joe	31
Philis	31
Siser	31
SUTHARD, Jno (overseer) (6 negroes)	
Adam	14
Bess	14
Cook	14
Hannah	14
James	14
Sarah	14
TAYLOR, Joseph (4 negroes)	
Hannah	25, 31
Joshua/Josuas	25, 31
Sarah	25, 31
Will	25, 31
TAYLOR, Judith (6 negroes)	
Adam	32
Bett	32
George	32
Kate	32
Nan	32
Tabb	32
THOMAS, David (1 negro)	
Patience	32
THOMAS, William (5 negroes)	
Betty	24
Harry	24
James	24
Judey	24
Sarah	24
THOMPSON, Eli/Ely (3 negroes)	
Aaron	25, 34
Kiza	25
Roz	34

Index "B" Slaves & Slaveholders 1759-001 to 1778-002 Tithable Lists

Surname, Given Name	page(s)
THOMPSON, Jesse (2 negroes)	
Sim	22
Will	22
THORNBERRY, Samuel (4 negroes)	
Jack	13
James	13
Sauny	13
Winifred	13
THORNTON, William (Captain) (9 negroes)	
Cate	23
Jack	23
Luke	23
Milley	23
Nann	23
Sambo	23
Sarah	23
Simon	23
Tom	23
THRELKELD, George (1 negro)	
Charles	18
TIMBERLAKE, Eppa (2 negroes)	
Geo./George	25, 32
Isabell/Isbel	25, 32
TOLLE, Roger (1 negro)	
Harry	14
TURNER, Edward (3 negroes)	
Betty	33
Luce	33
Nell	33
TURNER, Henry's Estate (4 negroes)	
Jane	10
Nan	10
Obier	10
Phillis	10
UNDERWOOD, Thomas (1 negro)	
Harry	34
UTTERBACK/OTTERBACK, John (3 negroes)	
Joe	30
Liz	30
Timby/Timpy	13, 30
WADDELL, John (1 negro)	
Jack	32
WAGENER, Peter (3 negroes)	
Essex	16
Neptune	16
Sarah	16
WAITE, W^m (4 negroes)	
Bob	19
Jack	19
Lucy	19
York	19

Surname, Given Name	page(s)
WAKE, John (3 negroes)	
James	32
Judas (2)	32, 32
Lot	32
WALLER'S Estate (8 negroes)	
Cyrus	10
Dye	10
Hannerboy	10
James	10
Joe	10
Lettice	10
Phillis	10
Winney	10
WALLER, Charles (4 negroes)	
Bacchus	16
Essea	16
Jack	16
Truelove	16
WALLER, W^m (3 negroes)	
Backus	10
Isaac	10
John	10
WASHINGTON, Laurence (6 negroes)	
George	20
Hannah	20
Jane	20
Joe	20
Sue	20
Winny	20
WATCHWAY, John (1 negro)	
Hannah	10
WATS, Francis (2 negroes)	
James	32
Nell	32
WATS/WATTS, Thomas	
Caleb/Calup	21, 34
Nell	4, 10
San	4
WATTS, John (1 negro)	
Mol	34
WEEKS, Alderson (2 negroes)	
Daniel	32
Nell/Nel	20, 32
WELCH, Silvester (3 negroes)	
Moses	32
Salley	32
Winney	32
WEVER, Jacob (2 negroes)	
Nance	25
Peter	25
WHEATLY, Jo^s (2 negroes)	
Judy	19
Sarah	19

Index "B" Slaves & Slaveholders 1759-001 to 1778-002 Tithable Lists

Surname, Given Name	page(s)
WHITLEDGE, Tho[s] (2 negroes)	
Bob	10
Phillis	10
WILLIAMS, George (2 negroes)	
Hannah	14
Jack	14
WINN, Ja[s] (Captain) (4 negroes)	
Harry	32
James	32
Moses	32
Sarah	32
WINN, Minor (5 negroes)	
Adam	10
Fryday	10
Moll	10
Rachel	10
Tony	10
WINN, Mynor's Estate (5 negroes)	
Grace	32
Jean	32
Paul	32
Sawny	32
Tony	32
WITHERS, Cane's Estate (6 negroes)	
Easter	13
Nan	13
Ned	13
Phillis	13
Sue	13
Thompson	13
WITHERS, James Sr. (9 negroes)	
Andrew	13
Cupid	13
Dick	13
Jinny	13
Jude	13
Parish	13
Phebe	13
Prince	13
Tom	13
WITHERS, Ja[s] (son of James) (4 negroes)	
Harry	19
Phillis	19
Robin	19
Sara	19
WITHERS, Tho[s] (3 negroes)	
Flowra	2
Jam	2
Jude	2
WITHERS, William (5 negroes)	
Dick	13
Dinah	13
Jack	13
WITHERS, William (cont.)	
Peter	13
Sarah	13
WOOD, Dickerson (1 negro)	
Luke	21
WOOD, John (7 negroes)	
Aaron	9
Bristor	9
Dick	9
James	9
Joe	9
Moll	9
Ned	9
WOOD, Joshua (1 negro)	
Joe	18
WOOD, Samuel (4 negroes)	
Joe	16
Lucy	16
Milly	16
Nan	16
WRIGHT, John (4 negroes)	
Bray	14
Dinah	14
Judah	14
Will	14
WRIGHT, John Jr. (3 negroes)	
Grace	2
Luce	2
Phill	2
YOUNG, Bryan (1 negro)	
Ned	32
YOUNG, Original (1 negro)	
Cupid	11
YOUNG, William (2 negroes)	
Harry	32
Henly	32

Index "C" Tithables 1782-001 to 1782-005

Surname, Given Name	page(s)
AGAR	
John	48
ALEXANDER'S QUARTER	
Phillip	62
ALLEN	
James	107
John	107
Robert	107
ALLISON	
W^m (Exor. to Kirk)	77
ANDERSON	
Cornealus	107
David	77
ARMSTRONG	
James	62, 107
William	107
ARNAL	
Jack	107
ASBURY	
George	77
Henry	77
Thomas	77
W^m	77
ASHBY	
John Sr. (Captain)	40
ATHEL	
Ben (overseer)	82
BACK	
Harmon	107
BADEN	
James	105
John	105
BAILEY	
Car (overseer)	53
James	108
James (overseer)	56
Simon	48
BALEY	
Green	105
John	90, 105
Joseph	105
Moses	80
Rice	105
Rite [Wright]	80
Stephan	104
W^m	80, 94
BALEY'S QUARTER	
Joseph	105
BALL	
John	62
Nicholas	80
BANISTER	
Augustine	78
BARBEE	
Andrew Jr.	108
Joseph	107
BARBER	
Thomas	49
BARBEY	
Andrew Sr.	108
Joseph	108
BARKER	
Charles	78
John	104
W^m	80
W^m Jr.	80
BARNETT	
Ambrose	48
BARTLETT	
John	78
Richard	77
Robert	79, 80
Thomas	77
W^m	78
BARTON	
Cuthbert (Clear Levy)	78
Joseph	113
Kinber	80
Levy	80
Prue	104
BASEY	
Richard	105
BASHAW	
Peter	80, 105
BASYE	
Josias	107
BATTALEY	
Bryan	63
BAYLEY	
Martin	105
BENNETT	
Daniel	108
BERKLEY	
W^m	78
BERRY	
George	78
Henry	77
W^m	78
BERRYMAN	
Benjamin	62
Maximilion	62
BISHOP	
William	37
BLACKABY	
Joseph	107

Index "C" Tithables 1782-001 to 1782-005

Surname, Given Name	page(s)
BLACKERBY	
Goduthern	108
BLACKWELL	
John	63
Samuel	49
Thomas	62
W^m	36
BLAND	
Charles	80
Mary	80
BLYTHE	
James	105
BOSWELL	
Elizabeth	48
BOWEN	
James	63
James (overseer)	62
BOWER	
Peter	63
BOWLING	
Francis	108
BOWMAN	
Peter (overseer)	69
BOWMER	
Peter	62
BOYD	
Samuel (Dr.)	48
BRADFORD	
John	64
BRADLEY	
Hugh	105
BRADY	
Hezekiah	81
Peregin	78
BRAGG	
Dozzer	117
BRAMBLET	
Ruben Jr.	108
BRAMBLETT	
John	62
Peggy	62
Reubin	62
BRAY	
John	117
BRENT	
George	87
George's Property	87
William	63
BRIDWELL	
William	107
BRIGGS	
William	107
BROHON	
Lettice	37
Thomas	37
BRONAUGH	
Maryan	44
Thomas [counted twice]	76
Thos	64
BROOKE	
Humphrey	48
BROOKS	
James	105
BROWN	
Dixson	107
Duke	38
George	46
Jehu	104
John	63, 107
Mary	107
William	46
BROWNING	
Calup	107
George	107
Jacob	107
BRUIN	
Michael	80
Tom	80
BRYAN	
Enoch	78
John	48, 62
BRYANT	
James	64
Peter	81
William	64
BULLETT	
Cudberth	42
Permenes	85
BULLITT	
Cuth.	40
Joseph	39
BULLIT'S QUARTER	
Cuth.	40
BURGIS	
Edward	107
Garnar	107
BURK	
John	107
BUSSY	
Corn^l	52
BUTLER	
Samuel	105
C[R]OSBY	
George	39
John	39

Index "C" Tithables 1782-001 to 1782-005

Surname, Given Name	page(s)
C[R]OSBY	
Uriah	39
William	39
CAMMEL	
Anquish	117
CAMMORON	
Anquish	108
CANTWELL	
John	79
CARRELL	
Elizabeth	79
CARTER	
Charles L.	49
Dale	79
George	81
Peter	79
CASE	
Samuel	81
CAUNNA	
Stephen	108
CHADDOX	
Charles	79
CHADWELL	
John	108
CHICHESTER	
Richard	49
CHICK	
John	79
CHILTON	
Charles	50
CHINN	
Christopher	81
Thomas (Loudoun Co.)	81
CHURHCILL	
Armisteads	64
CLARK	
Elias	35
CLARKSON	
Henry	108
CLEMDENEA	
John	108
CLERK	
Benjamin	79
COATS	
Thomas	82
COCHRUM	
Richens	79
Richard (overseer)	97
COLLINS	
Edmond	82
James	49, 50
John	109
COLVIN	
Charles	42
COMBS	
Catharine	82
Enniss	44
Robert	82
Sarah	44
CONAWAY	
William	42
CONSTABLE	
W^m	82
CONWAY	
Thomas Jr.	41
COOK	
John	108
COOKE	
John	49
COOPER	
Richard	45
COPPAGE	
Charles	37
William	37
COPPEDGE	
John	99
CORDER	
James	109
CORNWELL	
Jervis	79
John	79
CORUM	
Champ	46
Richard	46
COURTNEY	
W^m	79
W^m (under 21)	79
COVENDER	
John	79
COX	
Abraham	45
Zachariah	45
CRAFFORD	
William	108
CRAIG	
James (Rev^d)	64
John	64
CRAINE	
John	81
CRAWLEY	
Minoah	117
CRESWELL	
George (overseer)	74
CRIM	
Cattron	109

Index "C" Tithables 1782-001 to 1782-005

Surname, Given Name	page(s)	Surname, Given Name	page(s)
CRIM (cont.)		DOUDALL	
Jacob	109	Thomas	46
John	109	DOWDELL	
Joseph	109	Banner	46
Peter	109	James	37
CRIMM		DOWNING	
Harmon	109	W^m	82
CRISTI		DOWMAN'S QUARTER	
Charles	109	Rawleigh	66
CROOK		DRUMMOND	
Mary	40	Aaron	66
CROSBY		James	83
Uriell	81	DUFF	
CUMINGS		James	66
Elexander	45	James Sr.	66
George	45	John	66
John	45	DUNCAN	
Thomas	45	Charles	65
Willis	45	Houson	65
CUNDIFF		John Sr.	65
Isaac	81	Joseph	65
James	82	Joseph Jr.	65
CURTIS		Joseph Sr.	65
John	109	EDGE	
CUSSENBERRY		John	41
John	64	Simon	41
DALE		EDWARDS	
William	51	John	109
DARNALL		Martin	83
Jeremiah	65	Thomas	83
Joseph	65	ELLIOTT	
DAY		Samuel	66
Leonard	109	ELLIS	
DEANE		James	66
John	51	Jonathan	109
DEARING		Nathaniel	109
Jeremiah	109	ENGLISH	
John	109	Robert, Robt	66, 66
DENNERSON		EUSTACE	
James	109	Hack	42
DODD		EVINS	
Benjamin	66	Sammuel	109
James	65	FEAGINS	
John	109	Edward	84
Nathl Jr.	66	Elizabeth	95
Nathl Sr.	65	John	95
DOFANY		Rawleigh	84
George	41	FELINGS	
DONALDSON		William	109
John	82	FELKINGS	
DONEPHAN		John	109
Joseph	51	FICKLIN	
		Charly, Charles	66, 67

Index "C" Tithables 1782-001 to 1782-005

Surname, Given Name	page(s)
FIDLAR	
Thos	43
FIELDING	
Edward	84
FIELDS	
John	83
FISHBACK	
James	84
John (2)	84, 84
Josiah	83
Philip	84
W^m	84
FITZGIARRALD	
Tom	95
W^m	95
FITZHUGH	
George	51
Henry	52
William	51
FLATHERS	
Edward	84
FLECHER	
Benjamin	109
Moses	110
William	110
FLETCHER	
Joshua	95
Moses	109
FLING	
John	83
FLOWEREE	
Daniel (2)	95, 95
W^m	95
FLOWERS	
Andrew	84
FLOWRANCE	
W^m	83
FLYNN	
Michail	109
Valentine	110
FOLEY	
Briant	110
Enoch	95
James	95, 110
Thomas	110
W^m	104
FOOTE	
George's Estate	36
William	51
FORCE	
Lewis	103
FORD	
William	110

Surname, Given Name	page(s)
FOSTER	
Thomas	51
FOX	
Samuel	66
FRENCH	
Daniel	95
George	86, 104
John (2)	95, 95
FUEL	
Nathaniel	110
GABRIEL	
George	49
GARNER	
Charles	67
Charles JR.	67
GARRARD	
Anthony	110
GENN	
James	52
GEORGE	
Margarett	40
Parnack	52
GIBSON	
Abraham	85
John	47
Jonathan	47
Robert	52
GILLISON	
Mary (Mrs)	47
GLASCOCK	
George	85
Thomas	84
GLOVER	
Thomas	110
GOFF	
Joshua	67
GOODWIN	
Abraham	110
GORE	
Thos	63
GRANT	
Geo.	43
James	110
GRASTY	
George	67
GRAY	
Gerrard	36
Gerrard Jr.	36
GREEN	
Ann	52
Thomas	52
Thomas (overseer)	58
William	52

Index "C" Tithables 1782-001 to 1782-005

Surname, Given Name	page(s)	Surname, Given Name	page(s)
GREENLEES		**HAWKINS**	
Peter	110	John	86
GREENWOOD		**HEAGINS**	
Daniel	67	John	85
GRIFFIN		**HEALE**	
Henry	52	George	53, 87
GRIFFITHS		Philip	54
Elijah	85	Smith	53
Evan	85	W^m	86
John	84	**HEATON**	
GRIGSBY		William	111
Aaron	85	**HEDGMAN**	
Ann	85	John's Quarter	67
Betsey	85	**HEFFERLINS**	
Taliaferro	85	William	111
GRIMSLEY		**HEFLIN**	
William	110	Simon	110
GROVES		**HEGINS**	
William	110	W^m	86
GUTTRIDGE		**HELM**	
Allen	110	Thomas (Captain)	68
GUY		**HERMON**	
Samuel	52	John (overseer)	63
HADDOX		**HILL**	
Zekel	111	John	111
HALL		**HILLIARY**	
Robert	117	William	111
HAMBRICK		**HINSON**	
John	110	Robert	67
HAMMONS		**HITCH**	
John	62	Cristopher	110
HAMRICK		**HITT**	
William	87	Charles	110
HARDWICK		Harmon	85
William	53	Lazarus	110
HARRIL		Martin	85
W^m	107	**HOAGAN**	
HARRILL		John	53
Daniel	41	Rawleigh	53
HARRIS		**HODO**	
Elisha	111	Peter	37
James	110	Peter Jr.	37
Jesse	107	**HOGAN**	
Richard	111	James	36
Sammuel	111	John	36
Thomas	110	**HOGANS**	
HARRISON		Thomas	86
Benjamin	43	**HOLIDAY**	
George	87	Samuel	67
John Peyton	86	**HOLTZCLAW**	
HATHAWAY		Benjamin	54
James	54	Jacob	86
John (2)	86, 86	Josiah	68

Index "C" Tithables 1782-001 to 1782-005

Surname, Given Name	page(s)
HOOE	
Housin	53
HOPPER	
John	110
John (overseer)	53
John Sr.	110
Joseph	54
Mary	111
HORNER	
James	35
HORTON	
James	39
HOVELL	
William's Quarter	67
HUFMAN	
Benjamin	44
John	44
Margret	44
Peter	44
HULET	
William	111
HUME	
John	36, 68
Robert	111
William	67
HUMEMODY	
Henry	111
HUMES	
Andrew	110
HUMSTON	
Edward	43
HUNDON	
John	68
HUNTON	
James' Quarter	68
James	53
William	53
HU[R]ST	
Henry	111
Rosannah	111
JACKSON	
Dempsey	88
George	88
Joseph	88
JAMES	
Dinah	38
John	88
JARRARD	
William	111
JEFFERSON	
William	69
JENKINS	
Thomas	87
JENNINGS	
Augustain	69
Balis	69
Geo.	69
Lewis	69
JETT	
Francis	111
James	117
William	117
William (2)	111, 111
JINKINS	
George	42
JOHNSON	
Beede	111
George	88
Isaac	112
Moses	87
Tunis (2)	69, 69
Yellis	69
JONES	
Brerinton	47
Francis	87
Henry	38, 111
James	87
John	69, 111
John Warner	47
Peter	87
Sam/Samuel	82, 88
W^m	39, 87
KEARNS	
John	44
KEIRNES	
Daniel	69
KEITH	
Alexander	88
Isham	88
John	54
KENDALL	
Thomas	54
KENNEDEY	
John (overseer)	51
KENNER	
George	35
Mrs.	39
Robert	35
Mark (clear levy)	88
KERNS	
Robert	112
KIBBLE	
Anderson	89
John	89
W^m	89

Index "C" Tithables 1782-001 to 1782-005

Surname, Given Name	page(s)	Surname, Given Name	page(s)
KIDWELL		LINOR	
John	88	Phil	93
KING		LINTON	
Robert	112	W^m	90
William	112	LITTRELL	
KNOX		Francis	43
William's Quarter	69	James	43
LAING		John (2)	43, 43
Alexander's Property	90	Joshua	43
LAKE		Richard	43
Vinson	89	LOLLER	
W^m	89	James	89
LAMKIN		LOVE	
Chattin	42	Augustine	55
James	90	LOWRY	
LANE		George	54
William	112	LUCAS	
LARRANCE		Phill (overseer)	53
Edward	112	LUNSFORD	
Peter	112	Jemima	70
LATHAM		William	70
Geo.	73	LUTTRELL	
LAWRENCE		Edward	37
Edward	46	Edward (overseer)	39
Richard	46	Richard	41, 54
Rodham	46	Richard (overseer)	51
LAWS		Robert	42
Thomas	89	LYNN	
LAWSON		William	70
Gavin's Quarter	70	MacCADE	
LEACH		James	112
Burdett	89	MADDOX	
George	85, 89	George	70
George (overseer)	95	George (overseer)	73
James (2)	89, 89	Thomas Sr. (levy free)	70
Thomas	89	MARKHAM	
Vall	100	James	45
W^m	89	John's Quarter	41
LEACHMAN		MARKWELL	
Thomas	89	Joseph	88
W^m	89	MARR	
LEE		Daniel	70
Hancock	70	MARTIN	
Stephen	35	Charles	56, 71
Henry's Estate	90	John	44, 112
LEWIS		Maryan	112
Britian	43	MASSEY	
James	43	Thomas	112
Zacariah (Captain)	44	MATTHEW	
LINN		Benjamin	91
Alex^r	70	Edward	90
James	70	Isaac	91
William	70	Nathan	91

Index "C" Tithables 1782-001 to 1782-005

Surname, Given Name	page(s)
MATTHEW (cont.)	
Simon	90
MATTHEWS	
Richard (levy free)	70
MAUZEY	
Bettey	45
John	36
McBEE	
John	113
McCLANAHAME	
Moore	55
McCLENACHAN	
Andrew	90
David	90
McCORMACK	
John	71
Stephen	71
McCORMICK	
John	112
McCOY	
John	37
McLANAHAME	
James	55
McMILLIAN	
John	90
Joseph	90
McQUEEN	
Charles	112
MEDLEY	
John	39
John (overseer)	41
MERCER	
John F.'s Estate	101
METCALFE	
John	55
William	55
MILLER	
Elizabeth (Mrs)	46
James	39
MILLON	
Thomas	64
MINTER	
Joseph	56
Mary	55
MONDAY	
John	91
Robert	91
W^m	102
MONROE	
John	113
MOONEY	
Nicholas	55

Surname, Given Name	page(s)
MOORE	
John	102
W^m	101
MOREHEAD	
Alexander	41
Charles	91
John Jr.	112
John Sr.	112
Presley	90
Samuel	42
W^m	91
MORGAN	
Charles	112
James	91
John	91
Simon	91
Spencer	39
William (Leeds Parish)	112
MORRISON	
Daniel	101
Hugh	101
MUCHETT	
John	96
MULLIKAN	
Burton	55
MURREY	
Enoch	101
James	102
Reuben	102
MUSCHETT	
James	55
MUSE	
Battle	101
NASH	
Traverse	56
NAWLS	
W^m (2)	92, 92
NEAL	
Christopher	92
NEALE	
Benjamin	56, 117
James	56
Mathew	117
Thomas	56
NEGROES	
Aaron	48, 50, 53, 54, 55, 60, 60, 68, 68 74, 78, 86, 87, 88, 91, 92, 116
Abe	37, 108, 108
Abel	49, 53, 54, 59, 86
Abigail	77, 86
Abner	39
Abraham	37, 45, 55, 74, 75, 102
Abram	50, 50, 50, 53, 56, 64, 64

Index "C" Tithables 1782-001 to 1782-005

Surname, Given Name	page(s)
NEGROES (cont.)	
Adam	40, 46, 47, 48, 49, 50, 51, 53, 57, 57, 57, 58, 71, 75, 80, 81, 81, 83, 105, 112
Ady	99
Aga	90
Agatha	40, 97
Agg	97
Agga	93, 104
Aggai	55, 57
Aggaitha	54
Aggay	50
Aggy	64, 68, 69, 71, 71, 79
Agor	78, 78, 78
Aker	70
Alce	66, 70, 116
Alec	69
Alex	40
Alexander	52, 68, 90
Alex^r	37
Alic	68
Alice	50, 50, 51, 52, 53, 58, 85, 96, 100, 106, 106
Alin	43
Alis	47
Allen	112
Alley	73, 102
Ally	60
Amay	71
Ambrose	50
Amelia	107, 112
Amey	43, 43, 70, 70, 75, 85, 88, 93, 97, 97, 101, 104
Ammy	69
Amos	49, 50, 51
Amy	42, 49, 50, 54, 99
Andrew	52, 87, 101
Ann	51, 75, 99, 111
Anne	53
Anney	64
Anthony	46, 50, 51, 51, 51, 53, 54, 69, 79
Antony	39, 42, 44, 45, 80
Arch	36, 40, 95
Arguile	100
Armistead	95
Aron	39, 41, 114
Augustin	55
Baccus	55, 80
Baeris	88
Bailey	48
Baley	90

Surname, Given Name	page(s)
NEGROES (cont.)	
Bally	53
Barbra	67
Bartley	36
Barton	56
Bash	36
Bathsheba	50
Beck	37, 43, 43, 49, 49, 51, 52, 53, 56, 63, 77, 77, 80, 98, 99
Beecher	68
Bell	65, 69
Bellow	43
Ben	35, 36, 38, 38, 39, 40, 43, 46, 47, 47, 47, 48, 49, 51, 54, 56, 58, 61, 62, 63, 64, 65, 68, 68, 68, 69, 70, 74, 74, 75, 76, 77, 77, 82, 83, 85, 91, 97, 98, 98, 101, 102, 103, 108, 112, 112, 115, 117
Berkey	102
Bess	39, 45, 45, 58, 74, 75, 78, 78
Bet	38, 60, 77, 77, 78, 80, 80, 81, 81, 82, 85, 85, 88, 90, 93, 95, 97, 98, 98, 99, 100, 100, 100, 100, 103, 112, 115
Betsy	68, 97
Bett	41, 44, 46, 46, 48, 50, 51, 53, 55, 57, 64, 65, 69, 69, 69, 71, 73, 74, 112, 117
Bettey	112
Betty	43, 44, 48, 49, 49, 49, 50, 50, 50, 50, 50, 50, 51, 52, 53, 54, 60, 82, 82, 106
Bill	49, 49, 70, 88
Billey	50
Billy	50, 52, 64
Blandford	70
Boatswain	82, 101
Bob	36, 41, 43, 48, 51, 52, 52, 52, 53, 54, 54, 60, 62, 64, 71, 71, 75, 79, 85, 97, 107, 107, 110, 112
Boron	97
Bosen	65
Braddock	51
Bray	69
Brick	86
Bridget	98
Brister	40, 40, 45, 101
Bristol	48
Britain	65
Briton	75
Brook	74

175

Index "C" Tithables 1782-001 to 1782-005

Surname, Given Name	page(s)
NEGROES (cont.)	
Bryan	51
Bryant	96
Buckery	47
Caesar	50
Cager	64
Caiff	81
Cain	49, 65, 74, 93
Captain	51, 101, 101
Carter	60
Cary	35
Cas	99
Caskus	68
Cate	35, 36, 37, 39, 39, 42, 42, 45, 47, 47, 48, 63, 63, 64, 65, 69, 73, 73, 74, 76, 79, 79, 84, 86, 87, 93, 93, 100, 100, 101, 102, 102, 107, 107, 108, 115, 116
Cantena	35, 101
Cato	38, 67, 73, 79
Ceaser	74
Cela	99
Celey	47
Celia	36, 38, 50, 50, 58, 60
Ceni	73
Cesar	60, 98, 99
Chany	51
Charity	50, 50, 66, 69, 69, 110, 110
Charles	36, 37, 38, 42, 43, 44, 45, 46, 47, 49, 50, 51, 52, 53, 53, 54, 57, 57, 57, 57, 58, 60, 60, 62, 63, 63, 63, 64, 65, 67, 71, 71, 74, 77, 78, 81, 85, 86, 87, 94, 94, 99, 99, 100, 109, 112, 112, 113, 116, 116
Charlot	38, 68
Charlott	44, 73
Charlotte	47, 50, 53, 58, 59, 69, 88, 99, 99, 99
Charrity	68, 71, 107, 107
Child (of Dinah)	37
Chloe	59, 60
Chloey	70, 72, 73
Chris	103
Cis	116
Ciss	37
Clare	110
Clares	109
Clarey	45, 74
Claris	48
]Clary	38, 85
Clo	116

Surname, Given Name	page(s)
NEGROES (cont.)	
Cloe	38, 40, 43, 43, 55, 65, 95, 98, 101
Cloey	42
Cogger	77
Cook	108
Cooper	85
Cris (2)	105, 105
Criss	49
Cuff	87
Cuffey	94
Cuffy	82
Cumber	94
Cupid	48, 48, 101
Currier	77
Cynar	49
Cyonis	91
Cyrus	49
Daffiney	107
Dakey	57
Dan	51
Danel	116
Danial	114
Daniel	37, 39, 40, 40, 42, 44, 44, 47, 48, 49, 49, 50, 51, 53, 55, 56, 57, 58, 59, 60, 60, 62, 62, 63, 64, 65, 68, 70, 71, 72, 74, 76, 77, 81, 83, 84, 86, 86, 92, 92, 94, 95, 98, 99, 103, 104, 105, 105, 107, 112, 114, 114, 115
Daphney	49, 88, 98
Darca	81, 90
Darcus	49, 53, 53
Dark	46, 81
Davey	43
David	35, 36, 36, 41, 42, 47, 50, 58, 63, 64, 65, 66, 82, 84, 90, 92, 93, 93, 98, 101, 105, 106, 117
Davy	49, 55
Delf	58
Delila	50
Delphia	74
Denbe (2)	36, 36
Dennis	51, 52, 53
Derende	73
Dianah	113
Dianna	99
Dick	35, 36, 36, 40, 42, 43, 46, 48, 48, 49, 49, 49, 49, 50, 51, 51, 51, 51, 52, 52, 53, 55, 56, 62, 63, 64, 65, 66, 67, 67, 73, 73, 73, 73, 74, 75, 78, 80, 81, 81, 84, 86, 93, 96, 97, 97, 99, 100,

Index "C" Tithables 1782-001 to 1782-005

Surname, Given Name	page(s)	Surname, Given Name	page(s)
NEGROES (cont.)		NEGROES (cont.)	
Dick (cont.)	108, 108, 110, 112	Fenny	95
Dido (2)	50, 50	Fielding	86
Dimbo	77, 78	Fill	96
Dimby	85	Fillis	109
Dimont	73	Florah	74, 97
Dinah	36, 36, 37, 38, 40, 41, 41, 47, 48, 49, 50, 50, 50, 54, 56, 58, 65, 69, 71, 73, 74, 75, 75, 77, 81, 81, 85, 90, 90, 91, 91, 97, 97, 97, 99, 99, 101, 106, 107, 112, 114	Fortin	39
		Fortune	53, 58, 60, 60
		Fran	63, 108
		Frank	35, 37, 41, 42, 42, 43, 43, 44, 48, 49, 49, 50, 50, 50, 51, 51, 53, 54, 54, 56, 58, 58, 60, 65, 67, 68, 69, 77, 78, 82, 82, 85, 87, 91, 95, 95, 96, 96, 97, 99, 99, 103, 103, 108
Diner	107, 108, 115		
Doctor	95		
Dol	37, 43		
Doll	50, 50, 65, 85, 111	Franny	65
Dolly	48	Gabriel	50, 50, 68, 82, 90, 93, 94
Dominy	86	Geo.	39, 42
Donnice	86	George	35, 37, 41, 41, 42, 42, 43, 43, 44, 44, 46, 47, 48, 49, 49, 50, 50, 53, 54, 54, 54, 55, 58, 58, 60, 62, 62, 62, 63, 69, 70, 71, 74, 74, 74, 75, 80, 85, 91, 94, 95, 96, 96, 97, 98, 100, 101, 101, 101, 101, 104, 104, 106, 107, 109, 110, 110, 112, 113, 115, 116
Dorithy	74		
Doss	50		
Dosse	50		
Duddley	59		
Duke	36, 57		
Dy	38		
Easter	52, 63, 66, 75, 75, 111, 111, 109, 112, 115		
Edam	96	Gerrard	69
Eddy	50	Gibby	91
Edmond	53, 60, 68, 93, 93	Gilbert	48, 97
Edmund	53	Giles	58
Edward	50	Gill	77
Elgan	98	Gillis	73
Eli	82	Ginn	111
Elige	111	Glascow	113
Elijah	56, 69, 99	Glasgo	74
Elizabeth	78, 91, 101, 101	Gloucester	78, 95
Ellen	55	Godfrey	51
Emanuel	49, 64, 68, 95	Grace	35, 43, 48, 53, 58, 60, 62, 63, 65, 68, 68, 70, 73, 82, 95, 103, 114, 115
Ennis	112		
Enoch	40, 68		
Ephraim	65, 74, 98	Grii	97, 98, 104
Eppa	88	Grimage	44
Essex	44	Grinage	79
Ester	74, 76	Guilford	58
Esther	41, 44, 45, 45, 48, 49, 50, 56, 77, 91, 98, 100	Gumby	50
		Guss	115
Eve	48, 50, 71, 86, 108	Guy	55, 69
Ezable	38	H[illegible]	57
Ezekiel	50	Hagar	53
Fanna	112	Hager	73, 114
Fanney	38, 70, 87, 98	Hagner	44
Fanny	50, 52, 60, 63, 111	Haley (2)	43, 43

Index "C" Tithables 1782-001 to 1782-005

Surname, Given Name	page(s)	Surname, Given Name	page(s)
NEGROES (cont.)		**NEGROES (cont.)**	
Hampton	50	Jack	36, 38, 38, 38, 41, 42, 44, 44, 46, 47, 49, 50, 51, 52, 53, 53, 54, 54, 57, 58, 59, 59, 60, 60, 60, 63, 65, 68, 69, 71, 73, 75, 77, 81, 85, 85, 87, 90, 94, 94, 95, 98, 99, 103, 103, 108, 112, 113, 113, 115
Hanah	54, 55, 55, 62, 62, 63, 63, 63, 65, 68, 68, 71, 71, 74, 75		
Hannah	36, 39, 40, 40, 40, 40, 42, 42, 43, 43, 44, 44, 45, 46, 48, 49, 49, 50, 50, 50, 51, 53, 53, 53, 54, 54, 55, 56, 57, 57, 58, 58, 58, 59, 63, 67, 73, 77, 78, 80, 84, 85, 87, 88, 88, 88, 90, 92, 93, 93, 95, 95, 96, 97, 97, 97, 97, 97, 97, 98, 98, 99, 99, 99, 99, 99, 100, 100, 101, 102, 102, 103, 107, 108, 109, 111, 112, 112, 113, 114, 117	Jacob	44, 49, 49, 50, 50, 50, 50, 51, 53, 55, 56, 58, 59, 63, 66, 68, 73, 86, 87, 94, 96, 97, 107, 115
		Jaffrey	63
		Jaive	39
		Jaley	65
		Jallace	49
		James	35, 36, 38, 38, 39, 41,42, 44, 46, 47, 47, 48, 48, 49, 49, 49, 50, 50, 50, 51, 51, 53, 53, 54, 54, 55, 56, 56, 57, 59, 59, 59, 60, 60, 60, 60, 62, 62, 62, 62, 62, 62, 63, 63, 64, 64, 66, 67, 69, 70, 71, 73, 74, 79, 81, 84, 84, 85, 87, 88, 88, 90, 91, 92, 94, 94, 95, 96, 97, 98, 99, 102, 103, 103, 106, 112,112, 114, 115, 115, 116
Hannar	114		
Hannibal	60		
Harry	40, 40, 43, 44, 45, 47, 48, 49, 49, 49, 50, 50, 50, 50, 51, 51, 53, 56, 57, 57, 57, 58, 58, 59, 60, 60, 60, 63, 64, 64, 65, 68, 69, 73, 74, 74, 76, 78, 78, 79, 80, 80, 81, 83, 84, 85, 87, 88, 92, 92, 94, 95, 97, 97, 98, 98, 99, 103, 102, 103, 107, 114, 114, 116, 116		
		Jane	48, 48, 48, 49, 49, 49, 50, 50, 50, 50, 50, 50, 51, 51, 52, 54, 56, 58, 59, 60, 60, 64, 65, 69, 81, 84, 84, 85, 86, 86, 87, 88, 88, 88, 88, 88, 91, 91, 93, 96, 96, 97, 98, 99,99, 99, 99, 102, 103, 103, 103, 104, 108, 110, 113, 113, 117
Hary	62		
Hath	46		
Haver	43		
Heath	113		
Hendley	94, 104		
Henna	109		
Henny	87, 87, 95		
Henry	35, 36, 39, 41, 47, 55, 70, 75, 81, 82, 91, 95, 97, 99, 112, 117	Janey	48
Hester	79, 85, 85, 103, 116	Jarrard	78, 84, 85, 97
Hethey	35	Jean	36, 39, 42, 43, 62, 66, 68
Hettey	47	Jeane	112
Hollan	40	Jeanny	45
Humphrey (2)	77, 77	Jeany	40, 43
Humpprey	59	Jeary	40
Isaac	35, 38, 46, 47, 50, 50, 53, 54, 54, 54, 56, 58, 59, 63, 71, 74, 75, 81, 82, 87, 98, 100, 106, 112, 113	Jeffery	35, 51, 65, 91
		Jeffrey	66, 75, 116
		Jefry	115
		Jemima	50, 99
Isabell	50	Jen	41
Isac	35, 39	Jeney	37, 43
Isbell	90, 101	Jenney	35, 36, 63, 71, 73, 113
Isham	43	Jenny	35, 40, 43, 50, 54, 66, 68, 71, 74, 107
Ismuth	53		
Issham	100	Jeny	44
		Jeremiah	116
		Jeremy	96

Index "C" Tithables 1782-001 to 1782-005

Surname, Given Name	page(s)
NEGROES (cont.)	
Jerimiah	36
Jerrard	36
Jerremy	56
Jerry	39, 50, 50, 52, 87, 97, 98, 100, 102
Jes	93, 94, 117
Jess	64, 74
Jesse	43, 49, 55, 58, 108
Jeter	59
Jim	115
Jin	37, 62
Jinkins	42
Jo	87, 116
Joan	50, 51, 59, 60
Joanna	50
Jobe	116
Joc	60
Jock	87
Joe	38, 41, 42, 42, 43, 47, 49, 50, 51, 51, 51, 57, 58, 58, 59, 60, 68, 69, 71, 74, 77, 78, 82, 83, 83, 86, 87, 96, 98, 98, 99, 101
Joel	55
John	36, 36, 39, 39, 43, 43, 49, 50, 50, 50, 51, 53, 53, 66, 84, 86, 87, 94, 94, 97, 98, 104, 115, 116, 117
Johua	38
Jonathan	60, 97
Jonco	49
Jone	94, 94, 96, 96, 97, 110
Joseph	50, 95, 108, 114
Josh	43
Joshua	38, 43, 49, 54, 60, 63, 64, 100
Joy	116
Jubey	40
Jud	79
Juda	63, 67
Judah	36, 46, 49, 77, 81, 87, 90, 91, 91, 93, 93, 94, 95, 98, 98
Judath	114
Jude	38, 38, 38, 38, 40, 41, 42, 43, 44, 46, 46, 51, 55, 59, 62, 75, 81, 82, 85, 85, 85, 91, 91, 92, 92, 99, 103, 103, 107, 112, 115
Judith	40, 51, 58, 97
Judy	49, 50, 50, 51, 52, 55, 55, 56, 57, 58, 60, 60, 63, 63, 64, 65, 66, 68, 68, 68, 74, 74, 75, 75, 76
Julen	111
June	48
Jupiter	56

Surname, Given Name	page(s)
NEGROES (cont.)	
Kate	49, 49, 49, 50, 51, 51, 53, 53, 55, 55, 57, 57, 58, 59, 60, 60, 64, 66, 114, 114
Kelley	103
Keziah	35, 50
King	77, 103
Kit	92
Kitty	66
Larke	43
Lazarus	62
Leak	88
Leanna	82, 87
Lee	66
Leet	111
Leevinah	64
Leir	85
Lemon	50, 53, 54
Let	77, 81, 81, 82, 84, 86, 86, 92, 100, 100, 100, 100
Lett	38, 38, 39, 44, 49, 49, 50, 50, 50, 53, 53, 56, 57, 57, 58, 59, 63, 69
Letty	50, 53, 53, 54, 55, 59
Lever	108
Levina	49
Levinah	67, 70
Levy	82
Lewis	39, 42, 48, 49, 60, 64, 65, 68, 70, 71, 96, 96, 99, 99, 102, 114
Lid	38, 79, 95, 99, 103
Lidd	115
Lidda	81
Liddy	49, 101
Lidia	35, 47
Lidy	63, 67, 75
Lil	42
Lilly	50, 64
Limass	35, 52
Lin	77
Liney	43
Linney	36, 112
Lis	41
Liza	108
Lizah	97
Lize	37
Lizza	50
Lizzy	113
London	69, 84, 95, 97, 99, 101
Lot	100, 103
Lott	71, 117
Loudon	42, 43, 43

Index "C" Tithables 1782-001 to 1782-005

Surname, Given Name	page(s)	Surname, Given Name	page(s)
NEGROES (cont.)		NEGROES (cont.)	
Luce	36, 38, 42, 43, 62, 63, 67, 68, 69, 85, 85, 94, 99, 99, 100, 107, 112, 112, 113, 115, 115, 115	Milly	35, 40, 45, 46, 47, 47, 58, 72, 107
Lucey	107	Mima	50, 50, 52, 58, 62, 97, 108
Lucie	64, 76	Mime	46, 46, 113
Lucinda	47, 98	Mimey	42, 66, 74, 82, 83, 94, 99, 115
Lucy	35, 39, 39, 40, 40, 41, 41, 43, 47, 47, 48, 48, 49, 49, 50, 50, 50, 50, 51, 51, 51, 53, 53, 54, 55, 56, 56, 58, 58, 59, 60, 60, 63, 64, 65, 65, 65, 65, 68, 69, 70, 71, 72, 72, 73, 74, 75, 87, 91, 91, 94, 95, 95, 95, 99, 103, 106, 107, 108	Mimy	42, 45, 117
		Minard	101
		Miney	43
		Minny	114
		Minor	94
		Minta	100
		Mirian	50
		Mirreah (2)	97, 97
		Mirta	98
Lucy Sr.	57	Mirtiller	86
Luis	36, 55	Mol	42, 43, 98
Luke	54	Moll	36, 36, 42, 48, 53, 70, 78, 94, 96, 96, 96, 100, 107, 108, 110
Lule	74		
Luse	40	Molley	48, 49, 57, 64
Lyd	112	Mollo	101
Lyda	37	Molly	51, 114
Lydda	55	Monday	91
Lydia	40	Monico (2)	83, 83
Lynn	101	Morocco	54
Mack	51	Moses	38, 39, 39, 40, 49, 50, 57, 57, 58, 62, 65, 65, 65, 66, 69, 71, 74, 74, 75, 77, 78, 86, 86, 93, 93, 96, 100, 100, 102, 102, 103, 114, 115
Major	52		
Malbrough	81		
Manual	54		
Manuel	49, 50, 82, 86, 88, 97, 113		
Margaret	50, 87	Mosses	46
Margery	86	Mountain	93
Margues	68	Murf	43
Margus	68	Murray	54
Martha	49, 50, 50, 54, 81, 81	Murriah	98
Mary	36, 37, 38, 42, 43, 46, 49, 51, 51, 53, 54, 54, 54, 55, 57, 60, 63, 64, 69, 79, 84, 84, 84, 85, 87, 87, 94, 94, 96, 97, 98, 99, 100, 103, 103, 111, 112, 115	Muter	49
		Nace	53, 87
		Hag[t]	35
		Nall	66
		Nan	37, 38, 39, 40, 42, 42, 46, 49, 49, 49, 51, 54, 55, 58, 59, 59, 62, 63, 65, 69, 70, 72, 73, 74, 82, 83, 83, 84, 85, 86, 86, 90, 90, 92, 94, 94, 98, 113, 115
Mason	62, 97, 99, 112		
Mass	59		
Matt	48		
Matthew	87		
Meligan	66	Nan Jr.	75
Mescheck	100	Nance	36, 42, 42, 44, 56, 62, 66, 68
Mill	67, 80, 83, 85, 85, 110, 112	Nancy	43, 43, 50, 51, 58, 87, 108
Mille	116	Nann	50, 51, 117
Miller	67	Nanny	47, 52, 53, 60, 60, 69
Milley	46, 48, 49, 50, 53, 59, 59, 60, 63, 65, 68, 68, 69, 73, 74, 75, 82, 82, 88, 88, 93, 93, 94, 94, 97, 97, 99, 101, 103, 106	Nat	87, 95
		Nath[l]	75
		Natt	64, 70
		Nead	107

Index "C" Tithables 1782-001 to 1782-005

Surname, Given Name	page(s)	Surname, Given Name	page(s)
NEGROES (cont.)		NEGROES (cont.)	
Ned	39, 39, 40, 43, 43, 49, 50, 50, 51, 52, 54, 54, 54, 55, 55, 56, 56, 56, 57, 57, 60, 86, 90, 93, 93, 94, 98, 116	Phil	43, 93, 97, 98
		Philander	50
		Philip	103
		Phillis	38, 38, 39, 42, 43, 101
Nedd	48, 53	Phill	49, 51, 53, 54, 55, 59, 64, 65, 101, 114
Neilson	100		
Nel	43, 88	Phillis	48, 49, 50, 57, 62, 62, 62, 63, 65, 68, 68, 73, 74, 74, 75, 77, 78, 78, 86, 86, 86, 99, 99, 101, 102, 104
Nell	36, 39, 39, 40, 40, 42, 45, 46, 46, 50, 51, 51, 51, 51, 55, 64, 69, 74, 74, 75, 76, 81, 94, 94, 97, 97, 97		
Nelley	98	Phoebe	77
Nelly	42, 54, 56, 57, 59	Pinder	68
Nelson	50, 50, 53, 55, 98, 114	Plat	37
Neriate	101	Plato	68
Nero	55	Platoe	45
Newman	46	Poll	41, 98, 103, 103
Newton	95	Polley	78, 87
Nib	39	Polly	47, 54, 79, 79
Nick	63, 71	Pompie	47
Nimrod	46	Pompy	44, 97
Norah	92	Pressley	98
Nott	50	Primos	65
Oliver (2)	60, 60	Prince	57, 58, 64, 65, 67
Orange	53, 84	Pris	94, 98, 98, 103
Orson	100	Priscilla (2)	81, 81
Ovid	74	Priss	46, 51, 75, 93
Pallace	67	Prue	73, 100
Parker	77	Punch	64
Pat	65, 77, 86, 99, 99	Quacko	55
Patience	36, 41, 50, 50, 82, 100, 100	Rachal	62
Patrick	78	Rachel	42, 43, 45, 49, 50, 50, 50, 51, 53, 53, 56, 56, 57, 58, 59, 59, 62, 64, 69, 71, 73, 76, 82, 86, 87, 87, 95, 95, 99
Patt	37, 37, 41, 49, 50, 51, 51, 53, 54, 65, 67, 69, 107, 113		
Patty	83, 95	Ralf	81, 86
Paul	43, 110	Ralph	50, 50, 53, 59, 75
Peg	40, 49, 49, 57, 77, 83, 90, 91, 91, 95, 96, 96, 97, 104, 104, 113	Randolph	94
		Ren	66
Pegg	36, 36, 50, 54, 56, 62, 62, 65, 111, 112	Reuben	85, 90, 97, 106
		Rewben	103
Peggy	53, 97	Rhoda	54, 107
Pen	69	Richmond	56
Pendar	74	Ridge	46
Penny	50	Robert	48, 108
Peter	35, 38, 39, 40, 40, 41, 43, 43, 43, 44, 44, 46, 48, 49, 49, 49, 50, 50, 51, 52, 52, 53, 53, 54, 54, 55, 57, 58, 58, 58, 62, 65, 65, 66, 68, 68, 69, 69, 70, 71, 71, 73, 73, 74, 75, 82, 87, 87, 91, 98, 98, 100, 100, 101, 102, 103, 109, 114, 117	Robin	47, 47, 50, 50, 53, 53, 54, 54, 55, 68, 81, 93, 98, 98, 114, 117
		Roger	40, 74
		Rose	39, 43, 47, 47, 48, 50, 51, 52, 55, 60, 61, 62, 63, 66, 67, 70, 74, 82, 85, 86, 86, 90, 90, 91, 91, 92, 97, 98, 99, 99, 99, 102,

Index "C" Tithables 1782-001 to 1782-005

Surname, Given Name	page(s)	Surname, Given Name	page(s)
NEGROES (cont.)		NEGROES (cont.)	
Rose (cont.)	103, 103, 104, 107, 107, 108, 109, 112, 115	Sesor	111
		Seth	46
Ross	64, 66, 76	Shad.	100
Rubin	47	Shadrach	49
Ruth	54, 69	Shadrack	53
Sal	80, 81, 81, 84, 84, 97, 99, 99, 100, 101, 102	Shadrick	64, 70, 75
		Sharlet	113
Sall	40, 41, 45, 50, 50, 55, 57, 58, 62, 63, 63, 64, 66, 68, 69, 69, 74, 90, 90, 94, 103, 113	Sharper	63, 64
		Sherlett	36
		Ship	68
Sally	51	Shurley	50
Sam	35, 36, 37, 39, 44, 44, 44, 46, 50, 50, 50, 50, 52, 54, 55, 56, 58, 58, 60, 60, 62, 63, 66, 65, 65, 67, 68, 69, 70, 73, 75, 77, 77, 80, 81, 81, 85, 86, 94, 97, 107, 107, 113, 116	Sib	95
		Sie	60
		Silla	50
		Sillar	106
		Siller	60, 64, 113
		Silva	45, 46
Sambo	62, 68, 99	Silvey	48
Sampson	55, 55, 82	Silvy	82
Samuel	55, 75	Simon	48, 51, 57, 57, 58, 74, 95, 96, 100
Sancco	43		
Sanco	43	Sinah	95
Sanda	108	Siner	40
Sarah	35, 36, 36, 37, 40, 41, 42, 43, 44, 45, 46, 48, 49, 50, 50, 50, 50, 51, 51, 52, 53, 53, 53, 54, 54, 55, 56, 57, 58, 59, 59, 60, 62, 63, 63, 65, 67, 68, 69, 69, 71, 74, 75, 75, 80, 80, 82, 82, 85, 85, 85, 85, 86, 88, 89, 89, 90, 90, 93, 95, 97, 98, 98, 100, 101, 101, 102, 103, 112, 114	Single	50
		Sip	116
		Sipio	71
		Sisley (2)	87, 87
		Sisley (2)	96, 96
		Siss	68
		Sisser	75
		Solomon	35, 49, 52, 52, 53, 57, 59, 68, 73, 74, 79, 80, 92, 92, 93, 93, 97, 100, 102
Sary	46, 112		
Sauney	99, 103, 106	Sook	53, 68
Sawney	50, 64, 81	Sookey	64
Scelia (2)	50, 50	Spencer	40, 53, 64, 69, 93, 95
Scelia (2)	50, 50	Squire	98
Sciah	59	Stepan (2)	84, 84
Scilla	52, 53, 53	Stephan	81, 86, 86, 94, 97, 98, 98
Scillar	52	Stephen	44, 50, 53, 62, 75
Scipeo	45	Strother	50
Scipio	52, 54, 58, 70	Subbinia	98
Sealey	63, 98	Suck	37, 39, 42, 44, 51, 65, 71, 73, 73, 81, 93, 93, 112
Seaser	115		
Sebre	50	Suckey	93
Sela	45	Sucky	40
Selah (2)	101, 101	Sue	40, 46, 49, 51, 51, 59, 71, 84, 85, 87, 94, 94, 96, 98, 100
Selea	108		
Selia	51	Sukey	50, 51
Sen	43	Susanah	62, 62, 68, 113
Sepio	37, 80, 99, 101, 101	Susannah	50
Seppi	73	Sylva	50

Index "C" Tithables 1782-001 to 1782-005

Surname, Given Name	page(s)
NEGROES (cont.)	
Synar	53
Tab	38, 82, 100, 117
Tamer	52, 74
Teanah	40
Temp	65
Tener	68, 77
Tenor	52
Thomas	98
Thos	47
Tibby	101
Tiers	116
Tiller	53
Tilly	54
Tim	63
Timatha	41
Titus	68, 98, 108
Toba	67
Tobe	88, 100
Toby	49, 49, 52
Tolbert	50
Toliver	74
Tom	36, 36, 37, 40, 41, 43, 44, 45, 48, 48, 49, 49, 49, 50, 50, 51, 53, 54, 54, 54, 56, 56, 58, 59, 59, 59, 60, 60, 60, 61, 62, 63, 63, 64, 64, 64, 65, 65, 65, 65, 68, 68, 68, 69, 69, 72, 72, 73, 73, 74, 74, 75, 77, 78, 79, 79, 83, 85, 86, 86, 87, 88, 90, 90, 90, 91, 92, 93, 94, 95, 96, 96, 97, 97, 97, 97, 97, 100, 101, 112, 114, 117
Tone	99
Toney	42, 43, 48, 61, 65, 65, 67, 69, 90, 91, 101
Tong	65
Tony	50
Troy	75
Truelove (2)	101, 101
Truley	54
Trulove	44
Tuner (Turner?)	62
Ugene	47
Unnamed	114
Unnamed (girl)	115
Ursley	75
Val	94, 96
Venes	66
Venus	54, 61, 64, 66, 102, 102
Vicey	47
Vick	108
Vilat	41

Surname, Given Name	page(s)
NEGROES (cont.)	
Vilet	38, 62, 107
Vina	92
Viney	44
Vinson	63
Violet	48, 57, 58, 114
Violett	87, 92, 97
Virgin	46
Weaver	42
West	90
Whip	68
Wil (2)	43, 43
Wil (2)	43, 43
Wilkins	100
Will	35, 36, 36, 38, 38, 39, 39, 40, 40, 41, 41, 42, 45, 45, 46, 47, 48, 48, 48, 49, 49, 49, 49, 50, 52, 54, 57, 60, 61, 63, 64, 64, 65, 65, 65, 66, 66, 68, 68, 68, 68, 68, 69, 71, 74, 74, 75, 75, 75, 76, 76, 80, 82, 85, 87, 87, 88, 90, 91, 93, 93, 93, 94, 95, 99, 101, 101, 103, 105, 106, 107, 110, 112, 112
William	91, 108, 114, 116
Williby	80, 97
Willis	51, 60
Willoughby	69
Wilson	50
Win	65
Windsor	50
Winea	107, 112, 112
Winey	44
Winn	97
Winna	106
Winney	35, 36, 38, 41, 49, 50, 50, 50, 53, 53, 53, 55, 56, 56, 56, 56, 58, 59, 59, 62, 63, 63, 66, 68, 69, 71, 74, 75, 83, 85, 85, 85, 86, 94, 94, 95, 97, 97, 97, 97, 98, 99, 99, 102, 102, 103, 103, 104, 104, 110, 110, 114
Winny	42, 42, 42, 52, 52, 54, 55, 63, 64, 69, 74, 107, 116
Woner	64
Young Abigail	77
Zachariah	47, 63, 70, 74
YOUNG NEGROES	
Abrener	96
Amy	64
Billy	64
Harry	79

Index "C" Tithables 1782-001 to 1782-005

Surname, Given Name	page(s)	Surname, Given Name	page(s)
YOUNG NEGROES (cont.)		OSBORN	
Let	96	W^m	92
Mill	79	OWENS	
Moses	64	Bethell	93
Rose	96	John	93
Scipio	64	John (Pignut)	92
Suky	64	Joshua	93
Tom	64	Joshua (overseer)	82
Unnamed	82, 92	W^m (2)	93, 93
Will	79	PAIN	
Unnamed (of Lucy)	55	Charles	44
Tramp	107	PARKER	
Unnamed child	51, 51, 58, 111	Alexander	57
		John	44
NEILSON		Richard	56
Thomas	36	PARR	
NELSON		James	72
John	36	PAWLING	
John (Blacksmith)	71	Isachar	48
John (Elk Run)	41	PAYNE	
William	41	Ann	113
NEWBY		Francis	114
Betty	56	Thomas	113
NEWHOUSE		William	113
Jonathan	92	W^m	114
NEWTON		PEAK	
Abraham	113	W^m	94
NICKOLS		PEARCE	
Samuel	113	John	72
NORMAN		PEARLE	
Clem	113	Charity (wife of W^m)	93
Ezekel	113	Edward	113
Isack	113	Samuel	94
Jesse	113	W^m	94
John	113	PERSON	
Martin	113	John	42
William	113	PETERS	
NORRISS		Elizabeth	35
John	92	James	42
W^m	92	John	35
NORTHCUTT		Mary	45
Jeremiah	37	PETTIT	
NORTON		Nathaniel	56
John	44	Obadiah	56
OBANNON		Samuel	56
Benjamin	92	PEYTON	
James	93	Henry	93
John	93	PHILLIPS	
Joseph	93	Abner	71
Samuel	92	Elias	71
Will	93	PICKARD	
ORGAN		William	45
Samuel	56		

Index "C" Tithables 1782-001 to 1782-005

Surname, Given Name	page(s)
PICKET	
W^m	112
PICKETT	
John	97
Sanford	97
Wm Sanford	97
PIDGE	
John	94
PINCKARD	
James	94
PINKSTONE	
Henry	93
PIPER	
Benjamin	113
PORTER	
Charles	57
Martin	56
Samuel	56
Thomas	57
Thomas Jr.	57
William	42
PREAILE	
John	94
PREAST	
John	113
Mason	113
Rodam	113
PRESTON	
Jacob	72
Jeremiah	72
John	72
Joshua	72
William Jr.	71
William Sr.	72
PRIEST	
Thos (levy free)	46
PRIM	
W^m	93
PROUDFOOT	
John	92
PUTIR	
George Sr.	45
Joseph	45
QUSSENBERY	
James	114
RANDELL	
William	114
RANDOLL	
John	114
RANSDELL	
John	57
Thomas	96
Whorton (Captain)	96

Surname, Given Name	page(s)
RANSDELL (cont.)	
Whorton's Quarter	96
W^m	96
REALY	
Thomas	47
Thos Jr.	47
RECTOR	
Charles	96
John	42
RED	
Allan	57
REVELY	
John	59
RICE	
W^m	96
RICTOR	
Harman	38
RIDDLE	
William	114
RIGHLEY	
John	114
Thomas	114
RIXSEY	
Richard	114
ROACH	
James	38
John	58
ROBERTSON	
John	96, 114
Joseph	96
Nat	90
Nathaniel	96
William	114
ROBISON	
Benjamin	57
Stephen	57
ROE	
Alexander	57
ROGERS	
Edward	57
George	57
George Jr.	57
Henry (2)	114, 114
James	114
John	114
Steaven	114
ROOCH [ROACH?]	
Robert	57
William	57
ROSE	
Jesse	41
William	41

Index "C" Tithables 1782-001 to 1782-005

Surname, Given Name	page(s)
ROUTT	
James	72
Peter	72
RUSAW	
William	46
RUSSELL	
William	72
W^m	43
RUST	
John	96
Matthew	96
Samuel	96
SANDERS	
John	58
Robert	58
William	58
SAUNDERS	
James	99
W^m	99
SCOTT	
Alexander	99
Elizabeth	99
James (Prince William Co.)	98
John (Rev^d)	98
Robert	97
SEATON	
John	98
W^m	35
SELMAN	
Ann	115
SETTLE	
Joel	115
SHACKELFORD	
Benjamin	114
George	58
James	58
James Jr.	58
SHANKS	
John	73
SHARP	
Ann	72
SHAW	
Charles	111
SHIRLEY	
Benjamin	58
John	58
SHOEMATE	
Benj^a	73
James	73
John (2)	73, 73
William	73
SHUMAKE	
Baley	40

Surname, Given Name	page(s)
SHUMAKE (cont.)	
Daniel	45
James	45
John Sr.	40
SHUMATE	
John	115
Samuel	115
Thomas	41
Tolliver	38
SIDDALL	
Job	58
John	58
SILVEY	
Abraham (overseer)	77
Abraham's Property	99
SINCLAIR	
James	72
John	97
William, W^m	73, 99
SINGER	
George	39
John	39
John Jr.	39
SINGLETON	
Standley	97
Tonshend	97
SINKLER	
Robert	115
SKINKER	
W^m (Prince William Co.)	98
SMITH	
Berryman	115
John	41, 102, 115, 116
John Jr.	115
Joseph	99
Mary	97
Rich^d	97
William	115
William (Carter's Run)	115
William (Carter's Run)	116
William Sr. (Hicory)	115
SMOOT	
James	115
John	115
Leonard	115
SMOOTE	
John	115
SNYDER	
Jacob	115
SPILLER	
Jeremiah	41
Phill	41
Phill Sr.	39

Index "C" Tithables 1782-001 to 1782-005

Surname, Given Name	page(s)	Surname, Given Name	page(s)
STAGE		THARP	
Richard	99	James (overseer)	68
STALARD		THOMAS	
Walter (overseer)	40	Aaron	106
STARK		Benjamin	106
James	37	David	100
Jeremiah	37	Elisha	100
STEELE		THOMPSON	
George	59	James (Rev^d)	100
Samuel	59	THOMSON	
STEVENSON		Eli	116
James	72	James	35
STEWART		Jesse	116
Allen	59	THORNBERRY	
George	79	Francis	59
William	59	Henry	59
William, W^m (Rev^d)	39, 58, 97	John	59
W^m (Rev^d) Quarter	39	Samuel Jr.	59
STONE		Samuel Sr.	59
Benjamin	115	Thomas	59
John	59	William	59
John (overseer)	49	THRAILKILL	
Menoah	98	Elijah	41
STROTHER		Elijah's Quarter	41
Reuben	99	TOLLE	
STROTHERS		George	106
William	115	Roger	106
SUDDOTH		Sarah	106
James	115	TOMLET'S	
Larrance	115	Quarter	75
SULLIVAN		TOMLIN	
Sarah	99	John Jr.	60
SUTTLE		John Sr.	60
Francis	49	Samuel	60
William	49, 59	W^m	60
SWENSON		TRIPLETT	
John	72	Francis	116
TATE		William	116
Peter	100	TUELLAS [TULLOS?]	
TAYLOE		Rodam	45
James (overseer)	52	TURBERVILLE	
TAYLOR		George's Quarter	73
Benjamin	100	TURNER	
Charles	100	Edward	106
Elizabeth	73	John	73, 100, 106
Henry	60	Samuel	106
Isaac	100	UTESLER	
Joseph	100	Christian	101
Judith	100	UTTERBACK	
Nimrod	60, 73	Agnes	38
Peter	73	Chas	38
Peter (overseer)	67	Harmon	101
W^m	106	Harmon (overseer)	98

Index "C" Tithables 1782-001 to 1782-005

Surname, Given Name	page(s)
UTTERBACK (cont.)	
Henry (levy free)	41
John	101
VANN	
Zachariah	64
VAUGHAN	
John	101
W^m	101
VOWLS	
Richard	74
WADDLE	
James	103
John	103
W^m	103
WAKE	
John	103
WALLER	
Charles	44
Edward	38
WATSON	
William	75
WATTS	
John	103
WATTSON	
Thomas	60
WAY	
John	116
WEATHERLY	
James	116
WEATHERS	
Cain	76
WEAVER	
Jacob	117
John	76
Tilman	40
WELCH	
Cilvester (2)	102, 102
William	116
WEST	
Charles	102
WHAILIN	
Patrick	102
WHEATLEY	
James	74
John	75
Joseph	75
WHEATLEY	
Charles	40
David (2)	40, 40
WHITE	
John (overseer)	98
William	60
W^m	103
WHITING	
Francis	60
WHITLEY	
William	116
WILKINS	
William Sr.	75
WILLIAMS	
John	93
Jonas	75
Paul	74
WILLIBY	
John	102
WILLIS	
Ursely	75
WILLSON	
Richard	116
WINN	
James	102
Margaret	103
Minor	103
WITHERS	
James	74, 116
Jesse (overseer)	75
Lewis	75
Thomas Sr.	74
WOOD	
Dickerson	116
James	35
John	36
WOODARD	
Charles	103
Luke	103
WOODFORD	
Catesby	49, 60
WOODYARD	
Lewis	116
WRIGHT	
John (Captain)	75
Reuben (overseer)	68
WYNNE	
John	116
YOUNG	
James	61
Original	35
William	104
Willm Jr.	104

Index "D" Slaves & Slaveholders 1782-001 to 1782-005 Tithable Lists

Surname, Given Name	page(s)
ALEXANDER, Phillip (16 negroes)	
Ben	62
James (2)	62, 62
James (2)	62, 62
Pegg (2)	62, 62
Phillis (2)	62, 62
Rose	62
Sall	62
Sam	62
Sambo	62
Stephen	62
Tom	62
Tuner	62
ALLEN, James (1 negro)	
Vilet	107
ALLISON, Wm. ("Exor. to Kirk") (14 negroes)	
Beck	77
Ben	77
Bet (2)	77, 77
Charles	77
Cogger	77
Currier	77
Daniel	77
Dimbo	77
Esther	77
Moses	77
Peg	77
Tener	77
ARNAL, Jack (3 negroes)	
Bob	107
Diner	107
Nead	107
ASBURY, Wm (3 negroes)	
King	77
Lin	77
Phillis	77
ASHBY, John Sr. (Captain) (13 negroes)	
Daniel (2)	40
Jeany	40
Judith	40
Lucy	40
Lydia	40
Milly	40
Sall	40
Spencer	40
Sucky	40
Teanah	40
Will (2)	40, 40
BALEY, Joseph (3 negroes)	
Daniel (2)	105, 105
Will	105
BALEY, Moses (9 negroes)	
Baccus	80

Surname, Given Name	page(s)
BALEY, Moses (cont.)	
Dick	80
George	80
Hannah	80
Mill	80
Sal	80
Sarah (2)	80, 80
Sepio	80
BALL, John (10 negroes)	
Charles	62
Daniel	62
George	62
Jin	62
Jude	62
Luce	62
Nance	62
Phillis	62
Rachel	62
Winney	62
BARBEE, Andrew Jr. (1 negro)	
Mima	108
BARBEE, Joseph (4 negroes)	
Cate	107
Charrity	107
Jacob	107
Rose	107
BARBEY, Andrew Sr. (10 negroes)	
Dick	108
Eve	108
Hannah	108
Jesse	108
Joseph	108
Liza	108
Lucy	108
Nancy	108
Rose	108
William	108
BARBEY, Joseph (1 negro)	
Lever	108
BARKER, John (8 negroes)	
Agga	104
Grii	104
John	104
Peg (2)	104, 104
Phillis	104
Winney (2)	104, 104
BARKER, Wm (1 negro)	
Adam	80
BARNETT, Ambrose (15 negroes)	
Aaron	48
Bett	48
Bob	48
Claris	48

Index "D" Slaves & Slaveholders 1782-001 to 1782-005 Tithable Lists

Surname, Given Name	page(s)	Surname, Given Name	page(s)
BARNETT, Ambrose (cont.)		BERRY, Henry (5 negroes)	
Dick	48	Beck	77
George	48	Ben	77
Glasgow	48	Sam (2)	77, 77
Janey	48	Tom	77
Lewis	48	BERRY, W^m (6 negroes)	
Molley	48	Charles	78
Sarah	48	Elizabeth	78
Silvey	48	Harry	78
Tom	48	Phillis (2)	78, 78
Violet	48	Polley	78
Will	48	BERRYMAN, Benjamin (2 negroes)	
BARTLETT, Thomas		Jean	62
Abigail	77	Mason	62
Dinah	77	BERRYMAN, Maximilion (16 negroes)	
Frank	77	Ben	63
Gill	77	Daniel	63
Hannah	77	George	62
Humphrey (2)	77, 77	Hanah	62
Jack	77	James	62
Joe	77	Joshua	63
Judah	77	Milley	63
Let	77	Nan	62
Parker	77	Rachal	62
Pat	77	Sarah	62
Phoebe	77	Sarah	63
Young Abigail	77	Susanah	62
BARTLETT, W^m (1 negro)		Vinson	63
Dimbo	78	Winny	63
BARTON, Levy (1 negro)		Zachariah	63
Williby	80	BLACKABY, Joseph (10 negroes)	
BASHAW, Peter (3 negroes)		Amelia	107
Beck	80	Cate	107
Bet (2)	80, 80	George	107
BATTALEY, Bryan (1 negro)		Jenny	107
Cate	63	Jude	107
BERKLEY, W^m (8 negroes)		Lucey	107
Aaron	78	Moll	107
Agor (3)	78, 78, 78	Rhoda	107
Bet	78	Will	107
Hannah	78	Winea	107
Harry	78	BLACKERBY, Goduthern (4 negroes)	
Moses	78	Cook	108
BERRY, George (10 negroes)		Fran	108
Bess (2)	78, 78	Moll	108
Dick	78	Titus	108
Frank	78	BLACKWELL, John (16 negroes)	
Gloucester	78	Fanny	63
Jarrard	78	George	63
Joe	78	Grace	63
Moll	78	Hanah	63
Patrick	78	Harry	63
Tom	78	Jacob	63

Index "D" Slaves & Slaveholders 1782-001 to 1782-005 Tithable Lists

Surname, Given Name	page(s)	Surname, Given Name	page(s)
BLACKWELL, John (cont.)		BLACKWELL, W^m (cont.)	
James	63	Tom	36
Judy	63	Will	36
Lidy	63	Winney	36
Lucy	63	BLAND, Mary (1 negro)	
Mary	63	Will	80
Nan	63	BOSWELL, Elizabeth (10 negroes)	
Sealey	63	Bailey	48
Susanah	63	Ben	48
Will	63	Dolly	48
Winney	63	Esther	48
BLACKWELL, Samuel (16 negroes)		Eve	48
Amos (2)	49, 49	Grace	48
Bill (2)	49, 49	James (2)	48, 48
Cynar	49	Jane	48
Cyrus	49	Simon	48
Dinah	49	BOWEN, James (2 negroes)	
Frank	49	Hannah	63
Jane (2)	49, 49	Judy	63
Kate	49	BOWER, Peter (9 negroes)	
Lett	49	Charles (2)	63
Muter	49	Hanah	63
Toby (2)	49, 49	Juda	63
Tom	49	Phillis	63
Will	49	Sarah	63
BLACKWELL, Thomas (10 negroes)		Tim	63
Bob	62	Tom	63
Daniel	62	Winney	63
Dick	62	BOYD, Samuel (Dr.) (9 negroes)	
George	62	Adam	48
Grace	62	Cate	48
James	62	Cupid	48
Lazarus	62	Dick	48
Mima	62	Frank	48
Peter	62	June	48
Vilet	62	Lucy	48
BLACKWELL, W^m (21 negroes)		Matt	48
Bartley	36	Tom	48
Bash	36	BRADLEY, Hugh (4 negroes)	
Bob	36	Adam	105
Celia	36	Cris (2)	105, 105
David	36	David	105
Dinah	36	BRADY, Hezekiah (1 negro)	
Henry	36	Sawney	81
Jack	36	BRAGG, Dozzer (2 negroes)	
James	36	Jane	117
Jenney	36	Mimy	117
John (2)	36, 36	BRENT, George (5 negroes)	
Luis	36	Antony	80
Mary	36	Harry (2)	80, 80
Nell	36	Sam	80
Pegg (2)	36, 36	Solomon	80
Sarah	36		

Index "D" Slaves & Slaveholders 1782-001 to 1782-005 Tithable Lists

Surname, Given Name	page(s)
BRENT, William (21 negroes)	
Beck	63
Cate	63
Charles	63
David	63
Dick	63
Easter	63
Fran	63
Hanah	63
Isaac	63
Jack	63
Jaffrey	63
James	63
Jenney	63
Lett	63
Luce	63
Nick	63
Sall (2)	63, 63
Sam	63
Sharper	63
Tom	63
BRIGGS, William (6 negroes)	
Bob	107
Charrity	107
Daniel	107
Hannah	107
Rose	107
Sam	107
BROHON, Lettice (3 negroes)	
Frank	37
Sarah	37
Tom	37
BRONAUGH, Maryan (2 negroes)	
Daniel	44
Sam	44
BRONAUGH, Thomas (10 negroes)	
Ben	64, 76
Daniel	64, 76
Harry	64, 76
Judy	64, 76
Kate/Cate	64, 76
Lucie	64, 76
Nell	64, 76
Rachel	64, 76
Ross	64, 76
Will	64, 76
BROOKE, Humphrey (15 negroes)	
Betty	48
Cupid	48
Daniel	48
Dinah	48
Hannah	48
Harry	48

Surname, Given Name	page(s)
BROOKE, Humphrey (cont.)	
Jane	48
Lucy	48
Milley	48
Moll	48
Nedd	48
Peter	48
Phillis	48
Rose	48
Will	48
BROWN, George (3 negroes)	
Nell	46
Newman	46
Silva	46
BROWN, John (1 negro)	
Rose	63
BROWN, Mary (2 negroes)	
Luce	107
Tramp (child)	107
BROWNING, Calup (1 negro)	
Daffiney	107
BRYAN, John (7 negroes)	
Bristol	48
Gilbert	48
Hary	62
Jane	48
Robert	48
Toney	48
Will	48
BRYANT, James (3 negroes)	
Abram (2)	64, 64
Prince	64
BULLETT, Cudberth/Cuthbert (25 negroes)	
Antony	42
Cate (2)	42
Charles	42
Cloey	42
George	42
Hannah (2)	42, 42
Jack	42
James	42
Jinkins	42
Joe	42
Jude	42
Loudon	42
Luce	42
Mimey	42
Mimy	42
Nan	42
Nance (2)	42
Philis	42
Rachel	42
Toney	42

Index "D" Slaves & Slaveholders 1782-001 to 1782-005 Tithable Lists

Surname, Given Name	page(s)	Surname, Given Name	page(s)
BULLETT, Cudberth/Cuthbert		CARTER, Charles L. (cont.)	
Winny (2)	42, 42	Bathsheba	50
BULLITT, Cuth[bert] (11 negroes)		Beck	49
Adam	40	Ben	49
Brister	40	Betty (7)	49, 50
Cloe	40	Billey	50
Jeary	40	Caesar	50
Jubey	40	Charity (2)	50, 50
Moses	40	Charlotte	50
Nell	40	Criss	49
Peter	40	Daniel (3)	49, 50
Sarah	40	David	50
Sue	40	Delila	50
Tom	40	Dick (4)	49, 50
BULLITT, Joseph (12 negroes)		Dido (2)	50, 50
Bess	39	Dinah (2)	50, 50
Cate	39	Doll (2)	50, 50
Geo.	39	Doss	50
Jean	39	Dosse	50
Lett	39	Eddy	50
Lewis	39	Edward	50
Ned (2)	39, 39	Esther	50
Nell	39	Eve	50
Peter	39	Ezekiel	50
Phillis	39	Fanny	50
Will	39	Frank (3)	50, 50, 50
BURGIS, Garnar (7 negroes)		Gabriel (2)	50, 50
Dinah	107	George (2)	50, 50
Harry	107	Gumby	50
Lucy	107	Hampton	50
Milly	107	Hannah (3)	50, 50, 50
Patt	107	Harry (5)	49, 50
Sam	107	Isaac (2)	50, 50
Winny	107	Isabell	50
CANTWELL, John (4 negroes)		Jack	50
Cate (2)	79. 79	Jacob (4)	50, 50, 50, 50
Cato	79	Jallace	49
Solomon	79	James (5)	49, 50
CARRELL, Elizabeth (3 negroes)		Jane (4)	50, 50, 50, 50
Lid	79	Jemima	50
Harry	79	Jenny	50
Mill	79	Jerry (2)	50, 50
CARTER, Charles L. (190 negroes)		Joan	50
Aaron	50	Joanna	50
Abram (3)	50, 50, 50	Joe (2)	49, 50
Adam	49	John (4)	49, 50
Adam	50	Jonco	49
Aggay	50	Joseph	50
Alice (2)	50, 50	Judy (3)	49, 50
Ambrose	50	Kate (2)	49, 50
Amos	50	Keziah	50
Amy	50	Lemon	50
Anthony	50	Lett (2)	50, 50

Index "D" Slaves & Slaveholders 1782-001 to 1782-005 Tithable Lists

Surname, Given Name	page(s)	Surname, Given Name	page(s)
CARTER, Charles L. (cont.)		CARTER, George (12 negroes)	
Letty	50	Charles	81
Lilly	50	Dark	81
Lizza	50	Dick	81
Lucy (4)	49, 50	Dinah	81
Manuel (2)	49, 50	Harry	81
Margaret	50	Jack	81
Martha (2)	50, 50	Judah	81
Mima	50	Jude	81
Mirian	50	Let	81
Molley	49	Priscilla (2)	81, 81
Nan (2)	49, 49	Suck	81
Nann	50	CARTER, Peter (2 negroes)	
Ned (2)	50, 50	Bob	79
Nell	50	Harry	79
Nelson (2)	50, 50	CHADDOX, Charles (1 negro)	
Nott	50	James	79
Patience	50	CHICHESTER, Richard (45 negroes)	
Patt (2)	49, 50	Abram	49
Peg	49	Amy	49
Pegg	50	Beck	49
Peter	50	Betty	49
Peter (2)	49, 49	Cain	49
Philander	50	Charles	49
Phillis	50	Daphney	49
Rachel	50	Darcus	49
Rachel (2)	50, 50	Davy	49
Ralph (2)	50, 50	Emanuel	49
Robin (2)	50, 50	Esther	49
Roger	50	Frank	49
Rose	50	George	49
Sall (2)	50, 50	Hannah (2)	49, 49
Sam (2)	50, 50	Jack	49
Sarah (2)	50, 50	Jacob (2)	49, 49
Sawney	50	James	49
Scelia (4)	50, 50, 50, 50	Jane	49
Sebre	50	Jesse	49
Shurley	50	Joshua	49
Silla	50	Judah	49
Single	50	Kate	49
Stephen	50	Let t	49
Strother	50	Levina	49
Sue	49	Lewis	49
Sukey	50	Liddy	49
Suky	50	Lucy	49
Susannah	50	Martha	49
Sylva	50	Milley	49
Tolbert	50	Moses	49
Tom (3)	49, 50	Nan	49
Will (4)	49, 50	Ned	49
Wilson	50	Peg	49
Windsor	50	Peter	49
Winney (3)	50, 50, 50	Phill	49

Index "D" Slaves & Slaveholders 1782-001 to 1782-005 Tithable Lists

Surname, Given Name	page(s)
CHICHESTER, Richard (cont.)	
Phillis	49
Rachel	49
Sarah	49
Shadrach	49
Solomon	49
Suky	49
Tom	49
Winney	49
CHICK, John (3 negroes)	
Grinage	79
Hester	79
Mary	79
CHILTON, Charles (20 negroes)	
Bett	50
Celia (2)	50, 50
Charles	50
Dinah	50
Harry	50
Jane (2)	50, 50
Lett	50
Lucy	50
Milley	50
Mima	50
Moses	50
Nancy	50
Patience	50
Penny	50
Sam	50
Sarah (2)	50, 50
Tony	50
CHINN, Christopher (17 negroes)	
Adam	81
Bet (2)	81, 81
Caiff	81
Daniel	81
Dick	81
Henry	81
Isaac	81
Jane	81
Let	81
Malbrough	81
Nell	81
Ralf	81
Sall (2)	81, 81
Sam (2)	81, 81
CHINN, Thomas (Loudoun Co.)(3 negroes)	
Dinah	81
James	81
Stephan	81

Surname, Given Name	page(s)
CHURCHILL, Armisteads (38 negroes)	
Aggy	64
Anney	64
Bett	64
Billy	64
Cager	64
Cate	64
Charles	64
David	64
Dick	64
Emanuel	64
Harry	64
James (2)	64, 64
Jane	64
Jess	64
Joshua	64
Leevinah	64
Lewis	64
Lilly	64
Lucy	64
Mary	64
Molly	64
Natt	64
Phill (2)	64, 64
Punch	64
Sall	64
Sawney	64
Shadrick	64
Sharper	64
Siller	64
Sookey	64
Spencer	64
Tom (2)	64
Venus	64
Will	64
Woner	64
CLARK, Elias (6 negroes)	
David	35
Henry	35
Jenny	35
Milly	35
Peter	35
Sarah	35
CLARKSON, Henry (11 negroes)	
Abe (2)	108
Ben	108
Cate	108
Dick	108
Diner	108
Jack	108
Jane	108
Sanda	108
Selea	108

Index "D" Slaves & Slaveholders 1782-001 to 1782-005 Tithable Lists

Surname, Given Name	page(s)
CLARKSON, Henry (cont.)	
Vick	108
CLEMDENEA, John (2 negroes)	
Frank	108
Robert	108
CLERK, Benjamin (1 negro)	
Jud	79
COLLINS, Edmond (8 negroes)	
Ben	82
Frank (2)	82, 82
Henry	82
Jude	82
Nan	82
Sampson	82
Sarah	82
COLLINS, John (2 negroes)	
Henna	109
Peter	109
COMBS, Catharine (3 negroes)	
Cuffy	82
David	82
Sarah	82
COMBS, Enniss (5 negroes)	
Charlott	44
Esther	44
Harry	44
Lett	44
Viney	44
COMBS, Robert (1 negro)	
Boatswain	82
COMBS, Sarah (4 negroes)	
Daniel	44
George	44
Hagner	44
James	44
CONAWAY, William (8 negroes)	
Amy	42
Frank	42
Geo.	42
Joe	42
Lewis	42
Moll	42
Nell	42
Will	42
CONWAY, Thomas Jr. (11 negroes)	
David	41
George	41
Henry	41
James	41
Jen	41
Lucy	41
Patt	41
Peter	41

Surname, Given Name	page(s)
CONWAY, Thomas Jr. (cont.0	
Sall	41
Tom	41
Will	41
COOKE, John (5 negroes)	
Abel	49
Betty	49
George	49
Harry	49
Mary	49
COPPAGE, Charles (2 negroes)	
Dinah	37
Unnamed Child (of Dinah)	37
COPPAGE, William (2 negroes)	
Jeney	37
Sepio	37
CORNWELL, Jervis (1 negro)	
Tom	79
CORNWELL, John (1 negro)	
Will	79
COURTNEY, W^m (5 negroes)	
Aggy	79
Anthony	79
Polly (2)	79, 79
Tom	79
COX, Abraham (3 negroes)	
Charles	45
Harry	45
Nell	45
CRAIG, James (Rev^d) (9 negroes)	
Amy	64
Billy	64
Bob	64
Moses	64
Scipio	64
Sukey	64
Tom (2)	64, 64
Winny	64
CRAINE, John (5 negroes)	
Adam	81
Darca	81
Lidda	81
Martha (2)	81, 81
CRAWLEY, Menoah (1 negro)	
Tom	117
CRIM, Cattron (4 negroes)	
Charles	109
Easter	109
George	109
Hannah	109
CROOK, Mary (3 negroes)	
Enoch	40
Harry	40

Index "D" Slaves & Slaveholders 1782-001 to 1782-005 Tithable Lists

Surname, Given Name	page(s)
CROOK, Mary (cont.)	
Nan	40
C[R]OSBY, George (4 negroes)	
Ben	39
Daniel	39
Henry	39
Jerry	39
CUNDIFF, Isaac (1 negro)	
Robin	81
DALE, William (4 negroes)	
Hannah	51
Nann	51
Ned	51
Sarah	51
DARNALL, Jeremiah (9 negroes)	
Bett	65
David	65
Hanah	65
Jack	65
Judy	65
Milley	65
Moses	65
Peter	65
Toney	65
DARNALL, Joseph (4 negroes)	
Franny	65
Lucy	65
Tom	65
Will	65
DEARING, John (1 negro)	
Clares	109
DODD, Benjamin (1 negro)	
Jenny	66
DODD, John (2 negroes)	
Fillis	109
Rose	109
DODD, Nath¹ Jr. (2 negroes)	
Rose	66
Venus	66
DODD, Nath¹ Sr. (10 negroes)	
Bosen	65
Cate	65
Dinah	65
Jaley	65
Jeffery	65
Lucy (2)	65, 65
Moses (2)	65, 65
Will	65
DONALDSON, John (1 negro)	
Unnamed (young negro)	82
DOUDALL, Thomas (7 negroes)	
Bett (2)	46, 46
Charles	46
DOUDALL, Thomas (cont.)	
Hannah	46
Isaac	46
Milley	46
DOWDELL, James (10 negroes)	
Abe	37
Abraham	37
Charles	37
Dol	37
Jin	37
Nan	37
Patt (2)	37, 37
Plat	37
Suck	37
DOWNING, W^m (22 negroes)	
Bet	82
Betty (2)	82, 82
Eli	82
Gabriel	82
Grace	82
Isaac	82
Joe	82
Leanna	82
Let	82
Levy	82
Manuel	82
Milley (2)	82, 82
Mimey	82
Patience	82
Peter	82
Rachel	82
Rose	82
Silvy	82
Tab	82
Will	82
DOWNMAN, Rawleigh (21 negroes)	
Alce	66
David	66
Dick	66
Easter	66
Frank	66
Jeffrey	66
John	66
Kate	66
Kitty	66
Lee	66
Meligan	66
Mimey	66
Moses	66
Nall	66
Nance	66
Ren	66
Ross	66

Index "D" Slaves & Slaveholders 1782-001 to 1782-005 Tithable Lists

Surname, Given Name	page(s)	Surname, Given Name	page(s)
DOWNMAN, Raleigh (cont.)		FEAGINS, Edward (2 negroes)	
Sall	66	Cate	84
Venes	66	Harry	84
Will	66	FEAGINS, Elizabeth (4 negroes)	
Winney	66	Lucy (2)	95
DUFF, James (1 negro)		Will	95
Will	66	Winney	95
DUNCAN, Charles (12 negroes)		FEAGINS, John (1 negro)	
Bell	65	Joseph	95
Britain	65	FICKLIN, Charles (2 negroes)	
Daniel	65	Levinah	67
Doll	65	Pallace	67
Frank	65	FIELDING, Edward (8 negroes)	
Lucy	65	Daniel	84
Primos	65	Dick	84
Prince	65	John	84
Sam (2)	65, 65	Let	84
Sarah	65	Mary (2)	84, 84
Suck	65	Nan	84
DUNCAN, Houson (2 negroes)		Sue	84
Ben	65	FIELDS, John (1 negro)	
Pegg	65	Mimey	83
DUNCAN, John Sr. (5 negroes)		FISHBACK, John (4 negroes)	
Patt	65	James (2)	84
Temp	65	London	84
Tom	65	Mary	84
Toney	65	FISHBACK, Josiah (10 negroes)	
Will	65	Ben	83
DUNCAN, Joseph Jr. (18 negroes)		Daniel	83
Cain	65	Harry	83
Charles	65	Joe	83
Cloe	65	Mill	83
Dick	65	Monico (2)	83, 83
Ephraim	65	Peg	83
Grace	65	Tom	83
Harry	65	Winney	83
Lewis	65	FISHBACK, Philip (1 negro)	
Nan	65	Jarrard	84
Pat	65	FITZGIARRALD, W^m (3 negroes)	
Peter	65	Harry	95
Phill	65	Sarah	95
Phillis	65	Tom	95
Tom (2)	65, 65	FITZHUGH, George (22 negroes)	
Tong	65	Alice	51
W^m	65	Anthony	51
EDWARDS, Thomas (1 negro)		Beck	51
Joe	83	Betty	51
EUSTACE, Hack (5 negroes)		Captain	51
David	42	Dan	51
Mary	42	Frank (2)	51, 51
Mol	42	Harry	51
Weaver	42	Jack	51
Winny	42	James	51

Index "D" Slaves & Slaveholders 1782-001 to 1782-005 Tithable Lists

Surname, Given Name	page(s)	Surname, Given Name	page(s)
FITZHUGH, George (cont.)		FITZHUGH, W^m (cont.)	
Jeffery	51	Willis	51
John	51	FLATHERS, Edward (6 negroes)	
Lucy	51	David	84
Mack	51	Hannah	84
Molly	51	Jane (2)	84
Nan	51	Sal (2)	84, 84
Rachel	51	FLETCHER, Joshua (1 negro)	
Sally	51	Sib	95
Sukey	51	FLOWEREE, Daniel (15 negroes)	
Unnamed negro child (2)	51, 51	Arch	95
FITZHUGH, Henry (13 negroes)		Cloe	95
Alexander	52	Dinah	95
Beck	52	Hannah	95
Billy	52	Henny	95
Bob	52	Henry	95
Dennis	52	Jack	95
Easter	52	Jane	95
Judy	52	Lid	95
Major	52	London	95
Nanny	52	Nat	95
Sarah	52	Patty	95
Scilla	52	Rachel (2)	95, 95
Tamer	52	Sinah	95
Will	52	FLOWRANCE, W^m (4 negroes)	
FITZHUGH, W^m (37 negroes)		Adam	83
Anthony (2)	51	Nan (2)	83, 83
Ben	51	Patty	83
Bett	51	FOLEY, James (10 negroes)	
Bryan	51	Armistead	95
Chany	51	Bet	95
Charles	51	Bob	110
Dennis	51	Charity	110
Dick (2)	51, 51	Daniel	95
Godfrey	51	Doctor	95
Harry	51	Emanuel	95
James	51	Fenny	95
Jane	51	Gloucester (2)	95, 95
Joan	51	Hannah	95
Joe (2)	51, 51	Judah	95
Jude	51	Lucy	95
Judith	51	Newton	95
Kate (2)	51, 51	Peg	95
Lucy (2)	51, 51	Simon	95
Mary (2)	51, 51	Will	110
Nancy	51	FOLEY, Thomas (4 negroes)	
Nell (3)	51, 51, 51	Charity	110
Patt	51	George	110
Phill	51	Mill	110
Rose	51	Moll	110
Simon	51	FOLEY, W^m (1 negro)	
Sue (2)	51, 51	George	104
Tom	51		

Index "D" Slaves & Slaveholders 1782-001 to 1782-005 Tithable Lists

Surname, Given Name	page(s)
FOOTE, George's Estate (14 negroes)	
Charles	36
Denbe (2)	36, 36
Dick	36
Duke	36
Hannah	36
Judah	36
Linney	36
Luce	36
Moll (2)	36, 36
Nance	36
Sherlett	36
Tom	36
FOOTE, William (13 negroes)	
Adam	51
Ann	51
Bob	51
Daniel	51
Dick	51
Jane	51
Joe	51
Judy	51
Patt	51
Peter	51
Priss	51
Sarah	51
Selia	51
FOSTER, Thomas (6 negroes)	
Amos	51
Braddock	51
Dick	51
Jacob	51
Nell	51
Suck	51
FOX, Samuel (7 negroes)	
Charity	66
Jacob	66
James	66
Jean	66
Judy	66
Peter	66
Sam	66
FRENCH, John (6 negroes)	
Frank (2)	95
George	95
Grace	95
James	95
Spencer	95
GENN, James (5 negroes)	
Charles	52
Dick	52
Jerry	52
Scillar	52

Surname, Given Name	page(s)
GENN, James (cont.)	
Solomon	52
GEORGE, Margarett (8 negroes)	
Agatha	40
Alex	40
Arch	40
Dick	40
Hannah	40
Hollan	40
Jude	40
Lucy	40
GEORGE, Parnack (9 negroes)	
Bob (2)	52, 52
Jack	52
Ned	52
Peter (2)	52, 52
Rose	52
Scipio	52
Winny	52
GIBSON, Abraham (1 negro)	
Jude	85
GIBSON, Jonathan (28 negroes)	
Adam	47
Alis	47
Ben (2)	47, 47
Cate	47
Celey	47
Charles	47
Charlotte	47
Daniel	47
David	47
Dinah	47
Henry	47
Hettey	47
Isaac	47
James	47
Joe	47
Lidia	47
Lucy	47
Milly	47
Polly	47
Robin	47
Rose	47
Rubin	47
Tho[s]	47
Ugene	47
Vicey	47
Will	47
Zachariah	47
GILLISON, Mary (Mrs.) (9 negroes)	
Ben	47
Buckery	47
George	47

Index "D" Slaves & Slaveholders 1782-001 to 1782-005 Tithable Lists

Surname, Given Name	page(s)
GILLISON, Mary (Mrs.) (cont.)	
Harry	47
Lucinda	47
Lucy	47
Milly	47
Nanny	47
Rose	47
GLASCOCK, George (8 negroes)	
Bet (2)	85, 85
Bob	85
Jack	85
Jude	85
Nan	85
Sarah	85
Will	85
GLASCOCK, Thomas (3 negroes)	
Orange	84
Stepan (2)	84, 84
GRASTY, George (14 negroes)	
Barbra	67
Charles	67
Dick	67
Frank	67
Hannah	67
Juda	67
Lidy	67
Luce	67
Mill	67
Miller	67
Patt	67
Rose	67
Toba	67
Toney	67
GREEN, Ann (9 negroes)	
Alice	52
Betty	52
Dick	52
Fanny	52
Jane	52
Mima	52
Sam	52
Toby	52
Winny	52
GREEN, Thomas (1 negro)	
Limass	52
GREENLEES, Peter (4 negroes)	
Clare	110
Dick	110
Jane	110
Jone	110
GREENWOOD, Daniel (2 negroes)	
Sam	67
Sarah	67

Surname, Given Name	page(s)
GRIFFIN, Henry (3 negroes)	
Andrew	52
Solomon	52
Tenor	52
GRIFFITHS, Evan (2 negroes)	
George	85
Sarah	85
GRIGSBY, Ann (14 negroes)	
Alice	85
Amey	85
Ben	85
Clary	85
Cooper	85
Dimby	85
Frank	85
Hester	85
Jack	85
James	85
Jane	85
Mill (2)	85, 85
Winney	85
GRIGSBY, Betsey (13 negroes)	
Charles	85
Doll	85
Harry	85
Hester	85
Jarrard	85
Leir	85
Luce (2)	85, 85
Mary	85
Reuben	85
Rose	85
Sarah	85
Sue	85
GRIMSLEY, William (1 negro)	
Winney	110
GUTTRIDGE, Allen (1 negro)	
Winney	110
HARDWICK, William (3 negroes)	
Bett	53
Rachel	53
Sarah	53
HARRIS, Elisha (1 negro)	
Hannah	111
HARRIS, Richard (1 negro)	
Fanny	111
HARRIS, Sammuel (4 negroes)	
Doll	111
Easter (2)	111, 111
Unnamed child	111

Index "D" Slaves & Slaveholders 1782-001 to 1782-005 Tithable Lists

Surname, Given Name	page(s)
HARRISON, Benjamin (53 negroes)	
Amey (2)	43, 43
Beck	43
Bellow	43
Ben	43
Bob	43
Cloe (2)	43
Dick	43
Dol	43
Frank	43
George (2)	43, 43
Grace	43
Haley (2)	43, 43
Hannah (2)	43, 43
Haver	43
Isham	43
Jean	43
Jeany	43
Jeney	43
Jenny	43
Jesse	43
John (2)	43, 43
Josh	43
Loudon (2)	43, 43
Lucy	43
Mary	43
Mimey	43
Mol	43
Murf	43
Nancy (2)	43, 43
Ned	43
Nel	43
Peter (2)	43
Phil	43
Phillis	43
Rachel	43
Rose	43
Sancco	43
Sanco	43
Sarah	43
Sen	43
Tom	43
Toney	43
Wil (2)	43, 43
HARRISON, George (15 negroes)	
Charles	87
Frank	87
Henny (2)	87, 87
Jack	87
Jerry	87
Jo	87
Jock	87
Judah	87

Surname, Given Name	page(s)
HARRISON, George (cont.)	
Mary	87
Nace	87
Nancy	87
Tom	87
Violett	87
Will	87
HARRISON, John Peyton (2 negroes)	
Brick	86
Dick	86
HATHAWAY, James (15 negroes)	
Frank	54
Hanah	54
Hannah	54
Jack	54
Jenny	54
Joshua	54
Lemon	54
Mary (2)	54, 54
Patt	54
Pegg	54
Sarah	54
Tom	54
Will	54
Winny	54
HATHAWAY, John (8 negroes)	
Phillis (2)	86, 86
Rachel	86
Rose	86
Sam	86
Stephan	86
Tom	86
Winney	86
HEALE, George (74 negroes)	
Aaron	53
Abel	53
Abram	53
Adam	53
Alice	53
Andrew	87
Anne	53
Anthony	53
Bally	53
Beck	53
Betty	53
Cate	87
Charles (2)	53, 53
Cuff	87
Daniel	53
Darcus (2)	53, 53
Dennis	53
Dick	53
Esther	53

Index "D" Slaves & Slaveholders 1782-001 to 1782-005 Tithable Lists

Surname, Given Name	page(s)	Surname, Given Name	page(s)
HEALE, George (cont.)		HEALE, George (cont.)	
Fanney	87	Frank	54
Fortune	53	George (3)	54, 54, 54
Frank	53	Isaac	54
Grace	53	James (2)	54
Hagar	53	Letty	54
Hannah (2)	53, 53	Luke	54
Hannah	87	Manual	54
Harry	53	Martha	54
Jacob	53, 87	Ned (3)	54, 54, 54
James (2)	53, 53,	Polly	54
James	87	Rhoda	54
Jane	87	Robin (2)	54, 54
John	87	Ruth	54
Kate	53	Sarah	54
Leanna	87	HEALE, W^m (30 negroes)	
Letty (2)	53, 53	Aaron	86
Lucy (2)	53, 53	Abel	86
Lucy	53, 87	Abigail	86
Margaret	87	Adam	86
Mary	87	Cate	86
Matthew	87	Charles	86
Milley	53	Daniel (2)	86, 86
Nanny	53	Dominy	86
Nat	87	Donnice	86
Nedd	53	Eve	86
Nelson	53	Fielding	86
Peggy	53	Hannah	86
Peter	53	Jacob	86
Peter (2)	87, 87	Jane (2)	86, 86
Phill	53	Joe	86
Polley	87	John	86
Rachel	53	Manuel	86
Ralph	53	Margery	86
Robin	53	Mirtiller	86
Scilla (2)	53, 53	Moses (2)	86, 86
Shadrack	53	Nan (2)	86, 86
Sisley (2)	87, 87	Pat	86
Solomon	53	Phillis	86
Spencer	53	Sarah	86
Stephen	53	Stephan	86
Sue	87	HEDGMAN, John (22 negroes)	
Synar	53	Alic	68
Tiller	53	Ben	68
Will	87	Frank	68
Winney (2)	53, 53	Grace	68
HEALE, Philip (26 negroes)		Hanah (2)	68
Aaron	54	Harry	68
Abel	54	Jack	68
Aggaitha	54	Jean	68
Amy	54	Joe	68
Betty	54	Judy (2)	68, 68
Charles	54	Lucy	68

Index "D" Slaves & Slaveholders 1782-001 to 1782-005 Tithable Lists

Surname, Given Name	page(s)
HEDGMAN, John (cont.)	
Robin	68
Sam	68
Ship	68
Siss	68
Sook	68
Tom	68
Whip	68
Will	68
Winney	68
HELM, Thomas (Captain) (14 negroes)	
Aaron	68
Enoch	68
Grace	68
Lewis	68
Luce	68
Nance	68
Peter	68
Phillis	68
Pinder	68
Plato	68
Sambo	68
Solomon	68
Titus	68
Will	68
HITCH, Cristopher (2 negroes)	
George	110
Paul	110
HITT, Harmon (8 negroes)	
Dinah	85
Hannah	85
Jude	85
Sam	85
Sarah	85
Tom	85
Winney (2)	85, 85
HOAGAN, John (2 negroes)	
George	53
Lett	53
HOGANS, Thomas (5 negroes)	
Let (2)	86, 86
Ralf	86
Rose	86
Tom	86
HOLTZCLAW, Benjamin (1 negro)	
Murray	54
HOOE, Housin (8 negroes)	
Edmond	53
Edmund	53
Hannah	53
Jack	53
Lett	53
Nace	53

Surname, Given Name	page(s)
HOOE, Housin (cont.)	
Patt	53
Sook	53
HOVELL, William (4 negroes)	
Cato	67
Dick	67
James	67
Prince	67
HUMSTON, Edward (12 negroes)	
Alin	43
Betty	43
Charles	43
Davey	43
Frank	43
Joe	43
Jude	43
Liney	43
Luce	43
Paul	43
Wil (2)	43
HUNDON, John (7 negroes)	
Charlot	68
Edmond	68
Gabriel	68
Peter	68
Sarah	68
Susanah	68
Tom	68
HUNTER, James (26 negroes)	
Aaron	68
Aggy	68
Alexander	68
Beecher	68
Ben (2)	68, 68
Betsy	68
Caskus	68
Charrity	68
Daniel	68
Emanuel	68
Jacob	68
Jenny	68
Judy	68
Margues	68
Margus	68
Milley (2)	68, 68
Phillis	68
Sall	68
Sithy	68
Tener	68
Tom	68
Will (3)	68, 68, 68

Index "D" Slaves & Slaveholders 1782-001 to 1782-005 Tithable Lists

Surname, Given Name	page(s)
HUNTON, William (17 negroes)	
Bob	53
Charlotte	53
Harry	53
Isaac	53
Ismuth	53
Jack	53
Kate	53
Lemon	53
Mary	53
Moll	53
Orange	53
Peter	53
Robin	53
Sarah (2)	53, 53
Tom	53
Winney	53
JACKSON, Joseph (3 negroes)	
Amey	88
Jane (2)	88, 88
JAMES, Dinah (19 negroes)	
Cato	38
Charles	38
Charlot	38
Clary	38
Ezabel	38
Jack	38
Joe	38
Jude (2)	38, 38
Luce	38
Mary	38
Moses	38
Nan	38
Philis (2)	38, 38
Tab	38
Vilet	38
Will	38
Winney	38
JAMES, John (4 negroes)	
Bet	88
Hannah (2)	88, 88
Manuel	88
JARRARD, William (4 negroes)	
Elige	111
Julen	111
Mary	111
Sesor	111
JENNINGS, Augustain (7 negroes)	
Aggy	69
Bell	69
Ben	69
Bett	69
Moses	69

Surname, Given Name	page(s)
JENNINGS, Augustain (cont.)	
Sall	69
JENNINGS, Balis (4 negroes)	
Alec	69
Sam	69
Toney	69
Willoughby	69
JENNINGS, Lewis (10 negroes)	
Bray	69
Charity	69
Frank	69
Joe	69
Lucy	69
Rachel	69
Sall	69
Spencer	69
Tom	69
Winny	69
JETT, Francis (1 negro)	
Pegg	111
JETT, James (4 negroes)	
Bett	117
David	117
Lott	117
Tab	117
JOHNSON, Beede (3 negroes)	
Ann	111
Ginn	111
Leet	111
JOHNSON, Moses (5 negroes)	
Aaron	87
Isaac	87
Joe	87
Rachel (2)	87, 87
JOHNSON, Tunis (3 negroes)	
George	69
Harry	69
Mary	69
JOHNSON, Yellis (2 negroes)	
James	69
Nell	69
JONES, Brerinton (1 negro)	
Pompie	47
JONES, Henry (4 negroes)	
Fanney	38
Joshua	38
Jude	38
Lett	38
JONES, John (9 negroes)	
Bett	69
Charlotte	69
Gerrard	69
Guy	69

Index "D" Slaves & Slaveholders 1782-001 to 1782-005 Tithable Lists

Surname, Given Name	page(s)
JONES, John (cont.)	
Jane	69
Nanny	69
Pen	69
Peter	69
Ruth	69
JONES, W^m (2 negroes)	
Abner	39
Lucy	39
KEITH, Alexander (10 negroes)	
Bill	88
Daphney	88
Hannah	88
James	88
Jane (2)	88, 88
Leak	88
Sarah	88
Tom	88
Will	88
KEITH, Isham (11 negroes)	
Aaron	88
Baeris	88
Charlotte	88
Eppa	88
Harry	88
James	88
Jane	88
Milley (2)	88, 88
Nel	88
Tobe	88
KEITH, John (12 negroes)	
Bob	54
Jane	54
Lucy	54
Mary	54
Morocco	54
Nan	54
Nelly	54
Peter (2)	54, 54
Sam	54
Tilly	54
Tom	54
KENNER, George (2 negroes)	
Catena	35
James	35
KENNER, Mrs. (10 negroes)	
Antony	39
Cate	39
Fortin	39
Hannah	39
Isac	39
Jaive	39
John	39

Surname, Given Name	page(s)
KENNER, Mrs. (cont.)	
Lucy	39
Moses	39
Suck	39
KIBBLE, W^m (2 negroes)	
Sarah (2)	89, 89
KNOX, William (19 negroes)	
Ammy	69
Anthony	69
Bett	69
Cate	69
Charity	69
Dinah	69
Elijah	69
Jack	69
London	69
Luce	69
Milley	69
Nan	69
Patt	69
Peter	69
Sarah (2)	69, 69
Tom	69
Will	69
Winney	69
LAMKIN, James (5 negroes)	
Isbell	90
Nan (2)	90, 90
Reuben	90
Sarah	90
LARRANCE/LAWRENCE, Edward (25 negroes)	
Adam	46
Dark	46
Dick	46
Ennis	112
Hannah	112
Hath	46
Henry	112
Jack	46
Jeane	112
Jude (2)	46, 46
Mary	46
Mason	112
Mime (2)	46, 46
Mosses	46
Nan	46
Ridge	46
Rose	112
Sam	46
Sarah	46
Sary	46, 112
Seth	46
Sue	46

Index "D" Slaves & Slaveholders 1782-001 to 1782-005 Tithable Lists

Surname, Given Name	page(s)
LARRANCE/LAWRENCE, Edward (cont.)	
Virgin	46
LARRANCE, Peter (3 negroes)	
Bettey	112
George	112
Jack	112
LAWSON, Gavin (8 negroes)	
Aker	70
Bill	70
Blandford	70
Daniel	70
Lucy	70
Moll	70
Peter	70
Sam	70
LAYTON, Robert (2 negroes)	
Augustin	55
George	55
LEE, Hancock (18 negroes)	
Abram	70
Alce	70
Amey (2)	70, 70
Ben	70
Fanney	70
George	70
Grace	70
Henry	70
James	70
Levinah	70
Lewis	70
Nan	70
Nat	70
Rose	70
Scipio	70
Shadrick	70
Zachariah	70
LEE, Henry's Estate (15 negroes)	
Alexander	90
Baley	90
Bet	90
Darca	90
Dick	90
Dinah (2)	90, 90
Gabriel	90
Jack	90
Peg	90
Sall	90
Sarah	90
Tom	90
West	90
Will	90
LEWIS, James (2 negroes)	
Larke	43
Ned	43
LEWIS, Zacariah (Captain) (9 negroes)	
Bett	44
George	44
Jack	44
Jude	44
Peter	44
Stephen	44
Suck	44
Tom	44
Winey	44
LITTRELL, Richard (3 negroes)	
Beck	43
Harry	43
Peter	43
LOVE, Augustine (7 negroes)	
Daniel	55
Ellen	55
Joel	55
Jude	55
Nell	55
Phill	55
Samuel	55
LOWRY, George (13 negroes)	
Anthony	54
Ben	54
Bess	54
Bob	54
Dinah	54
Hannah	54
Isaac	54
Jack	54
Phill	54
Scipio	54
Tom	54
Truley	54
Venus	54
LUNSFORD, Jemima (1 negro)	
Chloey	70
MARKHAM, James (5 negroes)	
Abraham	45
Clarey	45
Milly	45
Rachel	45
Scipeo	45
MARKHAM, John's Quarter (9 negroes)	
Bett	41
Esther	41
Joe	41
Jude	41
Lucy	41

Index "D" Slaves & Slaveholders 1782-001 to 1782-005 Tithable Lists

Surname, Given Name	page(s)
MARKHAM, John's Quarter (cont.)	
Patience	41
Poll	41
Will	41
Winney	41
MARTIN, Charles (13 negroes)	
Aggy	71
Bob (2)	71, 71
Charles	71
Charrity	71
George	71
Hanah	71
Jerremy	56
Lott	71
Peter	71
Rachel	71
Sipio	71
Sue	71
MARTIN, John (2 negroes)	
Nance	44
Peter	44
MASSEY, Thomas (3 negroes)	
Amelia	112
Luce	112
Winea	112
MAUZEY, Bettey (4 negroes)	
Hannah	45
Jeanny	45
Sall	45
Will	45
MAUZEY, John (9 negroes)	
Ben	36
Cate	36
Dinah	36
Jean	36
Jerimiah	36
Jarrard	36
Patience	37
Sarah	37
Will	37
McCORMACK, Stephen (18 negroes)	
Adam	71
Aggy	71
Bett	71
Charles	71
Daniel	71
Dinah	71
Eve	71
Hanah	71
Isaac	71
James	71
Jenney	71
Joe	71
McCORMACK, Stephen (cont.)	
Lucy	71
Moses	71
Nick	71
Sarah	71
Suck	71
Will	71
McCORMICK, John (2 negroes)	
James	112
Jude	112
McCOY, John (4 negroes)	
Alex^r	37
Ciss	37
Mary	37
Sam	37
McLANAHAME, James (10 negroes)	
Aggai	55
Davy	55
Hannah	55
Lydda	55
Ned (2)	55, 55
Robin	55
Sam	55
Sampson	55
Winney	55
McQUEEN, Charles (1 negro)	
Will	112
MERCER, John F's Estate (41 negroes)	
Amey	101
Andrew	101
Ben	101
Boatswain	101
Brister	101
Captain (2)	101, 101
Catena	101
Cloe	101
Cupid	101
David	101
Dinah	101
George (3)	101, 101, 101
Hannah	101
Isbell	101
Liddy	101
London	101
Lynn	101
Milley	101
Minard	101
Mollo	101
Neriate	101
Peter	101
Philis	101
Phill	101
Phillis	101

Index "D" Slaves & Slaveholders 1782-001 to 1782-005 Tithable Lists

Surname, Given Name	page(s)
MERCER, John F's Estate (cont.)	
Sal	101
Sarah (2)	101, 101
Selah (2)	101, 101
Sepio (2)	101, 101
Tom	101
Toney	101
Truelove (2)	101, 101
Will (2)	101, 101
METCALFE, John (6 negroes)	
Dick	55
Guy	55
Kate (2)	55, 55
Mary	55
Sall	55
MINTER, Joseph (8 negroes)	
Barton	56
Dick	56
Harry	56
Lett	56
Ned (2)	56, 56
Rachel	56
Winney	56
MINTER, Mary (5 negroes)	
Baccus	55
James	55
Lucy	55
Sarah	55
Unnamed baby (of Lucy)	55
MONDAY, John (12 negroes)	
Aaron	91
Adam	91
Frank	91
Gibby	91
Henry	91
Judah (2)	91, 91
Peg (2)	91, 91
Rachel	91
Rose	91
Tom	91
MONDAY, Robert (6 negroes)	
Ben	91
Elizabeth	91
Jeffery	91
Lucy (2)	91, 91
Rose	91
MONDAY, W^m (5 negroes)	
Ben	102
Cate (2)	102, 102
Jane	102
Sall	102
MONROE, John (1 negro)	
Jane	113

Surname, Given Name	page(s)
MOREHEAD, Alexander (4 negroes)	
Bop	41
Sarah	41
Timatha	41
Vilat	41
MOREHEAD, Charles (6 negroes)	
Dinah (2)	91
James	91
Monday	91
Peter	91
Will	91
MOREHEAD, John Sr. (18 negroes)	
Ben	112
Bet/Bett (2)	112, 112
Charles (2)	112, 112
Daniel	112
Dinah	112
Easter	112
Fanna	112
Hannah	112
Isaac	112
Linney	112
Luce	112
Lyd	112
Mary	112
Sarah	112
Suck	112
Will	112
MOREHEAD, Presley (12 negroes)	
Aga	90
David	90
Hannah	90
James	90
Judah	90
Ned	90
Rose (2)	90, 90
Sall	90
Tom (2)	90, 90
Toney	90
MOREHEAD, Samuel (7 negroes)	
Daniel	42
Dick	42
Frank	42
Jean	42
Lil	42
Nan	42
Suck	42
MOREHEAD, W^m (4 negroes)	
George	91
Jude (2)	91, 91
Toney	91

Index "D" Slaves & Slaveholders 1782-001 to 1782-005 Tithable Lists

Surname, Given Name	page(s)
MORGAN, Charles (5 negroes)	
Adam	112
Allen	112
Ben	112
Bob	112
Winea	112
MORGAN, Simon (5 negroes)	
Cyonis	91
Esther	91
Jane (2)	91, 91
William	91
MULLIKAN, Burton (2 negroes)	
Bett	55
Sampson	55
MURREY, James (6 negroes)	
Hannah (2)	102, 102
Peter	102
Phillis	102
Rose	102
Winney	102
MUSCHETT, James (19 negroes)	
Aaron	55
Abraham	55
Cloe	55
Hanah (2)	55, 55
Henry	55
Jacob	55
Jesse	55
Judy (2)	55, 55
Letty	55
Luis	55
Nan	55
Nelson	55
Nero	55
Peter	55
Quacko	55
Rose	55
Winny	55
NASH, Traverse (13 negroes)	
Elijah	56
Frank	56
Hannah	56
Jacob	56
James	56
Lucy	56
Ned	56
Nelly	56
Pegg	56
Richmond	56
Sam	56
Tom	56

Surname, Given Name	page(s)
NEALE, Benjamin (6 negroes)	
Abram	56
Daniel	56
Lucy	56
Rachel	56
Sarah	56
Winney	56
NEILSON, Thomas (7 negroes)	
Aaron	92
Daniel (2)	92, 92
Harry	92
Jude (2)	92, 92
Rose	92
NELSON, John (4 negroes)	
Arch	36
David	36
Dick	36
Sam	36
NELSON, John (Elk Run) (1 negro)	
George	41
NICKOLS, Samuel (1 negro)	
George	113
NORRISS, W^m (8 negroes)	
Harry	92
Kit	92
Let	92
Norah	92
Solomon (2)	92
Vina	92
Violett	92
NORTON, John (11 negroes)	
Antony	44
Betty	44
Charles	44
Frank	44
Grimage	44
Hannah (2)	44, 44
Jacob	44
Jeny	44
Pompy	44
Sam	44
OBANNON, Benjamin (1 negro)	
Nan	92
OBANNON, John (13 negroes)	
Amey	93
Cate	93
Dick	93
Gabriel	93
Jess	93
Judah (2)	93, 93
Phill	93
Sarah	93
Solomon	93

Index "D" Slaves & Slaveholders 1782-001 to 1782-005 Tithable Lists

Surname, Given Name	page(s)
OBANNON, John (cont.)	
Tom	93
Will	93
OBANNON, Samuel (1 negro)	
Hannah	92
ORGAN, Samuel (2 negroes)	
Beck	56
Jane	56
OSBORN, W^m (4 negroes)	
David	92
James	92
Tom	92
Unnamed young negro	92
OWENS, John (7 negroes)	
Agga	93
Milley	93
Moses	93
Robin	93
Suck (2)	93, 93
Suckey	93
OWENS, W^m (4 negroes)	
Cain	93
David	93
Edmond (2)	93, 93
PARKER, Alexander (12 negroes)	
Bett	57
Charles	57
Dakey	57
H[illegible]	57
Hannah	57
Harry	57
Jack	57
Lett	57
Peter	57
Sall	57
Sarah	57
Simon	57
PARKER, Richard (3 negroes)	
Esther	56
Isaac	56
Jupiter	56
PARR, James (1 negro)	
Milly	72
PAYNE, Ann (10 negroes)	
Dianah	113
Glascow	113
Hannah	113
Heath	113
Jenney	113
Nan	113
Sall	113
Samson	113
Siller	113

Surname, Given Name	page(s)
PAYNE, Ann (cont.)	
Susanah	113
PAYNE, Francis (5 negroes)	
Daniel	114
Grace	114
James	114
Moses	114
Winney	114
PAYNE, Thomas (2 negroes)	
Jack	113
Lizzy	113
PEARLE, Samuel (7 negroes)	
Charles (2)	94, 94
Jack	94
Lucy	94
Mary (2)	94, 94
Nan	94
PEARLE, W^m (16 negroes)	
Cuffey	94
George	94
Hendley	94
Jack	94
Jone	94
Milley (2)	94, 94
Moll	94
Nan	94
Ned	94
Sall	94
Sam	94
Tom	94
Will	94
Winney (2)	94, 94
PETERS, Elizabeth (9 negroes)	
Ben	35
Cate	35
Frank	35
George	35
Hethey	35
Isac	35
Lucy	35
Will	35
Winney	35
PETERS, James (3 negroes)	
George	42
Nelly	42
Sarah	42
PEYTON, Henry (15 negroes)	
Bet	93
Cate	93
Hannah (2)	93, 93
Jane	93
Milley	93
Moses	93

Index "D" Slaves & Slaveholders 1782-001 to 1782-005 Tithable Lists

Surname, Given Name	page(s)
PEYTON, Henry (cont.)	
Mountain	93
Ned (2)	93, 93
Priss	93
Solomon	93
Spencer	93
Will (2)	93, 93
PHILLIPS, Abner (1 negro)	
Lewis	71
PHILLIPS, Elias (4 negroes)	
Amay	71
Jack	71
Jenny	71
Winney	71
PICKET, W^m (5 negroes)	
Dick	112
James	112
Mill	112
Pegg	112
Tom	112
PICKETT, Wm Sanford (5 negroes)	
Gilbert	97
London	97
Tom	97
Winney (2)	97, 97
PIDGE, John (6 negroes)	
James	94
Jes	94
John	94
Jone	94
Sue (2)	94, 94
PINCKARD, James (1 negro)	
Stephan	94
PIPER, Benjamin (11 negroes)	
Charles	113
Isaac	113
Jack	113
Jane	113
Luce	113
Manuel	113
Mime	113
Patt	113
Peg	113
Sam	113
Sharlet	113
PORTER, Samuel (7 negroes)	
Ben	56
Dinah	56
James	56
Nance	56
Tom	56
Winney (2)	56, 56
PORTER, Thomas (2 negroes)	
Ned	57
Will	57
PREAILE, John (16 negroes)	
Cumber	94
Daniel	94
Gabriel	94
Harry	94
Jacob	94
James	94
John	94
Judah	94
Luce	94
Mimey	94
Minor	94
Nell (2)	94, 94
Pris	94
Randolph	94
Val	94
PRESTON, William Jr. (1 negro)	
Peter	71
PRIEST, Thos (levy free) (3 negroes)	
Nimrod	46
Priss	46
Will	46
RANSDELL, John (4 negroes)	
Charles	57
Daniel	57
Harry	57
Judy	57
RANSDELL, Whorton (3 negroes)	
Frank	96
Jane	96
Tom	96
RANSDELL, Whorton (Captain) (17 negroes)	
Dick	96
Edam	96
George (2)	96, 96
James	96
Jane	96
Jeremy	96
Joe	96
Moll	96
Moses	96
Peg (2)	96, 96
Simon	96
Sisley (2)	96, 96
Sue	96
Tom	96
REALY, Thomas (4 negroes)	
Cate	47
Jack	47
James	47

Index "D" Slaves & Slaveholders 1782-001 to 1782-005 Tithable Lists

Surname, Given Name	page(s)
REALY, Thomas (cont.)	
Robin	47
RED, Allan (3 negroes)	
Adam	57
Mary	57
Moses	57
RICTOR, Harman (2 negroes)	
Ben	38
Peter	38
RIXSEY, Richard (9 negroes)	
Aron	114
Danial	114
Hager	114
Hannar	114
Joseph	114
Sarah	114
Tom	114
Violet	114
William	114
ROACH, James (1 negro)	
Jude	38
ROBERTSON, Joseph (5 negroes)	
Bryant	96
Jone (2)	96, 96
Ned	96
Val	96
ROBISON, Benjamin (16 negroes)	
Adam	57
Aggai	57
Charles	57
Hannah	57
Harry	57
James	57
Joe	57
Lucy Sr.	57
Molly	57
Moses	57
Nelly	57
Peg	57
Rachel	57
Simon	57
Solomon	57
Violet	57
ROGERS, George (7 negroes)	
Adam	57
Charles	57
Duke	57
Kate (2)	57, 57
Lett	57
Prince	57
ROOCH, William (2 negroes)	
Ned	57
Phillis	57

Surname, Given Name	page(s)
ROUTT, James (2 negroes)	
Daniel	72
Lucy	72
ROUTT, Peter (3 negroes)	
Chloey	72
Tom (2)	72
RUSAW, George (8 negroes)	
Anthony	46
Ben	46
George	46
James	46
Judah	46
Milly	46
Nell	46
Peter	46
RUSSELL, William (2 negroes)	
Lucy	72
Nan	72
RUST, John (5 negroes)	
Frank	96
Hannah	96
Jacob	96
Moll (2)	96, 96
RUST, Matthew (3 young negroes)	
Abrener	96
Lett	96
Rose	96
RUST, Samuel (6 negroes)	
Alice	96
Fill	96
George	96
Lewis (2)	96, 96
Mary	96
SANDERS, Robert (6 negroes)	
Hannah	58
Jesse	58
Lucy	58
Peter	58
Sam	58
SAUNDERS, James (2 negroes)	
Sal	99
Sepio	99
SCOTT, Elizabeth (31 negroes)	
Ady	99
Amy	99
Beck	99
Bet	99
Cela	99
Charles	99
Charlotte	99
Daniel	99
Dianna	99
Frank	99

Index "D" Slaves & Slaveholders 1782-001 to 1782-005 Tithable Lists

Surname, Given Name	page(s)	Surname, Given Name	page(s)
SCOTT, Elizabeth (cont.)		SCOTT, John (Rev^d) (cont.)	
Hannah (2)	99	Nelson	98
Harry	99	Phil	98
James	99	Pris	98
Jane (4)	99, 99, 99, 99	Robin	98
Jemima	99	Rose	98
Jude	99	Thomas	98
Lewis	99	SEATON, W^m (5 negroes)	
London	99	Cary	35
Lucy	99	Isaac	35
Mason	99	Jeffery	35
Rose	99	Keziah	35
Sal	99	Sam	35
Sauney	99	SETTLE, Joel (3 negroes)	
Tone	99	Jack	115
Will	99	James	115
Winney	99	John	115
SCOTT, James (Prince William County) (19 negroes)		SHACKELFORD, Benjamin (17 negroes)	
		Beck	114
Beck	98	Daniel	114
Ben	98	Dinah	114
Bet (2)	98, 98	Hannah	114
Cesar	98	Harry (2)	114, 114
Cloe	98	Judath	114
Daniel	98	Kate (2)	114, 114
Daphney	98	Lewis	114
Elgan	98	Minny	114
James	98	Molly	114
Joe	98	Ned	114
Mary	98	Nelson	114
Mol	98	Peter	114
Murriah	98	Phill	114
Nan	98	Robin	114
Poll	98	SHACKELFORD, James (27 negroes)	
Pris	98	Adam	58
Stephen	98	Charlotte	58
Titus	98	Delf	58
SCOTT, John (Rev^d) (22 negroes)		Dinah	58
Ben	98	Fanny	58
Bridget	98	Fortune	58
David	98	Frank	58
Ephraim	98	George	58
George	98	Grace	58
Harry	98	Guilford	58
Jack	98	Hannah	58
James	98	Harry (2)	58, 58
Joe	98	Isaac	58
John	98	Jane	58
Judah (2)	98, 98	Joe (2)	58, 58
Lucinda	98	Judy	58
Mirta	98	Lett	58
Ned	98	Lucy	58
Nelley	98	Mima	58

Index "D" Slaves & Slaveholders 1782-001 to 1782-005 Tithable Lists

Surname, Given Name	page(s)	Surname, Given Name	page(s)
SHACKLEFORD, James (cont.)		SINCLAIR, John (cont.)	
Peter	58	James	97
Rachel	58	Manuel	97
Sall	58	Mima	97
Scipio	58	Nell	97
Violet	58	Sam	97
Winney	58	Sarah	97
SHOEMATE, James (1 negro)		Solomon	97
Ceni	73	Tom	97
SHOEMATE, John (10 negroes)		SINCLAIR, William (10 negroes)	
Alley	73	Bett	73
Cato	73	Charlott	73
Dick	73	Dick	73
Dinah	73	Gillis	73
Grace	73	Harry	73
Jenney	73	Jacob	73
Lucy	73	Nan	73
Milley	73	Phillis	73
Peter	73	Suck	73
Sam	73	Tom	73
SHUMAKE, Baley (4 negroes)		SINCLAIR, W^m (6 negroes)	
Brister	40	Cas	99
Harry	40	Hannah	99
Nell	40	Pat (2)	99, 99
Peter	40	Rachel	99
SHUMAKE, Daniel (2 negroes)		Tom	99
Bess	45	SINGLETON, Standley (11 negroes)	
Tom	45	Dinah	97
SHUMAKE, James (7 negroes)		Frank	97
Brister	45	Hannah (3)	97, 97, 97
Cate	45	Harry	97
Esther	45	Mason	97
Mimy	45	Milley	97
Platoe	45	Stephan	97
Sarah	45	Tom	97
Sela	45	Winn	97
SHUMATE, Samuel (1 negro)		SINKLER, Robert (5 negroes)	
Luce	115	Guss	115
SHUMATE, Thomas (1 negro)		James	115
Dinah	41	Jim	115
SILVEY, Abraham (1 young negro)		Lidd	115
Milley	99	Mimey	115
SINCLAIR, John (20 negroes)		SKINKER, W^m (Prince William County) (18 negroes)	
Agg	97	Esther	98
Amey	97	Fanny	98
Ben	97	Grii	98
Bet	97	Hannah (2)	98, 98
Dick	97	Harry	98
Dinah	97	Isaac	98
George	97	Jane	98
Grii	97	Jerry	98
Hannah (3)	97, 97, 97	Ned	98
Jacob	97		

Index "D" Slaves & Slaveholders 1782-001 to 1782-005 Tithable Lists

Surname, Given Name	page(s)
SKINKER, W^m (Prince William County) (cont.)	
Peter	98
Pressley	98
Robin	98
Sealey	98
Stephan	98
Subbinia	98
Sue	98
Winney	98
SMITH, John (8 negroes)	
Ben	115
George	115
Grace	115
Jefry	115
John	115
Jude	115
Luce	115
Mary	115
SMITH, John Jr. (1 negro)	
Nan	115
SMITH, Joseph (9 negroes)	
Ann	99
Charlotte (2)	99, 99
Hannah (2)	99, 99
Lewis	99
Lid	99
Mary	99
Rose	99
SMITH, Mary (11 negroes)	
Balley	97
Betsy	97
Bob	97
Boron	97
Henry	97
Jane	97
Mirreah (2)	97, 97
Tom	97
Violett	97
Williby	97
SMITH, William (Carter's Run) (1 negro)	
Mille	116
SMITH, W^m Sr. (Hickry) (11 negroes)	
Bet	115
Cate	115
Diner	115
Easter	115
Hannah	115
Jacob	115
James	115
Luce	115
Moses	115
Rose	115
Seaser	115

Surname, Given Name	page(s)
SPILLER, Phill Sr. (1 negro)	
Sam	39
STALARD, Walter (1 negro)	
Hannah	50
STARK, James (6 negroes)	
Beck	37
Cate	37
Daniel	37
George	37
Lize	37
Lyda	37
STEELE, Samuel (6 negroes)	
Abel	59
Charlotte	59
Jack	59
James (2)	59
Jane	59
STEWART, Allen (5 negroes)	
Joan	59
Lucy	59
Nan	59
Solomon	59
Tom	59
STEWART, William (5 negroes)	
James	59
Mass	59
Rachel	59
Sue	59
Winney	59
STEWART, William (Rev^d) (24 negroes)	
Alice	58
Ben	58
Bess	58
Celia	58
Charles	58
Daniel	58
David	58
Frank	58
George	58
Giles	58
Hannah	58
Jack	58
Jacob	58
Judith	58
Kate	58
Milly	58
Moses	58
Nan	58
Nancy	58
Peter	58
Sam	58
Sarah	58

Index "D" Slaves & Slaveholders 1782-001 to 1782-005 Tithable Lists

Surname, Given Name	page(s)
STEWART, William (Rev^d) (cont.)	
Simon	58
Tom	58
STEWART, W^m (Rev^d) (9 negroes)	
Aron	39
James	39
John	39
Moses	39
Nan	39
Nib	39
Nell	39
Rose	39
Will	39
STEWART, W^m (Rev^d) (26 negroes)	
Amey	97
Dick	97
Dinah	97
Florah	97
Harry	97
Jarrard	97
Jerry	97
John	97
Jonathan	97
Jone	97
Judith	97
Lizah	97
Mary	97
Milley	97
Nan (2)	97, 97
Peg	97
Peggy	97
Phil	97
Pompy	97
Reuben	97
Rose	97
Sal	97
Tom	97
Winney (2)	97, 97
STONE, John (3 negroes)	
Lett	59
Rachel	59
Sarah	59
STONE, Menoah (3 negroes)	
Sarah (2)	98, 98
Squire	98
STROTHER, Reuben (9 negroes)	
Charles	99
Dinah	99
Frank	99
Henry	99
Jack	99
Luce (2)	99, 99
Rose	99

Surname, Given Name	page(s)
STROTHER, Reuben (cont.)	
Sambo	99
STROTHERS, William (1 negro)	
Daniel	115
SULLIVAN, Sarah (9 negroes)	
Cesar	99
Dick	99
Diner	99
Elijah	99
Joe	99
Mimey	99
Phillis (2)	99, 99
Winney	99
TATE, Peter (7 negroes)	
Let (2)	100, 100
Minta	100
Moll	100
Moses	100
Peter	100
Sue	100
TAYLOR, Joseph (10 negroes)	
Arguile	100
Bet (2)	100, 100
Joshua	100
Mescheck	100
Meilson	100
Sal	100
Sarah	100
Shad.	100
Simon	100
TAYLOR, Judith (17 negroes)	
Adam	100
Alice	100
Bet	100
Cate (2)	100, 100
Charles	100
Esther	100
George	100
Hannah	100
Isaac	100
Jerry	100
Luce	100
Mary	100
Peter	100
Solomon	100
Tobe	100
Wilkins	100
TAYLOR, Peter (1 negro)	
Jack	73
THOMAS, David (7 negroes)	
Dick	100
Lot	100
Orson	100

Index "D" Slaves & Slaveholders 1782-001 to 1782-005 Tithable Lists

Surname, Given Name	page(s)	Surname, Given Name	page(s)
THOMAS, David (cont.)		THRAILKILL, Elijah (4 negroes)	
Patience (2)	100, 100	Aron	41
Prue	100	Dinah	41
Tom	100	Frank	41
THOMPSON, James (Rev^d) (7 negroes)		Lis	41
Bet	100	TOMLIN, John Jr. (13 negroes)	
Hannah	100	Tom	60
Issham	100	Bet	60
Let (2)	100, 100	Charles	60
Moses	100	Fortune (2)	60, 60
Tab	100	Jack	60
THOMSON, Eli (5 negroes)		James	60
Aaron	116	Jane	60
Cis	116	Joc	60
Jo	116	Joe	60
Ned	116	Kate	60
Tiers	116	Lucy	60
THOMSON, James (6 negroes)		Ned	60
Dick	35	TRIPLETT, Francis (6 negroes)	
Grace	35	Cate	116
Jenney	35	Charles	116
Limass	35	Clo	116
Nag^t	35	Harry	116
Solomon	35	James	116
THOMSON, Jesse (2 negroes)		John	116
Sip	116	TUELLAS, Rodam (5 negroes)	
William	116	Antony	45
THORNBERRY, Samuel Sr. (19 negroes)		Bess	45
Chloe	59	Esther	45
Duddley	59	Silva	45
Hannah	59	Will	45
Harry	59	TURBERVILLE, George (17 negroes)	
Humpprey	59	Cate (2)	73, 73
Jack	59	Chloey	73
Jacob	59	Derende	73
Jeter	59	Dick (2)	73, 73
Joe	59	Dimont	73
Kate	59	Hager	73
Letty	59	Hannah	73
Milley	59	James	73
Nan	59	Peter	73
Nelly	59	Prue	73
Phill	59	Rachel	73
Ralph	59	Seppi	73
Sarah	59	Solomon	73
Sciah	59	Suck	73
Winney	59	Tom	73
THORNBERRY, John (5 negroes)		TURNER, Edward (15 negroes)	
Daniel	59	Alice (2)	106, 106
Jude	59	Betty	106
Milley	59	David	106
Tom (2)	59, 59	Dinah	106
		George	106

Index "D" Slaves & Slaveholders 1782-001 to 1782-005 Tithable Lists

Surname, Given Name	page(s)
TURNER, Edward (cont.)	
Isaac	106
James	106
Lucy	106
Milley	106
Reuben	106
Sauney	106
Sillar	106
Will	106
Winna	106
UTTERBACK, Harmon (1 negro)	
Cate	101
UTTERBACK, Henry (levy free) (1 negro)	
Jack	41
UTTERBACK, John (5 negroes)	
Elizabeth (2)	101, 101
George	101
Joe	101
Tibby	101
VOWLS, Richard (2 negroes)	
Nell	74
Zachariah	74
WADDLE, John (5 negroes)	
Ben	103
Hannah	103
Jack	103
Winney (2)	103, 103
WAKE, John (13 negroes)	
Chris	103
Daniel	103
Harry	103
James	103
Jane	103
Jude (2)	103, 103
Lid	103
Lot	103
Lucy	103
Milley	103
Pris	103
Sarah	103
WALLER, Charles (5 negroes)	
Essex	44
Jack	44
Sam	44
Sarah	44
Trulove	44
WALLER, Edward (15 negroes)	
Ben	38
Bet	38
Celia	38
Cloe	38
Dinah	38
Dy	38

Surname, Given Name	page(s)
WALLER, Edward (cont.)	
Isaac	38
Jack (2)	38, 38
James (2)	38, 38
Johua	38
Lett	38
Lid	38
Will	38
WATSON, William (1 negro)	
Nell	75
WATTS, John (5 negroes)	
Bet	103
Kelly	103
Mary (2)	103, 103
Will	103
WEATHERS, Cain (2 negroes)	
Ester	76
Will	76
WEAVER, Jacob (8 negroes)	
Ben	117
Hannah	117
Henry	117
Jes	117
John	117
Nann	117
Peter	117
Robert	117
WEAVER, Tilman (5 negroes)	
Dinah	40
Hannah (2)	40, 40
Luse	40
Siner	40
WELCH, Cilvester (5 negroes)	
Alley	102
Jerry	102
Moses (2)	102, 102
Winney	102
WHEATLEY, David (4 negroes)	
Ben	40
Jenny	40
Ned	40
Peg	40
WHEATLEY, James (11 negroes)	
Daniel	74
Ester	74
George	74
Glasgo	74
Harry	74
Judy	74
Mimey	74
Nell	74
Rose	74

Index "D" Slaves & Slaveholders 1782-001 to 1782-005 Tithable Lists

Surname, Given Name	page(s)	Surname, Given Name	page(s)
WHEATLEY, James (cont.)		WHITLEY, William (cont.)	
Sall	74	Jean	116
Winney	74	Jeffrey	116
WHEATLEY, John (4 negroes)		WILKINS, William Sr. (18 negroes)	
Henry	75	Abraham	75
Lucy	75	Adam	75
Nath[1]	75	Amey	75
Will	75	Bess	75
WHEATLEY, Joseph (4 negroes)		Briton	75
Judy	75	Easter	75
Sarah	75	George	75
Shadrick	75	Hannah	75
Stephen	75	Jack	75
WHITE, William (6 negroes)		Jeffrey	75
Aaron	60	Nan Jr.	75
Betty	60	Peter	75
Bob	60	Priss	75
Jack	60	Sam	75
Jane	60	Samson	75
Tom	60	Samuel	75
WHITING, Francis (33 negroes)		Sarah	75
Aaron	60	Winney	75
Carter	60	WILLIAMS, Paul (18 negroes)	
Cesar	60	Abraham	74
Charles	60	Ben	74
Chloe	60	Charles	74
Daniel (2)	60, 60	Delphia	74
Frank	60	Dorithy	74
George	60	Ephraim	74
Grace	60	Florah	74
Hannibal	60	George	74
Harry	60	James	74
James	60	Lule	74
Jonathan	60	Milley	74
Joshua	60	Moses	74
Judy	60	Ovid	74
Kate	60	Pendar	74
Lewis	60	Phillis	74
Lucy	60	Tamer	74
Mary	60	Toliver	74
Nanny (2)	60, 60	Will	74
Oliver (2)	60, 60	WILLIS, Ursley (8 negroes)	
Rose	60	Ben	75
Sam (2)	60	Dick	75
Sarah	60	Dinah	75
Sie	60	Isaac	75
Siller	60	Phillis	75
Tom	60	Ralph	75
Will	60	Sisser	75
Willis	60	Ursley	75
WHITLEY, William (4 negroes)		WINN, James (9 negroes)	
Charles	116	Abraham	102
Harry	116	Berkey	102

Index "D" Slaves & Slaveholders 1782-001 to 1782-005 Tithable Lists

Surname, Given Name	page(s)	Surname, Given Name	page(s)
WINN, James (cont.)		WITHERS, Thomas Sr. (cont.)	
Harry	102	Dick	74
James	102	Dinah	74
Lewis	102	George	74
Sarah	102	Hanah	74
Solomon	102	Harry	74
Venus (2)	102, 102	Jess	74
WINN, Margaret (7 negroes)		Moses	74
Grace	103	Phillis	74
Hester	103	Roger	74
Jack	103	Solomon	74
Jane	103	Tom	74
Poll (2)	103, 103	Will	74
Sauney	103	Winney	74
WINN, Minor (13 negroes)		WOOD, Dickerson (2 negroes)	
Frank (2)	103, 103	Alce	116
Harry	103	Jeremiah	116
James	103	WOOD, James (1 negro)	
Jane	103	Lidia	35
King	103	WOODFORD, Catesby (12 negroes)	
Moses	103	Ally	60
Peter	103	Celia	60
Philip	103	Edmond	60
Rewben	103	Fanny	60
Rose (2)	103, 103	Harry (2)	60, 60
Sall	103	Jack	60
WITHERS, James (12 negroes)		James (2)	60, 60
Ben	74	Joan	60
Brook	74	Judy	60
Cain	74	Milley	60
Isaac	74	WRIGHT, John (Captain) (14 negroes)	
Jenny	74	Ann	75
Joe	74	Bob	75
Judy	74	Dinah	75
Lucy	74	Easter	75
Nan	74	Jean	75
Sarah	74	Jude	75
Simon	74	Judy	75
Tom	74	Lidy	75
WITHERS, James (7 negroes)		Milley	75
Danel	116	Moses	75
George	116	Tom	75
Hester	116	Troy	75
Jobe	116	Will (2)	75, 75
Joy	116	YOUNG, James (6 negroes)	
Winny	116	Ben	61
WITHERS, Thomas Sr. (19 negroes)		Rose	61
Aaron	74	Tom	61
Bess	74	Toney	61
Bett	74	Venus	61
Cate	74	Will	61
Ceaser	74		
Clarey	74		

Index "D" Slaves & Slaveholders 1782-001 to 1782-005 Tithable Lists

Surname, Given Name	page(s)
YOUNG, William (7 negroes)	
Amey	104
Daniel	104
George	104
Hendley	104
Jane	104
Rose (2)	104, 104

Other Heritage Books by Joan W. Peters:

Abstracts of Fauquier County, Virginia Birth Records, 1853-1896

Being of Sound Mind: An Index to the Probate Records in Fauquier County Virginia's Clerks Loose Papers and Superior and Circuit Court Papers, 1759-1919

Fauquier County, Virginia's Clerk's Loose Papers: A Guide to the Records, 1759-1919

Military Records, Certificates of Service, Discharge, Heirs, and Pensions Declarations and Schedules from the Fauquier County, Virginia Court Minute Books, 1784-1840

Military Records, Patriotic Service, and Public Service Claims from the Fauquier County, Virginia Court Minute Books, 1759-1784

Military Records, Pension Applications, Heirs at Law and Civil War Military Records from the Fauquier County, Virginia Court Minute Books, 1840-1904

Neglected and Forgotten: Fauquier County, Virginia French and Indian War, Revolutionary War and War of 1812 Veterans

Prince William County, Virginia General Index to Wills, 1734-1951

The Tax Man Cometh—Land and Property in Colonial Fauquier County, Virginia: Tax Lists from the Fauquier County Court Clerk's Loose Papers, 1759-1782

The Third Virginia Regiment of Foot, 1776-1778, with Flags Flying and Drums Beating Volume One: A History

The Third Virginia Regiment of Foot, 1776-1778, with Flags Flying and Drums Beating Volume Two: Biographies